ISBN 978-1-5283-0659-1
PIBN 10914638

1 MONTH OF
FREE
READING

at

www.ForgottenBooks.com

By purchasing this book you are eligible for one month membership to ForgottenBooks.com, giving you unlimited access to our entire collection of over 1,000,000 titles via our web site and mobile apps.

To claim your free month visit:

www.forgottenbooks.com/free914638

English
Français
Deutsche
Italiano
Español
Português

www.forgottenbooks.com

Mythology Photography **Fiction**
Fishing Christianity **Art** Cooking
Essays Buddhism Freemasonry
Medicine **Biology** Music **Ancient
Egypt** Evolution Carpentry Physics
Dance Geology **Mathematics** Fitness
Shakespeare **Folklore** Yoga Marketing
Confidence Immortality Biographies
Poetry **Psychology** Witchcraft
Electronics Chemistry History **Law**
Accounting **Philosophy** Anthropology
Alchemy Drama Quantum Mechanics
Atheism Sexual Health **Ancient History**
Entrepreneurship Languages Sport
Paleontology Needlework Islam
Metaphysics Investment Archaeology
Parenting Statistics Criminology
Motivational

THE

RACING CALENDAR:

CONTAINING

AN ACCOUNT OF

Plates, Matches, and Sweepstakes,

RUN FOR IN

GREAT-BRITAIN AND IRELAND,

IN THE YEAR

1805.

WITH AN ABSTRACT

OF

ENGAGEMENTS ENTERED INTO

FOR

FUTURE YEARS, &c.

———

BY

Edward and James Weatherby.

VOLUME THE THIRTY-THIRD.

LONDON:

PRINTED BY H. REYNELL, NO. 21, PICCADILLY;
AND SOLD AT THE PUBLISHERS OFFICE,
NO. 7, OXENDEN-STREET.

———

M,DCCC,VI.

Advertisement.

SUBSCRIPTIONS, Advertisements, and Intelligence, for the RACING CALENDAR, are received and carefully attended to, at the Publishers Office, No. 7, Oxenden-Street, near the Hay-Market; where may be had most of the Volumes from the Year 1727, to the present.

Subscription for the Sheet Calendars and Volume, One Guinea per Annum; the first Year's Subscription to be paid in Advance.

The Volume for 1805 (price 10s. 6d.) is sold by Mr. E. W. Rhodes, York; Mr. Toufey, Newcastle-upon-Tyne; Mr. Deardin, No. 19, Piccadilly, Manchester; Mr. Ormandy, Bookseller, Liverpool; Mr. Partridge, Stable-keeper, Bath; and at the Coffee-room, Newmarket.

CAUTION.

In Confequence of the many fatal Accidents which have happened by Horfes running too near the Pofts, the STEWARDS of NEWMARKET RACES have caufed the *large and fixed Pofts* on the Heath, to be furrounded with Turf-banks, about Five Feet in the Bafe, and floping to the Poft, at the Height of about Four Feet; *and in other Parts of the Courfe, particularly where there are Turns, they have adopted the Ufe of flender Pofts that will break on any ftrong Pref- fure,* which they earneftly recommend to the Notice of Stewards and Managers of Races in general.

CONTENTS.

RACES TO COME.

Racing

MXT

A LIST

LIST OF SUBSCRIBERS.

HIS Royal Highneſs the PRINCE OF WALES
His Royal Highneſs the DUKE OF YORK

His Serene Highneſs the Margrave of Anſpach

His Grace the Duke of Beaufort
His Grace the Duke of Devonſhire
His Grace the Duke of Grafton
His Grace the Duke of Hamilton and Brandon
His Grace the Duke of Leeds
His Grace the Duke of Portland
His Grace the Duke of Queenſberry
His Grace the Duke of Richmond
His Grace the Duke of St. Albans

The Moſt Noble the Marquis of Huntley
The Moſt Noble the Marquis of Tichfield

Right Honourable the Earl of Barrymore
Right Honourable the Earl of Belmore
Right Honourable the Earl of Beverley
Right Honourable the Earl of Bridgewater
Right Honourable the Earl of Caſſillis
Right Honourable the Earl of Clarendon
Right Honourable the Earl of Clermont
Right Honourable the Earl of Darlington
Right Honourable the Earl of Derby
Right Honourable the Earl of Eglinton
Right Honourable the Earl of Egremont
Right Honourable the Earl of Euſton
Right Honourable the Earl of Farnham
Right Honourable the Earl Fitzwilliam

Right

Right Honourable the Earl Grosvenor
Right Honourable the Earl of Harborough
Right Honourable the late Earl of Jersey
Right Honourable the Earl of Jersey
Right Honourable the Earl of Mansfield
Right Honourable the Earl O'Neil
Right Honourable the Earl of Roden
Right Honourable the Earl of Stamford & Warrington
Right Honourable the Earl of Strathmore
Right Honourable the Earl of Wilton
Right Honourable the Earl of Winchilsea

Right Honourable Lord Frederick Beauclerk
Right Honourable Lord Belhaven
Right Honourable Lord Charles Bentinck
Right Honourable Lord Frederick Bentinck
Right Honourable Lord Boringdon
Right Honourable Lord Brooke
Right Honourable Lord Viscount Braybrooke
Right Honourable Lord G. H. Cavendish
Right Honourable Lord Cawdor
Right Honourable Lord De Dunstanville
Right Honourable Lord Dundas
Right Honourable Lord Foley
Right Honourable Lord Graves
Right Honourable Lord Grey, 2 sets
Right Honourable Lord Hawke
Right Honourable Lord Heathfield
Right Honourable Lord Hinton
Right Honourable Lord Kensington
Right Honourable Lord Charles Kerr
Right Honourable Lord Leslie
Right Honourable Lord Lowther
Right Honourable Lord Charles Manners
Right Honourable Lord Viscount Maynard
Right Honourable Lord Milsintown
Right Honourable Lord Monson
Right Honourable Lord Montgomerie

Right

Right Honourable Lord Francis Godolphin Ofborne
Right Honourable Lord Paget
Right Honourable Lord Rous
Right Honourable Lord William Ruffell
Right Honourable Lord Vifcount Sackville
Right Honourable Lord Saye and Sele
Right Honourable Lord Sherborne
Right Honourable Lord Arthur Somerfet
Right Honourable Lord Ch. H. Somerfet
Right Honourable Lord Edward Somerfet
Right Honourable Lord Sondes
Right Honourable Lord Southampton
Right Honourable Lord Stawell
Right Honourable Lord Talbot
Right Honourable Lord George Thynne
Right Honourable Lord Yarborough

Right Honourable the Lord Chief Juftice of the Common Pleas

Honourable George Charles Agar
Honourable A. Cavend. Bradfhaw
Honourable Captain Cavendifh
Honourable Berkeley Craven
Honourable Champion Dymoke
Honourable Newton Fellowes
Honourable Edward Finch
Honourable George Germain
Honourable William Booth Grey
Honourable W. A. Harbord
Honourable George Herbert
Honourable Richard Hill
Honourable S. H. Lumley
Honourable William Lumley
Honourable William Villiers Manfel
Honourable M. Mathew
Honourable W. R. Maule
Honourable Thomas Moreton
Honourable G. H. Neville

Honourable

Honourable Thomas Parker
Honourable R. Lumley Savile
Honourable Joshua Vanneck
Honourable George Villiers
Honourable Horatio Walpole
Honourable George Watson
Honourable Charles Wyndham

Sir William Abdy, Bart.
Sir George Armytage, Bt.
Sir Willoughby Aston, Bt.
Sir Dav. Hunter Blair, Bt.
Sir Patrick Blake, Bart.
Sir R. Lynch Bloffe, Bart.
Sir T. C. Bunbury, Bt.
Sir C. M. Burrell, Bart.
Sir R. Sal. Cotton, Bart.
Sir Charles Douglas, Bt.
Sir Fred. Evelyn, Bart.
Sir H. Fetherston, Bart.
Sir T. Gascoigne, Bart.
Sir W. Gerard, Bart.
Sir Stephen Glynn, Bart.
Sir N. B. Gresley, Bart.
Sir Henry Grey, Bart.
Sir William Guise, Bart.
Sir C. Haggerston, Bart.
Sir Harry Harpur, Bart.
Sir R. B. Harvey, Bart.
Sir John Hawkins, Bart.
Sir G. Heathcote, Bart.
Sir Tho. D. Hesketh, Bt.
Sir H. P. Hoghton, Bart.
Sir John Honywood, Bt.
Sir H. Carr Ibbetson, Bt.
Sir Wm. Johnston, Bart.
Sir John Johnstone, Bart.

Sir John Lade, Bart.
Sir John Lawson, Bart.
Sir Robert Lawley, Bart.
Sir John F. Leicester, Bt.
Sir Robert Leighton, Bt.
Sir Henry Lippincott, Bt.
Sir Ed. Pryce Lloyd, Bt.
Sir H. M. Mainwaring, Bt.
Sir Jos. Mawbey, Bart.
Sir H. P. St. John Mildmay, Bart.
Sir F. Molyneux, Bart.
Sir Thomas Mostyn, Bt.
Sir Hugh Owen, Bart.
Sir Henry Peyton, Bart.
Sir George Pigot, Bart.
Sir John Shelley, Bart.
Sir Hugh Smith, Bart.
Sir Frank Standish, Bart.
Sir Thomas Stanley, Bt.
Sir M. M. Sykes, Bart.
Sir J. Throckmorton, Bt.
Sir Charles Turner, Bart.
Sir H. Tempest Vane, Bt.
Sir William Wake, Bart.
Sir Peter Warburton, Bt.
Sir H. Williamson, Bart.
Sir Watkin W. Wynn, Bt.

BED.

BEDFORDSHIRE.

Mr. W. Deere
W. Lee Antonie, Efq.
Mr. Ifaac Elger
G. W. Monk, Efq.

BERKS.

William. Angell, Efq.
Captain Athorpe
Mr. Baily
Stanlake Batfon, Efq.
George Blackfhaw, Efq.
Adam Blandy, Efq.
Mr. Z. Bolt
Ferdinando Bullock, Efq.
Mr. Charlwood
Mr. John Clode, Caftle
    Inn, Windfor
Ifaac Delamare, Efq.
Charles Dundas, Efq.
Mr. J. Eldridge
Mr. W. Frogley
Thomas Goodlake, Efq.
Brig. Gen. Lev. Gower
Mr. W. Grace
Mr. W. Gurley, the Star
    and Garter, Windfor
W. Hallett, Efq.
Mr. Houfe
Mr. W. Howlett
Mr. D. Johnfton
Mr. Kennett
Mr. B Kent
W. Mabbott, Efq.
Mr. Thomas Miller
Mr. W. Nottage
A. F. Nunes, Efq.

John Philips, Efq.
W. Poyntz, Efq.
J Ramfbottom, Jun. Efq.
Mr. J. Shackel
Mr. C. Simmonds
Mr. J. Slingfby
Thomas Smith, Efq.
Mr. W. Starling
Col. Stead
Mr. Sturges
Mr. J. Sutton
W. Thoyts, Efq.
Ex. Turnor, Efq.
Captain Vyfe
Mr. W. Wait
Mr. Weftbrook
Mr. G. White
Mr. Wroughton

BUCKINGHAMSHIRE.

John Harrifon, Efq.

CAMBRIDGESHIRE.

Mr. W. Adams
Robert J. A'Deane, Efq.
Mr. Baxter
Mr. W. Clift
M Dayrell, Efq.
Mr. W. Evans, the Grey-
    hound, Cambridge
Jofeph Girdler, Efq.
Mr. Golding
Mr. Goodiffon
G. Lev. Gower, Efq.
K. J. Haggerfton, Efq.
Lt. Col. Harwood
john Hibbert, Efq.
B. Keene, Efq.

G. W. Leeds, Efq.
Mr. Longchamp
J. Macnamara, Efq.
Mr. F. Neale
W. Ouley, Efq.
Thomas Panton, Efq.
Mr. Perren
Mr. Potter, the Ram Inn, Newmarket
Mr. Rickword
Mr. T. Rider
Mr. Robfon
Mr. F. Smallman
Mr. M. Stephenfon
Mr. J. Stevens
John Tharp, Efq.
R. G. Townley, Efq.
Mr. R. Weatherill

CHESHIRE.

D. Afhley, Efq.
James Bayley, Efq.
Mr. Barlow
The late R. S. Barry, Efq.
Mr. John Billington
Mr. Edw. Brifcoe
T. Langford Brooke, Efq.
Henry Cafe, Efq.
Tho. Cholmondeley, Efq.
Cha. Cholmondeley, Efq.
Mr. Foreft
Mr. Tho. Garnett
Mr. Hinchliffe
John Hollins, Efq.
Mr. Jackfon, Hotel, Chefter
Fr. Jodrell, Efq.
G. J. Legh, Efq.

Charles Leicefter, Efq.
H. A. Leicefter, Efq.
Mr. Monk
Mr. Munnerley
Mr. David Nutting
Thomas Parker, Efq.
P. Patten, Efq.
Mr. Reece
Jofeph Richardfon, Efq.
John Roylance, Efq.
Charles Shakerley, Efq.
Mr. Starkey
Thomas Tarleton, Efq.
Edward Townfend, Efq.
Mr. G. Whitley

CORNWALL.

J. C. Rafhleigh, Efq.

CUMBERLAND.

Thomas Pattenfon, Efq.

DERBYSHIRE.

Mr. Thomas Bates
John Borrow, Efq.
Mr. Charles Brown
T. Cave Browne, Efq.
Jofeph Butler, Efq.
Mr. B. Buxton
Mr. E. Dawfon
Mr. Read Denham
Mr. John Hall
W. Ludlam, Efq.
Mr. Marfhall
Sitwell Sitwell, Efq.
H. B. Thornhill, Efq.
Mr. Jof. Webfter

Col.

Col. Wilson
Mr. John Wray

DEVONSHIRE.

George Barbor, Esq.
Mr. Brutton
G. Buck, Esq.
Mr. Tho. Kempson
Mr. Rob. Rookes
Captain Weir
James Whyte, Jun. Esq
J. Hamlyn Williams, Esq.
Mr. J. Williams

DORSETSHIRE.

Tho. H. Bastard, Esq.
W. Churchill, Esq.
Mr. G. Clark
Lieut. Col. Cook
John Farquharson, Esq.
R. E. D. Grosvenor, Esq.
A. M. Mills, Esq.

DURHAM.

G. A. Askew, Esq.
Mr. Tho. Atkinson
George Baker, Esq.
William Beckwith, Esq.
Mr. R. Bone, Boot-maker, Durham
Tho. Chipchase, Jun. Esq.
John Cookson, Esq.
Mr. G. Fothergill
Mr. Harrison
John Hudson, Esq.
Mr. S. King
R. J. Lambton, Esq.
C. Mason, Esq.

John Nesham, Esq.
J. O'Callaghan, Esq.
Geo. Fred. Ord, Esq.
Thomas Shafto, Esq.
Mr. John Smith
Mr. John Stephenson
John Trotter, Esq.
W. Wetenhall, Esq.
Mr. W. Wilson

ESSEX.

Mr. Jos. Aldridge
F. H. Child, Esq.
Mr. Edwards, Crown Inn, Chesterford
Mr. Filewood
John Hay, Esq.
Mr. Lee
Mr. Leech
W. Newton, Esq.
Mr. Samuel Pearce
Col. Rigby
G. Wilson, Esq.
Mr. David Wood

GLOCESTERSHIRE.

Haynes Alleyne, Esq.
George Austin, Esq.
Mr. Barrett
Mr. W. Bloss
Chas. Boultbee, Esq.
John Browne, Esq.
Robert Canning, Esq.
Henry Cooke, Esq.
C. Cooper, Esq.
R. E. Cresswell, Esq.
Edward Cripps, Esq.
Mr. T. Darling

Mr.

Mr. Charles Day
Mr. John Dilly
Richard Eccles, Efq.
John Frampton, Efq.
Mr. Green
Chas Hanford, Efq.
Mr. James Heath
W. P. Hodges, Efq.
Mr. Jennings
Roynon Jones, Efq.
Mr. T Izard
Mr. Keek
J. P. Kellermann, Efq.
Col. Kingfcote
Mr. S King, Jun.
Mr. Kirkby
W. Lawrence, Efq.
P. Leverfage, Efq.
Mr. Jofeph Mares
Mr. Mills
John Paul Paul, Efq.
Captain Paul
Mr. Pettat
Barrington Price, Efq.
A. T. Rawlinfon, Efq.
Mr. Thomas Sadler
George Talbot, Efq.
J. Taylor, Efq.
Edm. Waller, Efq.
Mr. Wheeler
Capt. White

HAMPSHIRE AND SOUTHAMPTON.

Mr. Bell, the George Inn, Southampton
B. Blachford, Efq.
Harry Blunt, Efq.

H. Bonham, Efq.
Mr. Budd
Mr. J Cole
R B. Cox, Efq.
Mr David
Mr. John Day, the White Hart, Stockbridge
Mr. M. Dilly
Z. H. Edwards, Efq.
Mr. Charles Fifher
Mr. W. Friend
Edw. Morant Gale, Efq.
W. Gauntlett, Efq.
Charles Græme, Efq.
Mr. W. Hoad
James Holder, Efq.
Major Kington
Percival Lewis, Efq.
Mr. John Major
Mr. Martin
Mr. John Merrett
C. W. Michel, Efq.
J. C. Middleton, Efq.
B. Newland, Efq.
Mr. Payn
John Parlby, Efq.
I. Pickering, Efq.
W. Powlett Powlett, Efq.
G. W. Ricketts, Efq.
W. Stacpoole, Efq.
Mr. Strickland
Charles Taylor, Efq.
H. Villebois, Efq.
Mr. A. Weftlake
Mr. Wilkinfon
V. H. Wilmot, Efq.

HERE.

HEREFORDSHIRE.

Mr. J. Munſey, Crown and Sceptre, Hereford

HERTFORDSHIRE.

Mr. Bolton, Crown Inn, Hockrill
Mr. Bott
Thomas Brand, Eſq.
John Cheſbyre, Eſq.
Mr. W. Clarke
John Corrie, Eſq.
R. Denton, Eſq.
W. Hale, Eſq.
Joſeph Hankin, Eſq.
T. Haworth, Eſq.
R. T. Heyſham, Eſq.
Archer Houblon, Eſq.
Mr. N. Humfrey
Mr. Kerby
W. L. Kingſman, Eſq.
Mr. Orme
E. H. Delmé Radcliffe, Eſq
Benj. Stead, Eſq.
Thomas Stevenſon, Eſq.
Mr. Sturges
John Vaux, Eſq.
Mr. J. Wilſon

HUNTINGDONSHIRE.

Mr. Aiſlabie
H. Pointer Standley, Eſq.
J. Wardell, Eſq.
Taylor White, Eſq.

KENT.

Captain Barrett
Edw. Butler, Eſq.
Colonel Clayton
Mr. Cole
Meſſ. Collett & Tomſett
Mr. Croſoer
William Evelyn, Eſq.
Mr. Gildart
J. Haffenden, Eſq.
Captain Hall
G. Hawkins, Eſq.
Captain A. Henry
Capt. F. B. Hervey
Mr. Hughes
T. Jenkins, Eſq.
Mr. Kidman
Richard Leigh, Eſq.
Mr. J. Page
Tho. Pannwell, Eſq.
——— Ratcliff, Eſq.
T. Trevillon, Eſq.
J. Walpole, Eſq.
Edward Witts, Eſq.

LANCASHIRE.

Edward Ackers, Eſq.
Mr. D. Ainſworth
Aſſembly News-Rooms, Mancheſter
Fr. D. Aſtley, Eſq.
Athenæum, Liverpool
Mr. Atherton
Mr. W. Ball
Mr. Birch

Mr.

Mr. J. Bloomerley
Mr. Henry Booth
Mr. W. Brade, Jun.
Mr. Bradburn
Mr. Edward Brint
Mr. J. Brooke
Mr. Calcott
Mr. Carkwell
Caſtle Coffee - Room, Preſton
James Chadwick, Efq.
Mr. J. Chapman
Mr. W. Chapman
Mr. Claughton
Mr. T. Clay
John Clayton, Efq.
Mr. Edward Clayton
John Clifton, Efq.
Mr. Cowpe
Richard Croffe, Efq.
Mr. John Crowther
Mr. John Daxon
Mr. Charles Deardin
Mr. Edgar
John Entwifle, Efq.
Lieut. Col. Farrington
Mr. James Forfhaw
Mr. W. Fray
Mr Gilding
J. Gregfon, Efq.
Mr. John Greenall
Guildhall Coffee-Room, Preſton
Mr. W. Halftead
Mr. James Hamer
Mr. J Hamer, Jun.
Edward Hanfon, Efq.
Mr. Harris

Mr. Harrop
Mr. Thomas Hays
Mr. W. Holland
Mr. Richard Johnfon
Mr. J. Kennerley
E. N. Kirfhaw, Efq.
Chas. Knightley, Efq.
Mr. W. Lawfon, 2 fets
Mr. W. Lazonby
W. P. Litt, Efq.
Mr. Thomas Marfhall
Mr. Thomas Milne
Mr. R. Morris
Mr. John Oldham
John Parke, Efq.
Edw. Pedder, Jun. Efq.
Mr. Platt
Mr. J. Poftlewhite
Mr. John Preston
Mr. T. Rawfon
Mr. Richard Roberts
Mr. Bethell Robinfon
Mr. Peter Sephton
Townley Shawe, Efq.
Mr. Thomas Shaw
Mr. N. Shepherd
Mr. Richard Singleton
Charles Smith, Efq.
Mr John Smith
Mr. M. Storey
Mr. Leon Taytham
Wm. Trafford, Efq.
Mr. John Travis
Mr. Jos. Turner
Mr. Thomas Walch, 2 fets
Mr. W. Walker
Mr. Thomas Watfon
Mr. Geo. White

Mr.

Mr. Samuel Wright
Mr. Thos. Yellowly

LEICESTERSHIRE.

C. J. Apperley, Efq.
R. Aftley, Efq.
T. L. Bennett, Efq.
Tho. Boultbee, Efq.
Mr. Coates
Mr. Coombe
Mr. John Dixon
William Herrick, Efq.
Mr. Mowbray
Mr. Munton
Mr. F. Nedham
Cofmas Neville, Efq.
Peter Oliver, Efq.
Mr. John Pearfon
Mr. B. Rowland
Mr. Spencer, Bull's Head
  Inn, Leicefter
Mr. W. Whitehead

LINCOLNSHIRE.

Charles Allenby, Efq.
Capt. Allix
Mr. Tho. Binney
J. Cracroft, Efq.
Mr. John Dauber
John Douglas, Efq.
Mr. Gardiner
Robert Heathcote, Efq.
Dr. Jenkin
Nevile King, Efq.
Benjamin Lloyd, Efq.
George Manners, Efq.

Mr. Martin, the George
  Inn, Grantham
William Pennyman, Efq.
Mr. Pettitt
John Richardfon, Efq.
Mr. T. Scrivener
Mr. John Toulfon
John Uppleby, Efq.
Charles White, Efq.
Dr. J. Willis

LONDON
AND MIDDLESEX.

Mr. Aldridge
Mr. Anderfon
Mr. Charles Afhley
Meff. Bailey, Waller, Bai-
  ley and Co.
Mr. Bainton
Major Barnard
Mr. Bartley, Livery Sta-
  bles, Oxford-ftreet
C. N. Bayly, Efq.
Major Belfon
Thomas Beft, Efq.
J. Beft, Efq.
T. Beft, Efq.
Jofeph Bird, Jun. Efq.
D. Blake, Efq.
Mr. Bonnar
Mr. Boucher
L. Bouverie, Efq.
Mr. J. Braddock
Mr. H. Bradley
Mr. Brett
William Brien, Efq.
Mr. Charles Briggs

Mr.

Mr. E. Brockfop
John Brown, Efq.
William Brien, Efq.
Rob. Crowe Bryanton, Efq
C. Burgh, Efq.
Captain Burlton
Mr. Burlinfon
Robert Calvert, Efq.
Nicholfon Calvert, Efq.
Mr. Chalon, Horfe and
   Dog Painter, 24, Win-
   chefter-row, Padding-
   ton
Mr. Cauty
Henry Churchill, Efq.
John Claridge, Efq.
Mr. Claridge, 2 fets
Mr. Cloves
Edward Coleman, Efq.
Capt. Coftello
Mr. Courtney
Mr. Crofby
Mr. Cruckfhanks
J. Crutchley, Efq.
Mr. Cuddington
Capt. Darley
William Davis, Efq.
Mr. Defbrow
W. Difney, Efq.
Major Draper
Richard Eades, Efq.
Samuel Emden, Efq.
Richard Emmott, Efq.
Richard England, Efq.
Mr. Erriker
F. Eyre, Efq.
The late Mr. Fawell
Mr. Fearhom

Mr. Fitz
E. D. Fitzgerald, Efq.
Mr. J. Forth, Eclipfe Li-
   very Stables, Oxford-
   ftreet
Mr. Foxall
Mr. Fozard, Stable keep-
   er, Park-lane
F. Franco, Efq.
Geo. Fuller, Efq.
Mr. Gafkoin
Mr. James Gauft
Mr. W. Geary
V. George, Efq.
Mr. Goldham
George Goold, Efq.
Mr. Grifewood, Sadler,
   Moorfields
Gen. Grofvenor
Mr. James Hall
John Hall, Efq.
Mr. John Hall
Mr. Edward Harris
Mr. Thomas Harrifon
Mr. George Hart
Edward Hawes, Efq.
W. Haxall, Efq.
J. Hewetfon, Efq.
Mr. James Hill
E. Hilliard, Jun. Efq.
John Hilton, Efq.
Meff. Hodgfon and Gann,
   Piazza Coffee-houfe,
   Covent-garden
James Holbrook, Efq.
J. H. Hole, Efq.
Jonathan Hort, Efq.
John Hotham, Efq.
           Humphry

Messrs Griffin,
H. Howorth, Esq.
Mr. Hughes
Mr. Hull
Mr. Jacobs
H. Jadis, Esq.
Mr. W. Jay
J. Jones, Esq.
Mess. Jones & Yarrell
Mr. Joy, Bedford C. H.
Mr. James Kerby, 4 sets
J. Ch. Kinchant, Esq.
Mr. W. King
Mr. Ladbrooke
Warwick Lake, Esq.
Mr. Lane
Mr. Leach
Col. Leigh
H. L. Lindow, Esq.
Thomas Littler, Esq.
R. Lukin, Esq.
Mr. Lumley, Tun Coffee-house, St. James's-market
Mr. Makepeace, Goldsmith, Serle-street, London; Manufacturer of Gold and Silver Race Cups
Mr. Marshall, Portrait & Horse Painter, Beaumont-street
Mr. J. Martin
Mr. B. Martindale
Mr. Mason
Mr. E. Mayers
Thomas Mellish, Esq.
Mr. D. Mercer

Mr. Miles
W. Moorcroft, Esq.
Mr. Moorhouse, Livery Stables, Piccadilly
J. M. Mostyn, Esq.
Mr. Mountford
Mr. Newton, Cocoa-tree, St. James's-street
Mr. T. W. Nunn
A. D. O'Kelly, Esq.
W. Ogden, Esq.
Mess. Owen and Bentley
Mr. Pardy
Mr. Parker
John Payne, Esq.
Wm. Pittman, Esq.
Robert Polhill, Esq.
Mr. R. Powis
Mr. Prior
S. Pryce, Esq.
Mr. Ramsden
Mr. C. Richardson, Grand Hotel, Covent-garden
J. Sale, Esq.
Mr. Sartorius, Horse and Dog Painter, Spur-str. Leicester-square
Mr. Sex
Arthur Shakespear, Esq.
T. Shaw, Esq.
Mr. Sheward
Lieut. Silvertop
C. C. Smith, Esq.
W. Smith, Esq.
H. L. Spencer, Esq.
W. L. Spencer, Esq.
Mr. Stacie

Mr. Stevens, Coffee-houfe New Bond-ftreet
Thomas Stirling, Efq.
Mr. Talbot
Mr. Tate, Sadler, Upper Brook-ftr. Grofv.-fq.
Mr. Tatterfall, a fets
Mr. Tayler
Richard Tayler, Efq.
Richard Taylor, Efq.
Col. Thomas
Tho. Thornhill, Efq.
Captain Todd
Captain Tower
William S. Towers, Efq.
W. Trevanion, Efq.
P. Treves, Efq.
Francis Tyffen, Efq.
The Union Club
Mr. Walker
Mr. J. Watier
Mr. Wefton
Mr. Jofeph White, the Bufh-inn, Staines
Mr. White, Stable-keeper, Little Moorfields
Meffrs Willis, Thatched-houfe, St. James's-ftr.
Samuel Worrall, Efq.
George Worrall, Efq.
Mr. Yeatman, Coach & Horfes, Dover-ftreet

MONMOUTHSHIRE.

Capel Leigh, Efq.
Colonel Probyn

NORFOLK.

James P·evor, Efq.
Mr. Beevor, Jun.
Arthur Branthwayt, Efq.
W. Brooke, Efq.
Mr. Davis
R. Lee Doughty, Efq.
Anthony Hammond, Efq.
Mr. Hamond
Mr. H. Miller
John Mofeley, Efq.
Mr. Partridge
Mr. Powell
Mr. J. Watts
Robert Wilfon, Efq.
Major Wyndham

NORTHAMPTONSHIRE.

R. Andrew, Efq.
Mr. Benton
J. P. Clarke, Efq.
Mr. J. Cole
R. C. Elwes, Efq.
W. Harris, Efq.
Mr. Harrifon
W. Hopkinfon, Efq.
Samuel Ifted, Efq.
Mr. I. Johnfon
George Lynn, Efq.
G. Payne, Efq.
The Pytchley Hunt
Mr. S. Roberts
Mr. J. Scafe
Mr. Sharman
Mr. F. Siffon
Mr. R. Wakefield
Mr. H. Wright

NORTHUM-

NORTHUMBERLAND AND NEWCASTLE.

Mr. George Bates
Charles Brandling, Efq.
Mr. Clayton
Mrs. Hodgfon
Collingwood James, Efq.
Mr. W. Loftus.
R. Riddell, Efq.
Mr. Robfon
Geo. Silvertop, Efq.
Mr. J. Walker, Jun.
J. Wilkie, Jun. Efq.

NOTTINGHAMSHIRE.

Mr. Adwick
Mr. Thomas Barton
Jonas Bettifon, Efq.
Fr. H. Clay, Efq.
Robert Clifton, Efq.
Capt. Clifton
S. Duncombe, Efq.
Mr. J. Eyre
Mr. James Green
Mr. Lammin
Mr. W. Mabbott
Henry Fra. Mellifh, Efq.
2 fets
Mr. John Mills
John Mufters, Efq.
Mr. W. Pearfon
T. Rofe, Efq.
Thomas Thoroton, Efq.
Mr. Thoroton
Mr. S. Tupman

OXFORDSHIRE.

A. Annefley, Efq.
T. Raymond Barker, Efq.
Mr. Beechey
Dr. Berkeley
Mr. Cloafe, Jun.
Mr. Noah Crook
Wm. Holbech, Efq.
Benjamin Holloway, Efq.
Mr. T. Lovegrove
John Morant, Efq.
Mr. Powell
Pryfe Pryfe, Efq.
Mr. John Scott
Mr. Samuel Seckham
Geo. Fred. Stratton, Efq.
John Stratton, Efq.
J. Swann, Efq.
W. Tate, Efq.
Mr. J. Tuckwell
Mr. Whiting, Horfe and Groom, St. Giles's, Oxford
Wm. Willan, Efq.

RUTLANDSHIRE.

Mr. Thomas Fifher
Mr. W. Hubbard
Cambel Norris, Efq.
Lt. Col. Pierrepont

SHROPSHIRE.

Mr. James Armfon
C. Baldwyn, Jun. Efq.
J. Barnes, Efq.
Mr. Bate, Jun.
G. T. Brooke, Efq.

Mr.

Mr. Burton
Mr. Chapman
N. L. Charlton, Efq.
Wm. Childe, Efq.
Mr. John Chipp
Mr. Clay
Mr. Pens. Clarke
Mr. E. Colerick
Mr. Edward-Collier
Mr. R. Dukes
Cecil Forefter, Efq.
Mr. Edward George
Mr. Griffiths
Mr. Handley
Robert Hale, Efq.
W. E. Hammond, Efq.
Mr. John Hickman
Roger Kynnafton, Efq.
H. L. Lee, Efq.
Fr. Lloyd, Efq.
Thomas Mafon, Efq.
Mr. Ralphs
Mr. Sandford
Mr. Thomas Snaxton
John Thompfon, Efq.
Mr. Turner
James Vere, Efq.
Thomas Whitmore, Efq.

SOMERSETSHIRE.

Col. Andrews
John Band, Efq.
Mr. E. Bartley, Jun.
W. J. Chambers, Efq.
Nathaniel Dalton, Efq.
Rd. Doidge, Jun. Efq.
Mr. Thomas Egley
Ifaac Elton, Efq.

Charles Fielder, Efq.
Geo. Gee, Efq.
John Gordon, Jun. Efq.
Mr. John Harris
Lieut. Col. Horner
Mr. T. Jones
Mr. King
J. Fownes Luttrell, Efq.
Edward Lyne, Efq.
Philip John Miles, Efq.
Mr. Morgan, Jun.
Mr. Oaks
Mr. Partridge
Mr. John Sadler
Mr. Stevenfon
Mr. John Stokes
Mr. Rd. Taylor
Mr. N. Temple
Captain Webb
J. Wiltfhire, Efq.

STAFFORDSHIRE.

Mr. Charles Allport
Thomas Anfon, Efq.
Thomas Birch, Efq.
Mr. George Bowker
Mr. Thomas Carr
Richard Dyott, Efq.
Mr. Eld
Mr. R. Fryer
Mr. Gibbons
John Glover, Efq.
Mr. John Hawkes
William Inge, Efq.
John Lockley, Efq.
Mr. James Lord
Hugo Meynell, Efq.
Mr. Geo. Miller

Mr.

Mr. F. Milward
Mr. J. Painter
Robert Parker, Efq.
George Pigot, Efq.
Major Richard Pigot
Mr. T. Princep
Mr. Thomas Roberts
Mr. W. Saunders
Francis Stokes, Efq.
Mr. Stokes
John Swinfen, Efq.
Mr. W. Tinkler
John Turner, Efq.
Henry Vernon, Efq.
Lt. Col. Unwin
Mr. Wilday

SUFFOLK.
Mr. Abbey
Mr. F. Baker
Mr. Barlow, King's Head, Beceles
Mr. S. Barnard
H. W. Bunbury, Efq.
Mr. I. Cater
Mr. S. Chifney
Mr. Dennis Fitzpatrick
Mr. J. Edwards
G. Eyres, Efq.
Mr. Gedge
Mrs. Golding, the White Hart-inn, Newmarket
General Gwynn
John Harwood, Efq.
Mr. Hilton
Mr. Lacey
Mr. W. Leach
Geo. Leathes, Efq.
Mr. Phillipfon

J. H. Powell, Efq.
Mr. Prentice
Mr. Prince
R. G. Rookwood, Efq.
Wm. Schutz, Efq.
W. Smith, Efq.

SURREY.
John Barlow, Efq.
Eliab Breton, Efq.
John Browne, Efq.
H. Boulton, Efq.
Mr. Richard Bowman
Chr. Buckle, Efq.
Mr. Thomas Clark
Mr. Copper, the Wheel-Inn, Egham
Mr. James Dartnell
Mr. Thomas Dockeray
Mr. Doolan
John H. Durand, Efq.
Mr. W. Fenwick
Mr. Girling, the King John-inn, Egham
Mr. Halford
Mr. Joseph Hall
W. P. Hamond, Efq.
Mr. Johnson
Benjamin Ifaac, Efq.
Mr. Wm. Knight
Mr. Lack, the Eclipfe, Egham
James Lawrell, Efq.
Robert Lovelace, Efq.
Thomas Martin, Efq.
Mr. Moon, King's Arms, Godalmin

Mr. T. H. Morland
Thomas Page, Efq.
Mr. Richardfon
Henry Rycroft, Efq.
Mr. J. Scott
Mr. Thomas Smith
Mr. W. Thompfon
Hen. H. Townfend, Efq.
Mr. M. Turner
Mr. William Worley

SUSSEX.

J. Blagrave, Efq.
W. Brereton, Efq.
Edward Broughton, Efq.
Mr. Thomas Brown
Edward Byndlofs, Efq.
Mr. Peter Clayton
Mr. Donaldfon
Ifaac Eeles, Efq.
Dr. Goodwin
Mr. Thomas Grant
Charles Harrifon, Efq.
S. S. Heming, Efq.
T. Read Kemp, Efq.
Mr. Lamb
Mr. W. Meads
John Micklethwait, Efq.
J. Lewis Newnham, Efq.
Mr. Peck
Mr. Raggett
John Shakefpear, Efq.
Mr. J. Shoubridge
Mr. Shuckard
Mr. Silverfides
G. White Thomas, Efq.

Mr. Tilt
Mr. Wilkes

WARWICKSHIRE.

Mr. Richard Bevan
Mr. Cleeter
Mr. Jos. Cotton
Col. Dilke
Mr. John Eagle
Mr. J. Gilliver
Mr. Jofeph Gray
Mr. W. Greenall
Samuel Harper, Efq.
John Hawkes, Efq.
Robert Ladbroke, Efq.
Wm. Marfh, Efq.
Richard Sadler, Efq.
Mr. B. Shepheard

WESTMORELAND.

John Upton, Efq.

WILTS.

Mr. Bendry
J. Benett, Efq.
Henry Biggs, Efq.
Mr. Burnett
T. Coufens, Efq.
Thomas Crook, Efq.
Thomas Goddard, Efq.
Ch. Gordon Gray, Efq.
R. Jones, Efq.
Robert Mafkelyne, Efq.
Wm. Northey, Efq.
Mr. Samuel Pofton
R. Radclyffe,

R. Radclyffe, Efq.
Wm. Scrope, Efq.
Walter Spencer, Efq.
Mr. Weeks
W. Wyndham, Efq.

WORCESTERSHIRE.

Richard Bayzand, Efq.
Mr. Walter Benton
Rowland Berkeley, Efq.
Gen. Bingham
Mr. Calcott
Mr. B. Chufe
Danfey Danfey, Efq.
Mr. Wm. Davis
Mr. John Griffiths
W. Hicks, Efq.
Mr. Jacob Jones
Col. Newport
Mr. Palfrey
W. Pratleton, Efq.
W. A. Roberts, Jun. Efq.
Mr. Jofeph Smith, Jun.
James Squires, Efq.
Mr. J. Tilbrook
Mr. Wheeler
Mr. S. Wilkins

YORKSHIRE.

Mr. Jofeph Acred
James Allott, Efq.
The late Capt. Barlow
Mr. Bartholoman
John Bell, Efq.
Mr. Beft
R. Bower, Efq.
Mr. D. Burnell

Mr. William Carter
Col. Childers
Mr. Chippendale
J. W. Clough, Efq.
Mr. S. Clowes
Mr. Coupland
Major Creyke
Stephen Croft, Efq.
Robert Denifon, Efq.
Mr. Drabwell
Mr. R. Erfkine
Mr. Thos. Fergufon
W. Garforth, Efq.
John Grimftone, Efq.
Mr. John Grove
F. Hartley, Efq.
L. W. Hartley, Efq.
Fra. Hawkefworth, Efq.
W. N. W. Hewett, Efq.
Mr. James Hill
Ellis L. Hodgfon, Efq.
Har. Hudfon, Efq.
Mr. W. Hutchinfon
Mr. J. Hutchinfon
George Hutton, Efq.
Mr. Jackfon
J. Johnfon, Efq.
Mr. Kirby
Robt. Lafcelles, Efq.
William Lee, Efq.
Thomas Lloyd, Efq.
Lieut. Col. Marriott
W. H. Marfden, Efq.
J. Mafon, Efq.
Jofias Morley, Efq.
Mr. John Nalton
J. P. Nevile, Efq.
Conyers Norton, Efq.
Mr. T.

Mr. T. Outram
J. G. Parkhurst, Efq.
Mr. Peacock
Mr. Tho. Pearfon
Henry Peirfe, Efq.
Mr. W. Peirfe
Mr. Pilkington
Mr. T. Pinder
Mr. Porter
Mr. R. Rayner
Mr. Rhodes
Mr. Richardfon
Brooke Richmond, Efq.
Mr. Scafe
Mr. C. Simpfon
Mr. Jofeph Smith
W. Sotherton, Jun. Efq.
John Stapleton, Efq.
Bryan Stapleton, Efq.
J. Starkey, Efq.
Col. Surtees
Tatton Sykes, Efq.
Jofeph Thompfon, Efq.
T. Thornton, Efq.
J. Torre, Efq.
H. Verelft, Efq.
Mr. Trebeck
John Waftell, Efq.
Francis Watt, Efq.
P. Wentworth, Efq.
John Wharton, Efq.
Mr. Jofeph Wigfall
Edward Wilkinfon, Efq.
Mr. Thomas Wilkinfon
Chr. Wilfon, Efq. 2 fets
H. Witham, Efq.
J. A. S. Worley, Efq.
W. Wrightfon, Efq.

WALES.

Mr. J. Bradley
Col. Colby
Edward Corbet, Efq.
Mr. Gamble
Mr. Harley
John Humffreys, Efq.
Herbert Hurft, Efq.
Mr. John Jeffreys
R. H. Jenkins, Efq.
Mr. Robert Jenkins
Mr. Thomas Johnfon
Robert Jones, Efq. 2 fets
Thomas Parry Jones
Edward Lloyd, Efq.
Edward Lloyd, Efq.
Thomas Lloyd, Efq.
W. A. Madocks, Efq.
Col. Morgan
Mr. Morgan
Mr. David Owen
R. Manfel Philipps, Efq.
F. R. Price, Efq.
Richard Pulefton, Efq.
E. W. V. Salefbury, Efq.
Amos Strettell, Efq.
T. M. Talbot, Efq.
Mr. Templeman
Mr. R. Williams
C. A. Wighton, Efq.
Robert Wrixon, Efq.
Thomas Wyndham, Efq.

SCOTLAND.

George Baillie, Efq.
R. Baird, Efq.

Wm.

Wm. Blair, Efq.

Alexander Bofwell, Efq.

Geo. Jas. Campbell, Efq.

John Cathcart, Efq.

George Cuming, Efq.

Mr. George Dawfon

Alexander·Don, Efq.

J. T. Erfkine, Efq.

Mr. Robert Ewart

Francis Garden, Efq.

W. C. Graham, Efq.

Meff. W. Hagart and Sons for the Caledonian Hunt

James Hamilton, Efq.

Peter Hay, Efq.

Col. Maxwell Heron

Quintin Macadam, Efq.

R. Dundas M'Queen, Efq.

John Maitland, Efq.

Lt.-Col. W. Maxwell

R. A. Ofwald, Efq.

George Ramfay, Efq.

Fletcher Read, Efq.

IRELAND.

W. Congreve Alcock, Efq.

Wm. Batterfby, Efq.

Theobald Butler, Efq.

Fitz-M. Caldwell, Efq.

C. Carrol, Efq.

Abel Craven, Efq.

Hugh Croke, Efq.

D. Bowes Daly, Efq.

Patr. Daly, Efq.

Richard Deafe, Efq.

John Dennis, Efq.

Farming Society, Dublin

Robert Gore, Efq.

R. Hamilton, Efq.

Charles Hawkes, Efq.

Mr. Hunter

Mr. Kelly, Keeper of the Match-book, Kildare

J. Kirwan, Jun. Efq.

Col. Lumm

Eldred Pottinger, Efq.

Col. Ram

John Taylor, Efq.

R. Boyle Townfend, Efq.

Mr. Watts, Vet. Surgeon

John Whaley, Efq.

GERMANY.

His Excellency Count Lewis Stahremberg

EAST INDIES.

T. Thornhill, Efq.

NORTH AMERICA.

John Hoomes, Efq.

Marm. Johnfton, Efq.

Major-Gen. M'Pherfon

John Randolph, Efq.

C. Ridgeley, Efq.

John Tayloe, Efq.

Dr. Wm. Thornton

JAMAICA.

Benjamin Scott, Efq.

John Taylor, Efq.

Abftract

Abstract of Acts of Parliament

RELATIVE TO

HORSE RACING.

THAT from and after the twenty-fourth day of June, one thousand seven hundred and forty, no person or persons whatsoever shall enter, start, or run any horse, mare, or gelding, for any Plate, Prize, Sum of Money, or other thing, unless such horse, mare, or gelding, shall be truly and *bona fide* the property of, and belonging to, such person so entering, starting, or running the same horse, mare, or gelding: nor shall any one person enter and start more than one horse, mare, or gelding, for one and the same Plate, Prize, Sum of Money, or other thing; and in case any person or persons shall, after the said twenty-fourth day of June, one thousand seven hundred and forty, enter, start, or run any horse, mare, or gelding, not being the property, truly and *bona fide*, of such person so entering, starting, or running the same for any Plate, Prize, Sum of Money, or other thing, the said horse, mare, or gelding, or the value thereof, shall be forfeited; to be sued for and recovered, and disposed of in manner as is hereinafter mentioned; and in case any person or persons shall enter and start more than one horse, mare, or gelding, for one and the same Plate, Prize,

Prize, Sum of Money, or other thing; every such horse, mare, or gelding, other than the first entered horse, mare, or gelding, or the value thereof, shall be forfeited; to be sued for and recovered, and disposed of in manner as hereinafter is mentioned.

Any person that shall enter, start, or run, a horse, mare, or gelding, for less value than fifty pounds, forfeits the sum of two hundred pounds.

Every person that shall print, publish, advertise, or proclaim any money, or other thing to be run for, of less value than fifty pounds, forfeits the sum of one hundred pounds.

Provided, That every Race that shall be thereafter run for any Plate, Prize, or Sum of Money, be begun and ended in one day.

Horses may run for any sum on Newmarket-heath, in the counties of Cambridge and Suffolk, and Black Hambleton, in the county of York, without incurring any penalty.

And be it further enacted by the Authority aforesaid, That from and after the twenty-fourth day of June, one thousand seven hundred and forty, all and every Sum and Sums of Money to be paid for entering of any horse, mare, or gelding, to start for any Plate, Prize, Sum of Money, or other thing, shall go and be paid to the second best horse, mare, or gelding, which shall start or run for such Plate, Prize, or Sum of Money as aforesaid.

Provided also, That nothing therein contained shall extend or be construed to extend, to prevent the starting or running any horse, mare, or gelding, for any Plate, Prize, or other thing or things issuing out of, or paid for by, the rents, issues, and profits, of any lands, tenements, or hereditaments; or of, or by, the interest of any Sum or Sums of Money, chargeable with the same, or appropriated for that purpose.

DUTY

DUTY ON HORSES.

For every faddle-horfe, coach-horfe, &c. to be paid, and for every horfe, mare, or gelding, entered to ftart or run for any Plate, Prize, Sum of Money, or other thing whatfoever, the further fum of two pounds two fhillings.

And be it further enacted, That the owner of every horfe, mare, or gelding, entered to ftart or run for any Plate, Prize, Sum of Money, or other thing, fhall previous to the entering or ftarting fuch horfe, mare or gelding, pay the fum of two pounds, two fhillings, as the duty for one year; which faid money fhall be paid for the ufe of His Majefty, his heirs, and fucceffors, into the hands of the Clerk of the Courfe, Book-keeper, or other perfon authorifed to make the entry of fuch horfe, mare, or gelding, being to ftart or run for fuch Plate, Prize, Sum of Money, or other thing, as aforefaid; and if any owner of fuch horfe, mare, or gelding, fhall, previous to the ftarting, neglect or refufe to pay the faid fum of two pounds, two fhillings for fuch entrance, to the Clerk of the Courfe, Book-keeper, or other perfon authorifed to make the entry as aforefaid, the owner or owners of every fuch horfe, mare, or gelding, fhall forfeit and pay the fum of twenty pounds, to be recovered and applied in fuch manner as hereinafter is directed.

And be it further enacted, That every Clerk of the Courfe, Book-keeper, or other perfon fo receiving the faid fum of two pounds, two fhillings, as entrance money, fhall within fourteen days after the receipt thereof, give an account of all monies received

ceived by him for horfes fo entered to ftart as aforefaid, to the Diftributor of ftamps, in the county
where the Race was run, upon demand made by fuch
Diftributor, for the fame, and producing his appointment as Diftributor, under the hands and feals of three
of the Commiffioners of His Majefty's ftamp duties;
and in cafe of not accounting for, and paying the
fame, he fhall for every default, in not delivering
fuch accounts, pay the fum of one hundred pounds:
and for every default of payment of the monies due
on fuch accounts, forfeit and pay double the amount
of the monies due on the faid accounts, at the time
of fuch default.

And it is hereby enacted, That the faid head Diftributor of ftamps, to whom fuch money fhall be paid
as aforefaid, fhall make an allowance of one fhilling
in the pound to fuch Clerk of the Courfe, Book-
keeper, or other perfon as aforefaid, for all monies
fo accounted for and paid by him to fuch Diftributor
as aforefaid.

KING'S PLATE ARTICLES.

IT is His MAJESTY's Command, that thefe following Rules be obferved by the Owners and
Riders of all fuch Horfes, Mares, or Geldings,
as fhall run for His MAJESTY's PLATES at NEW-
MARKET.

I. EVERY horfe, mare or gelding that runneth
for the faid Plate fhall carry twelve ftone;
fourteen pounds to the ftone, three heats.*

II. Every perfon that putteth in a horfe, mare or
gelding, for the faid Plate, is to fhew fuch horfe,
mare or gelding, with the marks, name, and name
of the Owner, to be entered at the King's Stables
in Newmarket the day before they run; and fhall
then produce a certificate under the hand of the
breeder, that his horfe, mare, or gelding, be no
more than   years old the grafs before.

III. Every horfe, mare, or gelding, that runneth, is
to ftart between the hours of one and four in the
afternoon; and to be allowed half an hour between
each heat to rub.

IV. Every horfe, mare, or gelding, that runneth on
the wrong fide of the Pofts or flags, or is diftanced
in any of the heats, fhall have no fhare of the faid
Plate, nor be fuffered to run any more.

V. The horfe, mare, or gelding, that winneth any two
heats, winneth the Plate; but if three feveral horfes,
mares, or geldings, win each of them a heat, then
thofe three, and only they, to run a fourth heat;
and the horfe, mare, or gelding, that winneth the
fourth heat, fhall have the Plate.

* By order, this is altered to ONE HEAT, and different weights
are appointed.

VI. And

VI. And each horfe, mare, or gelding's, &c. place as he or they come in, by the ending Poft, each heat, as 1ft, 2d, 3d, &c. fhall be determined by fuch judges as fhall be appointed for that purpofe, by the Mafter of the Horfe. And in cafe any horfe, mare, or gelding, fhall be then, or after, proved to be above the age of   years the grafs before, the Owner or Owners of fuch horfe, mare, or gelding, fhall be made incapable of ever running for any of the King's Plates hereafter.

VII. As many of the riders as fhall crofs, joftle, or ftrike, or ufe any other foul play, as fhall be judged by fuch perfon or perfons as fhall be appointed by the Mafter of the Horfe, fuch rider fhall be made incapable of ever riding any horfe, mare, or gelding, for any of His Majefty's Plates hereafter; and fuch Owners fhall have no benefit of that Plate; but fuch Owners may be permitted to run any horfe, mare, or gelding, for any other of His Majefty's free Plates hereafter.

VIII. Every rider fhall, immediately after each heat be run, be obliged to come to the Ending Poft with his horfe, mare, or gelding, then and there to alight, and not before, and there to weigh to the fatisfaction of the judges appointed for that purpofe.

IX. And in cafe of neglect or refufal thereof, fuch owners and riders fhall be immediately declared incapable of running or riding any more, for this or any of His Majefty's Plates hereafter.

X. And in cafe any difference fhall arife, relating to their ages, or in their running, or to thefe His Majefty's orders, &c. the fame to be determined by fuch perfon or perfons who fhall be appointed by the aforefaid Mafter of the Horfe.

☞ *Thefe Articles will continue in force for fucceeding years, unlefs directed to the contrary by His Majefty.*

FORM

FORM OF A CERTIFICATE,

OF HAVING WON

A KING'S PLATE.

THESE are to certify, that His Majesty's Plate of a Hundred Guineas was won at
the   day of   180 , by
                     's chefnut horfe, called

A. B. Steward
C. D. Clerk of the Courfe.

E. { *Lord Lieutenant of the County.

To the Right Honorable the Earl of CHESTERFIELD, } Mafter of the Horfe to His Majefty. }

[*The Signature of the Lord Lieutenant alone is fufficient, but that can feldom be obtained without firft preducing to him a Certificate, figned by the Steward and Clerk of the Courfe.*]

N. B. The Certificate, when properly figned, is payable at fight to the winner of the Plate, (or to any other perfon, if endorfed by the winner) at the Office of the Clerk of His Majefty's Stables, in the King's Mews, London.

☞ Since the alteration in the Act of Parliament, refpecting Stamps for Receipts, the Clerk of the Stables requires the perfon prefenting a Certificate for payment to provide a Receipt Stamp of the proper value, which at prefent is two fhillings.

* If the Lord Lieutenant be out of the Kingdom, the Signature of the Perfon regularly deputed by him is admiffible The Certificate for the Afcot-Heath Plate, muft be figned by the Mafter of His Majefty's Hounds, inftead of the Lord Lieutenant.

TABLE

TABLE

SHEWING

What WEIGHTS Horfes are to carry that run for
GIVE and TAKE PLATES, from Twelve to
Fifteen Hands high; Fourteen Hands carrying
Nine Stone.

	ft.	lb.	oz.
TWELVE HANDS..................	5	0	0
And half a quarter of an inch	5	0	14
And a quarter........	5	1	12
A quarter and half a quarter	5	2	10
Half an inch	5	3	8
Half an inch and half a quarter	5	4	6
Three quarters of an inch..............	5	5	4
Three quarters and half a quarter	5	6	2
One inch........................ ...	5	7	0
One inch and half a quarter............	5	7	14
One inch and a quarter........	5	8	12
One inch a quarter and half a quarter..	5	9	10
One inch and a half	5	10	8
One inch and a half and half a quarter..	5	11	6
One inch and three quarters...	5	12	4
One inch three quarters and half a quarter	5	13	2
Two inches....................	6	0	0
Two inches and half a quarter...........	6	0	14
Two inches and a quarter.	6	1	12
Two inches a quarter and half a quarter..	6	2	10
Two inches and a half	6	3	8
Two inches and a half and half a quarter	6	4	6
Two inches and three quarters...	6	5	4
Two inches three quarters & half a quarter	6	6	2
Three inches	6	7	0
Three inches and half a quarter	6	7	14
Three inches and a quarter	6	8	12

Three

	ft.	lb.	oz.
Three inches a quarter and half a quarter	6	9	10
Three inches and a half	6	10	8
Three inches and a half and half a quarter	6	11	6
Three inches and three quarters...... ..	6	12	4
Three inches three quarters & half a quarter	6	13	2
THIRTEEN HANDS.	7	0	0
And half a quarter of an inch .. ..'.....	7	0	14
And a quarter.........................	7	1	12
A quarter and half a quarter............	7	2	10
And half an inch	7	3	8
Half an inch and half a quarter	7	4	6
Three quarters of an inch.............	7	5	4
Three quarters and half a quarter	7	6	2
One inch......................... ..	7	7	0
One inch and half a quarter............	7	7	14
One inch and a quarter.........	7	8	12
One inch a quarter and half a quarter. ..	7	9	10
One inch and a half	7	10	8
One inch and a half and half a quarter..	7	11	6
One inch and three quarters............	7	12	4
One inch three quarters and half a quarter	7	13	2
Two inches.........................	8	0	0
Two inches and half a quarter.........,	8	0	14
Two inches and a quarter.. ....,	8	1	12
Two inches a quarter and half a quarter..	8	2	10
Two inches and a half	8	3	8
Two inches and a half and half a quarter	8	4	6
Two inches and three quarters..........	8	5	4
Two inches three quarters & half a quarter	8	6	2
Three inches......................	8	7	0
Three inches and half a quarter	8	7	14
Three inches and a quarter ....:	8	8	12
Three inches a quarter and half a quarter	8	9	10
Three inches and a half....'........... .	8	10	8
Three inches and a half and half a quarter	8	11	6
Three inches and three quarters ....:	8	12	4
Three inches three quarters & half a quarter	8	13	2

FOUR-

	ft.	lb.	oz.
FOURTEEN HANDS....................	9	0	0
And half a quarter of an inch..........	9	0	14
And a quarter......................	9	1	12
A quarter and half a quarter	9	2	10
And half an inch	9	3	8
Half an inch and half a quarter........	9	4	6
And three quarters of an inch..........	9	5	4
Three quarters and half a quarter	9	6	2
One inch	9	7	0
One inch and half a quarter............	9	7	14
One inch and a quarter................	9	8	12
One inch a quarter and half a quarter....	9	9	10
One inch and a half	9	10	8
One inch and a half and half a quarter..	9	11	6
One inch and three quarters	9	12	4
One inch three quarters and half a quarter	9	13	2
Two inches........	10	0	0
Two inches and half a quarter	10	0	14
Two inches and a quarter........	10	1	12
Two inches a quarter and half a quarter	10	2	10
Two inches and a half ......,.	10	3	8
Two inches and a half and half a quarter	10	4	6
Two inches and three quarters........ ..	10	5	4
Two inches three quarters & half a quarter	10	6	2
Three inches	10	7	0
Three inches and half a quarter........	10	7	14
Three inches and a quarter	10	8	12
Three inches a quarter and half a quarter	10	9	10
Three inches and a half	10	10	8
Three inches and a half and half a quarter	10	11	6
Three inches and three quarters	10	12	4
Three inches three quarters & half a quarter	10	13	2
FIFTEEN HANDS................... ..	11	0	0

The accounts are to be produced by the Stewards annually on the third of June.

That in cafe any Gentleman who keeps running horfes, has caufe to complain of any feeder, rider, groom, boy, or other perfon, employed by him in, or intrufted with the knowledge of, trials, of having difcovered them, directly or indirectly, by betting, or wilfully in any other way, (unlefs allowed fo to do by his mafter); or if any perfon as aforefaid, living with any Gentleman, fhall be difcovered in watching trials himfelf, or procuring other perfons To to do, or by any unfair means whatfoever endeavouring to difcover trials; on fuch complaint being carried to any one of the Stewards, that Steward is to fummon a general Jockey Club meeting as foon as convenient; which meeting is to appoint a committee. of three members, to examine into the accufation; and in cafe they fhall be of opinion that the perfon or perfons is, or are, guilty of it, then the perfon fo found guilty fhall be difmiffed from the fervice of his mafter, and the faid perfon fhall not be employed by any member of the Jockey Club, in any capacity whatfoever; nor fhall any horfe, &c. fed or rode by him or them, or in the management of which he or they are concerned, be fuffered to ftart for Plate, Match, or Subfcription. And the names of the perfons found guilty of thefe offences fhall be expofed in the Racing Calendar, and inferted in a paper to be fixed up in the coffee-room at Newmarket.

That a copy of all the Stakes to be made for Matches, Subfcriptions, and Sweepftakes, and the day and hour of fhewing, or entering, fhall be fairly written out, and fixed up by order of the Stewards, on the fide of the chimney-piece, at each end of the coffee-room, on the Sunday evening before each meeting; to continue there each day of the meeting, as notice for ftaking, fhewing, or entering, and no other fhall be infifted upon.

A Day

A Day Book fhall be kept by the perfon appointed by the Stewards, and continue in the coffee-room, in which fhall be entered an account of all Matches, Subfcriptions, and Sweepftakes, to be run for each day, within that meeting, and as the different Stakes are made, the payments fhall be marked to the names of the perfons fo paying.

All Stakes fhall be made in cafh, bank bills, bank poft bills properly indorfed, bankers notes payable to bearer, or bankers notes payable to order, alfo properly indorfed; and not otherwife, without the confent of the party or parties prefent, concerned in the Match, Subfcription, or Sweepftakes, on whofe account fuch Stakes are made.

All Stakes for Matches, Subfcriptions, and Sweep-ftakes, fhall be made before ftarting for the fame; and in default thereof by any perfon, he fhall forfeit in like manner, as if he had not produced his colt, filly, horfe, or mare, to ftart, and fhall have no claim to the Stake or Stakes of the Match, Subfcription, or Sweepftakes, fhould his colt, filly, horfe, or mare, have ftarted and come firft; and this to remain in full force, as an eftablifhed agreement of the Jockey Club, unlefs fuch perfon has previoufly obtained the confent of the party or parties prefent, with whom he is engaged, to difpenfe with his making his Stake as aforefaid.—N. B. This Rule does not extend to Bets which are to be paid and received as if no fuch omif-fion had happened.

All forfeits unpaid before ftarting, for any Match, Subfcription, or Sweepftakes, fhall be paid to the per-fon appointed by the Stewards to receive the fame, at the coffee-room, before twelve o'clock at night, of the day fuch forfeits are determined; and each perfon making default therein, fhall forfeit and pay to the perfon fo appointed by the faid Stewards, after the rate of five pounds for every hundred pounds fo for-feited,

feited, which shall be disposed of by the said Stewards towards such uses as they shall think fit.

And in order to prevent frauds, notice shall be given, that if any person make any bet or bets, from signal or indication, after the race has been determined at the Post, such person is not entitled to receive, or liable to pay the same; as such bet or bets, is or are, fraudulent, illegal, and totally void: and that if any servant belonging to a member of the Society shall be found to have made, or be engaged in the making, any such bet or bets, he shall be dismissed his service, and no farther employed by any member of this Society.

That all forfeits or money paid on compromising any Match or Sweepstakes, shall, *bona fide*, be declared and entered in the day-book, in order that all betters may be put upon an equality with the persons who had the Match or Sweepstakes, and may thus ascertain in what proportion they are to pay or receive.

That the Stewards of the Jockey Club shall appoint some proper person to examine every colt or filly, being of the age of two, three, or four years, at the Ending Post, immediately after running, the first time any colt or filly shall start for any Plate, Match, Sweepstakes, or Subscription, at Newmarket, and the said appointed person is to sign a certificate of such examination, and his opinion thereupon, which certificate is to be hung up before eight o'clock the evening of the said day of running, in the coffee-house at Newmarket.—But for all Plates, Matches, Subscriptions, or Sweepstakes, where the colt or filly is required to be shewn before running, the examination as above-mentioned, shall be made at the time of shewing them, and the certificate of the person appointed shall immediately, in like manner, be fixed up in the coffee-room at Newmarket.

That

That the hours of starting shall be fixed up in the coffee-house by eight o'clock in the evening preceding the day of running; and it is expected that every groom shall start punctually at the time appointed; and any groom failing so to do shall forfeit five guineas each time to the Jockey Club. It is also expected, that every groom will attend to the regulations and orders which the Stewards of the Jockey Club may give, relative to the preservation of the course and exercise ground.

That no person do borrow or hire any horse, &c. not belonging to his avowed confederate, to run in a private trial, without entering the name of such horse, before the trial shall be run, in the book appointed to be kept for that purpose, in the coffee-room at Newmarket: and no persons to be deemed confederates who do not subscribe this article as such.

That all disputes relative to racing at Newmarket, shall, for the future, be determined by the three Stewards, and two Referees, to be chosen by the parties concerned. If there should be only two Stewards present, they are to fix upon a third person, in lieu of the absent Steward.

That if for any Sweepstakes or Subscription, the first two horses shall come in so near together, that the judge shall not be able to decide which won, those two horses shall run for such prize over again, after the last Match on the same day; the other horses which started for such Sweepstakes or Subscription, shall be deemed losers, and entitled to their respective places, as if the race had been finally determined the first time.

That all bets determined by one event shall be subject (as before agreed) to any compromise made by the Principals, and paid in proportion to such compromise: but that all double bets shall, for the future (on account of the frequent disputes which have arisen), be considered as play or pay bets.

When

When any Match or Sweepstakes shall be made, and no particular weight specified, the horses, &c. shall carry eight stone seven pounds each. And if any weight is given, the highest weight is, by this resolution, fixed at eight stone seven pounds.

No horse that is matched to run on the day of entrance, for any Plate, &c. shall be obliged to shew and enter at the hour appointed, but shall shew and enter within an hour after his engagements are over, provided such horse, &c. be named at the usual time of entrance, which is to be between the hours of eleven and one, for all Plates, Subscriptions, and Sweepstakes, where any entrance is required, and no other particular time specified.

That all bets depending between any two horses, either in Match or Sweepstakes, are null and void, if those horses become the property of one, and the same person, or his avowed confederate, subsequent to the bets being made.

That the *Cup* be challenged for on the Monday in the First Spring Meeting, and the horses named for it declared at six o'clock on the Saturday evening of the said meeting.

That the *Whip* be challenged for on the Monday or Tuesday in the Second Spring or Second October Meeting, and the acceptance signified, or the Whip resigned, before the end of the same meeting.

If challenged for and accepted in the Spring, to be run for on the Thursday in the Second October Meeting following; and if in the October, on the Thursday in the Second Spring Meeting, B. C. weight, 10st. and to stake 200gs each.

That after the 13th of April, 1777, the Proprietor of any horse, &c. engaged in Match or Sweepstakes, who shall declare his intention of not starting before eight o'clock on the evening preceding the engagement, to the Keeper of the Match-book, or either of

the

the Stewards, fhall be entitled to five per cent. and no more of the forfeit.

That after the first day of July, 1793, no perfon fhall be allowed to ftart any horfe, mare, or gelding, for Match, Sweepftakes, or Subfcription, unlefs he fhall have paid all former ftakes and forfeits to the keeper of the Match-book, by eight o'clock in the evening before ftarting.—This Rule was intended, and has fince been declared, to extend to Epfom, Afcot, Brighthelmfton, York, Doncafter, and all other places, befides Newmarket, where Races are run, and Engagements entered into, by Members of the Jockey Club, for Matches, Sweepftakes, or Subfcriptions. And it is recommended to the confideration of the Stewards of other Races, where Members of this Club are not amongft the Subfcribers.

That the ground fhall not be engaged for trials, by the proprietor of any ftable of running horfes, more than two days in the fame week.

That when any Match is made, in which croffing and joftling are not mentioned, they fhall be underftood to be barred.

That when any Match or Sweepftakes is made, in which no Courfe is mentioned, it fhall be underftood to be the Courfe ufually run by horfes of the fame age as thofe engaged, viz. if yearlings, the Yearling Courfe: if two years old, the Two Years Old Courfe: if three years old, Rowley's Mile: if four years old, Ditch-in: if five years old, or upwards, Beacon Courfe: and in cafe the horfes matched fhould be of different ages, the Courfe to be fettled by the age of the youngeft.

That all forfeits declared or incurred for any Match, Sweepftakes, or Subfcription, fhall be paid to the Keeper of the Match-book, before twelve o'clock on the evening the race is run, under the former penalty of five per cent. to the Jockey Club; and perfons making default herein, fhall not be al-

lowed

lowed the deduction for the timely declaration of such forfeits.

That horses, &c. entered for Plates or Subscriptions, shall not be required to be shewn, if such horse, &c. has before started at Newmarket; and that the owner of each horse, entered for a Plate or Subscription, shall declare to the Stewards, or the Keeper of the Match-book, the evening before, by eight o'clock, or when the list is read, at half past nine o'clock, whether his horse is intended to run or not, which declaration shall be deemed obligatory, if in the affirmative, unless the horse be taken ill or matched; and if in the negative, his name shall be erased from the list.

That the owners of horses, &c. engaged in Matches or Sweepstakes, in which the forfeits shall amount to one hundred guineas, or upwards, shall be entitled to a deduction of ten per cent. if they declare their forfeits by half an hour past nine o'clock in the evening preceding running.

That from May 2d, 1800, no gentleman shall try the horse of any other person, except his declared confederate, without giving notice of such trial, by inscribing the name of the horse or horses, or their pedigrees, with the names of their owners, before or immediately after such trial, in the book, at the coffee-house.

That all Bets made on the Derby or Oaks Stakes at Epsom, the Pavilion at Brighthelmston, the St. Leger at Doncaster, and also on the Newmarket Stakes, and the Oatlands Stakes in the Spring and October Meetings, be deemed Play or Pay Bets; and also, that all Bets between particular horses be null and void, if neither of the horses happen to be the winner, unless specified to the contrary.

That the Keeper of the Match-book be directed to charge the proprietors of such horses as receive forfeit, and shall be excused from appearing, with the same fees for the weights and scales, as if they had come over the Course.

Complaint being made of new and exorbitant demands, in various places, for the maintenance of Race Horses, and the Lads attending them, resolved,

That the Members of this Club will give a preference to such Stable Keepers, and Inn Keepers, whose charges are reasonable.

That in future, the ballots for Members of the Jockey Club shall be in the New Rooms, Newmarket; on the Tuesday in the First Spring Meeting, and the Tuesday in the Second October Meeting, in each year.

That the candidates shall be proposed by Members, and their names put up in the Card Room, in the Meetings preceding the ballots, viz. in the Craven, and First October Meetings.

That Nine Members at least be present at the ballot, and that Two black balls exclude.

That all Members of the New Rooms, at Newmarket, may become Members of the Coffee Room, by application to Mr. Weatherby, and causing their names to be inserted in the list of Subscribers.

RULES

RULES

HORSE-RACING IN GENERAL,

WITH A DESCRIPTION OF

A POST AND HANDICAP MATCH;

Horfes take their Ages from *May-day*.
1760 Yards are a Mile.
240 Yards are a Diftance.
Four Inches are a Hand.
Fourteen Pounds are a Stone.

CATCH Weights are, each party to appoint any perfon to ride without weighing.

Give-and-take Plates, are fourteen hands to carry a ftated weight, all above, or under, to carry extra, or be allowed, the proportion of feven pounds for an inch.

A Whim Plate, is weight for age, and weight for inches.

A Poft Match, is to infert the age of the horfes in the articles, and to run any horfe of that age, without declaring what horfe, till you come to the Poft to ftart.

A Handi-

A Handicap Match, is for *A. B.* and *C.* to put an equal fum into a hat, *C.* who is the handicapper, makes a match for *A,* and *B.* who, when they have perufed it, put their hands into their pockets, and draw them out clofed, then they open them together, and if both have money in their hands, the match is confirmed; if neither have money, it is no match. In both cafes, the handicapper draws all the money out of the hat; but if one has money in his hand, and the other none, then it is no match; and he that has money in his hand, is entitled to the depofit in the hat.

The horfe that has his head at the Ending Poft firft, wins the heat.

Riders muft ride their horfes to the Weighing Poft to weigh, and he that difmounts before, or wants weight, is diftanced.

If a rider fall from his horfe, and the horfe be rode in by a perfon that is fufficient weight, he will take place the fame as if it had not happened, provided he go back to the place where the rider fell.

Horfe plates or fhoes not allowed in the weight.

Horfes not entitled to ftart, without producing a proper certificate of their age, if required, at the time appointed in the articles, except where aged horfes are included, and in that cafe, a *junior* horfe may enter without a certificate, provided he carry the fame weight as the aged.

All bets are for the beft of the Plate, if nothing is faid to the contrary.

For the beft of the Plate, where there are three heats run, the horfe is fecond that wins one.

For the beft of the heats, the horfe is fecond that beats the other twice out of three times, though he doth not win a heat.

A confirmed bet cannot be off without mutual confent.

Either

Either of the bettors may demand Stakes to be made, and on refusal, declare the bet void.

If a party be absent on the day of running, a public declaration of the bet may be made on the Course, and a demand, whether any person will make Stakes for the absent party; if no person consent to it, the bet may be declared void.

Bets agreed to pay or receive in town, or at any other particular place, cannot be declared off on the Course.

At Newmarket, if a Match be made for a particular day, in any meeting, and the parties agree to change the day, all bets must stand, but if run in a different meeting, the bets made before the alteration are void.

The person who lays the odds, has a right to chuse his horse, or the field.

When a person has chosen his horse, the field is what starts against him, but there is no field without one starts with him.

Bets made for pounds are paid in guineas.

If odds are laid without mentioning the horse before it is over, it must be determined as the bets were at the time of making it.

Bets made in running, are not determined till the Plate is won, if that heat is not mentioned at the time of betting.

Where a Plate is won by two heats, the preference of the horses is determined by the places they are in the second heat.

Horses running on the wrong side of the Post, and not turning back, distanced.

Horses drawn before the Plate is won, are distanced.

Horses distanced, if their riders cross and jostle, when the articles do not permit it.

A bet made after the heat is over, if the horse betted on does not start, is no bet.

When three horses have each won a heat, *they only*
must

muſt ſtart for a fourth, and the preference between them will be determined by it, there being before no difference between them.

No diſtance in a fourth heat.

Bets determined, though the horſe does not ſtart, when the words Abſolutely, Run or Pay, or Play or Pay, are made uſe of in betting.

Example. I bet that *Mr. Robinſon's* bl. h. *Sampſon*, Abſolutely wins the King's Plate at *Newmarket* next Meeting, the bet is loſt though he does not ſtart, and won though he goes over the Courſe himſelf.

In running of heats, if it cannot be decided which is firſt, the heat goes for nothing, and they may all ſtart again, except it be in the laſt heat, and then it muſt be between the two horſes, that if either had won, the race would have been over, but if between two, that the race might not have been determined, then it is no heat, and the others may all ſtart again.

Horſes that forfeit, are the beaten horſes, where it is run or pay.

Bets made on horſes winning any number of Plates that year, remain in force till the firſt day of *May*.

Money given to have a bet laid, not returned, if not run.

To propoſe a bet, and ſay done firſt to it, the perſon that replies done to it, makes it a confirmed bet.

Matches and bets are void on the deceaſe of either party, before determined.

COLOURS

COLOURS WORN BY THE RIDERS.

H.R.H. the P. of Wales	Purple waistcoat, with scarlet sleeves, trimmed with gold, and black cap
Duke of Grafton	Sky blue, with black cap
Duke of Queensberry	Deep red, with black cap
Lord Grosvenor ⎫ Gen. Grosvenor ⎭ ..	Yellow, with black cap
Lord Derby	Black, with white cap
Lord Egremont......	Dark green, with black cap
Lord G. H. Cavendish	Deep Yellow
Sir Charles Bunbury	Pink and white stripe
Sir Frank Standish ..	Mazarine blue, and white cap
Mr. Panton.........	White, with red cap
Hon. C. Wyndham..	Yellow, with blue cap
Mr. Wentworth	White satin
Mr. Westell	Pink, with black cap
Lord Sondes ⎫ Hon. G. Watson ⎭ ..	Deep yellow
Mr. Wilson.........	Light blue, trimmed with black, and black cap
Lord Darlington	Pink and black stripe
Lord Sackville	White, with black cap
Mr. Delmé Radcliffe	Blue, trimmed with pink, and black cap
Lord Clarendon	Black waistcoat, with red cap
Sir J. Shelley ⎫ Mr. Howorth ⎭	Black, with white cap
Mr. Durand	Pink and white broad stripe
Mr. Sitwell	Green, with gold button-holes, and black cap
Duke of St. Albans ..	White, with black cap
Sir T. Gascoigne	White, with black sleeves, and black cap
Sir H. T. Vane	Lilac body, yellow sleeves, and black cap

Mr.

Mr. Ladbroke ...... Black body, light blue sleeves, and black cap

Mr. Galwey .... Straw colour, purple sleeves, and straw colour cap

Mr. Wardell .... Purple body, & yellow sleeves

Mr. Biggs .... Green, with red cap

Mr. Elton .... Yellow, with black cap

Mr. Girdler .... Black

Mr. H. F. Mellish .. White body, crimson sleeves, and crimson cap tied with a white ribband

Gen. Gower .... Pink, with black cap

Lord Foley .... Green and white stripe

Mr. Lake .... Purple, with black cap

Mr. Branthwayt ..... Red, with black cap

Mr. Robert Jones .... Black body, white sleeves, and black cap

Mr. G. Hutton ...... Yellow body, purple sleeves, and purple cap

Mr. Douglas .... Gold coloured body, black sleeves and cap

Sir Hedw. Williamson Straw colour, with black cap

Mr. Kellermann ..... Rose satin, and black cap

Ld F. G. Osborne .... White

Lord Stawell. ...... Blue, and brown cap

Mr. Norton ...... Brown body, red sleeves, and white cap

Lord Barrymore .... Purple and yellow stripe

Mr. Elwes .... Purple, and black cap

Mr. Glover .... White

Mr. Andrew .... Green body, black sleeves

Mr. Golding .... Yellow and purple stripe

Mr. Abbey .... Red, with black cap

Mr. R. Boyce .... Dark green, with black cap

THE

EXACT LENGTHS

OF THE

COURSES AT NEWMARKET.

	Miles.	Furls.	Yards.
The Beacon Courſe is	4	1	138
Laſt three miles of ditto	3	0	45
Ditch-in	2	0	97
The laſt mile and a diſtance of B. C...	1	1	156
Ancaſter Mile.............	1	0	18
Fox's Courſe........	1	6	55
From the turn of the Lands, in	0	5	184
Clermont Courſe (from the Ditch to the Duke's ſtand).	1	5	217
Acroſs the Flat	1	2	44
Rowley Mile	1	0	1
Ditch Mile................	0	7	178
Abingdon Mile	0	7	211
Two middle miles of B. C. ...	1	7	125
Two years old Courſe	0	5	136
Yearling Courſe............	0	2	147
Round Courſe	3	6	93
Duke's Courſe.............	4	0	184
Bunbury Mile	0	7	208
Dutton's Courſe	3	0	0

The new Round-about Courſe on the Flat, is about a mile and three quarters.

THE

RACING CALENDAR.

—

1805.

—

April.

—

MALTON Craven Meeting.

ON Tuesday, April the 2d, a Sweepstakes of 20gs each, for colts, 8ft. 3lb. fillies, 8ft. rifing 3 yrs old;—laft mile and half. (8 Subfcribers.)

Col. Childers's b. c. Langton, by Precipitate.... 1
Mr. Nalton's br. c. by Totteridge 2
Sir M. M. Sykes's b. c. Sir Reginald 3
Mr. Garforth's b. f. Laura 4
Ld Fitzwilliam's c. Norval 5
Mr. N. B. Hodgfon's gr. c. by Delpini 6
Mr. Watt's br. c. by Precipitate, dam by Javelin 7

7 to 4 agft Sir Reginald, and 6 to 1 agft Langton.

, The Craven Stakes of 10gs each, for two yr olds, 6ft. three yr olds, 8ft. four yr olds, 8ft. 9lb. five yr olds, 9ft. 1lb. six yr olds, 9ft. 5lb. and aged, 9ft. 7lb. —two miles.

Sir M. M. Sykes's c. Sir Launcelot, by Delpini, 2 yrs old	1
Mr. Burton's br. f. Heb, 3 yrs old	2
Mr. Robinson's ch. f. by Abba Thulle, 2 yrs old	3
Mr. Garforth's b. f. Zara, 3 yrs old.............	4
Ld Fitzwilliam's Ducat, 4 yrs old......	5
Mr. Croft's b. c. by Cardinal, 2 yrs old........	6

6 to 4 agst Ducat, and 5 to 1 agst Sir Launcelot.

Mr. Hill's b. m. Peggy O'Rafferty, beat Mr. Shepherd's h. Blue Peter, rode by Gentlemen, 12ft. 3lb. each, four miles, 100gs.——3 to 1 on Blue Peter.

Wednesday, Sweepstakes of 5gs each, for horses, &c. not thorough-bred, 12ft. each, rode by Gentlemen;—2-mile heats. (28 Subscribers.)

Mr. Tatton Sykes's Hudibras, by Huby	1	1
Mr. Teasdale's b. g. Experiment	2	2
Sir F. Boynton's b. g. by Overton	5	3
Mr. Thompson's b. g. Welton	4	4
Mr. G. Hotham's b. g. by Ruler, aged......	6	5
Mr. H. C. Leatham's b. g. by Acacia	7	6
Mr. Burton's b. g. by Magnum Bonum.....	3	7

7 to 4 agst Hudibras.

Fifty Pounds for three yr olds, 7ft. four yr olds, 8ft. 4lb. five yr olds, 8ft. 10lb. six yr olds and aged, 9ft.—heats, a mile and a half. Mares allowed 2lb. The winner of a fifty carrying 3lb. extra. (Ages as in May.)

Mr. Nalton's br. c. by Totteridge, 3 yrs old..	1	1
Mr. Ackers's f. Heb, 4 yrs old	8	2
Mr. Garforth's b. f. Zara, 4 yrs old	4	3

Mr.

Mr. Hutty's ro. c. by Ormond, 3 yrs old.... 6 4
Mr. Bell's b. c. Jack Tar, 3 yrs old 7 5
Mr. Calcraft's b. f. by Reftlefs, 3 yrs old.... 5 6
Mr. Barton's gr. c. by Aimator, 3 yrs old... 2 7
Mr. Burton's b. m. by Trumpator, aged.... 3 8
Mr. Robfon's ch. c. by Ormond, 3 yrs old.. 9 dis

6 to 4 agft Heb, 7 to 4 agft Mr. Nalton's c. and after the heat, 6 to 4 he won; foon after ftarting for the fecond heat, Mr. Robfon's colt leaped over the cords—his rider (J. Midgley) in endeavouring to bring him back, got hurt fo feverely, that he died the following day.

Ld Middleton's Blue Devil, by Beningbrough, 8ft. 6lb. recd. ft. from Mr. N. B. Hodgfon's Stretch, 7ft. 12lb. two miles, 100gs, h. ft.

SKIPTON, YORKSHIRE.

On Wednefday, April 3d, a Sweepftakes of 10gs each, with 20gs added; colts, 8ft. fillies, 7ft. 11lb. rifing three yrs old;—two miles. (7 Subfcribers.)
Mr. Hutton's br. c. Cleveland, by Overton 1
Sir H. Williamfon's b. c. by Hambleton........ 2
Capt. Chamberlain's gr. c. by Delpini.. 3

2 to 1 on Cleveland.

Sweepftakes of 10gs each, for hunters, 12ft. rode by Gentlemen;—2-mile heats. (6 Subfcribers.)
Capt. Chamberlain's gr. g. Whynot, by Slope 1 1
Mr. C. Parker's ch. h. by Cavendifh........ 2 2

2 to 1 on Whynot.

On Thurfday the 4th, a Sweepftakes of 10gs each, with 20gs added, for all ages, Craven weights;—two miles. (5 Subfcribers.)

Mr.

Mr. G. Hutton's ch. c. Saxoni, by Delpini, 4 yrs   1
Mr. Walker's ch. c. Sir Sidney, 3 yrs old .... , 2

2 to 1 on Saxoni.

A Maiden Plate of 50l. for all ages;—2-mile heats.

Mr. W. Hutchinson's br. c. Didapper, by
   Overton, 2 yrs old, a feather............   1   1
Mr. Dent's Sir Charles, 3 yrs old, 7ft. 10lb.   2   2
Mr. Harris's b. f. by Hammer, 2 yrs old, a
   feather...............................   3   3

Sir Charles the favorite.

NEWMARKET

CRAVEN MEETING.

On Monday, April 15th, the Craven Stakes, a Subscription of 10gs each, for all ages; Across the Flat. Two yr olds carrying 6ft. three yr olds, 8ft. four yr olds, 8ft. 9lb. five yr olds, 9ft. 1lb. six yr olds, 9ft. 5lb. and aged, 9ft. 7lb. (13 Subscribers.)

Sir H. Williamson's b. c. Ditto, by Sir Peter,
   4 yrs old   1
Gen. Sparrow's ch. c. Castrel, 3 yrs old   2
Ld Grosvenor's b. c. Agincourt, 3 yrs old... ..   3
Mr. Delmè Radcliffe's b. m. Aniseed, aged......   4
Mr. Ladbroke's b. f. Dora, 2 yrs old; Mr. F. Neale's ch. h. Quiz, 6 yrs old; Mr. Kellermann's ch. f. Mary, 4 yrs old; Mr. Mellish's b. h. Stockton, 5 yrs old; Ld Foley's gr. c. Sir Harry Dimsdale, 4 yrs old; Mr. Sitwell's b. f. Goosecap, by Moorcock, 2 yrs old; and Mr. Wardell's b. f. Lady Brough, 3 yrs old; also started, but the Judge could place only the first four.

6 to 4 agst Lady Brough, 3 to 1 agst Ditto, and 4 to
   1 agst Castrel.

Produce

Produce Sweepſtakes of 100gs each, h. ft. R. M. (7 Subſcribers.)

Sir C. Bunbury's b. f. Lydia, by Whiſker, 8ft.4lb. 1
Gen. Groſvenor's b. f. Graffini, 7ft. 13lb........ 2
Mr. Howorth's b. c. Sinbad, 8ft. 7lb. 3

7 to 2 on Lydia.

Sweepſtakes of 100gs each, h. ft. Acroſs the Flat. (4 Subſcribers.)

Ld Foley's b. c. Watery, by Waxy, 7ft. 9lb..... 1
Mr. Norton's b. c. Quid 8ft. 1lb............... 2

6 to 4 on Quid.

Gen. Groſvenor's b. c. Skirmiſher, by Buzzard, 8ft. beat Mr. Craven's b. c. Jockey, 8ft. 1lb. Acroſs the Flat, 100gs, h. ft.

6 to 4 on Jockey.

Mr. Watſon's b. c. by Grouſe, out of Dreadnought's dam, beat Mr. Sitwell's ch. f. ſiſter to Cockfighter, 8ft. each, Ab. Mile, 100gs, h. ft.

3 to 1 on the colt.

Ld Foley's br. c. Little Peter, by Sir Peter, 8ft. 6lb. beat Sir J. Shelley's b. c. Currycomb, 8ft. 4lb. Two yr old Courſe, 50gs.

7 to 4 on Little Peter.

Sir H. Williamſon's b. h. Walton, by Sir Peter, 8ft. 6lb. beat the D. of Grafton's b. m. Penelope, 8ft. 7lb. B. C. 200gs, h. ft.

5 to 4 on Penelope.

Mr. Watſon's ch. h. Trombone, by Trumpator, 8ft. 7lb. beat Sir J. Shelley's br. f. Julia, 8ft. 3lb. Ab. Mile, 100gs, h. ft.

2 and 3 to 1 on Julia.

A 3   D. of

D. of Grafton's br. f. Peliffe, by Whifkey, 7ft. 13lb. beat Mr. Ladbroke's b. c. Buftard, 8ft. 3lb. Acrofs the Flat, 100gs.——7 to 2 on Peliffe.

Mr. Mellifh's ch. c. Honefty, by Overton, beat Mr. Jones's b. c. Freedom, 8ft. 3lb. each, Acrofs the Flat, 100gs.——5 to 4 on Honefty.

Mr. T. Fifher's b. f. Two Shoes, by Afparagus, 7ft. beat Ld F. G. Ofborne's b. f. Elizabeth, 8ft. 11lb. D. I. 100gs, h. ft.

2 to 1 on Two Shoes.

Mr. Wyndham's b. c. Tallboy, by Totteridge, recd. ft. from Sir J. Shelley's b. c. Skipjack, by Moorcock, 8ft. 3lb. each, Two yr old Courfe, 200gs, h. ft.

TUESDAY.

Mr. Jones's ch. c. Junius, by Buzzard, beat Mr. Harris's b. c. Farmer, 8ft. each, Acrofs the Flat, 300gs, h. ft.——2 to 1 on Junius.

D. of St. Albans's b. c. Merryman, by Buzzard, 8ft. 7lb. beat Gen. Grofvenor's b. c. Skirmifher, 7ft. 4lb. Ab. M. 25gs.

6 to 4 on Merryman.

Mr. Mellifh's b. h. Eagle, by Volunteer, aged, 9ft. 7lb. beat Mr. Watfon's b. c. Dreadnought, 4 yrs old, 5ft. 8lb. Ab. M. 200gs.

7 to 4 on Eagle.

Sweepftakes of 50gs each, Two yr old Courfe.

D. of St. Albans's b. c. Merryman, 8ft. 9lb. 1
Mr. Mellifh's ch. c. Honefty, 7ft. 6lb. 2
Sir J. Shelley's br. f. Pufs, 7ft. 7lb. ...'.......... pd

7 to 4 and 2 to 1 on Honefty.

. The

The firſt Claſs of the Oatlands Stakes of 50gs each, h. ft. D. I. (11 Subſcribers.)

Mr. Kellermann's b. c. Alaric, by Petworth, 3 yrs old, 6ft. 10lb............................ 1

Mr. Wardell's b. f. Houghton Laſs, 3 yrs old, 7ft. 11lb. 2

Mr. W. Fenwick's b. f. Miſs Coiner, 3 yrs old, 6ft. 8lb................................... 3

Mr. Abbey's ch. m. Margery, 5 yrs old, 8ft. 2lb. 4

Mr. Branthwayt's ch. c. Woodcot, 3 yrs, 6ft. 12lb. 5

Mr. R. Boyce's ch. c. Brainworm, 3 yrs, 7ft. 3lb. 6

Sir J. Shelley's br. m. Julia, 5 yrs old, 8ft. 1lb... 7

6 to 4 agſt Houghton Laſs, 9 to 2 agſt Margery, 5 to 1 agſt Julia, and 6 to 1 agſt Alarie.

WEDNESDAY.

Subſcription Plate of 50l. for two yr olds carrying 7ft. three yr olds, 8ft. 7lb. and four yr olds, 9ft. Two yr old Courſe.

Gen. Sparrow's ch. c. Caſtrel, by Buzzard, 3 yrs 1

Mr. Sitwell's b. f. Gooſecap, 2 yrs old.......... 2

Mr. Wardell's b. f. Lady Brough, 3 yrs old 3

Mr. Forth's br. c. Artichoke, 2 yrs old 4

Mr. Howorth's br. c. Enterprize, 3 yrs old...... 5

5 to 2 and 3 to 1 on Caſtrel.

The ſecond Claſs of the Oatlands Stakes of 50gs each, h. ft. D. I. (11 Subſcribers.)

Mr. Lake's b. h. Giles, by Trumpator, 6 yrs old, 8ft. 4lb.... 1

Mr. Watfon's b. h. Duxbury, 5 yrs old, 8ft. 9lb. 2

D. of Grafton's b. f. Parafol, 4 yrs old, 9ft. 1lb. 3

Mr. R. Weatherill's ch. h. Flambeau, 6 yrs, 7ft. 9lb. 4

Mr. Collett's b. c. Phœnix, 4 yrs old, 6ft. 10lb... 5

Mr. Kellermann's ch. f. Mary, 4 yrs old, 7ft. 10lb. 6

Mr.

Mr. Wardell's b. f. Gratitude, 3 yrs old, 7ft. 13lb.   7

    5 to 4 agft Parafol, 3 to 1 agft Duxbúry, 6 to 1 agft Giles, and 6 and 7 to 1 agft Gratitude.

The following having declared forfeit by the 31ft day of December, paid only 10gs each, which was divided between the owners of the fecond horfes in the two Claffes.

Ld Sackville's b. h. Enchanter, 5 yrs old, 8ft. 7lb.
Mr. Wardell's b. f. Lady Brough, 3 yrs old, 8ft. 3lb.
Mr. Ladbroke's b. c. Buftard, 3 yrs old, 7ft. 10lb.
Mr. Abbey's br. f. Virgin, 3 yrs old, 6ft. 7lb.
Mr. Mellifh did not name

    Mr. Parker's b. h. Oliver, by Pot8o's, beat Mr. Taylor's b. h. 8ft. 7lb. each, B. C. 25gs.

           3 to 1 on Oliver.

    Sir H. Williamfon's b. h. Walton, recd. ft. from Mr. Mellifh's b. h. Stockton, 8ft. 7lb. each, B. C. 300gs, 100gs ft.

THURSDAY.

    D. of St. Albans's b. c. Merryman, by Buzzard, beat Mr. T. Fifher's b. f. Two Shoes, 8ft. each, Acrofs the Flat, 50gs.

        6 to 4 on Merrymán.

Sweepftakes of 20gs each, Acrofs the Flat.

Ld Foley's ch. h. Captain Abfolute, by John Bull,
    5 yrs old, 8ft. 3lb.   1
Sir J. Shelley's br. m. Julia, 5 yrs old, 7ft. 11lb.   2
Mr. Delmé Radcliffe's gr. f. Nitre, 4 yrs, 7ft. 12lb.   3
Ld Sackville's ch. h. Enchanter, 5 yrs, 8ft. 12lb.   4
Mr. Howorth's ch. h. Malta, 6 yrs old, 7ft. 3lb.   5

    2 to 1 agft Enchanter, 5 to 2 agft Capt. Abfolute, and 5 to 1 agft Julia.

                        Sub-

Subfcription Plate of 50l. D. M. two yr olds, 6ft. 10lb. three yr olds, 8ft. 5lb. four yr olds, 8ft. 13lb. five yr olds, 9ft. 4lb. fix yr olds and aged, 9ft. 8lb. With this condition, that the winner was to be fold for 200gs, if demanded, &c.

D. of Grafton's b. h. Pic Nic, by Mr. Teazle, 5 yrs   1
Mr. Delmé Radcliffe's b. g. Rebel, aged   2
Mr. Wardell's br. c Capias, 2 yrs old   3
Gen. Gower's b. f. by Gouty, out of Ifabel, 2 yrs old; Mr. Williams's gr. c. Blue Bell, by Buzzard, 2 yrs old; Ld F. G. Ofborne's b. f. Elizabeth, 4 yrs old; Sir J. Shelley's b. c. Skipjack, 2 yrs old; Mr. Craven's b. c. Jockey, 2 yrs old; Gen. Grofvenor's ch. f. Humming Bird, 3 yrs old; Mr. R. Goodiffon's ro. f. by Buzzard, out of Admiral's dam, 2 yrs old; Mr. Lake's b. c. Mameluke, 3 yrs old; and Mr. Abbey's b. g. Little John, 4 yrs old; alfo ftarted, but the Judge could place only the firft three.

6 to 4 agft Rebel, 5 to 1 agft Pic Nic, and 7 to 1 agft Capias.

Ld Foley's gr. c. Sir Harry Dimfdale, by Sir Peter, 8ft. beat Mr. Wilfon's b. c. Ditto, 8ft. 9lb. B. C. 200gs.——7 to 4 and 2 to 1 on Ditto.

Mr. Waftell's b. f. Lumbago, by Groufe, 8ft. beat Mr. Panton's ch. c. Dilettante, 8ft. 3lb. D. L. 50gs.

5 to 4 on Lumbago.

Mr. Mellifh's b. h. Eagle, aged, 9ft. 7lb. recd. ft. from Mr. Howorth's ch. h. Malta, 6 yrs old, 5ft. 8lb. Ab. M. 200gs, h. ft.

FRIDAY.

Mr. Hurft's c. by Fortunio, out of Millamant, 6ft. 4lb. recd. 100gs from Mr. Jones's b. c. Freedom, 7ft. Acrofs the Flat, 200gs.

CAT-

CATTERICK BRIDGE.

On Wednefday, April the 17th, the Craven Stakes of 10gs each, for two yr olds, 6ft. three yr olds, 8ft. four yr olds, 8ft. 9lb. five yr olds, 9ft. 1lb. fix yr olds, 9ft. 5lb. and aged, 9ft. 7lb.—one mile and a half. (5 Subfcribers.)

Ld Darlington's b. c. by Ormond, 4 yrs old...... 1
Mr. Riddell's b. c. by Beningbrough, 3 yrs old.... 2

4 to 1 on Ld Darlington's colt.

A Maiden Plate of 50l. for two yr old colts, 7ft. three yr olds, 8ft. 2lb. all above that age, 8ft. 10lb. Mares allowed 4lb.—2-mile heats.

Mr. Dent's b. c. Sir Charles, by Selim, 3 yrs   1   1
Mr. Stevenfon's b. f. Wafp, 4 yrs old   2   2
Mr. Field's b. c. Wafer, 3 yrs old...........   3   3

Wafer the favourite.

Produce Sweepftakes of 25gs each, h. ft. colts, 8ft. 3lb. fillies, 8ft.—two miles. (8 Subfcribers.)

Mr. W. Fletcher's b. c. Staveley, by Shuttle, 8ft.   1
Sir W. Gerard's bl. c. Barouche, 8ft. 3lb.   2
Ld Strathmore's b. c. out of Queen Mab, 8ft. 3lb.   3

Even betting on Staveley.

THURSDAY.

A Sweepftakes of 10gs each, for two yr old colts, 8ft. 3lb. and fillies, 8ft.—two miles. (8 Subfcribers.)

Mr. Wentworth's b. c. Silver-heel, by Hambleton   1
Mr. Riddell's b. c. by Overton, dam by Spadille   2
Mr. Lonfdale's ch. c. by Pipator, dam by Paymafter   3
Ld Strathmore's gr. f. by Overton, dam by Delpini;
and

and Sir H. Williamson's b. c. by Hambleton, dam by Laurel; alfo ftarted, but were not placed.

Mr. Lonfdale's colt the favourite, and 3 to 1 agft Silver-heel.

Sweepftakes of 20gs each, for two yr old fillies carrying 8ft.—a mile and half. (3 Subfcribers.)

Mr. Burton's b. f. by Beningbrough, out of Judy, walked over.

Mr. Burton's b. g. by Dubfkelper, aged, recd. ft. from Capt. Hawke's Mifs Topping, 6 yrs old, 12ft. each, four miles, 400gs.

DURHAM.

On Tuefday, April 23d, a Maiden Plate of 5ol. given by the City Members, for colts, 8ft. 3lb. and fillies, 8ft. rifing three yrs old;—2-mile heats.

Mr. Lonfdale's ch. c. by Pipator, dam by Pay-mafter..........................	1	1
Mr. Uppleby's b. c. by Precipitate, dam by Magnet (bolted)........................	2	2
Mr. Hutty's ro. c. Diogenes................	3	dr

Wednefday the 24th, a Maiden Plate of 5ol. given by the County Members; two yr olds, 6ft. three yr olds, 7ft. 9lb. four yr olds, 8ft. 4lb. five yr olds, 8ft. 9lb. fix yr olds and aged, 9ft.—3-mile heats.

Mr. Hutty's ro. c. Diogenes, by Ormond, 2 yrs old	3	2	1	1
Sir H. Williamfon's b. c. by Hambleton, 2 yrs old..................	2	1	2	2
Mr. Phillips's ch. c. Sir Frank, 2 yrs old (bolted)................	1	dis		

Thurfday,

Thursday the 25th, the Lambton Hunt Stakes of 5gs each, for hunters, 12ft.—2-mile heats. (12 Subscribers.)

Mr. Mason's ch. h. by Archer   1   1
Mr. Lambton's b. g. Ardent................   5   2
Col. Seddon's bl. h. Sweeper.. ....:.   4   3
Mr. Surtees's gr. m. Eliza   3   4
Mr. Allan's ch. m. Fanny   2   5

Friday the 26th, 50l. for two yr olds, 6ft. 4lb. three yr olds, 8ft. four yr olds, 8ft. 6lb. five yr olds, 8ft. 12lb. six yr olds and aged, 9ft. A winner of 50l. at any time, carrying 3lb. extra. of two fifties or a hundred, 5lb. extra. Mares allowed 3lb.—4-mile heats.

Mr. J. Thompson's b. c. Newcastle, by Waxy,
    3 yrs old......   1   1
Mr. Stevenson's b. f. Cantata, 4 yrs old......   3   2
Mr. W. Hutchinson's br. c. Didapper, 2 yrs   2   3

NEWMARKET

FIRST SPRING MEETING.

N. B. When any part of this Meeting happens in May, the Ages are considered as in April.

On Monday, April 29th, the first Class of the Prince's Stakes of 100gs each, h. ft. for colts carrying 8ft. 7lb. and fillies, 8ft. 4lb. Across the Flat. (5 Subscribers.)

Ld Grosvenor's b. c. Goth, by Sir Peter........   1
Sir C. Bunbury's b. f. Lydia................,..   2
Mr. Watson's b. c. brother to Gaoler........... 3

   5 to 2 on Lydia, 3 to 1 agst the brother to Gaoler, and 6 to 1 agst Goth.

Sweep-

Sweepſtakes of 200gs each, h. ft. 8ft. 3lb. R. M. (3 Subſcribers.)

Ld Foley's br. c. Little Peter, by Sir Peter...... 1
Mr. Delmè Radcliffe's b. c. Achmet... 2

5 to 2 on Little Peter.

Produce Sweepſtakes of 100gs each, h. ft. colts, 8ft. 4lb. fillies, 8ft. Acroſs the Flat. (7 Subſcribers.)
D. of Grafton's b. f. Dodona, by Waxy........... 1
Sir F. Standiſh's br. f. by Sir Peter, out of Storace 2
Mr. Watſon's ch. c. by Buzzard, out of Doubtful 3

2 to 1 on Dodona.

Sweepſtakes of 100gs each, h. ft. Ab. Mile. (5 Subſcribers.)
Sir J. Shelley's b. c. Currycomb, by Buzzard, 8ft. 1lb.......................... 1
Mr. Wilfon's ch. c. by Buzzard, out of Vixen, 8ft. 6lb.,................................. ... 2
Mr. Wyndham's b. c. Tallboy, 8ft.... ,....... 3
Mr. F. Neale's b. c. Punch, 8ft. 5lb..,........... 4

6 to 4 agſt Mr. Wilſon's colt, and 2 to 1 agſt Curry-comb.

Mr. Melliſh's b. h. Eagle, by Volunteer, aged, 9ft. 4lb. beat Mr. Wyndham's ch. m. Marianne, 6 yrs old, 7ft. 6lb. Ab. M. 200gs, h. ft.

7 to 4 on Eagle.

Mr. Melliſh's b. c. Didler, by Pegaſus, 7ft. 13lb. beat Mr. R. Boyce's ch. c. Brainworm, 8ft. 3lb. Ab. M. 100gs, h. ft.

Even betting, and 6 to 5 on Brainworm.

Sir J. Shelley's br. f. Puſs, by Hambletonian, recd. 8ogs from Gen. Groſvenor's f. Graſſini, 8ft. 7lb. each, Acroſs the Flat, 200gs, h. ft.

Ld Foley's ch. h. Captain Abfolute, by John Bull, 5 yrs old, recd. 5gs from Sir. J. Shelley's b. c. Strap, 4 yrs old, 8ft. each, B. C. 200gs.

Mr. R. Boyce's br. c. Sir David, by Trumpator, 3 yrs old, 8ft. 7lb. recd. 20gs. from Mr. Watfon's b. c. Dreadnought, 4 yrs old, 7ft. 10lb. R. M. 100gs.

Ld Foley's gr. c. Sir Harry Dimfdale, by Sir Peter, recd. 75gs from Mr. Howorth's Harefoot, 8ft. 7lb. each, B. C. 300gs, h. ft.

TUESDAY.

The Claret Stakes of 200gs each, h. ft. colts, 8ft. 7lb. fillies, 8ft. 2lb. D I. The owner of the fecond horfe received back his Stake. (5 Subfcribers.)

Ld Grofvenor's br. c. Bagatelle, by Sir Peter.... 1
Sir C. Bunbury's b. c. Young Whifkey......... 2
No betting.

Ld Stawell's b. f. Gloriana, by Coriander, 2 yrs old, 7ft. beat Mr. Panton's ch. c. Dilettante, 3 yrs old, 8ft. 7lb. Acrofs the Flat, 100gs, h. ft.
2 to 1 on Dilettante.

Ld Sackville's ch. h. Enchanter, by Pot8o's, 8ft. beat Mr. Mellifh's br. h. Pipylin, 8ft. 3lb. Ab. M. 50gs.——Even betting, and 6 to 5 on Pipylin.

Fifty Pounds by Subfcription, for four yr olds, 7ft. 9lb. five yr olds, 8ft. 3lb. fix yr olds, and aged, 8ft. 7lb. R. C.

Sir H. Williamfon's b. h. Walton, by Sir Peter, 5 yrs old 1
Mr. Mellifh's br. h. Pipylin, 5 yrs old 2
D. of Grafton's b. f. Parafol, 4 yrs old 3
6 to 4 on Walton, 7 to 4 agft Parafol, and 50 to 1 agft Pipyliu.

His

His Majesty's Plate of 100gs, for five yr old mares, carrying 10ft. R. C.

D. of Grafton's b. f. Parasol, by Pot8o's, 4 yrs old, walked over.

Mr. Norton's b. c. Quid, by Star, 8ft. 4lb. beat Mr. Wastell's Lumbago, 8ft. D. I. 50gs.

7 to 4 on Lumbago.

Mr. Watson's b. h. Lignum Vitæ, by Walnut, 8ft. 8lb. recd. 10gs from Sir J. Shelley's br. m. Julia, 7ft. 9lb. R. M. 50gs, h. ft.

Mr. Wastell's b. f. Lumbago, by Grouse, 5ft 13lb. recd. ft. from Ld Foley's b. c. Hippocampus, 8ft. 7lb. both 3 yrs old, Across the Flat, 200gs, h. ft.

Mr. Branthwayt's ch. c. Woodcot, by Guildford, 3 yrs old, 8ft. 2lb. recd. from Mr. Jones's b. c. Freedom, 2 yrs old, 7ft. 5½lb. Across the Flat, 25gs.

WEDNESDAY, May 1ft.

Ld Barrymore's b. c. Merryman, by Buzzard, 3 yrs old, 8ft. 7lb beat Sir J. Shelley's b. c. Currycomb, 2 yrs old, 7ft. 7lb. Ab. M. 100gs, h. ft.

5 and 6 to 4 on Currycomb.

The second year of the Newmarket Stakes of 50gs each, h. ft. colts, 8ft. 7lb. fillies, 8ft. 2lb. D. M. (20 Subscribers.)

Sir C. Bunbury's b. f. Lydia, by Whiskey...... 1
Mr. Biggs's ch. c. Bassanio.................. 2
Mr. Glover's ch. f. by Buzzard...............3
D. of Grafton's b. c. brother to Duckling; Mr.
  Wastell's br. c. brother to Whiskerandos; Ld
  Darlington's ch. c. Bumper; Ld Stawell's b. f.
  Gloriana; Mr. Watson's b. c. by Grouse, out of
  Dreadnought's dam; Ld Grosvenor's br. c. Jasper,
by

by Sir Peter; and Sir F. Standish's fister to Duxbury; also started, but the Judge could place only the first three.

3 to 1 agst Bassanio, 4 to 1 agst the brother to Whiskeraudos, and 5 to 1 agst Lydia.

Sweepstakes of 50gs each, Ab. M.

Mr. Ladbroke's b. f. Dora, by Driver, 8ft........ 1
Mr. Wilfon's ch. c. out of Vixen, 8ft. 5lb. 2
Mr. Sitwell's b. f. Goofecap, 8ft. 7lb.......... 3

6 and 7 to 4 agst Dora, and 7 to 4 agst Mr. Wilfon's colt.

Sweepstakes of 100gs each, h. ft. D. C.

Ld Foley's ch. h. Captain Abfolute, by John Bull,
  5 yrs old, 7ft. 5lb..... 1
Mr. Watfon's b. h. Duxbury, 5 yrs old, 8ft. 1lb. 2
Mr. Howorth's Harefoot, 5 yrs old, 7ft. 5lb.... pd

6 to 4 on Captain Abfolute.

Fifty Pounds by Subfcription, for three yr olds, 7ft. 4lb. four yr olds, 8ft. 7lb. and five yr olds, 9ft. D. C.

D. of Grafton's b. f. Parafol, by Pot8o's, 4 yrs old 1
Ld Foley's b. c. Hippocampus, 3 yrs old........ 2
Mr. Wardell's b. f. Houghton Lafs, 3 yrs old... 3
Mr. Ladbroke's br. c. Sir David, 3 yrs old...... 4
Ld F. G. Ofborne's b. f. Elizabeth, 4 yrs old.... 5
Mr. Howorth's br. c. Enterprize, 3 yrs old.. ... 6

Even betting on Hippocampus, 4 to 1 agst Parafol, and 4 to 1 agst Houghton Lafs.

Ld Foley's b. c. Watery, by Waxy, 3 yrs old, 8ft. 12lb. received 50gs from Mr. Howorth's br. c. Tramper, 2 yrs old, 7ft. Two yr old Courfe, 100gs,

THURS.

THURSDAY.

Mr. Howorth's br. m. Julia, by Whiſkey, 7ft. 4lb. beat Mr. Mellifh's br. h. Pipylin, 8ft. 7lb. Two yr old Courſe, 100gs, h. ft.

6 and 7 to 4 on Julia.

The ſecond Claſs of the Prince's Stakes of 100gs. each, h. ft. for colts carrying 8ft. 7lb. and fillies, 8ft. 4lb. Acroſs the Flat. (5 Subſcribers.)

Mr. Glover's ch. f. by Buzzard, out of Camilla   1
Ld Groſvenor's br. c. Jaſper. ; 2
Mr. Delmé Radcliffe's b. c. Achmet.. 3
Mr. Panton's b. c. Performer. 4

11 to 8 agſt Achmet, and 7 to 4 agſt the filly.

Mr. Mellifh's b. f. Lady Brough, by Stride, 7ft. 7lb. beat Ld Sackville's b. h. Whirligig, 8ft. 9lb. Acroſs the Flat, 25gs.

2 to 1 and 5 to 2 on Whirligig.

His Majeſty's Plate of 100gs, for four yr olds, 11ft. five yr olds, 11ft. 9lb. ſix yr olds and aged, 12ft. R. C. Sir H. Williamſon's b. h. Walton, 5 yrs, walked over.

FRIDAY.

Sweepſtakes of 100gs each, R. M.

Mr. R. Boyce's ch. c. Brainworm, by Buzzard, 3 yrs old, 9ft. 1
Mr. Branthwayt's ch. c. Woodcot, 3 yrs, 8ft. 7lb. 2
Mr. Mellifh's ch. c. Honeſty, 2 yrs old, 6ft. 7lb. 3

6 and 7 to 4 agſt Honeſty, 7 to 4 agſt Woodcot, and 5 to 2 agſt Brainworm.

Ld Darlington's ch. c. Bumper, by St. George, 8ft. 6lb. beat Mr. Craven's b. c. Jockey, 8ft. R. M. 50gs.——5 to 2 on Bumper.

Handicap Sweepſtakes of 15gs each, Ab. M. rode by Stable Boys.

Mr. Howorth's br. c. Tramper, by Whiſkey, 2 yrs old, 7ft. 2lb.................................. 1
Mr. Waſtell's b. f. Lumbago, 3 yrs old, 8ft. 10lb. 2
Mr. R. Boyce's b. c. Punch, 2 yrs old, 7ft. 1lb. - 3
Mr. Wilſon's ch. c. by Buzzard, out of Vixen, 2 yrs old, 7ft. 10lb. Mr. Watſon's b. c. brother to Gaoler, 2 yrs old, 7ft. 4lb. Mr. Melliſh's ch c. Honeſty, 2 yrs old, 7ft. 2lb. and Mr. Wyndham's b. c. Tallboy, 2 yrs old, 6ft. 12lb. alſo ſtarted, but the Judge could place only the firſt three.

6 and 7 to 4 agſt Lumbago, 7 to 4 agſt Tramper, 5 to 1 agſt Mr. Wilſon's colt, and 10 to 1 agſt Tallboy.

The New Claret Stakes of 200gs each, h. ft. colts carrying 8ft. 7lb. fillies, 8ft. 2lb. D. I. The owner of the ſecond horſe received back his Stake. (6 Subſcribers.)

Ld Darlington's b. c. Pavilion, by Waxy 1
Mr Melliſh's b. c. Sancho.... 2
Ld Egremont's b. c. Hannibal 3
D. of Grafton's br. f. Peliſſe................. 4

6 to 4 on Sancho, 3 to 1 agſt Hannibal, 5 to 1 agſt Peliſſe, and 7 to 1 agſt Pavilion.

Mr. Howorth's b. c. Heeltap, by Waxy, 3 yrs old, recd. ft. from Ld Darlington's ch. c. Bumper, 2 yrs old, 8ft. each, Acroſs the Flat, 200gs, h. ft.

May.

CHESTER.

ON Monday, May 6th, a Sweepſtakes of 15gs each, for maiden horſes; three yr olds, 5ft. 12lb. four yr olds, 8ft. five yr olds, 8ft. 10lb. ſix yr olds, 9ft. and aged, 9ft. 2lb. Mares allowed 3lb.—two miles. (6 Subſcribers.)

Mr. E. L. Hodgſon's ch c. by Pipator, 3 yrs old	1
Ld Groſvenor's ch. f. Mony Muſk, 4 yrs old....	2
Mr. C. Cholmondeley's b. c. Green Dragon, 4 yrs	3
Ld Grey's b. f. Georgina, 3 yrs old	4
Mr. B. Grey's b. c Foreſter, 4 yrs old	5

A Maiden Plate of 50l. three yr olds, a feather; four yr olds, 7ft 6lb. five yr olds, 8ft. 6lb. ſix yr olds, 8ft. 9lb. and aged, 9ft. 12lb. Mares allowed 3lb.— 4-mile heats.

Sir W. W. Wynn's b. c. by Buzzard, 3 yrs old	1	1
Ld Groſvenor's ch. c. Vandal, 4 yrs old..., .	2	2
Mr. C. Cholmondeley's br. c. Welch Rabbit, 4 yrs old	3	3

TUESDAY.

Fifty Pounds, the gift of T. Groſvenor and R. E. D. Groſvenor, Eſqrs. for three yr old colts, 6ft. 8lb.
fillies,

fillies, 6ft 6lb. and four yr old colts, 8ft. 4lb. and fillies, 8ft. 1lb.—2-mile heats.

Mr Brooke's b. c. Optician, by Telefcope, 4 yrs old	3	1	1
Ld Grofvenor's ch. f. Mony Mufk, 4 yrs	1	3	2
Mr. Bettifon's b. f by Sir Peter, 4 yrs old	4	2	dr
Mr. E. L Hodgfon's ch. c. by Pipator, 3 yrs old (ran againft a Poft)	2	dr	

The Earl of Chefter's Plate of 100gs; four yr olds, 8ft. 2lb. five yr olds, 8ft. 10lb. fix yr olds and aged, 9ft. Winners of one Plate, Match, or Sweepftakes, carrying 4lb. of two, 7lb. and of three or more, 10lb. extra.—thrice round.

Mr. Tarleton's b. c. Jack Tar, by John Bull, 4 yrs old	1
Mr Ackers's b. f. Heb, 4 yrs old	2
Mr. Gloffop's b. c. Skylark, 4 yrs old	3
Mr. C. Cholmondeley's b. c. Green Dragon, 4 yrs old	4
Mr. Lord's b. g. Cockfpinner, 5 yrs old	5
Sir W. W. Wynn's b. m. 6 yrs old	6

WEDNESDAY.

The City and Corporation Plate of 50l. for three yr olds, a feather; four yr olds, 7ft. 4lb. five yr olds, 8ft. 4lb. fix yr olds, 9ft. and aged, 9ft. 4lb. Mares allowed 3lb.—4-mile heats.

Mr. Clifton's b. h. Sir Ulic Mackilligut, by Whifkey, 5 yrs old	1	1
Mr Simpfon's ch. h. Rudftone, 5 yrs old	2	2
Sir W. W. Wynn's b. m. 6 yrs old	3	3

A Sweepftakes of 20gs each, for horfes, the property of the Subfcribers; four yr olds, 7ft. 12lb. five yr olds, 8ft. 10lb. fix yr olds, 9ft. 2lb. and aged, 9ft. 5lb. Mares and geldings allowed 3lb.—two miles. (6 Subfcribers.)

Mr.

Mr. Tarleton's b. c. Jack Tar, 4 yrs old.... .. 1
Ld Grey's br. c. Gayman, 4 yrs old 2
Mr. Clifton's b. f. Jofephine, 4 yrs old 3
Ld Grofvenor's b. h. Baron Bull, 5 yrs old...... 4

THURSDAY.

A Piece of Silver Plate, value 50l. the gift of Earl Grofvenor, for three yr olds, a feather; four yr olds, 7ft. 5lb. five yr olds, 8ft. 2lb. fix yr olds, 8ft. 11lb. and aged, 9ft. 1lb. Mares allowed 3lb.—4-mile heats.

Mr. Clifton's b. h. Sir Ulic Mackilligut,
5 yrs old 1 2 1
Mr. Brooke's b. c. Optician, 4 yrs old.... 2 1 2

FRIDAY.

The Ladies Purfe, value 50l. for three yr olds, a feather; four yr olds, 7ft. 5lb. five yr olds, 8ft. 5lb. fix yr olds, 8ft. 12lb. and aged, 9ft. 2lb. Mares allowed 3lb. A winner of one 50l. Plate carrying 3lb. extra. of two, 5lb. and of three or more, 8lb. extra.—4-mile heats.

Ld Grey's b. f. Georgina, by George,
3 yrs old 5 4 1 2
Mr. Ackers's b. f. Heb, 4 yrs old.... 1 2 2 2
Mr. Clifton's b. f. Jofephine, 4 yrs old 4 1 3 3
Mr. Lord's b. g. Cockfpinner, 5 yrs.. 3 3 4
Sir W. W. Wynn's b. c. by Buzzard,
3 yrs old .... 2 5 dr

A Handicap Stakes of 10gs each, with 20gs added by the Stewards; two miles, bona fide the property of the Subfcribers.

Ld Grofvenor's ch. c. Vandal, by John Bull, 4 yrs old, 8ft. 5lb............. 1
Mr. Crowther's b. c. Forefter, 4 yrs old, 8ft. 6lb. 2
Mr. Gloffop's b. c. Skylark, 4 yrs old, 8ft. 5lb. .. pd

GOOD.

GOODWOOD.

On Wednefday, May the 8th, the Goodwood Hunters Plate of 50gs, 12ft.—2-mile heats.

D. of Richmond's gr. h. You know me, by Gay	4	1	1
Mr. Wyndham's gr. h. Grey Surrey....	1	2	3
Sir G. Thomas's b. g. Leader	2	3	2
Mifs Le Clerc's b. m. Arachne	3	dr	

The Goodwood Club Subfcription, amounting to 50gs, rode by Gentlemen, 13ft.—2-mile heats.

Mr. W. Burrell's ch. g. Rinaldo, by Huby	3	1	1
Mr. P. Burrell's b. g. Quill-driver	1	3	2
Mr. R. Boulton's b. g. Mafter Morton,.	4	2	3
Gen. Lennox's br. g. Watchman........	5	4	dr
Sir C. M. Burrell's ch. g. Sarpedon......	2	dr	

The Skirters Plate, 13ft.—2-mile heats.

D. of Richmond's Rolla, by Precipitate..	3	1	1
Mr. Dickens's gr. g. Slindon ... ... \.	1	2	2
Mr. Græme's Gommel M'Gralahan ...	2	3	3

THURSDAY.

Hunters Plate of 50gs, for four yr olds, 10ft. 4lb. five yr olds, 11ft. 6lb. fix yr olds, 12ft., and aged, 12ft. 2lb. Horfes that never won 50l. allowed 5lb. —2-mile heats.

Major Pigot's br. g. Black Dick, by Magpie, aged	2	1	1
Mifs Le Clerc's b. g. Bayard, aged	1	2	2

Handicap Plate;—two miles.

Mr. W. Burrell's Rinaldo, 13ft.	1
Mr. R. Boulton's Mafter Morton, 11ft.	2

Mr.

Mr. P. Burrell's Quill-driver, 12ft. 3
Sir C. Burrell's Sarpedon, 11ft. 7lb..... 4
Gen. Lennox's br. g. Watchman, 10ft. 7lb........ 5

The Ladies Plate of 60gs; King's Plate weights;—
2-mile heats.

Mr. Martin's Enchantrefs, by Volunteer, 5yrs 1 1
Mr. Hyde's ch. c. by Mr. Teazle, 4 yrs old.. 4 2
Major Pigot's Gary Owen, aged............ 3 3
Ld Egremont's b. g. by Driver, 5 yrs old ... 2 dr

NEWMARKET

SECOND SPRING MEETING.

On Monday, May 13th, Mr. Wyndham's ch. m.
Marianne, by Mufti, aged, 8ft 4lb. beat Mr. Mellifh's b. h. Stockton, 6 yrs old, 8ft. 2lb. R. M. 100gs.

2 to 1 on Marianne.

Mr. R. Boyce's ch. h. Bobtail, by Precipitate,
aged, 8ft. 9lb. beat Mr. Mellifh's b. c. Sancho, 4yrs
old, 7ft. 12lb. R. M. 500gs.——6 to 4 on Sancho.

Ld Darlington's ch. c. Bumper, by St. George,
8ft. beat Mr. Howorth's br. c. Tramper (who ran
out of the Courfe). 8ft. 4lb. Ab. M. 100gs.

Even betting.

Sweepftakes of 100gs each, h. ft. Acrofs the Flat.

Mr. Ladbroke's br. c. Buftard, by Buzzard,
7ft. 12lb. 1
Ld Foley's b. c. Hippocampus, 8ft. 5lb. 2
Ld Grofvenor's br. c. Bagatelle, 7ft. 4lb........ 3

6 to 5 and 5 to 4 on Hippocampus, 3 to 1 agft Bagatelle, 7 to 2 and 4 to 1 agft Buftard.

Mr.

Mr. R. Boyce's b. c. Punch, by Y. Woodpecker, 3 yrs old, 6ft. 12lb. beat Mr. Mellish's b. f. Lady Brough, 4 yrs old, 8ft. 9lb. Two yr old Courfe, 50gs.

3 to 1 on Lady Brough.

Sweepſtakes of 200gs each, h. ft. D. I. (4 Subfcribers)

Ld Darlington's b. c. Pavilion, by Waxy, 8ft. 2½lb. 1
Mr. Norton's b. c. Quid, 7ft. 2

7 to 4 on Pavilion.

Sweepſtakes of 200gs each, h. ft. Laſt three miles of B. C. (3 Subfcribers.)

Mr. Mellish's b. c. Sancho, by Don Quixote, 7ft. 13lb. recd. ft. from the other two.

Ld Grofvenor's b. f. Meteora, by Meteor, 8ft. recd. ft. from Mr. Sitwell's ch. f. fifter to Cockfighter, 8ft. 1lb. D. M. 200gs, h. ft.

Sir J. Shelley's br. f. Puſs, by Hambletonian, 8ft. recd. 80gs from Ld Foley's c. by Ambrofio, out of Jeſſica, 8ft. 4lb. R. M. 200gs, h. ft.

Gen. Grofvenor's b. c. Skirmiſher, by Buzzard, 8ft. 4lb. recd. 35gs from Sir J. Shelley's b. c. by Moorcock, dam by Dungannon, 8ft. 1lb. Two yr old Courfe, 100gs, h. ft.

Ld Grofvenor's br. c. Jaſper, by Sir Peter, recd. 60gs from Mr. Watfon's b. c. brother to Gaoler, 8ft. 2lb. each, R. M. 200gs, h. ft.

TUESDAY.

Mr. Panton's b. c. Performer, by Coriander, beat Ld Stawell's b. f. Gloriana, 8ft. each, Acrofs the Flat, 100gs.——6 to 4 on Gloriana.

Ld

Ld Barrymore's b. c. Merryman, by Buzzard, 4 yrs old, 8ft. 9lb. beat Mr. Wyndham's br. c. by Waxy, bought of Sir F. Poole, 3 yrs old, 7ft. 10lb. Two yr old Course, 50gs.——3 to 1 on Merryman.

Mr. Mellish's b. c. Didler, by Pegasus, 7ft. 13lb. beat Sir J. Shelley's br. m. Julia, 8ft. 7lb. Two yr old Course, 200gs, h. ft.

6 to 5 on Didler.

Fifty Pounds, for three yr old colts carrying 8ft. 4lb. and fillies, 8ft. R. M.

Ld Grosvenor's b. f. Violantè, by John Bull, out
 of a sister to Skyscraper........................ 1
Mr. Grisewood's ch. c. Honesty 2
Mr. Sitwell's b. f. Goosecap................... 3
D. of Grafton's b. f. Farce..................... 4
Mr. Wardell's br. c. Capias 5
Mr. Ladbroke's b. f. Dora..................... 6

7 to 4 agst Violantè, 3 to 1 agst Dora, 4 to 1 agst Goosecap, 4 to 1 agst Capias, and 8 to 1 agst Honesty.

Fifty Pounds by Subscription, for four yr olds, 7ft. 8lb. five yr olds, 8ft. 6lb. six yr olds, 8ft. 12lb. and aged, 9ft. 2lb. Dut. C. With this condition, that the winner was to be sold for 200gs, if demanded, &c.

Ld F. G. Osborne's b. f. Elizabeth, by Waxy,
 5 yrs old................................. 1
Mr. Abbey's b. g. Little John, 5 yrs old........ 2
Mr. Wastell's b. f. Lumbago, 4 yrs old 3

5 to 4 agst Lumbago, 7 to 4 agst Little John, and 5 to 2 agst Elizabeth.

Mr. Howorth's b. c. Heeltap, by Waxy, 8ft. 9lb. recd. 20gs from Mr. Wilson's ch. c. by Buzzard, out of Vixen, 7ft. 12lb. R. M. 50gs.

WEDNESDAY.

Mr. Watson's b. h. Dreadnought, by Buzzard, 8ft. 11lb. beat Mr. Howorth's br. c. Tramper (who ran out of the Course) 7ft. 7lb. Two yr old Course, 100gs.——5 to 4 on Tramper.

Mr. Wilson's b. f. Maiden, by Sir Peter, 8ft. 1lb. beat Mr. Ladbroke's b c. Buftard, 8ft. 7lb. R. M. 100gs.——6 to 4 on Buftard.

Mr. R. Boyce's ch. h. Bobtail, by Precipitate, 8ft. beat Mr. Mellifh's b. h. Eagle, 9ft. 2lb. Ab. M. 500gs.

7 to 4 on Eagle.

Mr. Mellifh's b. c. Didler, by Pegafus, 8ft. 8lb. beat Mr. Wilson's b. f. Maiden, 8ft. R. M. 50gs.

5 and 6 to 4 on Didler.

Sweepstakes of 50gs each, h. ft. D. M.

Gen. Sparrow's ch. c. Caftrel, by Buzzard, 8ft. 9lb. 1
Ld Foley's b. c. Watery, 7ft. 9lb... 2
Ld Foley's br. c. Czar Peter, 7ft 4lb......... . 3
Ld Barrymore's b c. Merryman, 7ft. 3lb. 4
Ld Grofvenor's b. c. Agincourt, 7ft. 6lb........ 5
Mr. Wardell's Houghton Lafs, 8ft. 4lb. Mr. R. Boyce's Brainworm, 8ft. Mr. Branthwayt's Woodcot, 7ft. 8lb. and Mr. Kellermann's Alaric, 7ft. 3lb.... .... pd ft.
2 to 1 agft Caftrel, 5 to 2 agft Watery, 4 to 1 agft Agincourt, 5 and 6 to 1 agft Merryman, and 7 to 1 agft Czar Peter.

Sweepstakes of 20gs each, for two yr olds, 7ft. and three yr olds, 8ft. 7lb. Yearling Courfe. · With this condition, that the winner was to be fold for 100gs, if demanded, &c.

Mr. Mellifh's b. f. Mifs Allerthorpe, by Buzzard, 2 yrs old 1

Mr.

Mr. Sitwell's ch. f. sister to Cockfighter, 3 yrs old   2

Mr. Wilson's ch. c. by Buzzard, 3 yrs old....... 3

Mr. Payne's br. c. by Waxy, 3 yrs old; Mr. Panton's b. f. Fugue, 3 yrs old; and Sir J. Shelley's br. f. Puss, 3 yrs old; also started, but the Judge could place only the first three.

2 to 1 agst Mr. Wilson's colt, 3 to 1 agst Miss Aller-thorpe, and 7 to 2 agst Fugue.

Ld Foley's b. c. Watery, by Waxy, 4 yrs old, 8ft. 12lb. beat Ld Darlington's ch. c. Bumper, 3 yrs old, 7ft. 1lb. Ab. Mile, 100gs.

5 to 4 on Watery.

Mr. Mellish's br. h. Pipylin, 8ft. 12lb. and Mr. Ladbroke's ch. c. Prospero, 8ft. 1lb. Ab. M. 25gs, ran a dead beat.——6 to 4 on Prospero.

The Jockey-club Plate of 50gs, for four yr olds, 7ft. 2lb. five yr olds, 8ft. 3lb. six yr olds, 8ft. 9lb. and aged, 8ft. 11lb. B. C.

D. of Grafton's b. m. Parasol, by Pot8o's, 5 yrs   1

Sir H. Williamson's b. h. Walton, 6 yrs old.... 2

Mr. Delmè Radcliffe's ro. c. Petruchio, 4 yrs old   3

6 to 4 on Walton, and 7 to 4 agst Parasol.

THURSDAY.

Gen. Grosvenor's b. f. Graffini, by Gouty, 8ft. beat Ld F. G. Osborne's b. c. by Overton, dam by Highflyer, out of Fair Barbara, 8ft. 7lb. Ab. Mile, 100gs, h. ft.——2 to 1 on Graffini.

Fifty Pounds, for three yr olds, 6ft. 2lb. four yr olds, 8ft. five yr olds, 8ft. 7lb. six yr olds and aged, 8ft. 12lb. Two middle miles of B. C. With this condition, that the winner was to be sold for 100gs, if demanded, &c.

         Mr.

Mr. Abbey's b. g. Little John, by Calomel, 5 yrs   1
Mr. Crouch's br. c. brother to Whiſkerandos, 3 yrs   2
D. of Grafton's b. c. brother to Duckling, 3 yrs. .   3
Mr. Kellermann's gr. f. Iphigenia, 4 yrs old; Mr.
Perren's b. c. Spot, by Pipator, 4 yrs old; Mr.
Panton's ch. c. Dilettante, 4 yrs old; Mr. Craven's
b. c. Jockey, 3 yrs old; Mr. R. Boyce's b. g. Diſ-
mal, 4 yrs old; and Mr. Wyndham's br. c. by
Waxy, 3 yrs old; alſo ſtarted, but the Judge could
place only the firſt three.

5 to 2 agſt Iphigenia, 5 to 2 agſt Little John, and 4
to 1 agſt Dilettante.

Mr. Wilſon's f. Maiden, by Sir Peter, 8ſt. 4lb.
beat Ld Foley's br. c. Czar Peter, 8ſt. D. M. 25gs.

6 to 4 on Czar Peter.

Mr. Watſon's b. c. Dreadnought, by Buzzard,
8ſt. 7lb. beat Gen. Groſvenor's ch. f. Humming Bird,
7ſt. 8lb. Two yr old Courſe, 50gs.

7 to 4 on Dreadnought.

Ld Sackville's ch. h. Enchanter, by Pot8o's, beat
Mr. Melliſh's br. h. Pipylin, 8ſt. each, B. C. 100gs.

5 to 2 on Enchanter.

Ld Foley's b. c. Hippocampus, by Coriander,
4 yrs old, 8ſt. 4lb. beat Mr. Watſon's b. h. Duxbury,
6 yrs old, 8ſt. 6lb. Laſt three miles of B. C. 100gs.

5 and 6 to 4 on Hippocampus.

Mr. Norton's b. c. Quid, by Star, 8ſt. 2lb. beat
Mr. Lake's b. h. Giles, 9ſt. D. I. 100gs.

5 and 6 to 4 on Giles.

Gen. Groſvenor's b. c. Skirmiſher, by Buzzard,
8ſt. 2lb. beat Mr. R. Boyce's b. c. Punch, 8ſt. Two
yr old Courſe, 50gs.——6 to 4 on Punch.

Sweep.

Sweepftakes of 100gs each, h. ft. for colts carrying 8ft. 3lb. and fillies, 8ft. Ab. M.

Ld Grofvenor's br. c. Knight Errant, by Sir Peter, out of Peggy Bull, recd. 45gs from the D. of Grafton's b. c. by Trumpator, out of Sea-fowl:—Gen. Grofvenor's b. f. Graffini, withdrew.

Mr. Wardell's b. f. Houghton Lafs, 8ft. 9lb. recd. 70gs from Mr. Branthwayt's ch. c. Woodcot, 8ft. Two yr old Courfe, 100gs.

MIDDLEHAM.

On Wednefday, May the 15th, a Sweepftakes of 20gs each, for three yr old colts, 8ft. 3lb. and fillies, 8ft.—two miles.

Mr. Riddell's br. c. by Overton, dam by Spadille   1
Mr. Mellifh's b. c. True Briton   2
Sir H. Williamfon's ch. f. by Hambleton   3
D. of Hamilton's b. f. by Spadille, dam by Dungannon... ....   pd

The Gold Cup, value 100gs, the remainder in fpecie, being a Subfcription of 10gs each, with 20gs added by the town, for all ages; four yr olds carrying 7ft. 10lb. five yr olds, 8ft. 6lb. fix yr olds, 8ft. 12lb. —four miles. (12 Subfcribers.)

Sir H. Williamfon's gr. h. Starling, by Sir Peter, 5 yrs old....   1
Sir W. Gerard's b. c. Young Chariot, 4 yrs old   2
Ld Belhaven's b. h. Brandon, 6 vis old.......   3
Mr. Baillie's gr. c. Orphan, by Overton, 4 yrs old; D. of Hamilton's br. f. by Walnut, 4 yrs old; Ld Belhaven's b. m. Lady Mary, 5 yrs old; and Mr. Riddell's b. c. by Beningbrough, 4 yrs old; alfo ftarted, but were not placed by the Judge..

C 3

YORK

YORK

SPRING MEETING.

On Wednefday, May 22d, Mr. Wentworth's ch. c. Hippolitus, by Beningbrough, beat Sir R. Winn's b. c. Mariner, 8ft. each, two miles, for 200gs, h. ft.

5 to 2 on Hippolitus.

Mr. Acred's b. f. Mifs Welham, by Screveton, out of Mifs Cogden, beat Mr. Hill's b. f. by Ormond, 8ft. each, two miles, 100gs, h. ft.

2 to 1 on Mifs Welham.

Mr. Robinfon's b. c. by Overton, out of Fanny, by Weafel, beat Mr. Nalton's c. by Star, dam by Slope, 8ft. each, the laft mile and half, 200gs, h. ft.

7 to 4 on Mr. Nalton's colt.

Mr. Bell's b. f. by Abba Thulle, beat Mr. Nutbrown's b. f. by Brough, 7ft. 7lb. each, four miles, 50gs.——3 to 1 on the winner.

Mr. Flint's b. h. Black Strap, by Volunteer, 8ft. 4lb. recd. ft. from Mr. Darley's gr. g. by Pallafox, 8ft. two miles, 200gs, h. ft.

THURSDAY.

A Sweepftakes of 20gs each, for two yr old colts, 8ft. 3lb. and fillies, 7ft. 13lb.—Two yr old Courfe. Thofe marked thus * allowed 3lb.　(7 Subfcribers.)

Mr. Walker's ch. c. brother to Sir John, by Stride　1
*Mr. Knapton's b. f. by a brother to Eagle, dam by Star..　2
Mr. Mellifh's b. c. Companion, by Beningbrough　3
Sir H. T. Vane's b. f. by Patriot, out of Hyperion's dam ....　4

*Mr.

*Mr. J. Hill's c. Talifman, by Totteridge, dam by
Highflyer 5

6 to 4 agft the winner.

Sweepftakes of 20gs each;—two miles. (4 Subfcribers.)

Ld Fitzwilliam's Sally, by Sir Peter, 9ft......... 1
Mr. W. Lee's Brunette, 8ft. 2lb................... 2

5 to 2 on Sally

Sweepftakes of 30gs each, 10gs ft.—laft three
miles. (6 Subfcribers.)

Mr. Garforth's gr. f. Vefta, by Delpini, 4 yrs old,
8ft. 1lb.................................... 1
Mr. Garforth's Evander, 4 yrs old, 8ft. 4lb....... 2
Ld Middleton's gr. h. Blue Devil, 6 yrs old, 9ft... 3
Mr. Flint's m. Spitfire, 5 yrs old, 8ft. 8lb......... 4

6 to 4 agft Blue Devil.

FRIDAY.

The Stand Plate of 50l. four yr olds, 7ft. 9lb. five
yr olds, 8ft. 4lb. fix yr olds and aged, 8ft. 10lb.—four
miles.

Mr. Hutton's ch. h. Saxoni, by Delpini, 5 yrs old 1
Mr. Garforth's gr. c. Evander, 4 yrs old........ 2
Mr. Mangle's b. c. by Walnut, 4 yrs old 3
Mr. Thompfon's b. c. Newcaftle, 4 yrs old.... 4
Sir H. Williamfon's gr. h. Starling, 5 yrs old..... 5

2 to 1 agft Saxoni, 5 to 2 agft Evander, and 3 to 1
agft Starling.

Sweepftakes of 20gs each, for three yr old colts, 8ft.
and fillies, 7ft. 12lb. laft mile and half. (6 Subfcribers.)

Mr. Fletcher's b. c. Staveley, by Shuttle........ 1
Ld Fitzwilliam's b. c. Caleb Quotem.......... 2

Sir

Sir T. Gafcoigne's gr. c. by Delpini 3
Mr. Mellifh's b. c. True Briton 4

6 and 7 to 4 on Staveley.

EPSOM.

On Thurfday the 30th of May, the firft year of a renewal of the Derby Stakes of 50gs each, h. ft. for three yr old colts, 8ft. 5lb. and fillies, 8ft.—the laft mile and half. (39 Subfcribers.)

The owner of the fecond horfe received 100gs out of the Stakes.

Ld Egremont's b. c. Cardinal Beaufort, by Go-
    hanna. 1
Ld Grofvenor's b. c. Plantagenet .... -. 2
Ld Grofvenor's b. c. Goth... ....,.... .. 3
Mr. Biggs's ch. c. Baffanio........ 4
Ld Foley's br. c. Little Peter......... 5
Ld Egremont's ch. c. Impoftor; Gen. Gower's b. c. by Coriander; H. R. H. the P. of Wales's b. c. Barbaroffa; Mr. Wilfon's b. c. Newmarket; Mr. Howorth's ch. c. Honefty; Mr. Glover's ch. f. by Buzzard; Mr. Jones's b. c. Freedom; Mr. Jones's ch. c. Junius; Mr. Beft's ch. c. by Dungannon; and Mr. Harris's b. c. Farmer; alfo ftarted, but were not placed.

7 to 4 agft Impoftor, 5 to 2 and 2 to 1 agft Plantage-net, 9 to 1 agft Little Peter, 9 to 1 agft Newmar-ket, 9 to 1 agft Baffanio, and 20 to 1 agft Cardi-nal Beaufort.

Mr. Beft's c. was thrown down by fome horfemen croffing the Courfe before all the race horfes had paffed—his rider (B. Norton) was much bruifed by the fall.

Mr.

Mr. Emden's Gipfy, by Guildford, 5 yrs old, 8ft. 11lb. beat Mr. Burt's br. f. Harriet, by Ofcar, 2 yrs old, 7ft. 11lb. the laft half mile, 100gs.

Mr. Durand's b. c. Quarter-mafter, by Guildford, out of Slamerkin, recd. ft. from Mr. Ladbroke's br. c. by Sir Peter, 8ft. each, the laft half mile, 50gs, h. ft.

Fifty Pounds, for horfes, &c. that had not won more than one 50l. Plate fince the 1ft of March, 1804; four yr olds, 7ft. 4lb. five yr olds, 8ft. 6lb. fix yr olds, 9ft. and aged, 9ft. 3lb. mares and geldings allowed 3lb.—2-mile heats.

Mr. F. Neale's ch. h. Quiz, by Buzzard, aged	1	1
Mr. Forth's ch. h. Brighton, aged.........	5	2
Mr. Browne's b. h. Surprife, aged..	4	3
Ld Egremont's b. f. by Precipitate, 4 yrs old	2	dr

5 to 4 on Quiz.

FRIDAY.

The firft year of a renewal of the Oaks Stakes of 50gs each, h. ft. for three yr old fillies carrying 8ft.— the laft mile and half. (27 Subfcribers)

The owner of the fecond filly received 100gs out of the Stakes.

Ld Grofvenor's b. f. Meteora, by Meteor.......	1
D. of Grafton's b. f. Dodona..	2
Sir F. Standifh's b. f. fifter to Duxbury	3
Mr. Howorth's Pimlico......	4
Mr. Glover's ch. f. by Buzzard........... ...	5
Ld Egremont's b. f. by Gohanna, out of Tag ..	6
Sir T. Gafcoigne's br. f. by Sir Peter, out of Violet	7
Mr. Dockeray's b. f. by Waxy, out of Macaria..	8

2 to 1 agft Dodona, 5 to 2 agft Pimlico, 7 to 2 and 3 to 1 agft Meteora.

Fifty

Fifty Pounds, for three and four-yr olds;—2-mile heats.

Mr. Fenwick's b. f. Miss Coiner, by Don Quixote, 4 yrs old, 8ft. 5lb..........   1   1

Mr. Ladbroke's ch. c. by Guildford, 3 yrs old, 7ft. 7lb. (bolted).................. . ..   2 dis .

SATURDAY.

A Sweepstakes of 10gs each, with 20gs added, for three yr old colts, 8ft. 2lb. and fillies, 8ft.—the last mile. The winner to be sold for 200gs, if demanded, &c.

Mr. Lake's b. c. by Gouty, out of Mademoiselle   1

Mr. Harris's b. c. Farmer   2

Mr. Wardell's br. c. Capias   3

Ld Egremont's b. f. by Gohanna..............   4

Mr. R. Boyce's b. c. Punch   5

Sweepstakes of 20gs each, with 20gs added, for two yr old colts, 8ft. 2lb. and fillies, 8ft.—the last half mile. (9 Subscribers.)

Mr. Lake's b. f. Rosabella, by Whiskey   1

Mr. Harris's b. c. Ploughboy, by Volunteer....   2

Mr. Durand's b. c. Quarter-master   3

Ld Egremont's b. f. by Gohanna, out of Camilla   4

Mr. Wardell's br. f. sister to Houghton Lass ...   5

Ld Foley's Little Peter, by Sir Peter, 8ft. beat Ld Egremont's Impostor, 8ft 7lb. the Derby Course, 200gs.——6 to 4 on Impostor.

Sweepstakes of 100gs each, h. ft.—the last mile. (4 Subscribers.)

Mr. R. Boyce's b. c. Punch, by Young Woodpecker, recd. 42gs from Mr. Wyndham.'s c. by Waxy—Mr. Ladbroke and Col. Kingscote drew Stakes.

Mr.

Mr. Jones's Freedom, by Buzzard, 6ft. ag^{ft} Mr. A. Craven's c. by Ambrofio, out of Jeffica, 5ft. 9lb. the laft half mile, 200gs—Freedom walked over.

The Surrey Yeomen's Plate of 50l. for three yr olds, 6ft. 2lb. four yr olds, 7ft. 12lb. five yr olds, 8ft. 12lb. fix yr olds, 9ft. 2lb. and aged, 9ft. 4lb. mares and geldings allowed 3lb.—4-mile heats.

Mr. F. Neale's Quiz, aged......	1	1
Mr. Wardell's Capiás, 3 yrs old	3	2
Mr. Hyde's ch. c. by Mr. Teazle, 4 yrs old	2	dis

June.

June.

GUILDFORD.

ON Tuesday the 4th of June, His Majesty's Plate of 100gs, for four yr olds, 10ft. 4lb. five yr olds, 11ft. 6lb. six yr olds, 12ft. and aged, 12ft. 2lb.——4-mile heats.

Sir H. Williamson's b. h. Ditto, by Sir Peter, 5 yrs old........................	1	1
Mr. Emden's br. m. Gipsy, 5 yrs old.......	2	dr

On Wednesday the 5th, the Town Plate of 50l. for three yr olds, 7ft. 4lb. and four yr olds, 8ft. 7lb. fillies and geldings allowed 2lb. The winner of a Plate or Sweepstakes, 3lb. extra. of two, 5lb. extra. The winner to be sold for 100gs, if demanded, &c.——2-mile heats.

Mr. Wardell's br. c. Capias, by Overton, 3 yrs	1	1
Mr. J. Sutton's b. f. by Waxy, 3 yrs old....	3	2
Mr. Best's ch. c. by Dungannon, 3 yrs old..	2	3

The Plate intended for Thursday, was not run for, only two horses being entered.

MAD-

MADDINGTON.

(STOCKBRIDGE COURSE.)

On Wednesday, June the 5th, the Maddington Stakes of 25gs each, 15 ft. and only 5gs if declared, &c. with 50gs added by the Club;—four miles.

Ld Sackville's b. c. Witchcraft, by Sir Peter, 4 yrs
  old, 10ft. 10lb. 1
Sir H. Lippincott's b. c. Mirror, 4 yrs, 10ft. 3lb. 2
Ld C. Somerset's ch. m. Daisy, aged, 10ft. 10lb. 3
Major Pigot's ch. g. Gary Owen, aged, 11ft. 4lb. 4
Mr. Scrope's b. h. Elemore, 5 yrs old, 11ft. 1lb.
  (broke down) 5
Mr. Germain's Whirligig, aged, 12ft. Ld E. Somerset's Sylvanus, 6 yrs old, 11ft. 10lb. Col. Kingscote's Viper, 6 yrs old, 11ft. 10lb. Mr. Hawkes's Little Printer, aged, 11ft. 7lb. Mr. Biggs's Washington, 4 yrs old, 10ft. 10lb. and Mr. Elton's Feather, 4 yrs old, 10ft. 7lb. having declared forfeit within the time prescribed; and Mr. Byndloss, Mr. Goddard, Mr. Bullock, and Mr. Stacpoole, who did not name, paid only 5gs each.

6 to 4 on Witchcraft.

Sweepstakes of 10gs each, with 50gs added by the Club, for four yr olds, 10ft. 7lb. five yr olds, 11ft. 6lb. six yr olds, 12ft. and aged, 12ft. 3lb. mares and geldings allowed 3lb.—two miles. (7 Subscribers.)

Ld Sackville's b. h. Whirligig, by Whiskey, aged 1
Col. Kingscote's b. c. La Mancha, 4 yrs old 2
Major Pigot's ch. h. Wheatear, 5 yrs old........ 3
Mr. Goddard's br. h. Young Eclipse, 6 yrs old.. 4

Whirligig the favorite.

Sweepſtakes of 10gs each, with 50gs added, for horſes that never won before the day of naming, carrying 11ſt. 7lb. mares and geldings allowed 3lb.— 2-mile heats. (5 Subſcribers.)

Ld E. Somerſet's ch. g. Sylvanus, by Volunteer, 6 yrs old......................	1	1
Mr. Bullock's br. g. Abelard, 5 yrs old.. ...	3	2
Mr. Howorth's gr. g. Badger, aged.........	2	dr

Sylvanus the favourite.

THURSDAY.

Sweepſtakes of 5gs each, with 100gs added, for horſes that never won 100gs at one time, except at Maddington, Bibury, or Kingſcote; four yr olds, 10ſt. 7lb. five yr olds, 11ſt. 6lb. ſix yr olds, and aged, 12ſt. horſes that never won any thing, allowed 4lb. mares and geldings allowed 3lb.—three miles. (14 Subſcribers.)

Sir H. Lippincott's b. c. Mirror, by Precipitate, 4 yrs old, 10ſt. 3lb................... ...	1
Major Pigot's Wheatear, 5 yrs old, 11ſt. 6lb.....	2

Mr. Howorth's Badger, aged, 11ſt. 7lb. and Mr. Biggs's Waſhington, 4 yrs old, 10ſt. 3lb. alſo ſtarted, but were not placed.

2 to 1 agſt Mirror, 5 to 2 agſt Wheatear, and 3 to 1 agſt Waſhington.

Handicap Plate of 50l.—one-mile heats.

Mr. Goddard's Young Eclipſe, by Y. Eclipſe, 6 yrs old, 11ſt. 7lb........	1	3	4	1
Major Pigot's Wheatear, 5 yrs old, 11ſt. 10lb......................	5	0	1	2
Sir H. Lippincott's Mirror, 4 yrs old, 10ſt. 10lb......................	2	4	2	dr
Ld E. Somerſet's Sylvanus, 6 yrs old, 10ſt. 12lb......................	4	0	3	dr

Ld

Ld C. Somerſet's Daiſy, aged, 10ft. 10lb. 3 dr
Mr. Howorth's Badger, aged, 10ft.
   (bolted) .... dis

Fifty Pounds for four yr olds and upwards;—heats,
about two miles and a quarter.

Ld Sackville's Whirligig, by Whiſkey, received the
   Plate without walking over.

MANCHESTER.

On Wedneſday, June the 5th, a Sweepſtakes of
10gs each, for three yr old colts, 8ft. 3lb. and fillies,
8ft. The winner of any Match, Plate, or Sweepſtakes, this year, 3lb. extra.—one mile. (10 Subſcribers.)

Sir W. Gerard's bl. c. Barouche, by Overton ... 1
Mr. Nalton's br. c. by Totteridge (3lb. extra) .. 2
Ld Wilton's b. c. by Alexander 3
     5 to 2 on Mr. Nalton's colt.

Seventy Pounds, for three yr old colts, 6ft. 10lb.
fillies, 6ft. 8lb. and four yr old colts, 8ft. 3lb. fillies,
8ft. A winner of one 50l. in the preſent year, 3lb.
extra. of two or more, 5lb. extra.—2-mile heats.

Ld Groſvenor's ch. f. Mony Muſk, by John Bull, 4 yrs old	6	1	1
Mr. Sitwell's b. f. Gooſecap, 3 yrs old ...	1	2	2
Mr. Wentworth's b. c. Silver-heel, 3 yrs	5	3	3
Mr. Taylor's b. c. by Marſk, 3 yrs old ...	4	4	dr
Mr. Nalton's br. c. by Totteridge, 3 yrs	2	dr	
Mr. Hanſon's b. f. by Precipitate, 3 yrs	3	dr	

    5 to 4 agſt the Totteridge colt.

On Thurſday the 6th, a Sweepſtakes of 10gs each,
for horſes, &c. not exceeding 14 hands; weight for
inches;—2-mile heats. (13 Subſcribers.)

                               Mr.

Mr. Hanson's ch. pony, 6ft. 3¼lb   1   1
Mr. Seddon's b. pony, Louisa, 7ft. 3¼lb.   3   2
Mr. Boardman's b. pony, Forest Lady, 8ft...   2   3
Mr. Hamer's br. pony Fortune, 6ft.........   4   dis

A Maiden Plate of 70l. for four yr olds, 7ft. 12lb. five yr olds, 8ft. 5lb. six yr olds and aged, 8ft. 12lb. mares allowed 3lb.—4-mile heats.

Mr. Baillie's gr. c. Orphan, by Overton, 4 yrs   1   1
Mr. Harris's b. c. by Hammer, 4 yrs old....   5   2
Mr Glossop's b. c. Skylark, 4 yrs old   2   3
Mr. Saunders's b. h. 5 yrs old   3   dis
Mr. Cooper's b. c. Draper, 4 yrs old   4   dis

On Friday the 7th, a Hunters Sweepstakes of 10gs each, 12ft.—four miles. (9 Subscribers.)

Mr. Rushton's b. g. Striver, by Standard, 5 yrs   1
Mr. Lockley's b. m. by Beningbrough, 6 yrs old   2

Eighty Pounds, for three yr olds, 6ft. 3lb. four yr olds, 7ft. 11lb. five yr olds, 8ft. 4lb. six yr olds, 8ft. 10lb. and aged, 9ft. 1lb. A winner of one 50l. this year, 3lb. extra. of two, 5lb. extra. mares and geldings allowed 2lb.—4-mile heats.

    N. B. The second horse to have 30l.

Mr. Thompson's b. c. Newcastle, by
   Waxy, 4 yrs old.....................   4   1   1
Mr. Clifton's b. h. Sir Ulic Mackilligut,
   5 yrs old   1   3   2
Mr. Lonsdale's gr. c. 3 yrs old (fell lame)   2   2   dis
Mr. Harris's b. h. Sir Rowland, 5 yrs old   3   4   dr
     Sir Ulic the favourite.

On Saturday, June the 8th, a Handicap Plate of 50l. given by the Stewards, for the beaten horses of the week;—2-mile heats.

Mr. Seddon's b. m. Louisa, a feather........   1   1
Mr. Johnson's b. f. 3 yrs old, 6ft. 4lb.   2   2
           NEWTON.

NEWTON.

On Wednesday, June 12th, 50l. for three and four yr olds;—two-mile heats.

Ld Wilton's b. c. by Alexander, 3 yrs old, 6ft. 10lb......... .... 1 1
Mr. Taylor's b. c. by Marske, 3 yrs, 6ft. 10lb. 2 2

Sweepstakes of 10gs each, with 20gs added, for three yr old colts, 8ft. 3lb. and fillies, 8ft.—two miles. (4 Subscribers.)

Sir W. Gerard's bl c. Barouche, by Overton ... 1
Mr. P. Patten's ch. f. by Pipator............... 2
Mr. M. Bankes's bl. c. by Overton... 3

Thursday, a Maiden Plate of 50l. for all ages, four yr olds, 7ft. 12lb.—four-mile heats.

Mr. Harris's b. c. by Hammer, 4 yrs old 1 2 1
Ld Grosvenor's ch. c. Vandal, 4 yrs old.. 3 1 2
Mr. Glossop's b. c. Skylark, 4 yrs old.... 2 3 dr

Friday, 50l. for all ages.—4-mile heats.

Mr. Thompson's b. c. Newcastle, by Waxy, 4 yrs old, 8ft......... .... 1 1
Mr. Harris's h. Sir Rowland, 5 yrs, 8ft. 4lb . 2 2

BEVERLEY.

On Wednesday, June 12th, a Sweepstakes of 20gs each, for three yr old colts, 8ft 3lb. and fillies, 8ft.— one mile and a half. (7 Subscribers.)

Sir M. M. Sykes's b. c. Sir Reginald, by Precipitate 1
Mr. Darley's ch. f. by Abba Thulle............. 2

Mr.

Mr. Hutty's ro. c. Diogenes, by Ormond.   3
Mr. Watt's b. f. out of Miss Judy   4

    Even betting on Mr. Watt's filly, and 2 to 1 agst
    Sir Reginald.

    A Sweepstakes of 20gs each, for all ages;—four
miles. (5 Subscribers.)

Sir M. M. Sykes's Sir Launcelot, by Delpini, 3 yrs
    old, 5ft. 12lb.   1
Mr. C. Bowman's b. m. Susan, 5 yrs, 8ft. 1lb. . . .   2

        10 to 1 on Susan.

    Thursday, 50l. for three and four yr olds; 2-mile
heats.

Major Bower's b. f. Miss Welham, by Screveton,
    3 yrs old, 7ft. 4lb, ...   1 1
Mr. Turner's b. f. 3 yrs old, 7ft. 4lb. 2 2
Mr. Watt's b. f. 3 yrs old, 7ft. 4lb. 3 3

    2 to 1, and after the heat 4 to 1, on Miss Welham.

    Friday, 50l. for all ages. No race.

    A Handicap Sweepstakes of 20gs each, for horses of
all denominations; heats, once round the Course.
Rode by Gentlemen. (6 Subscribers.)

Mr. Acklom's br. g. aged, 12ft. 4lb. 3 1 1
Mr Burton's b. g. 5 yrs old, 13ft. 1 2 3
Sir F. Boynton's m. Off she-goes, aged, 13ft.   2 3 2

    Saturday, a Maiden Plate of 50l. for three yr olds,
6ft. 4lb. four yr olds, 7ft. 7lb. five yr olds, 8ft. 7lb. six
yr olds, 9ft. and aged, 9ft. 4lb.—2-mile heats.

Mr. Robinson's ch. f. by Abba Thulle, out of
    Barnaby's dam, 3 yrs old. 1 1
Mr. Armstrong's b. m. Spitfire, 5 yrs old . . .   2 2
Mr. Hotham's b. c. Bounce, 3 yrs old 4 3

                            Col.

Col. King's gr. b. Hefsle, 6 yrs old........;.. 5 4
Mr. Philip's c. Sir Frank, 3 yrs old (bolted) 3 dis

6 to 4 agft the winner; after the 1ft heat, 6 to 4 fhe won.

Welter Stakes of 10gs each, for horfes, &c. 13ft. Rode by Gentlemen, twice round the Courfe. (8 Sub-fcribers.)

Ld Middleton's b. h. Bay Devil, by Jupiter...... 1
Sir M. M. Sykes's b. m. by Pegafus............ 2
Mr. Burton's ch. g. Ufurper.................. 3

Even betting on the mare, and 6 to 4 agft Bay Devil.

A Handicap Stakes, for horfes of all denominations, one mile and half; rode by Gentlemen. (9 Subfcribers.)

Mr. Thompfon's ch. f. Mifs Beverley, 4yrs, 11ft. 6lb. 1
Mr. C. Bowman's Stormer, 11ft. 11lb. 2
Capt. Maling's b. h. Recruit, 5 yrs old, 10ft. 12lb. 3
Mr. Acklom's b. m. Peg, 11ft. 9lb............. 4

TENBURY.

On Thurfday, June 13th, a Maiden Plate of 50l. for three yr olds, 6ft. four yr olds, 7ft. 7lb. five yr olds, 8ft. 6lb. fix yr olds, 8ft. 11lb, and aged, 9ft. mares and geldings allowed 3lb.—3-mile heats.

Mr. Anfon's gr. c. by Moorcock, out of
Eve, 3 yrs old 3 0 1 1
Mr. Richardfon's b. c. Forefter, 4 yrs 2 0 2 2
Mr. Bowker's b. c. Royal Oak, 3 yrs
old (bolted). . ... 1 dis.

ASCOT

ASCOT HEATH.

On Tuesday, June the 18th, the second and last year of a Sweepstakes of 10gs each, with 25gs added, for four yr olds, 7ft 9lb. five yr olds, 8ft. 5lb. six yr olds, 8ft. 11lb. and aged, 9ft. mares allowed 4lb. the winner to be sold for 300gs, if demanded, &c. —two miles and a half. (12 Subscribers.)

Mr. W. Fenwick's b. f. Miss Coiner, by Don Quixote, 4 yrs old 1
Mr. Abbey's ch. m. Margery, 6 yrs old 2
Ld Egremont's b. g. by Driver, 5 yrs old........ 3
Ld G. H. Cavendish's Duxbury, 6 yrs old...... 4
Sir C. Bunbury's Orlando, 6 yrs (broke down).. 5

Duxbury the favourite.

The second and last year of a Sweepstakes of 10gs each, with 25gs added, for three yr old colts, 8ft. 7lb. and fillies, 8ft. 2lb.　The winner of the Derby or Oaks Stakes, carrying 7lb. extra.—the New Mile. (12 Subscribers.)

Ld Grosvenor's Meteora, by Meteor (7lb. extra.) 1
Sir F. Standish's b. f. sister to Duxbury.. 2
Mr. Ladbroke's br. c. Wagtail........ 3
H. R. H. the D. of York's b. c. by Gouty.... ... 4
Mr. Batson's b. c. by Clayhall................. 5
Ld Egremont's b. c. by Gohanna 6
Mr. Wardell's Capias......... 7

6 and 7 to 4 agst Meteora.

His Majesty's Plate of 100gs for hunters; four yr olds, 11ft 2lb. five yr olds, 11ft. 9lb. six yr olds, 11ft. 12lb. and aged, 12ft. mares allowed 4lb.—4 mile heats.

Mr. Richardson's b. g. Lemon-squeezer, by Coriander, aged 1 1

Mr.

Mr. Emden's b. g. Contestor, 5 yrs old...... 2 2
Mr. Smith's b. g. Venture, 5 yrs old. 3 3

Mr. Emden's b. c. Latitat, by Waxy, beat Mr. Abbey's br. f. Virgin, 8ft. 7lb. each, two miles, 50gs, h. ft. Virgin the favourite.

Mr. Hyde's b. c. Little Coiner, by Coiner, 3 yrs. old, a feather, beat Mr. Peirse's br. m. Forest Lady, by Clayhall, 7ft.— miles, 50gs, h. ft.

Mr. R. M. Philipps's b. c. by Fortunio, 7ft. recd. 50gs from Mr. Jones's Freedom, 8ft. the New Mile, 100gs.

Wednesday, the 19th, 50l. for all ages. The winner to be sold for 350gs, if demanded, &c.—3-mile heats.

Mr. Fenwick's Miss Coiner, by Don Quixote,
 4 yrs old, 7ft. 4lb...... .... 1 1
Mr. Frogley's b. c. Triptolemus, 4 yrs, 7ft. 4lb. 2 2

Thursday, the 20th, 50l. for horses, the property of Huntsmen, Yeomen Prickers, &c.—4-mile heats.

Mr. Richardson's b. g. Lemon-squeezer, by
 Coriander, aged 1 1
Mr. Nottage's b. g. aged .... 2 dr

Fifty Pounds, for three yr old colts, 8ft. 3lb. and fillies, 7ft. 12lb. the winner of a Plate in 1803, carrying 4lb. extra.—heats, the New Mile.

Mr Ladbroke's br. c. Wagtail, by Young
 Woodpecker. 1 1
Mr. Branthwayt's b. c. by Pegasus..... .... 4 2
Mr. Frogley's ch. f. by a son of Cignet...... 2 3
Ld Stawell's b. f. Gloriana...... .... 5 4
Mr. Wardell's br c. Capias............... . 3 5
Mr. Batson's b. c. by Clayhall.............. 6 6

                                            Friday,

Sir F. Boynton's b. m. by Ruler..... ...... 3 2
Sir H. Williamson's cb. h. by Standard...... 2 3

Wednesday, the 26th, the Members Plate of 50l. for three yr olds, 7ft. 4lb. and four yr olds, 8ft. 7lb. A winner of a Plate or Sweepstakes since the first of March, carrying 3lb. of two, 5lb. extra. mares allowed 3lb. - heats, two miles and a quarter.

Mr. Lonsdale's cb. c. by Pipator, 3 yrs old .. 1 1
Sir A. Don's b. c. by Skyscraper, 4 yrs old.. 2 2
Mr. Watt's br. f. out of Miss Judy, 3 yrs old 3 3

Fifty Pounds for all ages, 4-mile heats.—No race for want of horses.

Thursday, the 27th, the Gold Cup, value 100gs, a Subscription of 10gs each, the surplus in specie; three yr olds, 6ft. 3lb. four yr olds, 7ft. 12lb. five yr olds, 8ft. 8lb. six yr olds and aged, 8ft. 13lb. mares allowed 3lb.—four miles. (17 Subscribers.)

Mr. Garforth's gr. m. Marcia, by Coriander, aged 1
Mr. R. Riddell's br. c. by Overton, 3 yrs old.... 2
Mr. Storey's b. h. Necho, 6 yrs old........... 3

High odds on Marcia.

The Freemen and Innkeepers Plate of 50l. for horses that never won that sum in Plate or Sweepstakes; three yr olds, 6ft. 10lb. four yr olds, 8ft. five yr olds and upwards, 8ft. 8lb. mares allowed 3lb.—3-mile heats

Mr. Peverall's ch. c. by Oberon, 4 yrs old.... 1 1
Sir A. Don's b c. by Skyscraper, 4 yrs old.. 3 2
Mr. Riddell's b. c. by Beningbrough, 4 yrs old 2 3

Friday, the 28th, the Town Subscription and Ladies Plate of 50l. for three yr olds, 7ft. four yr olds, 8ft. 3lb. five yr olds, 8ft. 10lb. six yr olds and aged, 9ft. mares allowed 3lb.—heats, two miles and three quarters.

Ld

Ld Belhaven's b. m Lady Mary, by Beningbrough, 5 yrs old 0 1 1
Sir H. Williamson's gr. h. Starling. 5 yrs. 0 2 2

4 and 5 to 1 on Starling.

Saturday the 29th, a Handicap Plate of 50l. for
the beaten horses of the week—Heats, two miles and
a quarter.

Mr. C. Bowman's b. m. Susan, by Overton,
5 yrs old, 8ft. 9lb. 5 1 1
Mr. Watt's b. f. by Beningbrough, 3 yrs
old, 6ft. 8lb....................... 1 4 3
Mr. Hodgson's gr. f. Priscilla, 4 yrs, 8ft. 5lb. 4 2 2
Mr. Richardson's b. f. by Screveton, 3 yrs
old, 6ft. 3lb. 3 3 4
Mr. Riddell's b. c. by Beningbrough, 4 yrs
old, 7ft. 12lb...................... 2 dr

Priscilla the favourite.

BIBURY.

On Tuesday, June the 25th, the Craven Stakes of
10gs each, with 50gs added, for three yr olds, 10ft.
four yr olds, 11ft. five yr olds, 11ft. 6lb. six yr olds,
and aged, 11ft. 12lb.—the New Mile. The winner
to be sold for 250gs, if demanded, &c. (7 Subscribers.)

H. R. H. the P. of Wales's b. g. Rebel, by Trum-
pator, aged............................ 1
Mr. Mellish's br. h. Pipylin, 6 yrs old........ 2
Mr. Goddard's br. h. Young Eclipse, 6 yrs old.. 3
Gen. Grosvenor's b. c. Skirmisher, 3 yrs old.. . 4
Mr. Cholmondeley's b. c. Bagatelle, 4 yrs old... 5

Even betting, Rebel agst the field.

The Sherborne Stakes of 50gs each, 30 ft. and only 10gs ft. if declared, &c.—four miles.

Mr. Howorth's ch. h. Wheatear, by Y. Wood-
pecker, 5 yrs old, 11ft. 0
H. R. H. the P. of Wales's ro. c. Petruchio,
4 yrs old, 10ft. 11lb................ ... 0 2
Sir H. Lippincott's b. c. Mirror, 4 yrs, 10ft. 3
Mr. Mellish's ch. h. Lismahago, 6 yrs old,
11ft. 5lb.................. 4
Gen. Grosvenor's ch. f. Humming Bird, 4 yrs
old, 10ft.... 5
Mr. B. Price's b. c. Grildrig, 4 yrs, 9ft. 8lb. 6
Ld Foley's Captain Absolute, 6 yrs old, 12ft. Mr.
Cholmondeley's Bagatelle, 4 yrs old, 10ft. 8lb. and
Col. Kingscote's La Mancha, 4 yrs old, 10ft. 6lb.
paid forfeit— 30gs each.

The following having declared forfeit within the time
prescribed, paid only 10gs each.

Mr. Byndlofs named Gary Owen, aged, 10ft. 8lb.
Mr. Rawlinson named Welsh Rabbit, 4 yrs, 9ft. 13lb.
Mr. Kellermann's Heeltap, 4 yrs old, 9ft 10lb.

5 to 2 agst Lismahago, 3 to 1 agst Wheatear, the
same agst Petruchio; after the dead heat, even
betting, and 6 to 5 on Petruchio.

Sir H. Lippincott's gr. g. Slate, by Mr. Teazle,
beat Mr. Miles's ch. g. by Waxy, out of Jemima,
both 5 yrs old, 10ft. each, two miles, 95gs.

2 to 1 on Slate.

Ld Foley's gr. h. Sir Harry Dimsdale, by Sir
Peter, 5 yrs old, 11ft. 3lb. beat Ld Sackville's Witchcraft, 4 yrs old, 9ft. 10lb. four miles, 100gs.

5 to 4 on Witchcraft.

Welter Stakes of 20gs each, for horses bona fide
the property of the Subscribers, that never started,
paid

paid or received ft. before the day of naming, carrying 13ft. each;—3-mile heats. (11 Subfcribers)

Ld F, Bentinck's b. g. Lothario, by Chance, 6 yrs
old, walked over—Mr. Hawkes's b. m. Toy, by
Afparagus, recd. a compromife of 10gs, and the
Stake returned.

H. R. H. the P. of Wales's b. m. Anifeed, by Coriander, 10ft. 5lb. recd. ft. from Mr. Scrope's Elemore, 10ft. the New Mile, 200gs, h. ft.

Ld E. Somerfet's ch. g. Sylvanus, by Volunteer,
6 yrs old, recd. ft. from Ld F. Bentinck's gr. g. Sir
Harry, by Active, aged, 12ft. each, three miles, 50gs,
h. ft.

WEDNESDAY.

Ld Sackville's Whirligig, by Whifkey, 12ft. beat
Mr. Mellifh's Lifmahago, 11ft. 6lb. three miles, 50gs.

Whirligig the favourite.

Sweepftakes of 25gs each, 15 ft. with 100gs added
by the Club, for all ages;—four miles. (11 Subfcribers.)

Ld Foley's Sir Harry Dimfdale, 5 yrs, walked over.

Major Pigot's Pipylin, by Sir Peter, 6 yrs old, beat
Mr. Mellifh's Gary Owen, aged, 12ft. each, two miles,
500gs.——6 to 4 on Pipylin.

Sweepftakes of 5gs each, with 50gs added, for
horfes that never won more than 100gs at any one
time, except at Bibury, Maddington, or Kingfcote;
three miles. (26 Subfcribers.)

Mr. Howorth's Wheatear, by Y. Woodpecker,
  5 yrs old, 11ft. 5lb.... 1
H. R. H. the P. of Wales's b. h. brother to Vivaldi,
  6 yrs old, 11ft. 9lb........................ 2

Sir

Sir H. Lippincott's b. c. Mirror, 4 yrs, 10ft. 4lb.   3
Mr. Mellish's Little Joey, 5 yrs, 11ft 5lb.   4

   5 to 4 agft brother to Vivaldi, and 6 to 4 agft
   Wheatear.

Handicap Plate of 50l.—2-mile heats.

Mr. Biggs's br. c. Wafhington, by Sir Peter,
   4 yrs old, 10ft. 2lb...   1   1
Sir H. Lippincott's ch. g by Waxy, out of
   Jemima, 5 yrs old, 10ft 8lb............   3   2
Major Pigot's ch. g. Gary Owen, aged, 11ft.   4   3
Mr. C. Cholmondeley's b. c. Green Dragon,
   4 yrs old, 10ft.......................   2   dr

   Even betting on Wafhington.

THURSDAY.

D. of St. Albans's Northampton, by John Bull,
11ft. beat Gen. Grofvenor's Humming Bird, 9ft. 10lb,
two miles, 25gs.——Northampton the favourite.

Ld Sackville's Witchcraft, by Sir Peter, 4 yrs old,
10ft. 3 lb. beat Ld Foley's Captain Abfolute, 6 yrs
old, 11ft. 6lb. three miles, 50gs.

   6 to 5 on Abfolute.

Mr. Mellifh's Little Joey, by Coriander, 5 yrs old,
12ft. beat Gen Grofvenor's Humming Bird, 4 yrs
old, 10ft. 11lb. from the end of the Wall, and once
round, 50gs.——2 to 1 on Little Joey.

Handicap Sweepftakes of 10gs each;—two miles.
(8 Subfcribers.)

H. R. H. the P. of Wales's b. h. brother to Vivaldi,
   by Woodpecker, 6 yrs old, 11ft. 10lb....   1
Mr. Goddard's Young Eclipfe, 6 yrs old, 11ft. ...   2
Mr. Harrifon's Chilton, aged, 11ft. 3lb........   3

                          Mr.

Mr. Mellish's Lismabago, 6 yrs old, 12ft...... 4

Mr. Hawkes's Little Printer, aged, 11ft. 7lb..... 5

Ld F. Bentinck's Lothario, by Chance, 6 yrs old, 11ft. 7lb. beat Gen. Grosvenor's Skirmisher, 3 yrs old, 9ft. 4lb. two miles and a half, 50gs.

6 and 7 to 4 on Skirmisher.

First Class of a Handicap Sweepstakes of 10gs each, with 25gs added by the Club;—two miles.

Ld Sackville's Whirligig, by Whiskey, aged, 12ft. 2lb.... ....,........ 1

Col Kingscote's La Mancha, 4 yrs old, 10ft. 2lb. 2

D. of St. Albans's Northampton, 6 yrs, 10ft. 9lb. 3

H. R. H. the P. of Wales's brother to Vivaldi, 6 yrs old, 11ft. 5lb........................ pd

2 to 1 on Whirligig.

Second Class of a Handicap Sweepstakes, as above.

Mr. Mellish's Pipylin, by Sir Peter, 6 yrs, 11ft. 7lb. 1

Gen. Grosvenor's Skirmisher, 4 yrs old, 9ft. 7lb. 2

Ld C. Somerset's Daisy, aged, 10ft. 11lb........ 3

Mr. Bar. Price's Grildrig, 4 yrs old, 10ft....... 4

Pipylin the favourite.

Fifty Pounds, for four yr olds and upwards;—heats, about two miles and a quarter.

H. R. H. the P. of Wales's Petruchio, by Stride, 4 yrs old, received the Plate without walking over.

FRIDAY.

The Barrington Stakes of 25gs each, 10 st. The winner to be sold for 150gs, if demanded, &c.—two miles. (7 Subscribers.)

H. R. H. the P. of Wales's Rebel, by Trumpator, walked over.——Mr. Cholmondeley's Northamp-

ton

ton reed 15gs; and Gen. Grofvenor's Skirmifher drew Stakes.

Mr. Howorth's Wheatear, by Young Woodpecker, 11ft. 9lb. beat Gen. Grofvenor's Humming Bird, 10ft. 7lb. the New Mile, 50gs.

6 to 1 on Wheatear.

Col. Kingfcote's La Mancha, by Don Quixote, 4 yrs old, 10ft. 4lb. beat Mr. Mellifh's Pipylin, 6 yrs old, 12ft. 4lb. the New Mile, 25gs.

2 to 1 on Pipylin.

Ld F. Bentinck's Lothario, by Chance, 10ft. 2lb. beat the D of St. Albans's Northampton, 10ft. 7lb. two miles and a half, 25gs.

5 to 4 on Northampton.

Handicap Plate of 50l.—heats, the New Mile.

Mr. Harrifon's ch. h. Chilton, by Pipator, aged, 10ft 12lb.............. ...	6	1	1
Col. Kingfcote's La Mancha, 4yrs, 10ft 1lb.	1	4	2
Major Pigot's Gary Owen, aged, 9ft. 4lb.	4	3	3
H. R H the P. of Wales's Rebel, aged, 12ft. 4lb......	2	2	dr
Mr. Goddard's Young Eclipfe, 6 yrs old, 11ft. 1lb	3	dr	
Mr. Mellifh's Pipylin, 6 yrs, 11ft. 9lb. ...	5	dr	

Even betting on Rebel; after the firft heat, 6 to 4 on La Mancha, and after the fecond heat, 7 to 4 on La Mancha.

D. of St. Albans's Northampton, 11ft. 13lb. recd. ft. from Mr. Howorth's Badger, 11ft. 2lb. three miles, 200gs, 50 ft.

July.

July.

IPSWICH.

ON Tuesday, July the 2d, His Majesty's Plate of 100gs, for three yr olds, 7ft. 11lb. and four yr olds, 9ft. 5lb. fillies allowed 3lb.—2-mile heats.

Sir J. Shelley's br. f. Houghton Lafs, by Sir Peter, 4 yrs old..... ..,...............	1	1
Mr. Wardell's br. c. Capias, 3 yrs old	3	2
Gen. L. Gower's b. c. Swinley, 3 yrs old ...	4	3
Ld Stawell's b. f. Gloriana, 3 yrs old	2	dr

5 to 2 and 3 to 1 on Houghton Lafs.

Wednefday the 3d, 50l. for all ages. The winner to be fold for 200gs, if demanded, &c.—heats, two miles and a quarter.

Mr. Wardell's br. c. Capias, by Overton, 3 yrs old, 7ft. 6lb............... .	0	1	1
Ld Stawell's b. f. Gloriana, 3 yrs, 7ft. 3lb.	0	2	dr

Capias the favourite.

Thurfday the 4th, the Town Purfe of 50l. for all ages;—2-mile heats, was won at two heats, by Mr. Neale's ch. m. Lady Rufhmere,

STAM-

STAMFORD.

On Tuefday, July the 2d, 5ol. for three yr old colts, 8ft. 2lb. and fillies, 8ft. that never won 5ol. in Plate, Match, &c.—heats, once round.

Mr. Williams's gr c. Blue Bell, by Buzzard	3	1	1
Mr. T Fifher's ch f. by Guildford......	1	4	3
Mr. Goodillon's ro. f Roanna..........	4	3	2
Mr Saile's b. c. brother to Duckling	5	2	4
Mr Watfon's br. c. brother to Gaoler....	2	dr	

 7 to 4 agft the brother to Duckling, and 2 to 1 agft the brother to Gaoler; after the firft heat, the field the favourite, and after the fecond heat, 2 and 3 to 1 on Blue Bell.

On Wednefday the 3d, the Town Plate of 5ol. for three yr olds, 6ft. 12lb. four yr olds, 8ft. 7lb. five yr olds, 9ft. 3lb. fix yr olds, 9ft. 8lb. and aged, 9ft. 10lb. mares and geldings allowed 3lb. The winner of a Plate or Sweepftakes this year, carrying 4lb. extra — heats, twice round.

Mr. Andrews's b. c. Fathom, by Trumpator, 3 yrs old	1	1
Mr. T. Fifher's b. f. Two Shoes, 4 yrs old..	2	2
Mr. Saile's brother to Duckling, 3 yrs old ..	4	3
Mr. Porter's b. f. Policy, 4 yrs old.........	3	4

 5 to 4 agft Fathom, and 2 to 1 agft Two Shoes; after the heat, 3 and 4 to 1 on Fathom.

On Thurfday the 4th, 5ol. given by the Truftees of the Marquis of Exeter, for all ages;—heats, thrice round.

Mr. T. Fifher's b. f. Two Shoes, by Afparagus, 4 yrs old, 6ft 13lb.	1	1
Mr. R. Weatherall's ch. h. Flambeau, aged, 9ft.	2	dr

 7 to 4 on Flambeau.

MOR.

MORPETH.

On Tuefday and Wednefday, the 2d and 3d of July,—no race, for want of horfes.

On Thurfday the 4th, 50l. for all ages;—4-mile heats.

Ld. Belhaven's Lady Mary, by Beningbrough, 5 yrs old...	1	1
Mr. Riddell's b. c. by Beningbrough, 4 yrs	2	2
Mr. Ilderton's b. f.	dis	

NEWCASTLE, STAFFORDSHIRE.

On Wednefday the 3d of July, a Maiden Purfe of 50l.—4-mile heats.

Mr. C. Cholmondeley's br. c. Welfh Rabbit, by Sir Peter, 4 yrs, 7ft. 2lb.	2	3	1	1
Mr. Billington's b. c. Forefter, 4 yrs old, 7ft. 2lb.	3	1	2	2
Mr. Clifton's ch. c. Welfh Harp, 3 yrs old, 6ft. 3lb.	1	2	3	3

A Sweepftakes of 10gs each;—four miles. (9 Subfcribers.)

Mr. Ackers's br. f. Heb, by Overton, 4 yrs, 7ft. 7lb.	1
Mr. Clifton's b. c. Coriolanus, 4 yrs old, 7ft. 9lb.	2

Thurfday the 4th, the Members Purfe of 50l.— 4-mile heats.

Mr. Clifton's b. c. Coriolanus, by Sir Peter, 4 yrs old, 7ft. 7lb.	2	1	1

Mr.

Mr. Lord's b. g. Cockfpinner, 5 yrs old,
8ft. 4lb.................................. 1 2 2
Mr. Billington's b. g. Bamford, 6 yrs old,
8ft. 13lb............................. 3 3 3

STOCKBRIDGE.

On Wednefday the 3d of July, 50l. for three yr
olds, 7ft. 5lb. and four yr olds, 8ft. 12lb. mares
and geldings allowed 2lb. The winner of one Plate
this year, 3lb. extra.—2-mile heats.

Mr. Fenwick's b. f. Mifs Coiner, by Don
Quixote, 4 yrs old 1 1
Mr. Branthwayt's ch. c. Woodcot, 4 yrs old.. 3 2
Mr. Day's br. c. Principle, 4 yrs old 2 3

Sweepftakes of 10gs each, for all ages, rode by
Gentlemen;—three miles. (6 Subfcribers.)

Sir H. Lippincott's Mirror, by Precipitate, 4 yrs old,
walked over.

Thurfday the 4th, a Maiden Plate of 50l. given by
the Members for the Borough; three yr olds, 6ft.
four yr olds, 8ft. five yr olds, 8ft. 12lb. fix yr olds,
9ft. 5lb. and aged, 9ft. 7lb. mares and geldings allowed 2lb.—4 mile heats.

Ld Sackville's br. c. Witchcraft, by Sir
Peter, 4 yrs old... .... 1 0 1
Mr. Ladbroke's b. f. Dora, 3 yrs old 2 0 2
Mr. Branthwayt's b. c. by Pegafus, 3 yrs dis
Mr. Martin's Difmal.................... dis
Mr. Sutton's Wren . ... dis

7 to 4 on Witchcraft, and after the dead heat, 3 to
1 he won.

Sweep-

Sweepftakes of 5gs each, for Welter horfes, &c. 12ft. each, rode by Gentlemen;—2-mile heats. (10 Subfcribers.)

Sir H. Lippincott's ch. g. Delegate, by Waxy,
5 yrs old....... .... 1 1
Mr. Sturges's gr. g. by the Arcot Arabian,
6 yrs old..........................,..... . 2 dr

6 to 4 on Delegate.

CARDIFF, GLAMORGANSHIRE.

On Wednefday the 3d of July, a Maiden Plate of 50l. for three yr olds, 7ft. four yr olds, 8ft. 6lb five yr olds, 9ft. fix yr olds, 9ft. 4lb. and aged, 9ft. 7lb. mares and geldings allowed 3lb.—2-mile heats.

Mr. Jones's ch. c. Junius, by Buzzard, 3 yrs   1   1
Mr. Hurft's b. c. by Fortunio, 3 yrs (ran out) 2 dis

Thurfday the 4th, the Sweepftakes not run for. ,

Friday the 5th, 50l. for all ages;—4-mile heats.

Mr. Hurft's ch. b. Jack-o'-the-green, by Buzzard, 5 yrs old, walked over.

BRIDGNORTH.

On Thurfday, July the 4th, a Sweepftakes of 10gs each, for all ages; three yr olds, 6ft. 10lb. four yr olds, 8ft.—four miles. (6 Subfcribers.)

Ld Stamford's br. c. Gayman, by Delpini, 4 yrs   1
Col. Kingfcote's br. c Hadley, 3 yrs old...... . 2

Fifty Pounds, given by J. Whitmore, Efq. for all ages;—2-mile heats.   Mr.

Mr. Clifton's b. f. Jofephina, by Sir Peter,
. 4 yrs old, 8ft. 7lb...................... 1 1
Mr. Emden's br. c. Latitat, 4 yrs old, 8ft. 9lb. 2 2

Friday the 5th, a Sweepftakes of 10gs each, for
three and four yr olds;—two miles. (7 Subfcribers.)
Ld Stamford's b. c. Young Rofcius, by Sir Peter,
3 yrs old, 7ft 7lb....................... .. 1
Mr. Clifton's Jofephina, 4 yrs old, 8ft. 6lb...... 2
Col. Kingfcote's Hadley, 3 yrs old, 7ft. 7lb...... 3

4 to 1 on Young Rofcius.

Hunters Sweepftakes of 10gs each, rode by Gen-
tlemen; 12ft. mares and geldings allowed 3lb.—
four miles. (10 Subfcribers.)
Ld F. Bentinck's b. g. Lothario, by Chance..... 1
Ld E. Somerfet's ch g Sylvanus 2
Mr. Emden's b. g. Contefter.... 3

. Fifty Pounds, given by I. H. Browne, Efq. for all
ages;—4-mile heats.
Ld Stamford's f. Georgina, by George, 3 yrs
old, a feather 1 1
Mr. Emden's Latitat, 4 yrs old, 7ft. 4lb. 2 2
Mr. Icke's b. g. Syphax, 6 yrs old, 8ft. 7lb.
(bolted)................... .... dis

NEWMARKET

JULY MEETING.

On Monday, July the 8th, Ld Grofvenor's b. f.
Meteora, by Meteor, 3 yrs old, 7ft 13lb. beat Mr.
Lake's b. c. Lynceus, 4 yrs old, 8ft 4lb. Two yr old
Courfe, 50gs.——2 to 1 on Meteora.

Mr.

Mr. Watfon's b. b. Dreadnought, by Buzzard, 5 yrs old, 8ft. 7lb. beat Ld Grofvenor's b. c. Agincourt, 4 yrs old, 8ft. 6lb. Ab. Mile, 100gs, h. ft.

5 to 4 on Agincourt.

Second and laft year of the July Stakes of 50gs each, 30gs ft. for two yr old colts, 8ft. 6lb. and fillies, 8ft. 4lb. Two yr old Courfe. (7 Subfcribers.)

Mr. Wilfon's b. c. brother to Merryman, by Buzzard 1
Mr. R. Boyce's ch. f. Wretch 2
Sir C. Bunbury's b. f. by Whifkey, out of Orange-
bud.. 3
D. of Grafton's b. c. by Groufe, out of Peppermint 4
Mr. Panton's br. c. by Whifkey, dam by Trumpator, out of Crane............................ 5

5 to 2 agft the brother to Merryman, 3 to 1 agft Mr. Panton's colt, 7 to 2 agft the D. of Grafton's colt, and 8 to 1 agft Wretch.

Mr. Waftell's b. f. Lumbago, by Groufe, 7ft. 9lb. recd. ft. from Mr. Howorth's f. Pimlico (dead) 6ft. D. I. 100gs, h. ft.

Mr. Watfon's Dreadnought, 9ft. recd. 20gs from Mr. R. Boyce's Punch, 7ft. 8lb. Two yr old Courfe, 50gs.

TUESDAY.

Mr. Watfon's b. c. by Groufe, out of Peppermint, 2 yrs old, 5ft. 7lb. beat the D. of Grafton's brother to Gaoler, 3 yrs old, 8ft. 7lb. Two yr old Courfe, 25gs.

5 to 4 on the winner.

July Stakes of 100gs each, h. ft. for three yr old colts, 8ft. 7lb. and fillies, 8ft. 3lb. Acrofs the Flat. (5 Subfcribers.)

Ld Grosvenor's b. c. Plantagenet, by John Bull..   1
Sir C. Bunbury's b. f. Lydia.... 2
D. of Grafton's b. f. by Grouse, out of Magic... 3

7 to 2, on Plantagenet.

The Town Plate of 50l. for three yr old colts,
8ft. 4lb. and fillies, 8ft.—last mile and a distance of
B. C. The late Mr. Perram, by his will, directed
his executors to pay 20gs to the winner of this Plate.

Ld Grosvenor's b. f. Violante, by John Bull....   1
Ld F. Osborne's b. c. brother to Hippocampus...   2
Mr. Elwes's br. c. by Buzzard........ 3
Mr. Forth's br. c. Artichoke........ 4
D. of Grafton's b. f. Farce................... 5

11 to 8 agst Violante, 2 to 1 agst the brother to
Hippocampus, and 5 to 1 agst Mr. Elwes's colt.

Mr. Watson's b. h. Duxbury, by Sir Peter, 8ft. 7lb.
recd. 15gs from the D. of Grafton's b. f. Lumbago,
7ft. 12lb. Ab. Mile, 50gs.

WEDNESDAY.

Ld F. G. Osborne's b. m. Elizabeth, by Waxy,
8ft. 7lb. beat Ld Grosvenor's b. c. Agincourt, 8ft. 1lb.
Across the Flat, 50gs.——6 to 4 on Agincourt.

Mr. Watson's b. h. Duxbury, by Sir Peter, 8ft. 6lb.
beat Mr. R. Boyce's Punch, 6ft. 11lb. Two yr old
Course, 50gs.——6 to 4 on Duxbury.

Fifty Pounds, for three yr olds carrying 6ft. 9lb.
four yr olds, 8ft. five yr olds, 8ft. 8lb. six yr olds,
8ft. 12lb. and aged, 9ft. D. I.

Ld Foley's ch. h. Captain Absolute, by John Bull,
    6 yrs old 1
Mr. Wardell's b. f. Gratitude, 4 yrs old........ 2

Sir

Sir C. Bunbury's b. m. Eleanor, aged.......... 3
Mr. Forth's ch. h. Brighton, aged............. 4

  6 to 4 agst Eleanor, 2 to 1 agst Gratitude, and 5 to
    2 agst Absolute.

  Mr. Watson's Dreadnought, 8ft. 4lb. agst Mr. Wilson's Maiden, 8ft. 2lb. R. M. 50gs—*a dead beat.*
       5 to 4 on Maiden.

  Mr. Wilson's brother to Merryman, 2 yrs old,
6ft. 3lb. recd. from Mr. Howorth's Pimlico (dead)
3 yrs old, 8ft. Two yr old Course, 50gs.

TOTNES.

  On Tuesday the 9th of July, a Sweepstakes of 5gs
each, for Hunters carrying 11st.—3-mile heats.—
{ Subscribers.)
Capt. Wall's ro. h. Ironsides, aged........... 1 1
Mr. Percy Burrell's br. g. Cyclops, aged 2 2
Capt. Fellowes's br. m. Creeping Jenny, 6 yrs 3 3
      High odds on Ironsides.

  Capt. French's b. g. Dare Devil, by Quetlavaca,
14ft. 7lb. beat Mr. Ord's bl. g. Soot-bag, 12ft. one
mile, 80gs.——2 to 1 on Dare Devil.

  Wednesday the 10th, the Town Plate of 50l.—
4-mile heats.
Mr. P. Burrell's b. g. Quill-driver, by Pipator,
    aged, 9ft. 4lb........................... 1 1
Mr. Foster's b. m. Maid of all Work, aged,
    9ft. 4lb.............................. dis
Capt. Ilbert's br. h. Phœnix, by Sir Peter,
    5 yrs old, 9ft. 1lb. (ran on the wrong side of
    a Post) .... dis
Capt. Wall's ro. h. Ironsides, 9ft. 7lb. (bolted) dis
      Ironsides the favourite.

A Sweep-

A Sweepſtakes of 20gs each, two miles, 12ſt. 7lb. —Owners on.

Mr. P. Burrell's br. g. Cyclops........ 1
Capt. French's b. g. Dare Devil... 2
Mr. Ord's ch. g. Feather Spring........ 3

6 to 4 on the winner..

Capt. Fellowes's Creeping Jenny beat Capt. Wall's Tartar, two miles, 50gs; rode by Gentlemen.

6 to 4 on the winner.

Thurſday the 11th, a Sweepſtakes of 5gs each, rode by Gentlemen;—2-mile heats. (6 Subſcribers.)

Mr. P. Burrell's b. g. Quill-driver, 12ſt. .. 5 1 1
Captain French's ch. g. Woodpecker,
  11ſt. 11lb. 3 3 2
Mr. Kempſon's b. m. Perdita, 11ſt. 11lb. 2 4 3
Capt. Wall's ro. h. Ironſides, 12ſt. 3lb. .. 1 2 dr
Capt. Fellowes's, br. m. Creeping Jenny,
  11ſt. 11lb. (fell, ſecond heat)........ 4 dis

Ironſides the favourite; after the heat even betting between him and Quill-driver; after the ſecond heat high odds on Quill-driver.

Mr. Foſter's Maid of all Work, 9ſt. 4lb. beat Capt. Fellowes's Creeping Jenny, 9ſt. 11lb. two miles, 50gs.

Even betting.

NANTWICH.

On Wedneſday the 10th of July, 50l. for three and four yr olds;—2-mile heats.

Mr. Cl. Cholmondeley's br. c. Welſh Rabbit,
  by Sir Peter, 4 yrs old, 8ſt. 8lb........... 1 1
Mr. Billington's b. c. Foreſter, 4 yrs, 8ſt. 5lb. 2 2
Mr. Denham's Optician recd. 10gs to withdraw.

On

On Thursday the 11th, 50l. for all ages;—4-mile heats.

Mr. Denham's b. c. Optician, by Telescope,
    4 yrs old, 7ft. 10lb.   1   1
Mr. Billington's b. g. Bamford, 6 yrs, 8ft. 5lb.   2   2
Mr. Lord's b. g. Cockspinner, 5 yrs old, 8ft.   3   3
Mr. Cholmondeley's ch. h. Northampton,
    6 yrs old, 8ft. 8lb............   4   4

LAMBERTON.

On Wednesday the 10th of July, a Hunters Sweep-stakes of 20gs each, 12ft. rode by Gentlemen;—4-mile heats. (3 Subscribers.)
Mr. Baillie's ch. g. by Star, walked over.

A Sweepstakes of 20gs each, for three yr olds;—two miles. (5 Subscribers.)
Ld Belhaven's b. c. by Star   1
Sir H. Williamson's ch. f. by Hambleton   2
Ld Montgomerie's gr. c. by Spadille   3

Thursday, 50l. for all ages;—4-mile heats.
Ld Belhaven's b. h. Brandon, by Beningbrough,
    6 yrs old.   1   1
Mr. Carnegie's ch. m. Miss Betsey, aged. ..   2   dr

LUDLOW.

On Thursday the 11th of July, a Sweepstakes of 10gs each, with 20l. added by the Town, for all ages;—four miles. (7 Subscribers.)

Ld Stamford's b. c. Gayman, by Delpini, 4 yrs old,
    7ft. 6lb............................,.........   1
Mr. Emden's br. m. Gipsy, 5 yrs, 8ft. 1lb.   2

         A Maiden

A Maiden Plate of 50l. for three yr olds, 6ft. four yr olds, 7ft. 7lb. five yr olds, 8ft. 6lb. six yr olds, 8ft. 11lb. and aged, 9ft. mares and geldings allowed 3lb.—3 mile heats.

Mr. Birch's ch. f. Lavinia, by Pipator, 3 yrs   1   1
Col. Kingſcote's b. c. Hadley, 3 yrs old.....   2   2
Mr. Saunders's br. f. Brown Beſs, 4 yrs old .   4   3
Mr. Icke's b. g. Romper-ſtomper, by Spear,
   6 yrs old........   3   dr

On Friday the 12tb, a Handicap Plate of 50l.— heats (the diſtance not mentioned in the liſt ſent us.)
Col. Kingſcote's b. c. Hadley, by Sir Peter,
   3 yrs old, 6ft. 2lb.....   3   1   1
Mr. Saunders's Brown Beſs, 4 yrs, 6ft. 7lb.   1   2   2
Mr. Emden's Latitat, 4 yrs old, 7ft. 2lb...   2   3   3

SWANSEA.

On Monday, July the 15th, 50l. for all ages;— 2-mile heats.

Mr. Jones's ch. c. Junius, by Buzzard, 3 yrs
   old, 7ft.....,.....................   1   1
Mr. Hurſt's b. c. Parſon Horne, 3 yrs old, 7ft.   2   2

Fifty Guineas, given by T. M. Talbot, Eſq. for Hunters, 12ft. each ;—4-mile heats.

Mr. Collins's b. h. Midas, by Whiſkey, 6 yrs   2   1
Mr. Jenkins's ch. g. Big Ben   1   dis

Tueſday the 16th, 50l. for three and four yr olds; —2-mile heats.

Mr. Jones's ch. c. Junius, 3 yrs old............   1
Mr. Hurſt's b. c. Parſon Horne, 3 yrs old .....   dis

Wed.

Wednesday the 17th, a free Plate of 50l. for all ages;—4-mile heats.

Mr. Jones's ch. c. Junius, 3 yrs old 1 1
Mr. Collins's b. h. Midas, 6 yrs old..... .. 3 2
Mr. Hurst's ch. h. Jack-o'-the-green, 5 yrs old 2 3

Mr. M. Philipps's b. f. Mary, by Stickler, 4 yrs old, beat Mr. Jones's g. Blacksmith, aged, 8ft. each, the last mile of the Course, 50gs.

WINCHESTER.

On Tuesday, July the 16th, His Majesty's Plate of 100gs, for all ages; four yr olds, 10ft. 4lb.—4-mile heats.

Ld Sackville's Witchcraft, by Sir Peter, 4 yrs 1 1
Mr. Ladbroke's Prospero, 4 yrs old........ 2 2
Mr. Abbey's Virgin, 4 yrs old 3 3

Even betting between Witchcraft and Prospero, and after the heat, 3 to 1 on Witchcraft.

Wednesday the 17th, 50l. for five yr olds, 8ft. 4lb. six yr olds, 9ft. and aged, 9ft. 6lb.—4-mile heats.

Ld Sackville's Whirligig, by Whiskey, aged 3 1 1
Mr. Abbey's Margery, 6 yrs old........ 1 2 2
Mr. Skinner's Duckling, 5 yrs old 5 4 3
Mr. Richardson's Lemon-squeezer, aged 4 3 dr
Mr. Neale's Quiz, aged............... 2 5 dr

Quiz the favourite.

Fifty Pounds, for three and four yr olds;—2-mile heats.

Mr. Fenwick's Miss Coiner, by Don Quixote, 4 yrs old, 8ft. 11lb...................... 1
Mr. Frogley's b. c. Triptolemus, 4 yrs, 8ft. 8lb. dis

10 to 1 on Miss Coiner.

Sweep-

Sweepſtakes of rogs each;—two miles. (7 Subſcribers.)

Mr. Abbey's Margery, by John Bull, 6 yrs old,
    11ft. 3lb.   1
Sir H. Lippincott's Mirror, 4 yrs old, 10ft. 6lb .   2
Mr. Branthwayt's Woodcot, 4 yrs old, 10ft. 6lb.   3

6 to 4 on the field.

Thurſday the 18th, a Maiden Plate of 50l. for
three yr olds, 6ft. four yr olds, 7ft. 12lb. five yr olds,
8ft. 7lb. ſix yr olds, 8ft. 13lb. 'and aged, 9ft. 2lb.—
4-mile heats.

Mr. Day's b. c. Principle (late Highflyer) by Moorcock, 4 yrs old....	2	1	1
Mr. Sutton's gr. f. Betſey, 4 yrs old......	1	4	4
Mr. Ladbroke's ch. c. by Guildford, 3 yrs	3	3	2
Mr. Sadler's b. c. Peregrine Pickle, 4 yrs	5	2	3
Mr. Frogley's gr. h. Starling, 5 yrs old..	4	5	5

Mr. Ladbroke's colt the favourite.

Fifty Pounds, given by the Members for the
County, for Hunters the property of reſident Freeholders, 12ft. each;—4-mile heats.

Mr. David's b. m. by John Bull, dam by Mercury, 5 yrs old........	1	1
Mr. Early's br. h. by Cottager, 5 yrs old....	2	2

This Plate remains in diſpute.

PRESTON.

On Tueſday, July the 16th, Sir W. Gerard's Barouche, by Overton, beat Ld Derby's brother to
Agoniſtes, 8ft. each, two miles, 100gs, h. ft.

5 to 2 on the winner.

A Maiden Plate of 50l. for three yr olds, 6ft. 10lb.
                                           four

four yr olds, 8ft. five yr olds, 8ft. 7lb. fix yr olds and aged, 8ft. 10lb. mares and geldings allowed 2lb.— 3-mile heats.

Mr. Clifton's ch. c. Welfh Harp, by Pipator, 3 yrs old....................	o	6	1	1
Mr. Mafon's gr. c. by Delpini, 3 yrs	7	1	2	3
Ld Strathmore's b. m. Viciffitude, 5 yrs	6	4	3	2
Mr. Turner's b. f. by Reftlefs, 3 yrs	o	5	4	dr
Mr. Taylor's b. c. by Hammer, 3 yrs	5	2	die	
Sir H. Williamfon's b. c. Surrender, 3 yrs old......	3	3	dr	
Ld Derby's brother to Agoniftes, 3 yrs old (bolted)...........	4	dr		

Wednefday the 17th, 50l. given by the Earl of Derby, for three yr olds, 7ft. 2lb. and four yr olds, 8ft. 4lb. fillies and geldings allowed 2lb. winners carrying 3lb. extra.—2-mile heats.

Mr. Lonfdale's b. c. Sir Charles, by Selim, 4 yrs old	1	1
Mr. Clifton's b. c. Coriolanus, 4 yrs old....	2	2
Mr. Robinfon's ch. f. by Abba Thulle, 3 yrs	3	3

Coriolanus the favourite.

Thurfday the 18th, the Members Plate of 50l. for all ages;—4-mile heats.

Mr. Lonfdale's b. c. Sir Charles, by Selim, 4 yrs old, 8ft. 5lb	1	
Mr. Harris's b. c. by Hammer, 4 yrs old, 8ft. 3lb....	2	dr

10 to 1 on the winner.

A Handicap Plate of 50l. for all ages;—three miles—Not run for.

Mr. Clifton's Sir Ulic Mackilligut, 5 yrs old, 8ft. 9lb. and Mr. Lonfdale's br. c. Sir Charles, 4 yrs old, 8ft. 3lb. recd. 10gs each; and Mr. Taylor's b. c. by Hammer, 3 yrs old, 6ft. was drawn.

BLAND.

BLANDFORD.

On Tuesday, July the 23d, 50l. for three and four yr olds;—2-mile heats.

Mr. Fenwick's b. f. Miss Coiner, by Don
   Quixote, 4 yrs old, 8ft. 2lb.... ...... 2 1 2
Mr. Abbey's bl. f. Virgin, 4 yrs, 7ft. 11lb. 1 2 dr

Fifty Pounds, for horses that have not won that value since March, 1804;—4-mile heats.

Mr. Dilly's b. f. Little Peggy, by Buzzard,
   4 yrs old, 7ft. 13lb.................. 1 1
Mr. Sutton's gr. f. Betsey, 4 yrs old, 7ft. 13lb. 2 2
Mr. Bishoffhanson's br. h. Serpent, aged,
   9ft. 10lb............................ 3 3

Wednesday the 24th, 50l. given by the Members for the County;—4-mile heats.

Mr. Fenwick's b. f. Miss Coiner, 4 yrs old,
   8ft. 3lb............................ 1 1
Mr. Abbey's ch. m. Margery, 5 yrs, 8ft. 12lb. 2 2
Mr. Frogley's gr. h. Starling, 5 yrs, 8ft. 12lb. 3 3

KNIGHTON.

On Tuesday, July the 23d, a Sweepstakes of 5gs each, with 10gs added, for all ages;—3-mile heats. (8 Subscribers.)

Ld C. H. Somerset's Daisy, by Buzzard,
   aged, 8ft 8lb......... .. .. 4 1 1
Mr. Emden's b. m. Gipsy, 5 yrs, 8ft. 4lb. 1 2 2
Mr. Browne's b. f. Maid of the Moor, 3 yrs
   old, 6ft. 5lb...................... 2 3 dr

                                                Mr.

Mr. Icke's b. g. Romper-ftomper, 6 yrs
old, 8ft. 6lb................... ... 3 4 dr

Gipfy the favourite. till after the fecond. heat, when
it was even betting.

Wednefday the 24th, 50l. by Subfcription for all
ages;—4-mile heats.

Ld C. H. Somerfet's Daify, aged, 8ft. 9lb . . 1 1
Mifs C. Saunders's br. f. Brown Befs, 4 yrs
old, 6ft. 11lb........ .... 2 2
Mr. Emden's Gipfy, 5 yrs old, 7ft. 11lb...... 3 3
Mr Icke's Romper-ftomper, 6 yrs, 8ft. 4lb... dis

5 to.4 on the field, and after the firft heat, 6 to 4 on
Daify.

BRIGHTON.

On Friday, July the 26th, the Smoaken Stakes of
20gs each, for three yr olds, 7ft. four yr olds, 8ft. 3lb.
five yr olds, 8ft. 9lb. fix yr olds, 9ft. 1lb. and aged,
9ft. 4lb —the laft mile.

H. R. H. the P. of Wales's Rebel, by Trumpator,
aged 1
Mr. Wardell's b. f. Gratitude, 4 yrs old. 2
Mr. Ladbroke's br. c. Buftard, 4 yrs old. 3
Mr. Howorth's Wheatear, 5 yrs old.. 4

6 to 4 agft Gratitude, 2 to 1 agft Buftard, and 5 to
1 agft Rebel.

Mr. Mellifh's Sancho, by Don Quixote, beat Ld
Egremont's Hannibal, 8ft. 7lb. each, the laft mile,
1000gs.—11 to 10 on Hannibal.

The third and laft year of the Pavilion Stakes of
100gs each, h. ft. for three yr old colts, 8ft. 3lb. and
fillies,

fillies, 8ft. The winner of the Derby Stakes carrying 7lb. extra.—the laft mile. (20 Subfcribers.)

Ld Egremont's b. c. Cardinal Beaufort, by Gohanna (7lb. extra.) 1
Sir C. Bunbury's b. f. Lydia.................... 2
Ld Grofvenor's br. c. Jafper..................... 3

6 to 4 on Cardinal Beaufort.

The fecond year of the renewed Sweepftakes of 10gs each, for three yr old colts, 8ft. 7lb. and fillies, 8ft. 4lb. The winner to be fold for 150gs, if demanded, &c.—the laft mile. (9 Subfcribers.)

Ld Egremont's b. c. Prodigal, by Gohanna 1
Mr. Howorth's b c. Scrip, by Pencil 2
Mr. Ladbroke's ch. c. Dudley............ 3

The winner was claimed.

Ld Barrymore's Merryman, by Buzzard, 8ft. 6lb. beat Sir J. Shelley's Currycomb, 7ft. 7lb. one mile, 100gs, h. ft.——11 to 8 on Currycomb.

Sweepftakes of 200gs each, h. ft.—four miles. (5 Subfcribers.)

H. R. H. the P. of Wales's Albion, by John Bull, 5 yrs old, 7ft. 6lb. 1
Mr. F. Neale's Bobtail, aged, 8ft. 2
Mr. Howorth's Harefoot, 5 yrs old, 6ft. 13lb... 3

5 to 4 on Bobtail.

SATURDAY.

The Somerfet Stakes of 50gs each, h. ft. for four yr olds, 7ft. 7lb. five yr olds, 8ft. 5lb. fix yr olds, 8ft. 11lb. and aged, 8ft. 13lb. mares allowed 3lb.— four miles. (16 Subfcribers.)

Sir

*Sir H. Williamfon's Walton, by Sir Peter, 6 yrs   1
Sir J. Shelley's Houghton Lafs, 4 yrs old........   2
Mr. Howorth's Enterprize, 4 yrs old..........   3
H. R. H. the P. of Wales's br. h. Orville, 6 yrs old   4
Mr. Mellifh's Lady Brough, 4 yrs old, did not weigh

* *A difpute having arifen upon this race, the Gentlemen
to whom it was referred, came to the following re-
folution, viz. that* Walton, Houghton Lafs, *and*
Enterprize, *not having run the proper Courfe, were
difqualified; that* Orville *being the only horfe that
fulfilled the conditions of the race, was entitled to the
Stakes.*

6 to 4 agft Lady Brough, 5 to 2 agft Walton, 3 to 1
agft Orville, 4 to 1 agft Houghton Lafs, and 10
to 1 agft Enterprize.

The fecond year of the renewed Petworth Stakes of
10gs each, for four yr olds, 7ft. 7lb. five yr olds,
8ft. 7lb. fix yr olds, 9ft. and aged, 9ft. 3lb. mares allowed 3lb. The winner to be fold for 250gs, if
demanded, &c.—four miles. (8 Subfcribers.)

Ld Egremont's b. f. by Precipitate, out of Cathe-
rine, 4 yrs old..............   1
H. R. H. the P. of Wales's b. g. Rebel, aged . ..   2
Mr. Howorth's ch. h. Wheatear, 5 yrs old......   3

5 to 4 agft Rebel, 6 to 4 agft Wheatear, and 3 to
1 agft the winner.

Fifty Pounds, for three yr olds, 7ft. 6lb. four yr
olds, 8ft. 11lb. and five yr olds, 9ft. 7lb. The winner of one Plate or Sweepftakes this year, carrying
3lb. of two, 7lb. extra. mares allowed 3lb.—heats,
the New Courfe.

*Mr. Howorth's b. c. Prodigal, by Gohanna,
3 yrs old... ....:   1   1
Mr. Ladbroke's b. f. Dora, 3 yrs old..... ..   2   2

H. R. H. the P. of Wales's ro. c. Petruchio,
4 yrs old............................. 3 dr

*It appearing upon enquiry, that none of these horses had
carried the proper weights for their qualifications, this
Plate was not given; and all bets upon it were
declared null and void.*

MONDAY the 29th.

Sweepstakes of 100gs each, the New Course. (4
Subscribers.)

Ld Darlington's Zodiac, by St. George, 4 yrs old,
8ft. 3lb......... ....: . 1
Mr. F. Neale's Brainworm, 4 yrs old, 7ft. 9lb . . 2

Even betting.

A Handicap Plate of 50l. for four yr olds and upwards;—heats, the New Course.

Mr. Ladbroke's Bustard, by Buzzard, 4 yrs
old, 8ft. 2lb. .... 1 .
H. R. H. the P. of Wales's brother to Vivaldi,
6 yrs old, 8ft. 7lb............ . .. .. 2 2
Mr. Wardell's Gratitude, 4 yrs old, 7ft. 3lb.. 3 3

7 to 4 agst the brother to Vivaldi, 2 to 1 agst Bustard, and 2 to 1 agst Gratitude.

Fifty Pounds, on the same conditions as Saturday's
Plate.

H. R. H. the P. of Wales's ro. c. Petru-
chio, by Stride, 4 yrs old............ 3 1 1
Mr. Ladbroke's b. f. Dora, 3 yrs old..... 1 3 3
Mr. Howorth's b. c. Prodigal, 3 yrs old.. 2 2 2

6 to 4 agst Petruchio, 2 to 1 agst Prodigal, and 3 to
1 agst Dora.

TUES-

TUESDAY.

The Egremont Stakes of 200gs each, h. ft. for three yr old colts, 8ft. 4lb. and fillies, 8ft.—the laft mile and half. (7 Subfcribers.)

H. R. H the P. of Wales's b. c. Barbaroffa, by Sir
Peter... 1
Sir C. Bunbury's br. f. Lydia................... 2
Ld Darlington's b. c. by Sir Peter, out of Æthe.. 3
Ld Egremont's ch. c. Impoftor................ 4

 7 to 4 agft Impoftor, 2 to 1 agft Lydia, 4 to 1 agft
  Ld Darlington, and 5 to 1 agft Barbaroffa.

Ld Egremont's Cardinal Beaufort, by Gohanna, 3 yrs old, beat Ld Barrymore's Merryman, 4 yrs old, 8ft. each, the laft mile, 200gs.

 5 to 4 on Cardinal Beaufort.

A Gold Cup, given by H. R. H. the P. of Wales, added to a Subfcription of 10gs each, for three yr olds, 6ft. four yr olds, 7ft. 8lb. five yr olds, 8ft. 6lb. fix yr olds and aged, 8ft. 12lb. mares allowed 3lb.— four miles. (21 Subfcribers.)

H. R. H. the P. of Wales's br. h. Orville, by Be-
ningbrough, 6 yrs old..... 1
Sir J. Shelley's b. f. Houghton Lafs, 4 yrs old.... 2
Mr. Mellifh's b. f. Lady Brough, 4 yrs old 3
Mr. Howorth's b. h. Harefoot, 6 yrs old 4

 5 and 6 to 4 on Houghton Lafs, 4 to 1 agft Lady
 Brough, and 6 to 1 agft Orville.

Mr. Mellifh's Honefty, by Overton, recd. 5gs com-promife from Mr. Neale's Punch (late Rara Avis) 8ft. 2lb. each, the Mile, 200gs, h. ft.

    G 2   Fifty

Fifty Pounds, for four yr olds and upwards. The winner to be fold for 150gs, if demanded, &c.—Not run for.

Mr. Howorth's Wheatear being the only horſe entered, recd. 20gs.

HAVERFORD-WEST.

On Monday, July 29th, 50l. for horſes, &c. bred in the Principality of Wales;—4-mile heats.

Capt. Mathias's bl. m. Creeping Jane, by Ramah Droog, 5 yrs old, 8ſt. 3lb.	1	2	1
Mr. Hurſt's b. c. Parſon Horne, 3 yrs old, a feather.........	2	1	2
Capt. Vaughan's b. f. 3 yrs old, a feather, (bolted)	dis		

Tueſday the 30th, a Maiden Plate of 50l. for all ages;—2-mile heats.

Capt. Sutton's gr. g. Piccalilly, by Pickle, aged, 9ft. 1lb........	1	1
Capt. Vaughan's b. f. Creeping Beſs, 4 yrs old, 7ſt. 4lb..........	2	2
Mr. Hurſt's b. g. 4 yrs old, 7ſt. 4lb........	dis	

Wedneſday the 31ſt, 50l. for three yr olds, 7ſt. and four yr olds, 8ſt. 3lb. fillies and geldings allowed 3lb. a winner of one Plate carrying 3lb. of two, 5lb. and of three or more, 7lb. extra.—2-mile heats.

Mr. Hurſt's b. c. Parſon Horne, by Fortunio, 3 yrs old...........	1	1
Capt. Vaughan's b. f. Creeping Beſs, 4 yrs old	2	2
Mr. Robin's ch. c. by Paſtor, 2 yrs old......	3	dis

A Free Plate of 50l.—4-mile heats.

Mr. Collins's b. h. Midas, by Whiſkey, 6 yrs old, 8ſt. 11lb..........	1	1

. Mr.

Mr. Harrifon's b. h. Vividus, aged, 8ft. 13lb.
(broke down) .... 2 dis
Mr. Hurft's ch. h. Jack-o'-the-Green, 5 yrs
old, 8ft. 4lb. (broke down) .... dis

EDINBURGH.

On Monday, July 29th, 50l. for horfes, &c. carrying 11ft.—4-mile heats.

Mr. Baird's b. h. Young Trimmer, by Trim-
mer................................... 1 1
Mr. Denham's gr. g..................... 3 2
Mr. Bofwell's b. m. by Guftavus 2 3
Mr. Dudgeon's br. m. Kate. 4 4
Mr. Browne's b. m 5 5

Several others ftarted.

Tuefday, His Majefty's Plate of 100gs, for four yr
olds and upwards ;—4-mile heats.

Ld Belhaven's b. h. Brandon, by Beningbrough, 6
yrs old, walked over.

Wednefday, 50gs, for all ages;—4-mile heats.

Mr. Baillie's gr. c. Orphan, by Overton, 4 yrs
old, 7ft. 4lb. 1 1
Mr. Carnegie's ch. m. Mifs Betfey..... .... 2 dr

Thurfday, 50gs for real Hunters, 11ft.—4-mile
heats.

Mr. Baillie's ch. h. by Star................ 1 1
Mr. Denham's gr. g..................... 3 2
Mr. Dudgeon's br. m. Kate.............. 4 3
Mr. Browne's b. m. .... 2 dr.

Friday, the Ladies Purfe of 50gs, for four yr olds
and upwards;—4-mile heats.

Mr.

Mr. Baillie's gr. c. Orphan, by Overton, 4 yrs old, walked over.

Saturday, the Purfe for the beaten horfes of the week, was won by Mr. Kincaid's b. m. beating Mr. Carnegie's ch m. Mifs Betfey, and Mr. Warwick's Unfortunate Jack.

KNUTSFORD. ·

On Tuefday the 30th of July, a Maiden Plate of 50l.—3·mile heats.

Ld Grofvenor's ch. c. Vandal, by John Bull, 4 yrs old, 7ft. 12lb........	1	1
Mr. Thackfton's ch. c. by Walnut, 4 yrs old, 7ft. 12lb..........,..	2	2
Mr. Fielding's b. m. Drufilla, aged, 8ft. 10lb.	3	3

Wednefday the 31ft, a Sweepftakes of 10gs each, for all ages;—three miles. (11 Subfcribers.)

Mr. Smith's br. f. Heb, by Overton, 4 yrs old, 7ft. 12lb...................................	1
Mr. Clifton's b. h. Sir Ulic Mackilligut, 5 yrs old, 8ft. 10lb....................................	2

Subfcription of 5gs each, with 40gs added, for three yr olds;—2·mile heats.

Ld Wilton's b. c. Bucephalus, by Alexander, 8ft. 5lb......	1	2	1
Mr. Bowker's b. c. Royal Oak, 8ft. 2lb .	4	1	2
Ld Stamford's b. f. Georgina, 8ft. 5lb....	2	3	dr
Mr. Godden's b. c. dam by Sir Peter, 8ft. 2lb..........	3	dr	

Thurfday the 1ft of Auguft, a Plate of 60l. for all ages;—4-mile heats.

Mr. Clifton's b. h. Sir Ulic Mackilligut, by Whifkey, 5 yrs old, 9ft..........	3	1	1

Ld

Ld Grofvenor's ch. f. Mony Mufk, 4 yrs
old, 8ft. 1lb........................ ...   1   2   dr
Mr. Golden's b. m. Dutchefs, 5 yrs old,
8ft. 7lb.........   2   dr

SOUTHAMPTON.

On Wednefday, July the 31ft, a Cup of 50l. for
all ages; Doncafter. Cup weights;—3-mile heats.

Mr. Branthwayt's ch. c. Woodcot, by Guildford, 4 yrs old   1   1
Mr. Sutton's Wren (bolted).............   dis

Thurfday, Auguft the 1ft, 50l. for all ages;—
3-mile heats.

Mr. Branthwayt's ch. c. Woodcot, 4 yrs old,
7ft. 12lb.......   1   1
Ld Stawell's b. f. Gloriana, 3 yrs old, 6ft. 3lb.   2   2
Mr. Band's b. h. Cottager, 5 yrs old, 8ft. 4lb.   3   dr

Ladies Plate of 50l. for all ages;—3-mile heats.

Mr. Fermor's br. c. Principle, by Moorcock,
4 yrs old, 7ft. 10lb.   1   1
Mr. Abbey's bl. f. Virgin, 4 yrs old, 7ft. 4lb.   2   2
Ld Stawell's Gloriana, 3 yrs old, 6ft. 3lb....   3   3

Friday the 2d, 50gs, given by the Marquis of
Lanfdown, for maiden horfes of all ages;—3-mile
heats.

Mr. Branthwayt's c. Southton, by
Pegafus, 3 yrs old, 6ft....... .   2   2   0   1   1
Mr. Sutton's Wren............. .   3   1   0   2   dr
Mr. Sadler's b. c. Peregrine Pickle,
4 yrs old, 7ft. 7lb. (fell)...... 1 dis
Mr. Hyde's c. by Dungannon, 4 yrs
old, 7ft. 7lb................. . dis

Auguſt.

LEWES.

ON Thurſday the 1ſt of Auguſt, Mr. Melliſh's b. c. Sancho, by Don Quixote, beat Ld Darlington's br. c. Pavilion, 8ſt. 3lb. each, four miles, 3000gs, 000 ſt.——2 to 1 on Pavilion.

The third and laſt year of a Sweepſtakes of 10gs ich, for three yr old colts, 8ſt. 3lb. and fillies, 8ſt. ie winner of the Derby, Oaks, or Aſcot Stakes, carring 7lb. extra.—the laſt mile and half. (13 Subribers.)

d Darlington's b. c. by Sir Peter, out of Æthe..   1
d Egremont's b. c. Cardinal Beaufort (7lb. extra.)   2
Ir. Ladbroke's br. c. Wagtail   3
d Groſvenor's br. c. Jaſper....   4
l. R. H. the P. of Wales's b. c. Barbaroſſa   5

Even betting on Cardinal Beaufort, 3 to 1 agſt Wagtail, 4 to 1 agſt Barbaroſſa, and 4 to 1 agſt the winner.

Sweepſtakes of 100gs each;—two miles and a half.

H. R. H.

H. R. H. the P. of Wales's b. h. Albion, by John
Bull, 5 yrs old, 8ft. 2lb... 1
Mr. Ladbroke's b. h. Rumbo, 5 yrs old, 8ft.. .. 2
Sir W. W. Wynn's b. h. Afhton, 6 yrs old, 8ft. 4lb. 3
Sir H. Lippincott's gr. g. Slate, 5 yrs old, 7ft. .. 4

> 6 to 5 on Albion, and 5 to 2 agft Afhton.

Handicap Sweepftakes of 30gs each, 10gs forfeit,
if declared by fix o'clock the evening before running,
for horfes the property of Subfcribers; two miles
and a half. (10 Subfcribers.)

Mr. Wardell's b. f. Gratitude, by Shuttle, 4 yrs
old, 6ft. 8lb........................ 1
Ld Darlington's ch. c. Zodiac, 4 yrs, 8ft. 10lb.. 2
H. R. H. the P. of Wales's b. h. brother to
Vivaldi, 6 yrs old, 8ft. 3lb. 3
Sir W. W. Wynn's Afhton, 6 yrs old, 8ft. 11lb. 4
Ld Grofvenor's br. c. Jafper, 3 yrs old, 6ft. 7lb. pd

> 6 to 4 agft Zodiac, and 2 to 1 agft Gratitude.

His Majefty's Plate of 100gs, for four yr olds,
10ft. 4lb. five yr olds, 11ft. 6lb. fix yr olds, 12ft. and
aged, 12ft. 2lb.—4-mile heats.

H. R. H. the P. of Wales's br. h. Orville, by
Beningbrough, 6 yrs old.............. · 1 1
D. of Richmond's b. h. Rolla, aged 2 2

> 10 to 1 on Orville.

FRIDAY.

Mr. R. Boyce's Bobtail, by Precipitate, aged, 8ft. 7lb.
beat Mr. Mellifh's b. f. Lady Brough, 4 yrs old,
7ft. 6lb. four miles, 200gs, h. ft.

> 6 and 7 to 4 on Bobtail.

The County Plate of 50l. for all ages; four yr
olds, 7ft. 6lb. fix yr olds, 8ft. 5lb. having won once
this

this year, carrying 3lb. extra. if twice, 5lb. if thrice, 7lb. extra. mares and geldings allowed 3lb.—heats, two miles and a half.

Sir H. Williamson's Walton, by Sir Peter,
   6 yrs old 1 1
Mr. Mellish's Lady Brough, 4 yrs old ..... 2 dr

4 to 1 on Walton.

The first year of a Sweepstakes of 10gs each, for Hunters the property of the Subscribers, rode by Gentlemen, 12ft. mares and geldings allowed 3lb.—four miles. (10 Subscribers.)

Mr. Ch. Lennox's b. g. Bayard, by Precipitate .. 1
Mr. Newnham's ch. h. aged............. 2
Mr. C. Burgh's b. m. Slow and Easy, aged 3
Mr. Kemp's b. m. Lady Susan, aged.......... 4

7 to 4 agst Slow and Easy, and 2 to 1 agst Bayard.

The Town Plate of 50l. The winner to be sold for 250gs, if demanded, &c.—heats, two miles and a half.

H. R. H. the P. of Wales's b. g. Rebel, by
   Trumpator, aged, 8ft. 6lb.............. 1 1
Ld Egremont's b. f. by Precipitate, 4 yrs old,
   7ft. 8lb. .... 2 dr

2 to 1 on Rebel.

SATURDAY.

Mr. Mellish's Sancho, by Don Quixote, 4 yrs old, 7ft. 12lb. beat Mr. R. Boyce's Bobtail, 8ft. 9lb. the last mile, 200gs, h. ft.——7 to 4 on Sancho.

By a mistake of the person starting them, these horses ran a mile and quarter instead of a mile. On a reference to the Jockey-club, it was declared a valid race.

Sweep-

Sweepſtakes amounting to 50gs and upwards, 11ſt. —four miles. (3 Subſcribers.)

Mr. Hawk's b. g. Cockahoop, by Sir Peter, aged   1
Mr. Bailey's b. g. Starling, by Meteor, aged.... 2

2 to 1 on Starling.

Ld Barrymore's Merryman, by Buzzard, 7ſt. 8lb. beat Mr. Ladbroke's Brainworm, 7ſt. 10lb. the laſt mile, 100gs.——Even betting.

Mr. Melliſh's Lady Brough, by Stride, 4 yrs old, 8ſt. 5lb. beat Ld Barrymore's Little John, 5 yrs old, 8ſt. four miles, 100gs.——5 to 2 on Little John.

The Ladies Plate of 60gs, for three yr olds, 5ſt. 12lb. four yr olds, 7ſt. 7lb. five yr olds, 8ſt. 4lb. ſix yr olds, 8ſt. 9lb. and aged, 8ſt. 11lb. mares and geldings allowed 3lb.—four miles.

Sir H. Williamſon's b. h. Walton, by Sir Peter,
   6 yrs old 1
Ld Egremont's b. c. Cardinal Beaufort, 3 yrs old 2
Mr. Ladbroke's ch. c. Impoſtor, 3 yrs old...... 3
Mr. Howorth's b. c. Enterprize, 4 yrs old...... 4

   Even betting and 5 to 4, on Walton, and 6 to 4 agſt
   Cardinal Beaufort.

The firſt year of a Subſcription of 10gs each, for all ages;—four miles. (10 Subſcribers.)

H. R. H. the P. of Wales's Orville, by Beningbrough, 6 yrs old, 8ſt. 12lb....:.............. 1
Sir H. Williamſon's Walton, 6 yrs old, 8ſt. 12lb. 2

Even betting.

Handicap Plate of 50l. given by the Members for the Borough;—heats, two miles and a half.

Mr. Wardell's b. f. Gratitude, by Shuttle,.
   4 yrs old, 7ſt. 4lb......... .... 3 1 1
H. R. H.

H. R. H. the P. of Wales's brother to Vivaldi, 6 yrs old, 8ft. 2lb.. .... 1 . 4 3
Mr. Howorth's b. h. Harefoot, 6 yrs old,
8ft. 7lb........ .. .. 4 2 3
D. of Richmond's Rolla, aged, 7ft. 10lb.. 2 3 4

6 to 4 agſt Gratitude, and 7 to 4 agſt brother to
Vivaldi; after the fiſt heat, 5 to 2 agſt Gratitude, and 6 to 4 either Harefoot or Vivaldi won;
after the ſecond heat, 2 to 1 on Gratitude.

TAUNTON.

ON Tueſday, Auguſt the 6th, 50l. for horſes that
never won a Plate, Match, or Sweepſtakes, of that
value; three yr olds, 7ft. four yr olds, 8ft. 2lb. five
yr olds, 8ft. 12lb. ſix yr olds, 9ft. 3lb. and aged,
9ft. 6lb. mares and geldings allowed 2lb.—4-mile
heats. .

*Sir H. Lippincott's ch. g. Delegate, by Waxy, —.
5 yrs old..................... .... 1 1
Mr. Frogley's gr. h. Starling, 5 yrs old.... 4 2
Mr. Trafford's ch. g. Honeſt Tommy, 6 yrs 2 3
Mr. Popham's b. g. Young Snap, 5 yrs old .. 3 4

*The owner of the ſecond horſe diſputes the qualifica-
tion of Delegate, and claims the Plate.

A Sweepſtakes of 10gs each, for three yr olds,
6ft. 9lb. four yr olds, 8ft. 2lb. five yr olds, 8ft. 12lb.
ſix yr olds and aged, 9ft. 3lb. mares and geldings allowed 3lb.—4-mile heats. (6 Subſcribers.)

Mr. Cruckſhank's b. m. Duckling, by Grouſe,
5 yrs old........ ... . 1 1
Sir H. Lippincott's b. c. Mirror, 4 yrs old.. dis

Wed-

Wednefday the 7th, 50l. for three yr olds, 7ft. four yr olds, 7ft. 12lb. five yr olds, 8ft. 7lb. fix yr olds, 9ft. and aged, 9ft. 3lb.—4-mile heats.

Sir H. Lippincott's b. c. Mirror, by Precipi-
tate, 4 yrs old.. . . .,......... .... ..:   1   1
Mr. Skinner's b. m. Duckling, 5 yrs old.,...   3   2
Mr. Frogley's gr. h. Starling, 5 yrs old......   2   3
Mr. Dilly's b. f. Little Peggy, 4 yrs old.....   dis

NOTTINGHAM.

On Tuefday the 6th of Auguft, His Majefty's Plate of 100gs, for four yr olds, 10ft. 4lb. five yr olds, 11ft. 6lb. fix yr olds, 12ft. 'and aged, 12ft. 2lb.—4-mile heats.

Mr. Ackers's b. c. Newcaftle, by Waxy, 4 yrs.   1   1
Mr. Morris's ch. h. Tornado, aged   4   2
Mr. Harris's b. h. Sir Rowland, 5 yrs old....   2   dr
Mr. J. Peveral's ch. c. Damper, 4 yrs old....   3   dr

The County Members Plate of 50l. added to a Sweepftakes of 5gs each, for three yr old colts, 8ft. 2lb. and fillies, 8ft.—one-mile heats.

Mr. Sitwell's b. f. Goofecap, by Moorcock...   1   1
Gen. Grofvenor's b. c. Skirmifher....   2   2
Mr. Stagg's b. f. Maid of Iflington   3   dr

Wednefday the 7th, 50l. for four yr olds;—2-mile heats.

Mr. Clifton's b. f. Jofephina, by Sir Peter, 4 yrs old, 8ft. 7lb......................   1   1
Mr. J. Peveral's ch. c. Damper, 4 yrs, 8ft. 7lb.   2   2

Hunters Sweepftakes of 10gs each; 12ft.—four miles. (6 Subfcribers.)

Ld F. Bentinck's b. g. Lothario, by Chance, 6 yrs   1
Mr. Ward's b. h. by Achilles, dam by Matchem   2

Thurſday the 8th, a Maiden Plate of 50l. given by the Town, for three yr olds, 5ft. 10lb. four yr olds, 7ft. five yr olds, 8ft. ſix yr olds and aged, 8ft. 7lb. —4-mile heats.

Mr. Egerton's bl. c. Othello, by Overton, 3 yrs   1   1
Mr. Morris's ch. h. Tornado, aged.........   3   2
Gen. Groſvenor's gr. h. Ganymede, 5 yrs ...   2   3

OXFORD.

On Tueſday, Auguſt the 6th, the Gold Cup of 100gs value, the remainder in ſpecie, a Subſcription of 10gs each, for four yr olds, 7ft. 7lb. five yr olds, 8ft. 7lb. ſix yr olds, 9ft. and aged, 9ft. 4lb.—four miles. (15 Subſcribers.)

Mr. Fenwick's b. f. Miſs Coiner, by Don Quixote, 4 yrs old   1
Mr. Kellermann's ch. m. Mary, 5 yrs old   2
Mr. Kellermann's b. c. Alaric, 4 yrs (fell lame)   3

5 to 4 on Alaric.

The 50l. for all ages;—4-mile heats, was not run for, for want of horſes.

Wedneſday the 7th, a Hunters Sweepſtakes of 10gs each, for five yr olds, 11ft. 5lb. ſix yr olds and upwards, 11ft. 7lb. mares allowed 3lb.—four miles; rode by Gentlemen. (11 Subſcribers.)

Ld E. Somerſet's ch. g. Sylvanus, by Volunteer, 6 yrs old, walked over.

Fifty Pounds, for three yr olds, 7ft. and four yr olds, 8ft. 7lb. fillies allowed 3lb. winner of one Plate,

this

this year, carrying 3lb. of two, 5lb. extra.—2-mile heats.

Mr. Abbey's bl. f. Virgin, by Sir Peter, 4 yrs	1	1
Mr. Fenwick's b. g. Eunuch, 4 yrs old	2	dr

Thurfday the 8th, 50l. given by the Duke of Marlborough, for three yr olds, 6ft. 9lb. four yr olds, 8ft. 2lb. five yr olds, 8ft. 12lb. fix yr olds and aged, 9ft. 3lb. winners of one Plate this year, carrying 3lb. of two, 5lb. of three or more, 7lb. extra. mares and geldings allowed 3lb.—2-mile heats.

Mr. Abbey's ch. m. Margery, by John Bull, 6 yrs old	0	2	1	1
Mr. Kellermann's Mary, 5 yrs old ...	0	1	2	2

HUNTINGDON.

On Tuefday the 6th of Auguft, 50l. for three yr olds, 7ft. four yr olds, 8ft. 9lb. and five yr olds, 9ft. 3lb. mares and geldings allowed 3lb. the winner of one Plate or Sweepftakes in 1805, carrying 4lb. of two, 6lb. extra.—2-mile heats.

Mr. Elwes's b. f. Maiden, by Sir Peter, 4 yrs old...............	5	3	1	1
Mr. Stapleton's gr. f. by Delpini, 3 yrs	2	1	2	2
Mr. Andrew's b. c. Fathom, 3 yrs old (1 Plate).	1	2	3	dr
Mr. Williams's gr. c. Blue Bell, 3 yrs old (1 Plate)....................	4	4	dr	
Mr. Cave Browne's b. c. by Magic, 3 yrs old....	3	dr		

Wednefday the 7th, 50l. for four yr olds and upwards;—2-mile heats.

Mr. Fifher's b. f. Two Shoes, by Afparagus, 4 yrs old, 7ft. 10lb...............	1	2	1

Sir

Sir C. Bunbury's Eleanor, aged, 8ft. 11lb.   2   1   1
Mr. Elwes's Maiden, 4 yrs old, 7ft. 10lb.   3   3   3

Thurſday the 8th, 50l. for four yr olds and upwards;—4-mile heats. The winner with engagements to be ſold for 150gs, if demanded, &c.

Mr. Fiſher's b. f. Two Shoes, 6ft. 13lb.   1   1
Mr. Girdler's Capella, 5 yrs old, 7ft. 9lb...   2   2

CHELMSFORD.

On Tueſday, Auguſt the 6th, Her Majeſty's Plate of 100gs, for fillies; three yr olds, 7ft. 7lb. and four yr olds, 9ft.—2-mile heats.

Ld Groſvenor's b. f. Meteora, by Meteor, 3 yrs old, walked over.

Wedneſday the 7th, the Stewards Plate of 50l. for four yr olds, 7ft. 7lb. five yr olds, 8ft. 7lb. ſix yr olds, 8ft. 12lb. and aged, 9ft. mares and geldings allowed 3lb. winners of one Plate this year, carrying 3lb. of two or more, 6lb. extra.—4-mile heats.

Mr. Golding's ch. f. Timidity, 4 yrs old.....   1   1
Mr. Child's ch. m. Annette, aged   3   2
Mr. Turner's br. m. Crazy Jane, aged......   2   3

Thurſday the 8th, a Maiden Plate of 50l. for all ages;—2-mile heats—Not run for, for want of horſes.

Fifty Pounds for all ages;—2-mile heats.

Mr. Child's ch. m. Annette, by Volunteer, aged, 8ft. 11lb.   1   3   1
Mr. Cholmley's br. g. Piſtol, aged, 8ft. 11lb.   5   1   3
Mr. Stuart's br. h. aged, 9ft. :..........   2   2   2
Mr. Turner's b. g. Highflyer, aged, 8ft. 11lb.   4   dis

EXETER.

EXETER.

On Monday, August the 12th, a Sweepstakes of 5gs each, ridden by Gentlemen; King's Plate weights, four miles. (10 Subscribers.)

Mr. Herbert's br. f. Little Peggy, by Buzzard, 4 yrs old...., ... 1
Mr. Percy Burrell's b. g. Quill-driver, aged 2
Mr. Fellowes's b. g. Paul, 5 yrs old (bolted).... 3

Peggy the favourite.

A Maiden Plate of 50l. given by the Members for the County;—2-mile heats.

Capt. B. Wall's strawberry h. Ironsides (late Gourd) by Young Pumpkin, aged, 9ft.   1   1
Capt. Trafford's ch. g. Honest Tommy, 9ft...   2   2
Mr. Johnstone's b. g. by Acacia, 8ft. 11lb....   3 dr
Mr. Webb's b. m. by Artist, 8ft. 6lb........ dis

Ld Boringdon's Angelica, by Hyperion, recd. from Mr. Fellowes's m. (dead) by Skyscraper, out of Jessica, 8ft. 10lb. each, 2-mile heats, 100gs.

Tuesday the 13th, 50l. given by the Stewards, for Hunters, carrying 12ft.—4-mile heats.

Mr. P. Burrell's Quill-driver, by Pipator...   1   1
Capt. B. Wall's Ironsides....   2   2

A Plate of 50l. given by Lord Viscount Courtenay, for horses carrying Newmarket Cup weights, with extra. for winning;—4-mile heats.

Mr. Herbert's Little Peggy, 7ft. 13lb.   1   1
Mr. Fellowes's Paul, 8ft. 8lb.............   2 dr

Mr. Fellowes's g. Paul, by Skyscraper, 8ft. 5lb. beat Ld Boringdon's m. Juliet, by Buzzard, 8ft. 11lb. the last mile, for 50gs.——5 to 4 on Paul.

WORCESTER.

On Tuefday, Auguft the 13th, a Sweepftakes of 10gs each;—2-milé heats. (8 Subfcribers.)

Col. Kingfcote's b. c. La Mancha, by Don Quixote, 4 yrs old, 7ft. 4lb........	1	1
Mr. Lord's b. g. Cockfpinner, 5 yrs, 7ft. 13lb.	2	2
Mr. Darling's bl. h. Orotranto, 5 yrs, 8ft. 2lb.	3	3

A Plate of 50l. given by the Members for the City; —4-mile heats.

Ld Grofvenor's ch. c. Vandal, by John Bull, 4 yrs old, 7ft. 7lb..	2	1	1
Mr. Birch's ch. f. Lavinia, 3 yrs, 5ft. 11lb.	1	2	2
Ld Stamford's Georgina, 3 yrs, 5ft. 11lb.	dis		

On Wednefday the 14th, the Ladies Plate of 50l. for all ages; four yr olds, 7ft. 7lb.—2-mile heats.

Col. Kingfcote's b. c. La Mancha, 4 yrs	1	2	1
Ld Stamford's b. c. Gayman, 4 yrs old ...	2	1	2
Mr. Emden's br. c. Latitat, 4 yrs old.. .	3	3	dis

The Hunters Purfe of 50l. given by the Members for the County;—4. mile heats.

Mr. Bayzand's b. m. Creeping Gin, by Laurel, 6 yrs old, 11ft. 11lb.	1	1
Mr. Price's b. g. Rebel, 6 yrs old, 11ft. 11lb.	2	2
Mr. Wilkin's b. h. Crabftock, 5 yrs, 11ft. 6lb.	3	dis
Mr. T. Jones's bl. g. Volunteer, 4 yrs old, 10ft. 1lb. (fell)...............	dis	

On Thurfday the 15th, 50l.—4-mile heats.

Ld Stamford's b. c. Gayman, by Delpini, 4 yrs old, 7ft........	1	1
Mr. Goulding's b. m. Duchefs, 5 yrs, 7ft. 11lb.	2	2

DERBY.

DERBY.

On Tuesday, August the 13th, a Maiden Plate of 50l. given by the Duke of Devonshire, for three yr olds, 7st. 2lb. four yr olds, 8st. 5lb. five yr olds, 8st. 10lb. six yr olds, 8st. 12lb. and aged, 9st. mares and geldings allowed 2lb.—2-mile heats.

Mr. Cave Browne's b. c. Mountaineer, by Magic, 3 yrs old......................	1	1
Mr. Billington's b. h. Ratler, 5 yrs old......	4	2
Mr. Soden's b. f. by Abba Thulle, 4 yrs old..	3	3
Mr. Godden's b. c. 3 yrs old	6	4
Mr. Broadhurst's b. h. Woodlark, 5 yrs old..	2	5
Mr. Dyott's b. f. by Jupiter, 4 yrs old	5	6

Mr. Sitwell's b. f. Goosecap, 3 yrs old, recd. 10gs to withdraw.

On Wednesday the 14th, 50l. for all ages;—4-mile heats.

Mr. Ackers's b. c. Newcastle, by Waxy, 4 yrs old, 8st. ....,......	1	1
Mr. Egerton's bl. c. Othello, 3 yrs, 6st. 3lb...	3	2
Mr. Harris's b. h. Sir Rowland, 5 yrs, 8st. 3lb.	2	dr

On Thursday the 15th, 50l. for horses, &c. that never won more than that sum at any one time;—2-mile heats.

Mr. Browne's b. c. Mountaineer, 3 yrs old, 7st. 5lb.	1	1
Mr. Egerton's bl. c. Othello, 3 yrs old, 7st. 5lb.	2	2
Mr. Bowman's b. f. Miss Brown, 3 yrs, 7st.2lb.	3	3

CAN-

CANTERBURY.

On Tuefday, Auguft 13th, the firft year of a Sweepftakes of 10gs each, for three yr olds, 7ft. four yr olds, 8ft. 4lb. five yr olds, 8ft. 12lb. fix yr olds, 9ft. 1lb. and aged, 9ft. 2lb. mares and geldings allowed 3lb.—two miles. (8 Subfcribers.)

Mr. Ladbroke's br. c. Buftard, by Buzzard, 4 yrs   1
Mr. Forth's b. c. Artichoke, 3 yrs old   2
Mr. Howorth's b. c. Prodigal, 3 yrs old.........   3

Kentifh Hunters Stakes of 5gs each (with a Silver Fox's Head to the owner of the fecond horfe) 12ft.— 4-mile heats. (12 Subfcribers.)

Mr. S. Lufhington's b. g. Pigmy, by Driver..   1   1
Mr. Duppa's b. m.   2   2
Mr. Brydges's ch. h. Venture   3   3

On Wednefday the 14th, His Majefty's Plate of 100gs, for four yr olds, 10ft. 4lb. five yr olds, 11ft. 6lb. fix yr olds, 12ft. and aged, 12ft. 2lb.—4-mile heats.

Mr. Ladbroke's Buftard, 4 yrs old......... ...   1   1
Mr. Howorth's Harefoot, 6 yrs old.... ...   2   dr

A Maiden Plate of 50l. given by the County Members, for three yr olds, 6ft. four yr olds, 8ft. five yr olds, 8ft. 12lb. fix yr olds, 9ft. 5lb. and aged, 9ft. 7lb. mares allowed 2lb.—4-mile heats.

Mr. Forth's b. c. Artichoke, by Don Quixote,
   3 yrs old.............................   1   1
Mr. Ladbroke's ch. c. by Guildford, 3 yrs old   4   2
Mr. Emden's br. c. Experiment, 3 yrs old..   2   3
Mr. Goodiffon's ro. f. Roanna, 3 yrs old....   3   dr

On

On Thursday the 15th, the City Plate of 50l. for three yr olds, 6ft. 12lb. and four yr olds, 8ft. 7lb. fillies allowed 2lb. the winner of a Match this year, carrying 2lb. and of a Plate or Sweepstakes, 4lb. extra.—2-mile heats.

Mr. Hyde's c. by Mr. Teazle, 4 yrs old .	3	1	1
Mr. Goodisson's ro. f. Roanna, 3 yrs old	1	2	2
Mr. Emden's ch. f. Maid of Kent, 4 yrs	2	3	3

On Friday the 16th, 50l. for all ages;—4-mile heats.

Mr. Howorth's b. h. Harefoot, by Bening-brough, 6 yrs old, 9ft.	1	2	1
Mr. Forth's Artichoke, 3 yrs old, 5ft. 2lb.	2	1	2
Mr. Emden's br. c. Experiment, 3 yrs old, 5ft. (bolted)...........	dis		
Mr. Lushington's b. g. Pigmy, aged, 9ft. 3lb...........................	dis		
Capt. Conway's b. g. Jack Chance, aged, 9ft. 3lb..........	dis		

SALISBURY.

On Wednesday, August 14th, His Majesty's Plate of 100gs, for four yr olds, 10ft. 4lb. five yr olds, 11ft. 6lb. six yr olds, 12ft. and aged, 12ft. 2lb.— 4-mile heats.

Ld Sackville's br. c. Witchcraft, by Sir Peter, 4 yrs old..............................	1	1
Mr. Frogley's b. c. Triptolemus, 4 yrs old, (bolted).......... ....,	2 dis	

7 to 1 on Witchcraft.

Sweepstakes of 10gs each, for four yr olds, 10ft. 7lb. five yr olds, 11ft. 6lb. six yr olds, 12ft. and aged, 12ft.

1st. 2lb. thofe which had won once this year, carrying 3lb. twice, 5lb. three times or more, 7lb. extra.—3-mile heats; rode by Gentlemen.   (7 Subfcribers.)

Sir H. Lippincott's b. c. Mirror, by Precipitate, 4 yrs old........ .... 1 1
Mr. Goddard's b. h. Young Eclipfe, 6 yrs old 2 2

5 to 4 on Mirror.

Thurfday the 15th, the Members Plate of 50l. for four yr olds, 7ft. 7lb. five yr olds, 8ft. 5lb. fix yr olds, 9ft. and aged, 9ft. 4lb. winners of one Plate this year, carrying 3lb. of two or more, 5lb. extra.—4-mile heats.

Sir H. Lippincott's b. c. Mirror, 4 yrs old.... 1 1
Mr. Richardfon's b. g. Lemon-fqueezer, aged 2 2
Ld Sackville's Whirligig, aged (fell lame)... 3 dr

6 to 4 on Whirligig.

The City Bowl, for horfes, &c. carrying 10ft.—4-mile heats.

Mr. Richardfon's b. g. Lemon-fqueezer, by Coriander, aged, walked over.

Friday the 16th, a Maiden Plate of 50l. for three yr olds, a feather; four yr olds, 7ft. 4lb. five yr olds, 8ft. fix yr olds, 8ft. 10lb. and aged, 9ft. 3lb.—4-mile heats.

For this Plate three horfes were entered, one of which not being deemed a reputed racer, the Steward would not allow it to be a race; and, although after he had quitted the Courfe, the horfes ftarted, we are authorifed by him to confider it as nothing.

YORK

YORK

AUGUST MEETING.

On Monday, Auguſt the 19th, a Subſcription of 25gs each, for four yr olds, 7ſt. 9lb. five yr olds, 8ſt. 5lb. ſix yr olds, and aged, 8ſt. 10lb. Four yr old fillies allowed 4lb.—four miles. (11 Subſcribers.)

Mr. Garforth's gr. f. Veſta, by Delpini, 4 yrs old	1
Sir T. Gaſcoigne's b. c. by Sir Peter, 4 yrs old ..	2
Ld Darlington's br h. by Ormond, 5 yrs old....	3
Ld Fitzwilliam's b. m. Sally, 5 yrs old.........	4
D. of Hamilton's b. f. by Walnut, 4 yrs old....	5

Even betting and 5 to 4, on Veſta.

His Majeſty's Plate of 100gs, for four yr olds, 10ſt. 5lb. five yr olds, 11ſt. 6lb. ſix yr olds, 12ſt. and aged, 12ſt. 2lb.—four miles.

Mr. Garforth's gr. c. Evander, by Delpini, 4 yrs	1
Mr. Mellish's b. c. Quid, 4 yrs old	2
Sir M. M. Sykes's br. c. Sir Bertrand, 4 yrs old	3
D. of Hamilton's b. c. by Walnut, 4 yrs, broke down	

6 to 5 the field agſt Evander.

Produce Sweepſtakes of 100gs each, h. ft. for four yr olds;—four miles. (13 Subſcribers.)

Sir H. T. Vane's br. c. Maſter Betty, by Sir Peter, 8ſt. 7lb................................	1
Mr. Hewett's Miſs Eliza Overton, 8ſt. 2lb.	2

High odds on Maſter Betty.

Sweepſtakes of 200gs each, h. ft.—laſt mile and half. (3 Subſcribers.)
Ld Fitzwilliam's b. c. Caleb Quotem, by Sir Peter, recd. ft.

Mr.

Mr. Mellish's b. c. Didler, by Pegasus, 7ft. 12lb. recd. ft. from Sir H. Williamson's Firelock, 8ft. 1lb. last three miles, 100gs, h. ft.

TUESDAY.

A Sweepstakes of 20gs each, for two yr old colts, 8ft. and fillies, 7ft. 12lb.—Two yr old Course. (6 Subscribers.)

Sir H. Vane's b. f. by Patriot, out of Hyperion's dam 1
Mr. Mellish's b. f. Flighty, by Traveller............ 2
Mr. C. Burton's ch. c. by Stamford, out of Belle Fille 3
Ld Fitzwilliam's b. f. by Sir Peter, out of Matron 4

6 to 4 agst the winner.

Fifty Pounds for all ages;—4-mile heats.

Sir H. Williamson's gr. h. Starling, by Sir Peter, 5 yrs old, 8ft. 5lb............... 1 1
Mr. N. B. Hodgson's ch. h. Stretch, 5 yrs old, 8ft. 5lb.................................... 2 dr
Mr. Garforth's b. f. Zara, 4 yrs old, 7ft. .... 3 dr
Mr. Flint's b. c. Scampston, 3 yrs old, 5ft... dis

11 to 8 on Starling.

WEDNESDAY.

A Sweepstakes of 50gs each, h. ft. for three yr old colts, 8ft. 2lb. and fillies, 7ft. 13lb.—two miles. (5 Subscribers).

Ld Fitzwilliam's b. c. Sir Paul, by Sir Peter...... 1
Sir M. Sykes's b. c. Sir Launcelot............ 2
Mr. Wentworth's ch. c. Hippolitus 3

7 to 4 on Sir Launcelot, and high odds agst Sir Paul.

Fifty

Fifty Pounds added to one-third of the Subfcription Purfe, for five yr olds; 8ft. 7lb.—four miles.

Mr. Peirfe's b. h. Fergufon, by King Fergus   1
Ld Strathmore's b. h. Remembrancer (broke
   down)   2
Ld Fitzwilliam's b. m. Sally   3
D. of Hamilton's ch. h. by Walnut   4

2 to 1 on Remembrancer, and 5 to 2 agft Fergufon.

Sweepftakes of 100gs each, h. ft. for four yr old colts, 8ft. 4lb. and fillies, 8ft.—three miles. (7 Subfcribers.)

Sir H. Vane's Mafter Betty, by Sir Peter, walked over.

THURSDAY.

Produce Sweepftakes of 100gs each, h. ft. for three yr olds;—two miles. (7 Subfcribers.)

Mr. Hewett's br. f. Mifs Hornpipe Teazle, by Sir
   Peter, 7ft. 11lb.   1
Ld Fitzwilliam's Caleb Quotem, 8ft. 2lb.   2
Ld Strathmore's b. c. brother to Witchcraft, 8ft. 2lb.   3
Ld Fitzwilliam's Sir Paul, 7ft. 13lb.   4

5 and 6 to 4 either Caleb Quotem or Sir Paul won, and high odds agft Mifs Hornpipe.

Fifty Pounds added to one-third of the Great Subfcription, for fix yr olds, 8ft. 10lb. and aged, 9ft.—four miles.

Mr. Garforth's gr. m. Marcia, by Coriander, aged   1
Mr. Peirfe's b. h. Fergufon, 5 yrs old   2
Mr. Hewett's br. h. Blackftrap, aged   3

5 and 6 to 1 on Marcia.

FRIDAY.

The Gold Cup, a Subfcription of 20gs each, for three yr olds, 6ft. 3lb. four yr olds, 7ft. 8lb. five yr olds, 8ft. 6lb. fix yr olds and aged, 8ft. 12lb. mares allowed 3lb.—four miles. (5 Subfcribers.)

Mr. Garforth's Marcia, by Coriander, aged...... 1
Mr. Mellifh's b. c. Didler, 4 yrs old (broke down) 2

10 to 1 on Marcia.

Fifty Pounds added to one-third of the Great Subfcription, for four yr old colts, 8ft. 7lb. and fillies, 8ft. 4lb.—four miles.

Mr. Garforth's gr. f. Vefta, by Delpini........ 1
Mr. Mellifh's b. c. Quid. 2
Sir H. Vane's br. c. Mafter Betty 3

2 to 1 on Mafter Betty; even betting between Quid and Vefta.

Mr. Hewett's Mifs Hornpipe Teazle recd. ft. from Mr. Watt's b. f. by Beningbrough, out of Mifs Judy, 8ft. each, the laft mile, 50gs, 30 ft.

SATURDAY.

Handicap Sweepftakes of 50gs each, h. ft. for four yr olds;—two miles. (6 Subfcribers.)

Sir W. Gerard's b. c. Young Charlot, by Cha-
-riot, 7ft. 13lb........ 1
Sir T. Gafcoigne's b. c. by Sir Peter, 7ft. 5lb..... 2

5 and 6 to 4 on the lofer.

Sweepftakes of 30gs each, h. ft. for three yr old colts, 8ft. 2lb. and fillies, 7ft. 12lb.—laft mile and three quarters. (11 Subfcribers.)

Ld Fitzwilliam's Caleb Quotem, by Sir Peter ... 1

Mr.

Mr. Nalton's b. c. by Totteridge 2
Mr. Garforth's b. f. Laura....,............... 3
Ld Darlington's ch. c. Bumper............... 4
Sir M. Sykes's b. c. Sir Reginald 5
Sir R. Winn's b. c. Mariner................. 6

7 to 4 agft Caleb, and 4 to 1 agft Mr. Nalton's colt.

The Ladies Plate (Handicap) for all ages;—two miles.

Mr. Wardell's ch. h. Stretch, by Stride, 5 yrs old,
  8ft. 7lb...... 1
Sir T. Gafcoigne's c. by Sir Peter, 4 yrs, 8ft. 5lb. 2
Mr. Hewett's Mifs Eliza Overton, 4 yrs old, 8ft. 3
Mr. Mellifh's b. c. True Briton, 3 yrs, 6ft. 10lb. 4

2 to 1 and 5 to 2 on Stretch.

Col. Thornton's Louifa, by Pegafus, out of Nelly, 9ft. 6lb. (rode by Mrs. T.) beat Mr. Bromford's Allegro, fifter to Allegranti, 13ft.6lb. (rode by Buckle), two miles, 500gs.

NEWBURY.

On Tuefday, Auguft the 20th, a Maiden Plate of 50l. for three yr olds, 6ft. four yr olds, 7ft. 7lb. five yr olds, 8ft. 6lb. fix yr olds, 8ft. 11lb. and aged, 9ft.— 2-mile heats.

Sir H. Lippincott's gr. g. Slate, by Mr. Teazle,
  5 yrs old............................. 1 1
Mr. Biggs's br. f. Margaretta, 3 yrs old..... 5 2
Mr. Harris's b. c. Farmer, 3 yrs old........ 7 3
Mr. Bacon's b. f. Pet, 3 yrs old............ 2 4
Mr. Chinnock's Lottery, 3 yrs old. 4 5
Mr. Dockeray's b. f. Primrofe, 3 yrs old.... 3 6
Mr. Frogley's ch. f. 3 yrs old............... 6 dis

Fifty Pounds for three yr olds, 6ft. four yr olds,
7ft. 7lb.

7ft. 7lb. five yr olds, 8ft. 6lb. fix yr olds, 8ft. 12lb. and aged, 9ft. 1lb. mares and geldings allowed 3lb.—4-mile heats.

Mr. Fermor's br. c. Principle, by Moorcock, 4 yrs old	1	1
Ld Barrymore's b. g. Little John, 5 yrs old..	2	2
Mr. Pearce's ch. m. Laura, 5 yrs old........	3	dr

Wednefday the 21ft, a Handicap Plate of 50l. for all ages;—2-mile heats.

Mr. Bacon's b. f. Pet, by Cauftic, 3 yrs old, 5ft. 7lb.	1	1
Mr. Goddard's br. h. Young Eclipfe, 6 yrs old, 9ft. 6lb.	2	2
Mr. Angel's bl. g. Driver, aged, 8ft. 10lb. ...	3	3

HEREFORD.

On Wednefday the 21ft of Auguft, 50l. for all ages;—4-mile heats.

Mr. Day's b. m. Dutchefs, by Old Tat, 5 yrs old, 8ft. 1lb.	1	1
Mr. Birch's ch. f. Lavinia, 3 yrs old, 6ft. 5lb.	2	2
Mr. Price's b. h. Midas, 6 yrs old, 9ft. 3lb...	3	dis

On Thurfday the 22d, 50l. for three and four yr olds;—2-mile heats.

Mr. Birch's Lavinia, by Pipator, 3 yrs old, 7ft. 5lb.....	1	2	1
Ld Grofvenor's ch. c. Vandal, 4 yrs, 9ft.	2	1	2

Friday the 23d, 50l. for all ages;—4-mile heats.

Mr. Billington's b. g. Cockfpinner, by Moorcock, 5 yrs old, 8ft. 4lb.	0	1	1
Mr. Price's Midas, 6 yrs old, 9ft. 3lb. ...	3	2	2
Mr. Day's Dutchefs, 5 yrs old, 8ft. 7lb. ...	0	3	dr

NORTH-

NORTHAMPTON.

On Tuefday, Auguft the 27th, 50l. for three yr olds;—heats, about a mile and half.

Mr. Andrew's br. c. Fathom, by Trumpator, 8ft. 5lb.	1	1
Mr. Emden's br. c. Experiment, 8ft. 2lb....	2	2

Hunters Sweepftakes of 5gs each, for five yr olds, 10ft. 7lb. fix yr olds, 10ft. 11lb. and aged, 11ft.—heats, twice round. (31 Subfcribers.)

Mr. Andrew's br. h. Norval, by Jupiter, 5 yrs	1	1
Mr. Morris's ch. h. Tornado, aged	4	2
Mr. Pell's br. g. aged	3	3
Mr. John Fletcher's b. g. Star, 5 yrs old....	2	4
Mr. Cooch's bl. g. Black Prince, 6 yrs old .	dis	

On Wednefday the 28th, 50l. for all ages;—4-mile heats.

Mr. Elwes's b. f. Maiden, by Sir Peter, 4 yrs old, 7ft. 11lb.	2	1	1
Mr. Fifher's b. f. Two-fhoes, 4 yrs old, 8ft. 1lb.	1	2	2
Mr. Newman's b. g. Dragon, aged, 8ft. 11lb.	dis		

5 to 4 on Two-fhoes; after the firft heat, 7 to 4 on Two-fhoes, and after the fecond heat, 2 to 1 on Maiden.

Sweepftakes of 10gs each, for Hunters, 12ft.—four miles. (6 Subfcribers.)

Mr. Andrew's br. h. Norval, by Jupiter, 5 yrs..	1
Mr. Wilfon's b. g. Madman (late Telemachus)..	2

5 to 1 on Norval.

The Cup, value 50gs, for Hunters, 13ft. each;—heats, twice round the Courfe.

I 3

Mr.

Mr. Wilfon's ch. h. Hackney 3 1 1
Mr. Benton's b. blind h... .... 1 2 2
Mr. Drage's br. m. Carelefs............ 2 3 dr

Mr. Andrew's br. h. Norval, by Jupiter, recd. 8ogs ft. from Mr. Wilfon's b. g. Madman, 10ft. each, twice round the Courfe, 100gs.

READING.

On Tuefday, Auguft the 27th, the Gold Cup, value 80gs, the refidue in fpecie, a Subfcription of 10gs each, for all ages;—four miles. (16 Subfcribers.)

Mr. F. Neale's ch. h. Quiz, by Buzzard, aged, 9ft. 1
Mr. Fenwick's Mifs Corner, 4 yrs old, 7ft. 8lb.. 2
Mr. Abbey's ch. m. Margery, 6 yrs old, 8ft. 12lb. 3

Fifty Pounds for three yr olds, 7ft. 4lb. and four yr olds, 8ft. 7lb. fillies and geldings allowed 2lb.— 2-mile heats.

Ld Barrymore's b. c. Merryman, by Buzzard,
4 yrs old............................ 1 1
Mr. Frogley's b. c. Triptolemus, 4 yrs old.. 2 2

On Wednefday the 28th, 50l. for all ages;—4-mile heats.

Ld Barrymore's Little John, by Calomel, 5 yrs
old, 8ft. 6lb........................ . 1 1
Mr. Frogley's ch. f. 3 yrs old, 6ft.......... 2 dr

Thurfday the 29th, a Handicap Plate of 50l.— 2-mile heats.

Mr. Skinner's b. m. Duckling, by Groufe,
5 yrs old, 9ft....................... 1 1
Mr. Biggs's b. f. Margaretta, 3 yrs, 5ft. 10lb. 4 2
Mr. Pearce's Laura, 5 yrs old, 8ft. 7lb....... 2 3
Mr.

Mr. Sutton's gr. f. Betfy, 4 yrs old, 7ft. 9lb... 3 4
Mr. Dockeray's b. h. Balius, 8ft............. 5 5
Mr. Smith's b. g. Venture, 5 yrs old, 7ft. 12lb. 6 6
Mr. Fenwick's Eunuch, 4 yrs old, 7ft. 9lb.
(ran on the wrong fide of the Poft) ...... dis

CHESTERFIELD.

On Wednefday, Auguft the 28th, a Maiden Plate of 50l. given by the Duke of Devonfhire, for two yr olds, 5ft. 5lb. three yr olds, 7ft. 8lb. four yr olds, 8ft. 12lb. and five yr olds, 9ft. 8lb. Horfes that had ftarted once this year, if beat, allowed 3lb. if twice or more, 5lb. mares and geldings allowed 3lb.— 2-mile heats.

Mr. Gloffop's b. c. Skylark, by Moorcock,
   4 yrs old.................. .... 1 1
Mr. Richardfon's b. f. Woodbine, 3 yrs old.. 2 2
Mr. Kirby's b. f. Elizabeth, 3 yrs old 3 3
Mr. Saunders's b. c. 3 yrs old.. .... 4 4

The Gold Cup, value 60gs, a Subfcription of 5gs each, for all ages;—four miles. (12 Subfcribers.)
Mr. Sitwell's b. f. Goofecap, by Moorcock, 3 yrs old, 6ft. walked over.

Thurfday the 29th, 50l. for all ages;—4-mile heats.
Mr. Sitwell's b. f. Goofecap, 3 yrs, 6ft. 7lb. 1 1
Mr. Richardfon's b. f. Woodbine, 3 yrs, 5ft. 9lb. 3 2
Mr. Gloffop's b. c. Skylark, 4 yrs old, 8ft... 2 3

Sweepftakes of 10gs each, for all ages;—four miles. (7 Subfcribers.)
Mr. Gloffop's b. c. Skylark, 4 yrs old, walked over.

Mr.

Mr. Sitwell's old pony beat Mr. Eyre's bay pony, 6ft. each, diftance in, 50gs.

Mr. Sitwell's old pony, 6ft. 7lb. beat Capt. Short's pony, 5ft. 7lb. diftance in, 50gs.

Mr. Sitwell's old pony recd. ft. from Mr. Denham's b. g. 4 yrs old, 9ft. each, diftance in, 50gs.

BOROUGHBRIDGE.

On Wednefday, Auguft the 28th, the Gold Cup, value 100gs, the remainder in fpecie, a Subfcription of 10gs each, with 20gs added, for all ages;—three miles. (9 Subfcribers.)

Ld Strathmore's br. c. by Sir Peter, 3 yrs, 6ft. 8lb.   1
Mr. Kirby's gr. c. Evander, 4 yrs old, 7ft. 10lb.   2
Sir T. Gafcoigne's b. c. Corkleg, 4 yrs, 7ft. 10lb.   3
Ld Darlington's br. h. by Ormond, 5 yrs, 8ft. 5lb.   4
Sir A. Don's b. c. by Precipitate, out of Skyfweeper,
    4 yrs old, 7ft. 10lb.   5
Mr. Lonfdale's br. c. Sir Charles, 4 yrs, 7ft. 10lb.   6
Mr. Linton's b. f. by Hambletonian, out of Baron
    Nile's dam, 3 yrs old, 6ft. 8lb.   7
Even betting and 5 to 4, agft Evander, and 10 to 1 agft
    the winner.

Thurfday the 29th, a Maiden Plate of 50l. for three yr olds; 2-mile heats—Not run for, for want of horfes.

Friday the 30th, 50l. for all ages;—3-mile heats.

Ld Darlington's br. h. by Ormond, 5 yrs old,
    8ft. 3lb.   1   1
Mr. Lonfdale's b. c. Sir Charles, 4 yrs old,
    7ft. 12lb. (fell lame) . . . .   dis

September.

September.

RICHMOND.

ON Tuefday, September the 3d, a Maiden Plate of 50l. for three and four yr olds; 2-mile heats—Not run for, for want of horfes.

Mr. J. Mafon's gr. c. by Delpini, out of Dapple's dam, beat Mr. W. Hutchinfon's br. c. Didapper, 7ft. 10lb. each, two miles, 100gs.——5 to 4 on Didapper.

Wednefday the 4th, His Majefty's Plate of 100gs, for five yr old mares, 10ft. each;—four miles.

Ld Belhaven's b. m. Lady Mary, by Beningbrough ... 1
Ld Fitzwilliam's b. m. Sally 2
Mr. Bowman's b. m. Sufan.................. 3

    6 to 4 agft Lady Mary, and 2 to 1 agft Sally.

The Subfcription Cup of 10gs each, for all ages;— four miles.   (12 Subfcribers.)

Sir W. Gerard's br. c. Young Chariot, by Chariot, 4 yrs old, 7ft. 10lb..................... 1
Sir H. Williamfon's gr. h. Starling, 5 yrs, 8ft. 6lb. 2
Mr. Riddell's br. c. by Overton, 3 yrs, 6ft. 3lb.. 3
Ld Strathmore's b. c. by Sir Peter, 3-yrs, 6ft. 3lb. 4
                         Mr.

Mr. Trotter's b. f. by Delpini, 3 yrs old, 6ft. 1lb. 5

Mr. Cradock's b. c. by St. George, 4 yrs, 7ft. 10lb. 6

Mr. W. Hutchinson's br. c. Didapper, 3 yrs old,
6ft. 3lb.. 7

5 and 6 to 4 agft Young Chariot, 3 to 1 agft Starling, and high odds againft any other.

As the horfes were ftarting for the Cup, a very thick mift came on, which rendered it impoffible to fee them, and in confequence fome of the horfes fell in running.

Thurfday the 5th, 70l. for all ages;—2-mile heats.

Sir H. Williamfon's gr. h. Starling, by Sir Peter,
5 yrs old, 8ft. 5lb.......................... 1 1

Mr. Riddell's br. c. by Overton, 3 yrs, 6ft. 7lb. 2 2

Sir W. Gerard's Young Chariot recd. 20l. to withdraw.

WARWICK.

On Wednefday, September the 4th, His Majefty's Plate of 100gs, for all ages; four yr olds carrying 10ft. 4lb.—4-mile heats.

Mr. Fermor's br. c. Principle, by Moorcock,
4 yrs old........................... 4 1 1

Mr. Ackers's b. c. Newcaftle, 4 yrs old,
(broke down) ... . 5 2 dis

Mr. Howorth's br. c. Enterprize, 4 yrs old 3 3 dr

Col. Marriott's b. f. Maiden, 4 yrs old.. 0 dr

Mr. Clifton's b. c. Coriolanus, 4 yrs old.. 0 dr

Maiden and Coriolanus both broke down.

A Sweepftakes of 10gs each, for Hunters that never won, 12ft. each; mares and geldings allowed 2lb.— 2-mile heats. (17 Subfcribers.)

Mr. Andrew's br. h. Norval, by Jupiter, 5 yrs 1 1

Mr.

Mr. Lockley's b. g. Herfchell, 5 yrs old..... ·3 2
Ld Brooke's ch. g. Spur.................. 2 3

Fifty Pounds for four yr olds, 7ft. 10lb. five yr olds, 8ft. 5lb. fix yr olds, 8ft. 11lb. and aged, 9ft. The winner of one fifty this year, carrying 3lb. of two, 5lb. extra. mares allowed 2lb.—4-mile heats.

Mr. Skinner's b. m. Duckling, by Groufe, 5 yrs 1 1
Mr. Cholmondeley's br. c. Welch Rabbit, 4 yrs 2 2

Thurfday the 5th, a Maiden Plate of 50l. for three yr olds, 6ft. 4lb. four yr olds, 7ft. 7lb. five yr olds, 8ft. 3lb. fix yr olds, 8ft. 9lb. and aged, 8ft. 11lb. mares and geldings allowed 2lb.—2-mile heats.

Mr. Kellermann's b. c. Heel-tap, by Waxy,
   4 yrs old 2 1 1
Mr. Lockley's b. g. Herfchell, 5 yrs..... 1 2 3
Mr. Sanders's br. f. Brown Befs, 4 yrs old 3 3 2

Sweepftakes of 10gs each, for four yr olds, 7ft. 7lb. five yr olds, 8ft. 4lb. fix yr olds, 8ft. 10lb. and aged, 9ft.—2-mile heats.   (14 Subfcribers.)

Mr. Denham's b. c. Optician, by Telefcope,
   4 yrs old.......................... ... 1 1
Mr. Andrew's br. h. Norval, 5 yrs old 2 2
Mr. Kellermann's Mary, 5 yrs old......... 4 3
Mr. Howorth's Enterprize, 4 yrs old........ 3 4

Fifty Pounds for all ages; 4-mile heats.—Not run for, for want of horfes.

EGHAM.

On Tuefday, September the 3d, 50l. for all ages; —4-mile heats.

Ld Barrymore's b. g. Little John, by Calomel,
   5 yrs old; 8ft. 6lb. 1 1

Sir

Sir Joseph Mawbey's br. c. Heathpolt, 4 yrs
old, 7ft. 6lb......   2   2
Mr. Branthwayt's b.c. Southton, 3 yrs, 5ft. 12lb.   3   dr
Mr. Richardson's b. g. Lemon-squeezer, aged,
8ft. 11lb....   4   dr

     Little John the favourite.

   The Gold Cup of 100gs value, the remainder in
specie, a Subscription of 10gs each (the second horse
to receive back his stake) three yr olds, 6ft. 3lb.
four yr olds, 7ft. 10lb. five yr olds, 8ft. 6lb. six yr
olds, 8ft. 12lb. and aged, 9ft. mares and geldings
allowed 2lb.—four miles.   (22 Subscribers.)

Sir C. Bunbury's b. m. Eleanor, by Whiskey, aged   1
Mr. W. Fenwick's b. f. Miss Coiner, 4 yrs old..   2
Mr. Ladbroke's ch. c. Prospero, 4 yrs old.   3
Sir J. Shelley's b. f. Houghton Lass, 4 yrs old. ...   4
Mr. F. Neale's ch. h. Quiz, aged, bolted, and did not
come to the scales.

2 to 1 agst Houghton Lass, 2 to 1 agst Quiz, 6 and 7
    to 1 agst Eleanor.

   Mr. Emden's Gipsy, by Guildford, recd. ft. from
Mr. Abbey's Little John, 8ft. 13lb. each, four miles,
50gs, 10gs ft.

   Wednesday the 4th, the Ladies Plate of 50l. for
three and four yr olds ;—2-mile heats.

Mr. Fenwick's b. g. Eunuch, by Pegasus, 4 yrs
old, 8ft. 3lb.   1   1
Mr. Frogley's ch. f. 3 yrs old, 6ft. 12lb   4   2
Ld Barrymore's b. c. Merryman, 4 yrs, 8ft. 12lb.   2   3
Mr. Dockeray's b. f. Primrose, 3 yrs old, 7ft.   5   4
Mr. Lake's b. f. Virtuosa, 4 yrs old, 8ft. 4lb.   3   dr
Ld Egremont's ch. c. Cerberus, 3 yrs old, 7ft. 3lb.
(bolted)..   6   dis

     Merryman the favourite.

                         The

The Magna Charta Stakes of 50gs each, h. ft. for three yr olds;—the New Mile. (3 Subfcribers.)

Mr. Ladbroke's b. c. by Young Woodpecker, out of a fifter to Driver, walked-over.

A Sweepftakes of 20gs each, for all ages; two yr olds, a feather; three yr olds, 7ft. 7lb. four yr olds, 8ft. 9lb. five yr olds, 9ft. 3lb. fix yr olds, 9ft. 7lb. and aged, 9ft. 10lb.—two miles. (7 Subfcribers.)

Mr. Wardell's b. f. Gratitude, by Shuttle, 4 yrs   1
Sir J. Shelley's b. f. Houghton Lafs, 4 yrs old ..   2
Mr. Prior's ch. c. by Spear, out of Lilly, 3 yrs old   3
Mr. Forth's br. c. Artichoke, 3 yrs old   4
Gratitude the favourite.

Thurfday the 5th, the Town Plate of 50l. for all ages;—2-mile heats.

Sir C. Bunbury's b. m. Eleanor, by Whifkey,
    aged, 9ft. 6lb .... :..   1   1
Mr. F. Neale's Quiz, aged, 9ft. 6lb....   2   2
Ld Egremont's ch. c. Cerberus, 3 yrs, 6ft. 8lb.   3   dr
Ld Barrymore's Little John, 5 yrs, 8ft. 13lb.   4   dr
6 to 4 on Eleanor.

A Sweepftakes of 25gs each, for two yr old colts, 8ft. 5lb. and fillies, 8ft. 2lb.—the laft half of the New Mile. (11 Subfcribers.)

Ld Egremont's b. f. Jerboa, by Gohanna.... ... 1
Mr. C. C. Smith's br. c. Argus 2
Mr. Ladbroke's br. c. by Sir Peter 3
Mr. Wardell's b. f. fifter to Houghton Lafs...... 4
Mr. Lake's b. f. Rofabella, by Whifkey...... .. 5
Mr. Dockeray's bl. f. Honeyfuckle 6
Mr. Wardell's b. c. Ploughboy...... 7
Sir C. Bunbury's ch. c. by Whifkey 8

   2 to 1 agft Ploughboy, 5 to 2 agft Sir C. Bunbury's
    colt, 3 to 1 agft Rofabella, and 5 to 1 agft the
   winner.

Sir C. Bunbury's Eleanor, 9ft. 2lb. beat Mr. Ladbroke's c. by Y. Woodpecker, 6ft. 12lb. the New Mile, 100gs, h ft.——7 to 4 and 2 to 1 on Eleanor.

Friday the 6th, a Handicap Subscription of 20gs each, for horses of all ages;—heats, a mile and a half.

Sir J. Mawbey's b. c. Heath-polt, by Moor-cock, 4 yrs old, 8ft. 6lb........	3	1 1
Mr. Lake's b. f. Virtuofa, 4 yrs old, 8ft.	1	2 2
Mr. Harris's b. c. Farmer, 3 yrs, 7ft. 2lb.	2	3 dr

Heath-polt the favourite.

ABINGDON.

On Tuesday, September the 10th, the Members Purse of 50l. for all ages;—4 mile heats.

Mr. Neale's ch. h. Quiz, by Buzzard, aged, 9ft. 7lb.	1 1
Mr. Kellermann's ch. m. Mary, 5 yrs, 8ft. 3lb.	2 2

Hunters Sweepstakes of 5gs each;—2-mile heats. (10 Subscribers.)

Mr. Bowes's b. h. Burdock, by Cardock, 5 yrs old, 12ft. walked over.

Wednesday the 11th, a Sweepstakes of 5gs each, with 50l. added, for maiden horses of all ages;—2-mile heats. (7 Subscribers.)

Mr. Ladbroke's ch. c. Dudley, by Guild-ford, 3 yrs old, 6ft. 7lb......	5	1 1
Mr. Girdler's ch. m. Capella, 5 yrs, 8ft. 2lb.	1	2 2
Mr. Blandy's gr. f. Miss Countryman, 3 yrs old, 6ft. 4lb...	4	5 3
Mr. Scrope's b. f. by Gohanna, out of Tag, 3 yrs old, 6ft. 4lb.	2	3 dr

Mr.

Mr. Sutton's gr. f. Betfey, 4 yrs, 7ft. 7lb..   3   4 dr
Ld Abingdon's b. f. 3 yrs old, 6ft. 4lb..   6 dis

Hunters Sweepftakes of 5gs each;—2-mile heats.
(11 Subfcribers.)

Mr. Bunce's b. g. Grafshopper, 6 yrs old, 13ft. walked
over.

PONTEFRACT.

On Tuefday, September the 10th, a Sweepftakes
of 10gs each, with 20gs added, for all ages; four
miles. (10 Subfcribers.)

Mr. N. B. Hodgfon's gr. f. Prifcilla, by Delpini,
   4 yrs old, 7ft. 7lb.   1
Ld Darlington's br. h. Fergufon, 5 yrs, 8ft. 8lb.   2
     5 to 2 and 3 to 1 on Fergufon.

A Maiden Plate of 50l. for three yr olds, 7ft. 2lb.
and four yr olds, 8ft. 2lb. fillies allowed 3lb.—3-mile
heats.

Sir R. Winn's b. c. Mariner, by Precipi-tate, 3 yrs old....................	6	1	1
Mr. Flint's b c. Scampfton, 3 yrs old. ...	1	3	2
Mr. Richardfon's b. f. Woodbine, 3 yrs	5	4	3
Sir T. Gafcoigne's b. f. by Sir Peter, out of Violet, 3 yrs old (bolted the 3d heat)	4	2	4
Mr. Lumley Savile's b. f. by Patriot, 3 yrs	3	5	dr
Mr. Hotham's b. c. Bounce, 3 yrs old ...	2	dr	

   6 to 4 agft Sir T. Gafcoigne's filly, and 6 to 1 agft
     Mariner; after the firft heat, 5 to 4 agft Sir T.
     Gafcoigne's filly; and after the fecond heat, 3 to
     1 on Mariner.

Wednefday the 11th, a Sweepftakes of 30gs each,

1ogs ft. for three yr old colts, 8ft. 2lb. and fillies, 7ft. 13lb. the laſt mile and three quarters. (8 Subſcribers.)

Sir W. Gerard's bl. c. Barouche, by Overton....   1
Sir R. Winn's ch. c. Sound Judgment... :......   2

     3 and 4 to 1 on Barouche.

Sweepſtakes of 2ogs each, with 2ogs added, for three yr old fillies; the laſt mile and three quarters. (5 Subſcribers.)

Sir T. Gaſcoigne's ch. f. by Precipitate, out of Goldenlocks, 8ft. 3lb.........   1
Ld Strathmore's gr. f. by Overton, dam by Delpini   2
Sir E. Smith's gr. f. Betſey, by Overton; Sir R. Winn's b. f. Hypocrite, by Beningbrough; and Mr. E. L. Hodgſon's b. f. Cowſlip, by Moorcock; alſo ſtarted, but were not placed.

     2 to 1 agſt Ld Strathmore's filly.

The Gold Cup, value 150gs, a Subſcription of 1ogs each, with 7ogs added, for all ages; four miles. (8 Subſcribers.)

Ld Darlington's br. h. Ferguſon, by King Fergus, 5 yrs old, 8ft. 1olb.......................   1
Mr. Dent's b. c. Sir Charles, 4 yrs old, 7ft. 1olb.   2

     5 to 2 on Ferguſon.

Thurſday the 12th, a Sweepſtakes of 2ogs each, for two yr old colts, 8ft. and fillies, 7ft. 12lb. the laſt mile. (6 Subſcribers.)

Sir H. T. Vane's b. f. by Patriot, out of Hyperion's dam......   1
Ld Fitzwilliam's b. f. ſiſter to Sir Solomon.. ...   2
Mr. Wilkinſon's gr. c. Young Selim.......... ..   3
Mr. Burton's ch. c. Percy........   4

     6 to 4 on Young Selim, 2 to 1 agſt the winner, 5 to 1 agſt Ld Fitzwilliam, and 5 to 1 agſt Percy.
                           Fifty

Fifty Pounds for all ages;—4-mile heats.

Mr. Wardell's ch. h. Stretch, by Stride, 5 yrs old, 8ft. 5lb.	5	1	1
Sir T. Gafcoigne's ch. f. by Precipitate, 3 yrs old, 6ft. 4lb.	1	2	2
Ld Darlington's br. h. by Ormond, 5 yrs old, 8ft. 5lb.	3	3	4
Mr. Lonfdale's ch. c. by Pipator, 3 yrs old, 6ft. 5lb.	4	4	3
Mr. R. L. Savile's ch. c. by Stride, 3 yrs old, 6ft.	2	5	5

Even betting on Stretch; after the firft heat, 6 to 4 agft him, and after the fecond heat, 2 to 1 he won.

LICHFIELD.

On Tuefday, September the 10th, His Majefty's Plate of 100gs, for five yr olds, 8ft. 7lb.—3-mile heats.

Mr. Skinner's b. m. Duckling, by Groufe	4	1	1
Mr. Clifton's b. h. Sir Ulic Mackilligut ..	1	2	2
Mr. Fenwick's b. f. Mifs Coiner, 4 yrs old	2	dr	
Mr. Fermor's br. c. Principle, 4 yrs old .	3	dr	

Wednefday the 11th, 50l. for three and four yr olds, that never won a Plate of greater value;—2-mile heats.

Mr. Fenwick's b. g. Eunuch, by Pegafus, 4 yrs old, 8ft. 4lb.	2	1	1
Mr. Clifton's b. f. Jofephina, 4 yrs, 8ft. 7lb.	1	2	2

Sweepftakes of 10gs each, with 50gs added, for two yr olds, a feather; three yr olds, 6ft. 11lb. four yr olds, 8ft. 2lb. five yr olds, 9ft. fix yr olds and aged, 9ft. 5lb.

9ft. 5lb. mares and geldings allowed 3lb. two miles: (11 Subscribers.)

Mr. Denham's b. c. Optician, by Telescope, 4 yrs   1
Ld Grey's b. c. Gayman, 4 yrs old........   2
Mr. Clifton's b. f. Josephina, 4 yrs old.........   3
Mr. Anson's gr. c. by Moorcock, 3 yrs old.....   4
Mr. Glossop's b. c. Skylark, 4 yrs old..........   5

Thursday the 12th, 50l. for all ages;—4-mile heats.

Ld Grey's b. c. Gayman, by Delpini, 4 yrs
   old, 7ft. 10lb   1   1
Mr. Fenwick's b. f. Miss Coiner, 4 yrs, 8ft..   2   dr

Sweepstakes of 10gs each, for all ages, rode by Gentlemen, two miles. (11 Subscribers.)

Mr. Andrew's br. h. Norval, by Jupiter, 5 yrs
   old, 10ft. 9lb...............   1
Mr. Lockley's b. m. by Beningbrough, 6 yrs old,
   10ft. 12lb.................................   2
Mr. Dyott's b. f. by Jupiter, 4 yrs old, 9ft. 11lb.   3

Sweepstakes of 10gs each, for three yr old colts, 8ft. and fillies, 7ft. 11lb. two miles. -(8 Subscribers.)

Mr. Bowker's b. c. Royal Oak, by Telescope....   1
Ld Grey's b. f. Georgina......   2
Mr. Clifton's ch. c. Welsh Harp........   3
Mr. Anson's gr. c. by Moorcock   4

BEDFORD.

On Wednesday, September 11th, the Woburn Stakes of 10gs each, with 20gs added, for all ages;— 2-mile heats. (9 Subscribers.)

Mr. Howorth's ch. h. Wheatear, by Young
   Woodpecker, 5 yrs old, 9ft.   1   1
                                  H. R. H.

H.R.H. the P. of Wales's b. h. brother to
    Vivaldi, 6 yrs old, 9ft. 5lb............   2   2
Ld C. Somerfet's ch. m. Daify, aged, 9ft. 2lb.   4   3
Mr. Badley's b. g. Steady, 5 yrs old, 9ft.....   3 dr

Fifty Pounds, given by the Duke of Bedford, for
three yr olds; the winner to be fold for 200gs, if demanded, &c. heats, once round.

Ld Sackville's br. c. Capias, by Overton, 8ft.4lb.   0 ,1
Mr. Howorth's ch. f. by John Bull, 7ft. 12lb.   0 dr

Thurfday the 12th, a Handicap Plate of 50l.—
4-mile heats.

Ld Sackville's br. c. Capias, 3 yrs old, 7ft.   5   1   1
H.R.H. the P. of Wales's b. h. brother
    to Vivaldi, 6 yrs old, 9ft. 7lb...   1   3   2
Mr. Howorth's ch. h. Wheatear, 5 yrs old,
    9ft. 4lb........................   2   2 dr
Mr. Fletcher's b. g. Harebell, 5 yrs, 8ft.....   3 dr
Mr. Emden's b. c. Latitat, 4 yrs old, 8ft.   4 dr .

LINCOLN.

On Wednefday the 11th of September, His Majefty's Plate of 100gs, for four and five yr old mares;
2-mile heats.

Mr. Smith's br. f. Heb, by Overton, 4 yrs old,
    7ft. 6lb.   1   1
Mr. Fifher's b. f. Two Shoes, 4 yrs, 7ft. 11lb.   2   2
Mr. Weatherill's b. f. Haughty, 4 yrs, 7ft. 8lb.   3 dr .

A Sweepftakes of 10gs each for Hunters; 2-mile
heats. (15 Subfcribers.)

Col. King's gr. g. Hefle, by Delpini,
    11ft. 11lb.............   1   2   1
Mr. Warde's b. h. by Achilles, 12ft.   4   1   2

                                             Mr.

Mr. Harnew's b. g. Little Chance, 5 yrs old,
11ft. 11lb.. 5   3   dr
Mr. Manwaring's br. h. Hodge, 12ft.. . . . 2   4   dr
Mr. Monfon's b. m. Laborie, 5 yrs old,
11ft. 11lb.. 3   dr

Thurfday the 12th, the City Plate of 50l.—
2-mile heats.

Mr. White's br. c. Truth, by Totteridge,
3 yrs old, 6ft. 6lb. 1   2   1
Mr. Hutty's ro. c. Diogenes, 3 yrs, 6ft. 6lb. 2   1   2
Gen Grofvenor's b c. Skirmifher, 3 yrs
old, 6ft. 3lb. 3   3   3

The Welter Stakes of 10gs each, rode by Gentlemen; 2-mile heats. (9 Subfcribers.)

Sir M. M. Sykes's b. m. by Pegafus, 11ft. 11lb. 1   1
Col. King's gr. g. Hefle, 11ft. 11lb.. 3   2
Gen. Grofvenor's b. g. Glider, 11ft. 11lb.. . . . 2   3
Mr. Monfon's b. h. Leonidas, 5 yrs, 12ft.. . . . 4   4

On Friday the 13th, 70gs, for all ages; 2-mile heats.

Mr. Andrew's b. c. Fathom, by Trumpator,
3 yrs old, 6ft. 6lb.. 1   1
Mr. White's br. c. Truth, 3 yrs old, 6ft. 6lb. 2   2
Mr. Sitwell's b. f. Goofecap, 3 yrs old, 6ft. 6lb. 3   3

The Gold Cup, a Subfcription of 5gs each, for
maiden horfes, &c. of all ages; 2-mile heats. (10
Subfcribers.)

Mr. Bayly's b. f. Mifs Fanny Fancy, by Reft-
lefs, 3 yrs old, 6ft. 5lb.. 1   1
Mr. Monfon's ch. m Coquette, aged, 8ft. 11lb. 3   2
Mr. Grant's ch. c. Felix, 3 yrs, 6ft. 8lb.. . . . 2   3
Mr. Chaplin's b. h. by Spartacus, 5 yrs, 8ft. 4   4

Gen. Grofvenor's b. g. Glider, by Pegafus, 7ft. 3lb.
recd ft. from Ld F. Ofborne's b. m. Elizabeth, 8ft. 12lb.
both 5 yrs old, two miles, 50gs, h. ft.

                         SHREWS-

SHREWSBURY.

On Monday, September 16th, a Maiden Plate of 50l. given by the Members, for all ages; 4-mile heats.

Mr. Bowker's b. c. Royal Oak, by Telescope, 3 yrs old, 6ft..........................	1	1
Mr. Pemberton's b. c. Forester, 4 yrs, 7ft. 7lb.	4	2
Mr. Hall's b. f. Bridget, 3 yrs old, 5ft. 12lb.	2	3
Mr. Saunders's Brown Bess, 4 yrs old, 7ft. 5lb.	3	4
Mr. Moore's b. h. Slow and Easy, 4 yrs, 7ft. 7lb.	5	dr

Tuesday the 17th, 50l. for three and four yr olds; heats, twice round the Course.

Mr. Smith's br. f. Heb, by Overton, 4 yrs old, 8ft. 6lb........................	1	1
Sir W. W. Wynn's b. c. by Buzzard, 3 yrs, 7ft. 1lb.	2	2
Mr. Harris's b. c. All Steel, 4 yrs old, 8ft. 8lb.	4	3
Mr. Egerton's bl. c. Othello, 3 yrs old, 7ft. 1lb.	3	4

Wednesday the 18th, a Handicap Sweepstakes of 5gs each, to which the Town Subscription was added, for all ages; heats, twice round the Course. (6 Subscribers.)

Mr. Billington's b. g. Cockspinner, by Moorcock, 5 yrs old, 8ft. 12lb...............	1	1
Mr. Anson's gr. c. 3 yrs old, 6ft. 4lb.	4	2
Mr. Collins's b. h. Midas, 6 yrs, 8ft. 4lb. ...	5	3
Mr. Egerton's bl. c. Othello, 3 yrs old, 6ft. 6lb.	2	4
Mr. C. Cholmondeley's br. c. Welsh Rabbit, 4 yrs old, 7ft. 12lb.	3	5

Thursday the 19th, 50l. given by the Earl of Darlington, for all ages; 2-mile heats.

Mr. Smith's br. f. Heb, 4 yrs old, 8ft. 2lb. ...	1	1
Mr. Skinner's b. m. Duckling, 5 yrs, 8ft. 12lb.	2	2
Ld Grosvenor's ch. f. Mony Musk, 4 yrs, 8ft.	3	3

KINGS-

KINGSCOTE.

On Tuefday, September the 17th, Sir H. Lippincott's b. c. Mirror, by Precipitate, 10ft. 10lb. beat Mr. Biggs's br. c. Wafhington, 10ft. three miles, 100gs.

Even betting, and 6 to 5 on Wafhington.

The Welter Stakes of 5gs each, for horfes that never ftarted or recd. ft. before the firft day of Maddington Races, 1805, carrying 13ft.—2-mile heats. (27 Subfcribers.)

Mr. E. Cripp's b. g. Misfortune, by Oak, dam by Critic, aged.................	4	1	1
Sir H. Lippincott's ch. g. Delegate, 5 yrs	1	2	2
Ld C. Somerfet's ro. g. Gamboy, aged..	5	3	dis
Mr. Bullock's br. g. Abelard, 5 yrs.....	3	4	dr
Mr. G. Bowes's b. g. Burdock, 5 yrs old	2	dr	

High odds agft the winner.

The Kingfcote Stakes of 25gs each, 15 ft. 19 Subfcribers, 8 of whom having not named, or having declared forfeit on Whit-Monday, paid only 5gs each. N. B. 50gs added to this Stake by the Club; —three miles.

Sir H. Lippincott's Mirror, by Precipitate, 4 yrs old, 10ft. 6lb....	1
Mr. Glover's br. h. Herfchell, 5 yrs old, 10ft. 2lb.	2
Col. Kingfcote's La Mancha, 4 yrs old, 10ft. 8lb.	3
Capt. Hervey's Cinderella, 5 yrs old, 10ft. 2lb...	4
Ld C. Somerfet's br. c. Bagatelle, 4 yrs, 10ft. 7lb. fell	

La Mancha the favourite.

Mr.

Mr. Miller's br. h. Razor-back, agft. Mr. Royn. Jones's gr. h. Contract, 14ft. each, two miles.—*a dead beat.*

The Match between Mr. Jones's Junius and Mr. Stacpoole's f. by John Bull, was not run.

WEDNESDAY.

The Cup, a Subfcription of 10gs each; three miles. (10 Subfcribers)

Mr. Biggs's Wafhington, by Sir Peter, 4 yrs, 11ft. 1
Mr. Bullock's Abelard, 5 yrs old, 11ft. 13lb..... 2
Mr. Elton's b. c. Feather, 4 yrs old, 11ft. 3
Mr. Bowes's Burdock, 5 yrs old, 11ft. 13lb. 4

5 to 2 on Wafhington.

Sweepftakes of 5gs each, with 100gs added by the Club; four miles. (15 Subfcribers.)

Mr. Herbert's b. f. Peggy, by Buzzard, 4 yrs old,
 9ft. 13lb...., ... 1
Sir H. Lippincott's gr g. Slate, 5 yrs, 10ft. 13lb. 2
Mr. Douglas's br. h. Ducat, 5 yrs old, 10ft. 12lb. 3
Mr. Glover's Herfchell, 5 yrs old, 10ft. 13lb. 4

5 and 6 to 4 agft Peggy, and 2 to 1 agft Ducat.

Sweepftakes of 10gs each, with 50gs added by the Club; three miles. (7 Subfcribers.)

Ld C. Somerfet's Bagatelle, by Sir Peter, 4 yrs
 old, 10ft. 10lb............. 1
Sir H. Lippincott's Mirror, 4 yrs old, 11ft. 2
Col. Kingfcote's La Mancha, 4 yrs old, 11ft.... 3

5 to 4 agft Mirror, 6 and 7 to 4 agft Bagatelle.

Handicap Plate of 50l. one-mile heats.

Ld Brooke's ch. h. Marplot, by Waxy,
 5 yrs old, 11ft...................... 4 1 1

Sir

Sir H. Lippincott's Slate, 5 yrs, 11ft. 3lb.   1   3   2
Mr. Goddard's Young Eclipse, 6 yrs old,
   11ft. 7lb.   3   2   dr
Mr. Biggs's Washington, 4 yrs, 10ft. 10lb.   2   dr
Young Eclipse the favourite,

THURSDAY.

Ld F. Bentinck's Lothario, by Chance, 10ft. 5lb.
beat Ld Brooke's Sylvanus, 10ft. two miles, 50gs.
Even betting.

Handicap Plate of 50l. 2-mile heats.

Mr. Goddard's br. h. Young Eclipse, by
   Young Eclipse, 6 yrs old, 10ft. 10lb. ...   6   1   1
Mr. Biggs's Washington, 4 yrs, 10ft. 2lb..   1   3   4
Mr. Elton's Feather, 4 yrs old, 9ft. 10lb. .   2   2   3
Ld Brooke's Marplot, 5 yrs old, 11ft. 7lb.   5   4   2
Sir H. Lippincott's Mirror, 4 yrs, 11ft.6lb.   3   dr
Mr. Cripp's Misfortune, aged, 11ft.   4   dis

Misfortune came second the second heat, but the
   rider being short of weight, was deemed distanced.

Sir H. Lippincott's ch. g. Recluse, by a brother to
Druid, 5 yrs old, recd. 30gs compromise from Capt.
White's b. m. Crazy Jane, 6 yrs old, 10ft. each, one
mile, 50gs.

LEICESTER.

On Wednesday, September the 18th, the Gentlemen's Purse of 50l.—2-mile heats.
Ld Stamford's br. c. Gayman, by Delpini,
   4-yrs old, 8ft. 6lb........   1   3   1
Mr.

Mr. Andrew's b. e. Fathom, 3 yrs, 7ft. 2lb.   2   1   8
Mr. Fenwick's b. g. Eunuch, 4 yrs, 8ft. 6lb.   3   2   3

Fathom the favourite.

Thurfday the 19th, the Burgefses Purfe of 50l.—4-mile heats.

Mr. Fifher's b. f. Two Shoes, by Afparagus,
  4 yrs old, 7ft. 7lb................   1   2
Ld Stamford's br. c. Gayman, 4 yrs old,
  7ft. 7lb. (broke down) .....,.............   2 dr

Gayman the favourite.

Hunters Sweepftakes of 5gs each, 12ft.—2-mile heats. (12 Subfcribers.)

Mr. Morris's ch. h. Tornado, by Whirlwind,
  6 yrs old ..../.....   1   1
Mr. Sturges's gr. g. 6 yrs old   2   2

OSWESTRY.

On Monday, September the 23d, a Silver Cup, value 50l. for Hunters;—2-mile heats.

Mr. Youde's b. g. Nimrod, 5 yrs, 11ft. 4lb.   1   1
Mr. Kenyon's Blood Royal, aged, 12ft. 4lb...   3   2
Mr. Lloyd's b. g. 5 yrs old, 11ft. 4lb...... .   2   3

Tuefday the 24th, a Cup, value 50l. the gift of the Stewards, for Hunters, 11ft. each;—2-mile heats.

Mr. Lockley's b. m. by Beningbrough, 6 yrs   1   1
Mr. Youde's b. g. Nimrod, 5 yrs old........   2   2

Fifty Pounds for three and four yr olds;—2-mile heats.

Mr. Bowker's b. c. Royal Oak, by Telefcope, 3 yrs old, 7ft. 10lb............   1   3   1

Mr. Pemberton's b. c. Forester, 4 yrs old,
8ft. 2lb.   3   1   2

Sir W. W. Wynn's b. c. by Buzzard, 3 yrs
old, 7ft. 10lb.......:............. ...   2   2   dr

Wednesday the 25th, 50l. for all ages;—4-mile
heats.

Mr. Lord's b. g. Cockspinner, by Moorcock,
5 yrs old, 8ft. 6lb....   1   .

Sir W. W. Wynn's b. c. by Buzzard, 3 yrs old,
6ft. 3lb.   2   2

Sweepstakes of 5gs each, with 20gs added, for all
ages; the winner to be sold for 50gs, if demanded,
&c.—1-mile heats. (9 Subscribers.)

Mr. Lord's Cockspinner, 5 yrs, 11ft. 5lb.   1   2   1
Mr. C. Cholmondeley's b. c. Welsh Rab-
bit, 4 yrs old, 10ft. 7lb.......   5   1   2
Mr. Collins's b. h. Midas, 6 yrs, 11ft.12lb.   4   3   3
Mr. Harris's b. c. All Steel, 4 yrs, 10ft.7lb.   2   4   4
Sir W. W. Wynn's b. f. Highland Lass,
4 yrs old, 10ft. 4lb.   3   dr

DONCASTER.

On Monday, September 23d, His Majesty's Plate
of 100gs, for four yr olds, 10ft. 4lb. five yr olds,
11ft. 6lb. six yr olds, 12ft. and aged, 12ft. 2lb.—
four miles.

Mr. Mellish's b. c. Quid, by Star, 4 yrs old....   1
Mr. Kirby's gr. c. Evander, 4 yrs old...   2
Ld Darlington's b. h Ferguson,-5 yrs old......   3

6 to 4 on Evander.

Sweepstakes of 20gs each, for two yr old colts, 8ft.
and fillies, 7ft. 11lb. the last mile. (5 Subscribers.)

Ld

Ld Fitzwilliam's b. f. by Sir Peter, out of Matron   1
Mr. Mellish's b. f. Flighty.................... 2
Sir H. T. Vane's b. f. by Patriot 3

     2 to 1 on Sir H. Vane's filly.

The North Welter Stakes of 20gs each, rode by Gentlemen, 13ft. each; 2-mile heats. (4 Subscribers.)

Sir F. Boynton's b. g. by Overton, bought of Mr. Percival, walked over.

On Tuesday the 4th, the St. Leger Stakes of 25gs each, for three yr old colts, 8ft. 2lb. and fillies, 8ft. two miles. (27 Subscribers.)

Mr. Mellish's b. c. Staveley, by Shuttle....... .   1
Ld Fitzwilliam's b. c. Caleb Quotem 2
Ld Fitzwilliam's br. c. Sir Paul. 3
Mr. Mellish's b. c. Sir Launcelot.. 4
Col. Childers's b. c. Langton................. 5
Mr. Smith's b. c. Hippomenes; Mr. Hutton's br. c. Cleveland; Ld F. G. Osborne's b. c. Don Felix; Ld Darlington's b. c. by Sir Peter, out of Æthe; and Ld Grey's br. c. Young Roscius; also started, but the Judge placed the first five only.

  5 to 2 agst Cleveland, 4 to 1 agst Hippomenes, 4 to 1 agst Sir Launcelot, 5 and 6 to 1 agst Staveley, and 10 to 1 agst Caleb Quotem.

The Corporation Plate of 50l. for three yr olds, 6ft. four yr olds, 7ft. 7lb. five yr olds, 8ft. 3lb. six yr olds, 8ft. 11lb. and aged, 8ft. 12lb.—4-mile heats.

Ld Fitzwilliam's b. m. Sally, by Sir Peter,
  5 yrs old............................... 1 1
Mr. Wardell's ch. h. Stretch, 5 yrs old. 2 2
Mr. Thompson's ch. f. Eliza, 4 yrs old...... 3 3

  6 to 1 on Stretch, and after the heat, 7 to 4 on Sally.

WEDNESDAY.

The first year of the renewed Doncaster Stakes of 10gs each, with 20gs added, for any horse, &c. bona fide the property of a Subscriber, or his declared confederate; three yr olds, 6ft. four yr olds, 7ft. 7lb. five yr olds, 8ft. 3lb. six yr olds and aged, 8ft. 10lb. four miles. (16 Subscribers.)

Mr. Garforth's gr. m. Marcia, by Coriander, aged	1
Ld Strathmore's b. c. by Sir Peter, 3 yrs old....	2
Ld Fitzwilliam's br. c. Sir Paul, 3 yrs old......	3
Sir T. Gascoigne's b. c. by Sir Peter, 4 yrs old..	4
Mr. Mellish's b. c. Staveley, 3 yrs old..........	5

6 to 5 on Marcia.

The Gold Cup, value 100gs, for three yr olds, 6ft. four yr olds, 7ft. 7lb. five yr olds, 8ft. 3lb. six yr olds, 8ft. 11lb. and aged, 9ft. four miles.

Ld Fitzwilliam's b. c. Caleb Quotem, by Sir Peter, 3 yrs old............................	1
Sir W. Gerard's br. c. Young Chariot, 4 yrs old	2

Ld Darlington's b. c. Pavilion, 4 yrs old; Mr. Garforth's gr. f. Helen, 4 yrs old; Mr. N. B. Hodgson's gr. f. Priscilla, 4 yrs old; Mr. Mellish's b. c. Sir Launcelot, 3 yrs old; Sir R. Winn's b. c. Mariner, 3 yrs old; Ld Strathmore's b. h. Remembrancer, 5 yrs old; and Mr. Flint's b. m. Spitfire, 5 yrs old; also started, but the Judge placed only the first two.

5 to 2 agst Pavilion, 3 to 1 agst Sir Launcelot, 7 to 2 agst Caleb, 5 and 6 to 1 agst Young Chariot.

THURSDAY.

A Sweepstakes of 20gs each, with 20gs added, for three yr old fillies, 8ft. each; two miles. (6 Subscribers.)

Mr.

Mr. Hewett's Mifs Hornpipe Teazle, by Sir Peter   1
Ld Fitzwilliam's b. f. by Beningbrough 2
Sir T. Gafcoigne's br. f. by Sir Peter 3

3 to 1 on Hornpipe.

Sweepftakes of 10gs each, for Hunters, rode by Gentlemen, 12ft. each; four miles. (5 Subfcribers.)
Sir M. M. Sykes's b. m. by Pegafus 1
Mr. Mellifh's br. h. Hodge 2

One Hundred Pounds for three yr olds, 7ft. 5lb. and four yr olds, 8ft. 7lb. maiden colts allowed 2lb. and maiden fillies, 3lb.—2-mile heats.

Col. Childers's b. c. Langton, by Precipitate, 3 yrs old	6	1	1
Sir H. T. Vane's b. c. Mafter Betty, 4 yrs	1	5	4
Mr. Hutton's br. c. Cleveland, 3 yrs old	4	4	2
Sir W. Gerard's br. c. Young Chariot, 4 yrs old	3	2	3
Mr. Flint's b. c. Scampfton, 3 yrs old ...	5	3	5
Mr. Johnfon's br. c. Sir Andrew (late Norval) 3 yrs old	2	dr	

6 and 7 to 4 agft Chariot, 5 to 2 agft Mafter Betty, and 6 to 1 agft Langton.

Sir W. Hunloke's ch. f. Gallina, by Overton, beat Mr. Bond's b. f. by Moorcock, dam by Matchem, 7ft. each, two miles, 100gs, h. ft.

6 and 7 to 4 on Gallina.

Mr. Bailey's ch. pony, 7ft. beat Mr. Chamberlain's br. g. Tally O, 9ft. four miles, 100gs.

Mr. Hewett's Mifs Hornpipe Teazle, 8ft. 2lb. recd. forfeit from Mr. E. L. Hodgfon's b. f. by Moorcock, 7ft. 11lb. 10 oz. two miles, 100gs, h. ft.

Col. Childers's Langton, by Precipitate, recd. ft. from Ld F. G. Ofborne's Don Felix, 8ft. 2lb. each, two miles, 300gs, h. ft.

L 3

AYR.

On Tuesday, September the 24th, the second year of the Gold Cup, a Subscription of 10gs each— 2-mile heats. (14 Subscribers.)

Ld Caffillis's ch. g. Chancellor, by Trimmer,
6 yrs old............................... 1 1
Mr. Maule's br. f. by Overton, 4 yrs old .... 2 dr
Ld Montgomerie's gr. c. by Spadille, 4 yrs old 3 dr

A Purse of 50l. for all ages; 4-mile heats.

Ld Belhaven's ch. h. by Star......,...... .. 1 1
Major Cathcart's ch. g. by Walnut..... ... 2 2
Mr. Boswell's b. c. by Delpini...... .... . 3 dis

Wednesday, 50l. for all ages; 4-mile heats.

Ld Belhaven's Lady Mary, by Beningbrough, being the only one entered, received 10gs.

Thursday, 50l. for all ages.

Ld Belhaven's Lady Mary, walked over.

Sweepstakes of 25gs each, for three yr old colts, 8ft. 5lb. and fillies, 8ft. 3lb. two miles. (4 Subscribers.)

Ld Belhaven's c. by Star, walked over.

WALSALL.

On Wednesday, September 25th, 50l. for all ages; 3-mile heats.

Mr. Clifton's b. f. Josephina, by Sir Peter,
4 yrs old, 7ft. 6lb. ....v 1 1
Ld

Ld Grey's br. f. Georgina, 3 yrs old, 6ft. 2lb.   2   2
Mr. Saunders's br. f. Brown Bess, 4 yrs, 7ft. 1lb.   3   3

Thurfday the 26th, 50l. for all ages; 3-mile heats.

Mr. Skinner's b. m. Duckling, by Groufe,
   5 yrs old, 8ft. 6lb........   1   1
Mr. Clifton's ch. c. Welfh Harp, 3 yrs, 6ft. 3lb.   4   2
Mr. Gloffop's b. c. Skylark, 4 yrs old, 7ft. 7lb.   3   3
Mr. Anfon's gr. c. by Moorcock, 3 yrs old, ·
   6ft. 3lb...........................   2   4

BECCLES. ·

On Thurfday, the 26th of September, 50l. for all
ages; the winner to be fold for 200gs, if demanded,
&c. 4-mile heats.

Ld Barrymore's b. g. Little John, by Calomel,
   5 yrs old, 8ft..........   1   1
Mr. Emden's br. c. Latitat, 4 yrs old, 7ft. 5lb.   2   2
Major Wilfon's br. c. Trudge, by Buzzard,
   3 yrs old, a feather (bolted)...... ....   3 dis

On Friday the 27th, the Town Purfe of 50l. for all
ages; the winner to be fold for 150l. if demanded,
&c. 4-mile heats.

Ld Barrymore's Little John, 8ft. 5lb........   1   1
Mr. Emden's Gipfy, 5 yrs old, 8ft.   2   2
Mr. Smith's gr. m. aged, 8ft. 11lb.. ....   dis

A Sweepftakes of 3gs each, with 15gs added by the
Town, for horfes of all ages, that never ftarted for
Plate, Match, &c. of 50l. value, before the time of
naming; 3-mile heats. (12 Subfcribers.)

Col. Harbord's ch. c. Mafter Betty, by Delpini,
   3 yrs old, 7ft.....   1   1
Mr. Emden's br. c. Experiment, 3 yrs old, 7ft.   2 dr
                 DORCHESTER.

DORCHESTER.

On Friday, September 27th, a Subfcription Plate of 50gs, for four yr olds, 10ft. 6lb five yr olds, 11ft. 6lb. fix yr olds and aged, 12ft. two mile heats; rode by Gentlemen.

Capt. Tower's br. c. Wafhington, by Sir Peter,
   4 yrs old............................. .... 1 1
Col. Andrews's b. g. Quick, aged 3 2
Col. Colebrooke's ch. h. Combatant, aged.. . 4 3
Col. Rawfthorne's ch. g. Spot, aged.... ... 2 dr
Major Hilton's ch. g. Fire, aged, ran out of the Courfe.

October.

—

NEWMARKET

FIRST OCTOBER MEETING.

ON Monday, September 30th, Mr. Wilfon's ch. m. Marianne, by Mufti, 6 yrs old, 8ft. 6lb. beat Ld Foley's b. c. Watery, 8ft. Acrofs the Flat, 200gs, h. ft.——5 to 2 on Marianne.

Mr. Watfon's b. h. Dreadnought, by Sir Peter, 8ft. 9lb. beat Ld Foley's br. c. Little Peter, 8ft. Two yr old Courfe, 100gs,——5 to 4 on Little Peter.

Ld Foley's b. c. Hippocampus, by Coriander, 8ft. 8lb. beat the D. of Grafton's br. f. Peliffe, 8ft. Acrofs the Flat, 200gs, h. ft.——7 to 4 on Peliffe.

Ld Foley's ch. h. Captain Abfolute, by John Bull, 8ft. 5lb. beat Ld Sackville's ch. h. Enchanter, 8ft. B. C. 200gs, h. ft.——11 to 8 on Enchanter.

Firft year of a renewal of a Subfcription of 5gs each, for four yr olds, 7ft. 7lb. five yr olds, 8ft. 6lb.

fix

fix yr olds, 8ft. 13lb. and aged, 9ft. 2lb. B. C. (15 Subfcribers.) To be the property of a Subfcriber, or pay 50gs entrance.

D. of Grafton's b. m. Parafol, by Pot8o's, 5 yrs old, walked over.

Ld Foley's br. c. Czar Peter, by Sir Peter, 8ft. 10lb. recd. from Mr. Howorth's b. f. Pimlico (dead) 7ft. 3lb. B. C. 200gs.

Mr. R. Boyce's ch. h. Bobtail, by Precipitate, 8ft. 12lb. recd. 25gs from Sir C. Bunbury's b. m. Eleanor, 8ft. 6lb. Ab. M. 200gs, h. ft.

Ld Grofvenor's br. c. Jafper, by Sir Peter; or his br. c. Knight Errant, by Sir Peter; recd. 60gs from Mr. Watfon's c. by Buzzard, out of Doubtful; or his brother to Gaoler; 8ft. 2lb. each, Acrofs the Flat, 200gs, h. ft.

D. of Grafton's Parafol, 8ft. 6lb. recd. 50gs from Mr. Mellifh's Pipylin, 8ft. 5lb. B. C. 200gs, h. ft.

TUESDAY.

Ld Grofvenor's b. c. Agincourt, by John Bull, beat Mr. Ladbroke's b. c. Buftard, 8ft. each, R. M. 100gs, h. ft.——11 to 5 on Buftard.

Sweepftakes of 100gs each, h. ft. for three yr old fillies, carrying 8ft. 2lb. each, R. M. (8 Subfcribers.)
Sir C. Bunbury's br. f. Lydia, by Whifkey...... 1
Sir F. Standifh's b. f. fifter to Duxbury.... 2
D. of Grafton's b. f. Dodona.......... 3
Ld Grofvenor's br. f. Iris............... 4

5 and 6 to 4 agft Dodona, 2 to 1 agft Lydia, 5 and 6 to 1 agft the fifter to Duxbury.

Sweep·

- Sweepflakes of 100gs each, h. ft. D. I.

Mr. Lake's b. c. Lynceus, by Buzzard, 8ft. 5lb... **1**
Mr. Wyndham's b. c. Tallboy, 7ft. 6lb. **2**
Mr. Howorth's b. f. Pimlico (dead) 7ft. 6lb. pd ft

> 2 and 3 to 1 on Lynceus.

One-third of a Subfcription of 25gs each (firft year) for four yr old colts carrying 8ft. 7lb. and fillies, 8ft. 4lb. D. I. (16 Subfcribers.)

Mr. Mellifh's b. f. Lady Brough, by Stride **1**
Ld Foley's br c. Czar Peter **2**
D. of Grafton's br. f. Peliffe..... .... **3**
Mr. Ladbroke's b. c. Buftard........ .. .. **4**
Ld Grofvenor's b c. Agincourt........ .... **5**

> 6 to 4 agft Czar Peter, 2 to 1 agft Peliffe, and 5 to 1 agft Lady Brough.

Mr. R. Boyce's ch. c. Brainworm, by Buzzard, 7ft. 11lb. recd. forfeit from Mr. Mellifh's b. c. Didler, 8ft. 7lb. Two yr old Courfe, 100gs, h. ft.

WEDNESDAY.

Ld F. G. Ofborne's ch. c. Superftition, by Buzzard, beat Gen. Grofvenor's b. c. Have-at-'em, 8ft. each, Two yr old Courfe, 100gs, h. ft.

> 2 to 1 on Superftition.

Sweepftakes of 50gs each, Ab. M.

Mr. Wilfon's ch. m. Marianne, by Mufti, 9ft. 1lb. **1**
D. of Grafton's b. f. Farce, 3 yrs old, 6ft. 8lb. .. **2**
Sir J. Shelley's b. c. Curryeomb, 3 yrs old, 7ft. 2lb. pd

> 3 to 1 on Marianne.

Mr. Mellifh's b. c. Sancho, by Don Quixote, 8ff. 9lb. beat Mr. R. Boyce's br. c. Sir David, 7ft. 13lb, both 4 yrs old, R. M. 500gs.

> 11 to 8 on Sir David.

One

One-third of a Subfcription of 25gs each, for three yr old colts carrying 8ft. 6lb. and fillies, 8ft. 3lb. D. I. (16 Subfcribers.)

Ld Grofvenor's b. f. Meteora, by Meteor 1
Sir C. Bunbury's br. f. Lydia . . . . . , ... 2
Mr: Delmé Radcliffe's br. c. Pedeftrian 3
Mr. Ladbroke's ch. c. Rubbifh 4

6 to 4 agft Meteora, 2 to 1 agft Pedeftrian, and 3 to 1 agft Lydia.

Fifty Guineas, free for any horfe, &c. four yr olds carrying 7ft. 4lb. five yr olds, 8ft. 5lb. fix yr olds, 8ft. 11lb. and aged, 9ft. B. C.

D. of Grafton's b. m. Parafol, 5 yrs old, walked over.

THURSDAY.

Sir C. Bunbury's b. m. Eleanor, by Whifkey, 9ft. 7lb. beat Ld Foley's br. c. Czar Peter, 8ft. D. I. 100gs.——5 to 4 on Eleanor.

The Town Plate of 50l. for three yr old colts, 8ft. 7lb. and fillies, 8ft. 3lb. D. I.
The late Mr. Perram, by his will, direfted his executors to pay 30gs to the winner of this Plate.

Ld Grofvenor's b. f. Violanté, by John Bull 1
Mr. Moorhoufe's br. c. brother to Whifkerandos 2
Sir C. Bunbury's br. f. Lydia 3
Sir F. Standifh's b. f. fifter to Duxbury 4
Mr. J. Stevens's b. c. by Young Woodpecker 5
Mr. Thompfon's ch. f. by Buzzard 6

Even betting on Violanté, 5 to 2 agft Lydia, and 3 to 1 agft the fifter to Duxbury.

Mr. Andrew's br. h. Norval, by Jupiter, 5 yrs old, 8ft. 12lb. beat Mr. Perren's ch. f. by Guildford, 3 yrs old, 7ft. 5lb. R. M. 100gs, h. ft.——5 to 2 on Norval.

His

His Majesty's Plate of 100gs, for four yr olds carrying 10ft. 4lb. five yr olds, 11ft. 6lb. six yr olds, 12ft. and aged, 12ft. 2lb. R. C.

D. of Grafton's b. m. Parasol, 5 yrs old, walked over.

MALTON.

On Monday, October the 7th, a Sweepstakes of 20gs each, for all ages; two miles. (8 Subscribers.)

Mr. Garforth's gr. m. Marcia, by Coriander, aged, walked over.

Sweepstakes of 20gs each, for three yr old fillies, carrying 8ft. 2lb. one mile and a half. (4 Subscribers.)

Mr. Garforth's b. f. Laura, by Traveller 1
Mr. Acred's b. f. Miss Welham........ 2
Mr. Pickering's b. f. Miss Cheesecake........ . 3

5 to 4 on Laura.

On Tuesday the 8th, a Sweepstakes of 20gs each, for three yr old colts, 8ft. 4lb. two miles. (4 Subscribers.)

Mr. G. Hutton's br. c. Cleveland, by Overton ... 1
Sir M. M. Sykes's b. c. Sir Reginald 2

5 and 6 to 4 on Cleveland.

A Maiden Plate of 50l. for three yr old colts, 8ft. 4lb. and fillies, 8ft. 2lb. heats, a mile and a half.

Mr. Robinson's b. f. by Beningbrough.. . 1 3 1
Mr. E. L. Hodgson's b. f. Cowslip 2 1 2
Mr. Hotham's b. c. Bounce 3 2 3

2 to 1 on the winner.

Wednesday the 9th, 50l. for all ages; 3-mile heats.

Mr. G. Hutton's br. c. Cleveland, by Overton, 3 yrs old, 6ft. 12lb.	4	1	1
Mr. Hutty's ro. c. Diogenes, 5 yrs, 7ft. 1lb.	1	4	5
Mr. Thompson's ch. f. Eliza, 4 yrs old, 7ft. 10lb.	5	3	2
Mr. Garforth's gr. f. Helen, 4 yrs, 7ft. 10lb.	3	2	dr
Mr. Robinson's ch. f. by Abba Thulle, 3 yrs old, 6ft. 10lb...........	2	dr	

STIRLING.

On Tuesday October the 8th, 50l. for all ages; 4-mile heats.

Ld Belhaven's b. m. Lady Mary, by Beningbrough, 5 yrs old..........	1	1
Sir A. Don's b. c. by Precipitate, 4 yrs old. ..	2	2

Wednesday, 50l. for all ages; heats, two miles and a half.

Ld Belhaven's b. m. Lady Mary, 5 yrs old....	1	1
Sir A. Don's b. c. by Skyscraper, 4 yrs old .	2	2

Thursday, 50l. for all ages; 4-mile heats. Not run for.

Ld Belhaven's Lady Mary, being the only horse entered, received 20l.

The Subscription Purse of 50l. for beaten and drawn horses, was won by

Sir A. Don's b. c. by Precipitate, out of Skysweeper, 4 yrs old; beating Mr. Kincaid's b. g. by Overton.

CARLISLE.

CARLISLE.

On Wednefday the 9th of October, His Majefty's Plate of 100gs, for three yr olds and upwards, carrying weight for age and qualifications; 4-mile heats.

Mr. W. Hutchinfon's br. c. Didapper, by
    Overton, 3 yrs old, 6ft.............. 3 1 1
Mr. Riddell's br. c. by Overton, 3 yrs, 6ft. 1 2 dr
D. of Hamilton's b. f. Hafty, 4 yrs, 7ft. 4lb. 2 3 dr

On Thurfday the 10th, 50l. given by the Earl of Carlifle, for all ages; 4-mile heats.

Mr. W. Hutchinfon's b. c. by Pipator,
    out of Serina, 4 yrs old, 7ft. 8lb...,.. 2 1 1
D. of Hamilton's Hafty, 7ft. 5lb.......... 1 2 2

Friday the 11th, the City Members Plate of 50l. for three and four yr olds; 2-mile heats.

Mr. W. Hutchinfon's Didapper, 8ft. 5lb.... . 1 1
Mr. Riddell's br. c. by Overton, 7ft. 12lb... 2 2

NORTHALLERTON.

On Thurfday, October the 10th, a Sweepftakes of 10gs each, with 20gs added, for three yr olds, 6ft. 7lb. four yr olds, 7ft. 10lb. five yr olds, 8ft. 3lb. fix yr olds and aged, 8ft. 8lb. mares allowed 2lb.—2-mile heats.

Sir W. Gerard's br. c. Young Chariot, by
    Chariot, 4 yrs old................. 5 1 1
Ld Fitzwilliam's b. m. Sally, 5 yrs old.. 1 3 2
Ld Darlington's br. h. by Ormond, 5 yrs 4 4 3
Mr. N. B. Hodgfon's gr. f. Prifcilla, 4 yrs 3 2 dr
Mr. Dent's br. c. Sir Charles, 4 yrs old 2 5 dr
    5 to 4 the field agft Young Chariot.

On'

On Friday the 11th, 50l. for three and four yr olds; 3-mile heats—Not run for, for want of horfes.

On Saturday the 12th, 50l. for three yr olds, 6ft. 7lb. four yr olds, 7ft. 11lb. five yr olds, 8ft. 9lb. fix yr olds, 8ft. 12lb. and aged, 9ft. mares allowed 2lb. a winner of 50l. fince the firft of March laft, carrying 3lb. of two, or a King's Plate, 5lb. extra.— 4-mile heats.

Mr. N. B. Hodgfon's gr. f. Prifcilla, by Delpini, 4 yrs old	3	1	1
Mr. Trotter's b. f. by Delpini, 3 yrs old	4	4	3
Ld Fitzwilliam's b. m. Sally, 5 yrs old (ran on the wrong fide of the poft the third heat)	1	2	dis
Sir E. Smith's gr. f. Betfey, 3 yrs old	2	3	dr

6 to 4 on Prifcilla.

NEWMARKET

SECOND OCTOBER MEETING.

On Monday, October the 14th, Mr. Elwes's br. c. Chriftopher, by Buzzard, 8ft. 4lb. beat Mr. Andrew's b. c. Fathom, 8ft. Acrofs the Flat, 100gs, h. ft.

7 to 4 on Chriftopher.

Sweepftakes of 100gs each, Two yr old Courfe.

Gen. Gower's b. c. Swinley, by Coriander, 3 yrs old, 7ft. 8lb.	0	1
Mr. Watfon's Dreadnought, 5 yrs, 8ft. 8lb.	0	2
Mr. Mellifh's b. c. Didler, 4 yrs old, 9ft.	pd	

6 and 7 to 4 on Dreadnought, and after the dead heat, the fame.

Ld

Ld Grofvenor's b. f. Meteora, by Meteor, 3 yrs old, 8ft. beat Ld Barrymore's b. c. Merryman, 4 yrs old, 8ft. 1lb. R. M. 100gs.——2 to 1 on Meteora.

A Gold Cup, value 80gs, the remainder in fpecie, a Subfcription of 10gs each, Acrofs the Flat. (9 Subfcribers.)

Mr. Ladbroke's br. c. Buftard, by Buzzard, 4 yrs
old, 6ft. 8lb.......:..........   1
Sir C. Bunbury's b. m. Eleanor, aged, 8ft. 13lb. .   2
Mr. Andrew's b. c. Fathom, 3 yrs old, 4ft. 13lb.   3
Mr. Wilfon's ch. c. by Buzzard, 3 yrs, 4ft. 12lb.   4
Mr. R. Boyce's ch. h. Bobtail, aged, 9ft. 5lb ...   5
Mr. Lake's b. f. Virtuofa, 4 yrs old, 5ft. 6lb....   6

2 to 1 agft Eleanor, 7 to 2 agft Bobtail, 5 and 6 to 1 agft Boftard.

Mr. Wilfon's b. c. Newmarket, by Waxy, 3 yrs old, 7ft. 7lb. beat the D. of Grafton's br. f. Peliffe, 4 yrs old, 8ft. 9lb. Acrofs the Flat, 100gs.

11 to 8 on Peliffe.

One-third of a Subfcription of 25gs each (firft year) for five yr olds, 8ft. 5lb. fix yr olds, 8ft. 11lb. and aged, 9ft. B. C. (16 Subfcribers.)

D. of Grafton's b. m. Parafol, by Pot8o's, 5 yrs..   1
Ld Foley's gr. h. Sir Harry Dimfdale, 5 yrs old...   2

2 to 1 on Parafol.

Ld Grofvenor's b. f. Violantè, by John Bull, 3 yrs old, 8ft. 10lb. recd. from Ld Foley's b. f. Our Blowing, 2 yrs old, 7ft. 2lb. Two yr old Courfe, 100gs.

Mr. R. Boyce's br. c. Sir David, by Trumpator, recd. ft. from Mr. Mellifh's b. c. Didler, 8ft. 2lb. each, Two yr old Courfe, 100gs, h. ft.

Mr. R. Boyce's Sir David, recd. 110gs from the D. of Grafton's Peliffe, 8ft. each, R. M. 200gs.

M 3   Mr.

Mr. Howorth's b. c. by Skyfcraper, recd. 30gs from the D. of Grafton's ch. c. Firebrand, 8ft. 7lb. each, Acrofs the Flat, 200gs, h. ft.

TUESDAY.

Mr. R. Boyce's ch. f. Wretch, by Gohanna, 7ft. 11lb. beat the D. of Grafton's b. f. Merrythought, 8ft. Two yr old Courfe, 100gs, h. ft.

Even betting, and 5 to 4 on Merrythought.

Ld Foley's br. c. Little Peter, by Sir Peter, 8ft. beat the D. of Grafton's b. f. Dodona, 8ft. 6lb. Acrofs the Flat, 200gs.——5 to 2 on Little Peter.

Fifty Pounds for two yr old colts carrying 8ft. 2lb. and fillies, 8ft. Two yr old Courfe.

Ld Grofvenor's ch. f. Norah, by John Bull 1
D. of Grafton's b. f. Merrythought 2
Mr. Wilfon's b. c. Pantaloon 3
Mr. R. Boyce's b. f. Orange Girl 4
Ld F. G. Ofborne's ch. c. Superftition ; Mr. Golding's
    b. f. Merrymaid ; and Sir F. Standifh's bl. c. by
    Mr. Teazle ; alfo ftarted, but the Judge could place
    only the firft four.

5 to 4 agft Pantaloon, 4 to 1 agft Merrymaid, 6 to 1
    agft Merrythought, and high odds agft Norah.

The third and laft year of a renewal of the October Oatlands Stakes, B. M. a Subfcription of 30gs each, 10gs ft. if declared by ten o'clock on Monday night.

Ld Grofvenor's b. f. Violantè, by John Bull, 3 yrs
    old, 7ft. 10lb. 1
Ld Foley's b. c. Watery, 4 yrs old, 7ft. 10lb. 2
Sir F. Standifh's fifter to Duxbury, 3 yrs, 6ft. 9lb. 3
D. of Grafton's b. f. Lumbago, 4 yrs old, 7ft. 1lb. 4
Mr. D. Radcliffe's b. g. Rebel, aged, 9ft. 5lb. 5

Mr.

Mr. Wyndham's br. c. Tallboy, 3 yrs old, 5ft. 4lb. 6
Mr. Howorth's ch. h. Wheatear, 5 yrs old, 7ft. 7lb. 7

> 6 to 4 agft Violantè, 5 to 1 agft Lumbago, 5 and
> 6 to 1 agft Rebel, 6 to 1 agft the fifter to Dux-
> bury, and 6 to 1 agft Wheatear.

The following declared forfeit by the time prefcribed, and 5 Subfcribers omitted to name.

Mr. F. Neale's ch. h. Bobtail, aged, 9ft. 12lb. D. of
Grafton's b. m. Parafol, 5 yrs old, 9ft. 9lb. Mr.
Wilfon's ch. m. Mai ianne, aged, 9ft. 3lb. Ld Sack-
ville's ch. h. Enchanter, 6 yrs old, 9ft. 2lb. Ld G.
H. Cavendifh's b. h. Duxbury, 6 yrs old, 8ft. 10lb.
Mr. Andrew's br. h. Norval, 5 yrs old, 8ft. 3lb.
Mr. Watfon's b. h. Dreadnought, 5 yrs old, 8ft.
Mr. Lake's Lynceus, 4 yrs old, 7ft. 6lb. Mr. D.
Radcliffe's b. c. Pedeftrian, 3 yrs old, 7ft. 2lb. and
Gen. Gower's b. c. Swinley, 3 yrs old, 6ft. 12lb.

Mr. Andrew's Norval, by Jupiter, 9ft. recd. 35gs
from Mr. Perren's ch. f. by Guildford, 7ft. 7lb. Acrofs
the Flat, 100gs, h. ft.

Mr. Wilfon's ch. c. by Buzzard, 3 yrs old, 6ft. 13lb.
recd. from Sir J. Shelley's Strap, 5 yrs old, 8ft. 5lb.
D. I. 100gs.

Ld Foley's br. c. Czar Peter, by Sir Peter, 8ft. 6lb.
recd. 60gs from Mr. Howorth's ch. c. Honefty, 7ft.
B. C. 200gs, h. ft.

Sweepftakes of 100gs each, for fillies, 8ft. D. I.
(3 Subfcribers.)

D. of Grafton's b. f. Dodona, by Waxy, recd. 65gs.

WEDNESDAY.

Sweepftakes of 25gs each, Two yr old Courfe.

Mr. Ladbroke's br. c. Wormwood, by Young
Woodpecker, 8ft. 2lb. 1
Gen.

Gen. Gower's b. c. Swinley, 7ft. 10lb.......... 2
Ld Sackville's br. c. Capias, 7ft. 3

   5 to 4 agft Wormwood, 5 to 2 agft Capias, and 5 to
   2 agft Swinley.

Gen. Gower's b. c. Agincourt, by John Bull, 4 yrs
old, beat Mr. Andrew's br. h. Norval, 5 yrs old,
8ft. 2lb. each, R. M. 50gs.——6 to 4 on Agincourt.

Mr. R. Boyce's b. c. Sir David, by Trumpator, 4
yrs old, 8ft. 6lb. beat Ld Foley's ch. h. Captain Abfolute, 6 yrs old, 8ft. 7lb. from the ftarting poft of
the Two middle miles, to the end of the Flat, 100gs,
h. ft.——13 to 8 on Abfolute.

The Town Plate of 50l. for three yr olds, 7ft. 4lb.
four yr olds, 8ft. 4lb. five yr olds, 8ft. 11lb. fix yr olds,
9ft. 1lb. and aged, 9ft. 4lb. Two middle miles—with
this condition, that the winner was to be fold for
100gs, if demanded, &c.

Mr. Wyndham's b. c. Tallboy, by Totteridge, 3 yrs 1
Mr. Panton's b. c. Performer, 3 yrs old......... 2
Mr. Perren's ch. f. by Guildford, 3 yrs old...... 3
Mr. Girdler's ch. m. Capella, 5 yrs old 4
Mr. Thompfon's ch. f. by Buzzard, 3 yrs old.... 5

   7 to 4 agft Performer, and high odds againft each
  of the others.

Ld Sackville's ch. h. Enchanter, by Pot8o's, 6 yrs
old, beat Mr. Mellifh's b. f. Lady Brough, 4 yrs old,
8ft. each, B. C. 50gs.——13 to 8 on Lady Brough.

   Ld Foley's br. c. Czar Peter, recd. from Mr. Andrew's Norval, 8ft. each, D. I. 25gs.

THURSDAY.

  Sir J. Shelley's b. c. Currycomb, by Buzzard, 3 yrs
                              old,

old, 8ft. 7lb. beat Mr. Wilfon's b. c. Pantaloon, 2 yrs old, 7ft. 7lb. Two yr old Courfe, 100gs.

5 to 4 on Currycomb.

Ld Foley's br. c. Little Peter, by Sir Peter, 8ft. 1lb. beat Mr. Wilfon's b. c. Newmarket, 8ft. 4lb. Acrofs the Flat, 100gs.——5 and 6 to 4 on Newmarket.

Ld Grofvenor's br. f. Iris, by Sir Peter, 8ft. beat Sir J. Shelley's Currycomb, 8ft. 12lb. Ab. M. 75gs.

11 to 8 on Iris.

Ld Foley's b. c. Watery, by Waxy, 4 yrs old, 8ft. 7lb. beat Mr. Ladbroke's Wormwood, 3 yrs old, 7ft. 13lb. Ab. M. 50gs.——11 to 10 on Wormwood.

Mr. R. Boyce's ch. c. Brainworm, by Buzzard, 8ft. 5lb. beat Gen. Gower's b. c. Agincourt, 8ft. Two yr old Courfe, 50gs.

Even betting, and 5 to 4 on Brainworm.

Ld Sackville's b. c. Witchcraft, by Sir Peter, 4 yrs old, 8ft. 9lb. beat Mr. Elwes's br. c. Chriftopher, 3 yrs old, 7ft. 9lb. D. I. 100gs, h. ft.

6 to 4 on Witchcraft.

Mr. Barnes's ch. f. by Whifkey, 8ft. reed. 20gs from Mr. Payne's c. by Waxy, 8ft. 7lb. Y. C. 50gs, h. ft.

HOLYWELL HUNT.

On Tuefday, October the 15th, the Members Annual Plate of 50gs, for horfes, &c. carrying 13ft. 2-mile heats.

Sir W. W. Wynn's b. m. by Speculator......	1	1
Mr. Lloyd Lloyd's ch. m. Wagtail..........	2	2
Ld Kirkwall's ch. g. Murphy....	3	dr
Sir E. P. Lloyd's b. g. Blenheim.....:.....	4	dr
		On

On Thurſday the 17th, a Sweepſtakes of 15gs each, for horſes that never ſtarted, paid or recd. forfeit before the 1ſt of September, 1805; five yr olds, 11ſt. 11lb. ſix yr olds, 12ſt. 4lb. and aged, 12ſt. 6lb. the winner of a Cup carrying 7lb. extra. two miles. (Subſcribers.)

Mr. Cholmondeley's b. m. by Beningbrough .	1	1
Mr. E. L. Loyd's ch. m. Wagtail.	2	2
Ld Kirkwall's ch. g. Murphy.	3	3

A Sweepſtakes of 5gs each, rode by jockies; five yr olds, 11ſt. 11lb. ſix yr olds, 12ſt. 4lb. and aged, 12ſt. 6lb.—1-mile heats. (Subſcribers.)

Mr. Cholmondeley's b. m. by Beningbrough	1	2	1
Sir W. W. Wynn's b. m. by Speculator...	2	1	2
Ld Kirkwall's ch. g. Murphy	3	dr	

KELSO RACES and CALEDONIAN HUNT
UNITED MEETINGS.

On Monday, October the 21ſt, a Sweepſtakes of 20gs each, for all ages; four miles. (3 Subſcribers.)

Sir H. Williamſon's gr. h. Starling, by Sir Peter, walked over.

His Majeſty's Plate of 100gs, given to the Hunt, free for any horſe, &c. 12ſt.—4-mile heats.

Sir H. Williamſon's gr. h. Starling, 5 yrs old	1	1
Ld Belhaven's b. h. Brandon, 6 yrs old	2	2

6 to 4 on Brandon; after the heat, 6 to 4 on Starling.

Tueſday the 22d, 50gs given by the Hunt, for four yr olds and upwards; 4-mile heats.

Ld

Ld Belhaven's m. Lady Mary, by Beningbrough, 5 yrs old, walked over.

The Kelfo Plate of 5ol. for three and four yr olds; 2-mile heats.

Mr. Baillie's gr. c. Orphan, by Overton, 4 yrs
old, 8ft. 7lb. 1 1
Sir A. Don's b. c. by Skyfcraper, ditto...... 2 2
    5 to 4 on Orphan; after the heat, 3 to 1 he won.

Sir J. Maxwell's br. m. beat Mr. F. Sitwell's ro. g. four miles.

Wednefday the 23d, 50gs given by the Hunt, for four yr olds and upwards; 4-mile heats.

Sir H. Williamfon's Starling, 5 yrs, 8ft. 3lb. 1 1
Ld Belhaven's Brandon, 6 yrs old, 8ft. 9lb... 2 2
    7 to 4 on Starling; after the heat, 2 to 1 he won.

Thurfday the 24th, 50gs given by the Hunt, for Hunters that never won, and the property of Members of the Hunt; 12ft. each; 4-mile heats.

Mr. Baird's h. Young Newbyth, by Newbyth 1 1
Sir J. Maxwell's b. g. by Antæus........... 2 2

Friday the 25th, 50gs given by the Hunt, for four yr olds and upwards; 4-mile heats.
Sir H. Williamfon's gr. h. Starling, walked over.

Saturday the 26th, the Kelfo Plate of 5ol. for three yr olds and upwards; 4-mile heats.
Ld Belhaven's b. m. Lady Mary, walked over.

BLICKLING,

BLICKLING, Norfolk.

On Tuesday the 22d of October, a Sweepstakes of 5gs each, for horses that never started before the day of naming (1st September) three yr olds, 7st. 5lb. four yr olds, 8st. five yr olds, 9st. six yr olds, 9st. 5lb. mares and geldings allowed 3lb.—2-mile heats. (11 Subscribers.)

Col. Harbord's ch. c. Master Betty, by Delpini, 3 yrs old 1   1
Major Wilson's br. c. Trudge, 3 yrs old.... 2   2
Col. Wyndham's br. c. Yorkshire Lad, 3 yrs   3 dr

A Sweepstakes of 2gs each, for horses bred in the county of Norfolk, qualified as above; two yr olds, 6st. 7lb. three yr olds, 7st. 7lb. four yr olds, 8st. 3lb. five yr olds, 9st. six yr olds, 9st. 5lb.—one-mile heats. (25 Subscribers.)

Col. Harbord's b. f. Czarina, by Saxe Cobourg, 2 yrs old.............. 1   1
Mr. Gunton's gr. f. Allegranti, 3 yrs old 4   2
Col. Harbord's b. m. Luna, 6 yrs old (bolted) 2 dis
Mr. Doughty's ch. c. Mr. Teazle, 4 yrs old (bolted)............... .... 3 dis

Wednesday the 23d, Welter Stakes of 5gs each, carrying 13st. rode by Gentlemen; 2-mile heats. (10 Subscribers.)

Col. Wyndham's b. g. Blickling, 6 yrs old .. 1 , 1
Mr. Hussey's gr. g. Smoaker, aged.. .... 2 dr

Produce Sweepstakes of 30gs each, for two yr olds; one mile. (3 Subscribers.)

Col. Harbord's b. f. Czarina, by Saxe Cobourg.. 1
Mr. Thomlinson's b. f. by Wonder............ 2

Mr. Doughty's ch. c. Mr. Teazle, by Mr. Teazle, 4 yrs old, 8st. 6lb. beat Mr. Gunton's gr. f. Allegranti, 3 yrs old, st. lb.   miles, 50gs.

PENRITH.

PENRITH.

On Thurfday, October the 17th, 50l. given by the Gentlemen of the Inglewood Hunt, for three yr olds, 7ft. 7lb. and four yr olds, 8ft. 5lb. A winner of one 50l. in the prefent year carrying 3lb. extra. of two, or of a Match or Sweepftakes of 100l. value, 5lb. extra. 2-mile heats.

Mr. W. Hutchinfon's br. c. Didapper,
  by Overton, 3 yrs old 1 3 1
Mr. Peverell's ch. c. by Oberon, 4 yrs old   2 1 dt
Mr. E. Theakftone's ch. c. by Walnut .. 3 2 dr

Saturday the 19th, 50l. given by the Town of Penrith, for horfes of all ages, weight for age, 3-mile heats, was won by

The D. of Hamilton's b. f. Hafty, by Walnut, 4 yrs old, beating Mr. Hutchinfon's b. c. Antipator, by Pipator, 4 yrs old.

NEWMARKET

HOUGHTON MEETING.

On Monday, October the 28th, Mr. Mellifh's ch. m. Marianne, 8ft. 7lb. agft Mr. R. Boyce's ch. c. Brainworm, 7ft. 7lb. Ab. Mile, 100gs—*a dead beat.*

11 to 10 on Marianne.

Mr. R. Boyce's br. c. Sir David, by Trumpator, 4 yrs old, 7ft. beat Ld Foley's gr. h. Sir Harry Dimfdale, 5 yrs old, 8ft. laft three miles of B. C. 200gs.

11 to 8 on Sir Harry Dimfdale.

D. of Grafton's b. f. Lumbago, by Groufe, 8ft. 9lb. beat Mr. Andrew's b. c. Fathom, 7ft. 11lb. Two yr old Courfe, 50gs.——5 to 2 on Lumbago.

Mr. Mellifh's b. f. Lady Brough, by Stride, 4 yrs old, 6ft. 11lb. beat Mr. R. Boyce's ch. h. Bobtail, aged, 8ft. 7lb. D. I. 200gs.——5 to 4 on Bobtail.

Ld Sackville's br. c. Witchcraft, by Sir Peter, beat Ld Foley's b. c. Watery, 8ft. each, D. I. 50gs.

11 to 8 on Witchcraft.

Sir C. Bunbury's b. f. Lydia, by Whifkey, 8ft. 6lb. recd. 80gs from Mr. Wilfon's b. c. Newmarket, 8ft. 3lb. R. M. 200gs, h. ft.

Ld Foley's b. c. Hippocampus, by Coriander, 4 yrs old, 7ft. 10lb. recd. ft. from H. R. H. the P. of Wales's br. h. Orville, 6 yrs old, 8ft. 11lb. B. C. 300gs, h. ft.

Mr. Watfon's ch. c. Sorrel, by Volunteer, 4 yrs old, recd. from Sir J. Shelley's b. c. Sir Launcelot, 3 yrs old, 8ft. each, D. M. 200gs.

Mr. Andrew's br. h. Norval, by Jupiter, 10ft. 1lb. recd. 35gs from Mr. Perren's ch. f. by Guildford, 8ft. D. I. 100gs, h. ft.

TUESDAY.

Mr. Wilfon's b. c. Pantaloon, by Buzzard, 2 yrs old, 7ft. 5lb. beat Mr. Lake's b. f. Virtuofa, 4 yrs old, 8ft. 7lb. Two yr old Courfe, 25gs.

2 to 1 on Virtuofa.

Mr. Ladbroke's br. c. Wormwood, by Y. Woodpecker, 3 yrs old, 8ft. 7lb. beat Mr. Mellifh's b. f. Flighty, 2 yrs old, 5ft. 11lb. Two yr old Courfe, 25gs.

13 to 8 on Wormwood.

A Gold Cup, value 80gs, the remainder in fpecie, a Subfcription of 10gs each, D. I. (9 Subfcribers.)

Mr.

Mr. Cave Browne's ch. h. Stretch, by Stride, 5 yrs
old, 8ft... . . ..….. 1
Sir C. Bunbury's b. m. Eleanor, aged, 9ft. 7lb... 2
Mr. Mellish's b. f. Lady Brough, 4 yrs, 8ft. 4lb. 3
Ld Barrymore's b. f. Gratitude, 4 yrs old, 7ft. 9lb. 4
Mr. Wyndham's b. c. Tallboy, 3 yrs old, a feather 5

> 5 to 2 agst Eleanor, 7 to 2 agst Lady Brough, 4 to
> 1 agst Stretch, 5 to 1 agst Gratitude, and 7 to 1
> agst Tallboy.

Fifty Pounds, for two yr olds carrying a feather;
three yr olds, 7ft. 5lb. four yr olds, 8ft. 9lb. five yr
olds, 9ft. 3lb. fix yr olds, 9ft. 7lb. and aged, 9ft. 10lb.
laft three miles of B. C. With this condition, that
the winner was to be fold for 300gs, if demanded, &c.

Mr. Moorhoufe's br. c. brother to Whifkerandos,
by Whifkey, 3 yrs old.................….... 1
Mr. Howorth's br. h. Norval, 5 yrs old........ 2
Ld F. G. Ofborne's ch. c. Superftition, 2 yrs old 3
Sir F. Standifh's br. h. brother to Stamford, 5 yrs 4
Mr. Lake's b. c. Lynceus, 4 yrs old... 5
Mr. A. Blofs's ch. c. by Delpini, 3 yrs old...,.. 6

> 6 to 4 agst brother to Stamford, and 5 to 2 agst the
> winner, who was claimed by the owner of the
> fecond horfe, according to the articles.

Mr. R. Boyce's ch. c. Brainworm, by Buzzard,
4 yrs old, 8ft. 7lb. beat Col. Todd's b. c. Hippomenes, 3 yrs old, 7ft. 7lb. Acrofs the Flat, 25gs.

> 6 and 7 to 4 on Hippomenes.

WEDNESDAY.

Sweepftakes of 100gs each, h. ft. 8ft. each, Two
yr old Courfe.

Mr. Watfon's b. c. Jumper, by Worthy... 1

Gen.

Gen. Grofvenor's b. c. Have-at-'em.......... 2
Mr. Howorth's c. by Sir Harry .... pd ft

2 to 1 on Jumper.

Mr. Watfon's b. h. Dreadnought, by Buzzard,
8ft. 3lb. beat Mr. Howorth's ch. h. Wheatear, 8ft.
Two yr old Courfe, 50gs.

5 to 4 on Dreadnought.

Ld Sackville's Witchcraft, 8ft. 8lb. beat Mr. Wilfon's Newmarket, 7ft. 8lb. D. I. 100gs.

5 to 2 on Witchcraft.

Sweepftakes of 50gs each, Acrofs the Flat.

Mr. Ladbroke's b. c. Buftard, by Buzzard, 4 yrs
old, 8ft. 2lb.............................. 1
Mr. Watfon's b. h. Duxbury, 6 yrs old, 8ft. 7lb. . 2
Mr. Howorth's ch. h. Wheatear, 5 yrs, 7ft. 3lb. 3

5 to 4 agft Buftard, 7 to 4 agft Duxbury, and 3 to
1 agft Wheatear.

Subfcription Plate of 50l. for two yr olds, 7ft. 4lb.
and three yr olds, 9ft. 4lb. fillies allowed 2lb. Two
yr old Courfe. With this condition, that the winner
was to be fold for 250gs, if demanded, &c.

N.B. For this Plate four horfes were faddled, viz. *Merrymaid,*
the *colt by Mr. Teazle, Tallboy,* and the *ch. f. by Buzzard—*
The betting was 5 to 4 agft the latter, and 2 to 1 agft Tallboy—
The firft three ftarted, and came in in the order they are mentioned—on enquiry, it was difcovered to be a falfe ftart; after
which, Mr. Mellifh drew Tallboy, and it was agreed all bets
fhould be off. The Plate was then run for as follows:

Mr. Wilfon's ch. f. by Buzzard, out of Gipfy, 2 yrs 1
Mr. Golding's b. f. Merrymaid, 2 yrs old 2
Sir F. Standifh's bl. c. by Mr. Teazle, 2 yrs old.. 3

2 to 1 on Mr. Wilfon's filly.

Ld Barrymore's b. f. Gratitude, by Shuttle, 4 yrs
old,

old, 8ft. 9lb. beat Col. Todd's Hippomenes, 3 yrs old, 8ft. Acrofs the Flat, 25gs.——Even betting.

Mr. C. Browne's ch. h. Stretch, 5 yrs old, 8ft. recd. ft. from Mr. W. Bayly's b. f. Fanny Fancy, 3 yrs old, 6ft. D. I. 100gs, h. ft.

THURSDAY.

D. of Grafton's b. f. Merrythought, by Totteridge, beat Mr. Mellifh's b. f. Flighty, 8ft. each, Firft half of Ab. M. 25gs.——5 to 2 on Merrythought.

Sir C. Bunbury's b. f. Lydia, by Whifkey, 8ft. 7lb. beat Sir J. Shelley's b. c. Currycomb, 6ft. 10lb. both 3 yrs old, Two yr old Courfe, 50gs, 40ft.

6 to 4 on Lydia.

Sweepftakes of 50gs each, Two yr old Courfe.

Gen. Gower's b. c. Swinley, by Coriander, 3 yrs old, 8ft. 1lb.....	1
Mr. Howorth's ch. c. Honefty, 3 yrs old, 7ft. 7lb.	2
Mr. Mellifh's b. f. Flighty, 2 yrs old, 6ft. ......,	3
Mr. Andrew's b. c. Fathom, 3 yrs old, 8ft.......	4

2 to 1 and 5 to 2 on Swinley.

Subfcription Handicap Plate of 50l. D. I.

Mr. Ladbroke's b. e. Buftard, by Buzzard, 4 yrs old, 7ft. 11lb..........	1
Sir C. Bunbury's b. m. Eleanor, aged, 9ft. 2lb. ...	2
Mr. R. Boyce's ch. h. Bobtail, aged, 9ft 2lb.....	3

Mr. D. Radcliffe's br. h. Orville, 6 yrs old, 8ft. 12lb. Ld Foley's ch. h. Captain Abfolute, 6 yrs old, 8ft. 8lb. Sir F. Standifh's brother to Stamford, 5 yrs old, 8ft. and Mr. Browne's b. f. Haughty, 4 yrs old, 6ft. 12lb. alfo ftarted, but the Judge could only place the firft three.

6 to 4 agft Eleanor, 5 to 2 agft Orville, and 5 to 1 agft Buftard.

N 3

Mr.

Mr. C. Browne's ch. h. Stretch, recd. 150gs from
r. Mellish's b. f. Lady Brough, 8ft. each, Ab. M.
ogs.

Mr. Ladbroke's c. Wormwood, by Young Wood-
cker, 8ft. 6lb. recd. ft. from Mr. Branthwayt's b. c.
uthton, 7ft. 12lb. R. M. 100gs, h. ft.

FRIDAY.

Mr. R. Boyce's Brainworm, by Buzzard, 8ft. 10lb.
it Sir J. Shelley's br. c. Mouftache, brother to
hifkerandos, 7ft. 7lb. Ab. M. 50gs.

6 to 4 on Brainworm.

Subfcription Handicap Plate of 50l. for two and
ree yr olds, Two yr old Courfe.

en. Gower's b. c. Swinley, by Coriander, 3 yrs
old, 8ft. 6lb..... ...., 1
l. Todd's b. c. Hippomenes, 3 yrs old, 8ft. 6lb. 2
of Grafton's b. f. Merrythought, 2 yrs, 6ft. 13lb. 3
r. Ladbroke's br. c. Wormwood, 3 yrs old, 9ft. 4lb.
Mr. D. Radcliffe's b. c. Pedeftrian, 3 yrs old, 9ft. 2lb.
Sir F. Standifh's b. f. fifter to Duxbury, 3 yrs old,
8ft. 6lb. Mr. Wilfon's b. c. Newmarket, 3 yrs old,
8ft. 4lb. Sir J. Shelley's Currycomb, 3 yrs old,
7ft. 13lb. Mr. Branthwayt's b. c. Southton, 3 yrs
old, 7ft. 13lb. Mr. W. Bayly's b. f. Fanny Fancy,
3 yrs old, 7ft. 10lb. and Mr. Watfon's b. c Jumper,
3 yrs old, 6ft. 1lb. alfo ftarted, but the Judge could
place only the firft three.

o 1 agft Swinley, 4 to 1 agft Newmarket, 6 to 1
agft Merrythought, and 7 to 1 agft Hippomenes.

Mr. R. Boyce's br. c. Sir David, by Trumpater, 8ft.
it Ld Foley's b. c. Hippocampus, 8ft. 5lb. D. I.
ogs.——6 to 4 on Hippocampus.

Mr.

Mr. Watson's b. h. Dreadnought, by Buzzard, 7ft. beat Mr. Mellish's ch. m. Marianne, 8ft. 7lb. Ab. M. 50gs.——11 to 8 on Marianne.

Mr. Watson's ch. c. Sorrel, by Volunteer, 6ft. 2lb. beat Mr. Mellish's Marianne, 8ft. 11lb. Ab. M. 25gs.

5 to 2 on Sorrel.

Ld Foley's br. c. Czar Peter, by Sir Peter, 8ft. 10lb. recd. 25gs from Mr. Howorth's Honesty, 7ft. D. I. 50gs.

Mr. Watson's b. h. Duxbury, by Sir Peter, 9ft. 12lb. recd. 5gs from Mr. Wilson's sister to Buzzard, 6ft. 7lb. Two yr old Course, 25gs.

SATURDAY.

Mr. Howorth's br. h. Norval, by Jupiter, 5 yrs old, beat the D. of Grafton's b. f. Lumbago, 4 yrs old, 8st. each, Two yr old Course, 25gs.—6 to 4 on Lumbago.

Mr. R. Boyce's ch. h. Bobtail, by Precipitate, 8ft. 10lb. beat Ld Foley's ch. h. Stretch, 7ft. 3lb. Ab. M. 50gs.——5 to 4 on Bobtail.

D. of Grafton's b. f. Dodona, by Waxy, 6ft. beat Mr. Mellish's b. f. Lady Brough, 8ft. 8lb. D. I. 50gs.

6 to 5 on Lady Brough.

Ld Foley's gr. h. Sir Harry Dimsdale, by Sir Peter, 8ft. 10lb. recd. from Mr. R. Boyce's br. c. Sir David, 7ft. 11lb. B. C. 50gs.

FIFE HUNT.

On Thursday, October 31st, 50l. for Hunters;— 4 mile heats.

Capt. Cathcart's b. g. by Restless............. 1 1
Mr. Panmure's b. g. by Moorcock............. 2 dis

Saturday,

BY BENINGBROUGH.

3 B. f. Mr. Robinson's, 50l. at Malton 1
3 B. f. Mr. Watt's, 40gs at Catterick.......... 1
6 B. m. Mr. Lockley's, a Cup at Ofweftry 1
5 B. m. Mr. Cholmondeley's, two Sweepftakes
at Holywell. 2
6 Blue Devil, Ld Middleton's, 50gs at Malton 1
6 Brandon, Ld Belhaven's, 50l. at, Lamberton,
and the King's Plate at Edinburgh 2
4 Firelock, Sir H. Williamfon's, 180gs at Newcaftle..... 1
6 Harefoot, Mr. Howorth's, 50l. at Canterbury 1
3 Hippolytus, Mr. Wentworth's, 200gs at York 1
5 Lady Mary, Ld Belhaven's, 50l. at Newcaftle,
50l. at Morpeth, the King's Plate at Richmond, 50l. at Ayr, two fifties at Stirling,
50gs and 50l. at Kelfo. 8
6 Orville, H. R. H. the Prince's, the Somerfet
Stakes, and the Cup with 200gs, at Brighton,
the King's Plate and 90gs at Lewes.. 4

BY BUZZARD.

3 B. c. Sir W. W. Wynn's, 50l. at Chefter.... 1
3 Blue Bell, Mr. Williams's, 50l. at Stamford.. 1
4 Brainworm, Mr. R. Boyce's, 200gs, 50gs, 50gs,
25gs, and 50gs, at Newmarket............ 5
4 Buftard, Mr. Ladbroke's, 200gs, the Cup,
100gs, and 50l. at Newmarket, 50l. at Brighton, 70gs and the King's Plate at Canterbury 7
4 Caftrel, Gen. Sparrow's, 50l. and 300gs at
Newmarket 2
3 Ch. c. Mr. Wilfon's, 100gs at Newmarket... 1
2 Ch. f. Mr. Wilfon's, 50l. at Newmarket..... 1
3 Ch. f. Mr. Glover's, the fecond Clafs of the
Prince's Stakes at Newmarket 1
3 Chriftopher, Mr. Elwes's, 100gs at Newmarket 1

3 Currycomb,

3 Currycomb, Sir J. Shelley's, 350gs and 100gs
  at Newmarket....................... .. 2

7 Daify, Ld C. Somerfet's, 45gs and 50l. at
  Knighton 2

5 Dreadnought, Mr. Watfon's, 100gs, 50gs,
  100gs, 20gs, 100gs, 50gs, and 50gs, at Newmarket 7

3 Freedom, Mr. R. Jones's, 200gs at Epfom.. 1

5 Jack-o'-the-green, Mr. Hurft's, 50l. at Cardiff 1

3 Junius, Mr. Jones's, 300gs at Newmarket, 50l.
  at Cardiff, and three fifties at Swanfea 5

4 Little Peggy, Mr. Herbert's, 50l. at Blandford,
  45gs and 50l. at Exeter, and 170gs at Kingfcote 4

4 Lynceus, Mr. Lake's, 150gs at Newmarket.. 1

4 Merryman, D. of St. Albans's, 25gs, 100gs,
  and 50gs, at Newmarket; Ld Barrymore's,
  100gs and 50gs at Newmarket, 100gs at
  Brighton, 100gs at Lewes, and 50l. at Reading 8

2 Our Blowing, Mr. Mellish's, 100gs at Newmarket 1

2 Pantaloon, Mr. Wilfon's, the July Stakes, 50gs,
  and 25gs, at Newmarket... 3

7 Quiz, Mr. F. Neale's, two fifties at Epfom, the
  Cup at Reading, and 50l. at Abingdon 4

3 Skirmisher, Gen. Grofvenor's, 100gs, 35gs,
  and 50gs, at Newmarket................. 5

2 Superftition, Ld F. Ofborne's, 100gs at Newmarket...................... 1

BY CALOMEL.

5 Little John, Mr. Abbey's, 50l. at Newmarket;
  Ld Barrymore's, 50l. at Reading, 50l. at Egham, and two fifties at Beccles............ 5

BY CARDOCK.

5 Burdock, Mr. Bowes's, 45gs at Abingdon.... 1

BY CAUSTIC.

3 Pet, Mr. Bacon's, 50l. at Newbury 1

BY CHANCE.

6 Lothario, Ld F. Bentinck's, the Welter Stakes (30gs exc.) 50gs, and 25gs, at Bibury, 90gs at Bridgnorth, 50gs at Nottingham, and 50gs at Kingscote............ 6

BY CHARIOT.

4 Young Chariot, Sir W. Gerard's, 150gs at York, the Cup at Richmond, and 60gs at Northallerton 3

BY COINER.

3 Little Coiner, Mr. Hyde's, 50gs at Afcot.... 1

BY CORIANDER.

8 Anifeed, H. R. H. the Prince's, 100gs at Bibury 1

3 Gloriana, Ld Stawell's, 100gs at Newmarket, and 50l. at Afcot 2

4 Hippocampus, Ld Foley's, 100gs, 200gs, and 150gs, at Newmarket................... 3

7 Lemon-fqueezer, Mr. Richardfon's, the King's Plate and 50l. at Afcot, and the Bowl at Salifbury 3

3 Little Joey, Mr. Mellifh's, 50gs at Bibury... 1

8 Marcia, Mr. Garforth's, the Cup at Newcaftle, one of the three Subfcription Purfes and the Cup at York, the Doncafter Stakes at Doncafter, and 140gs at Malton........ 5

3 Performer, Mr. Panton's, 100gs at Newmarket 1

3 Swinley, Gen. Gower's, 200gs, 150gs, and 50l. at Newmarket 3

BY DELPINI.

3 Gr. c. Mr. Mafon's, 100gs at Richmond.... 1

4 Evander,

4 Evander, Mr. Garforth's, the King's Plate at
York.. 1

4 Gayman, Ld Stamford's, 50gs at Bridgnorth,
8ogs at Ludlow, 5ol. at Worcester, 5ol. at
Lichfield, and 5ol. at Leicester............ 5

Hesle, Col. King's, 140gs at Lincoln....... 1

3 Master Betty, Col. Harbord's, 48gs at Beccles,
and 50gs at Blickling..................... 2

4 Priscilla, Mr. Hodgson's, 110gs at Pontefract,
and 5ol. at Northallerton 2

5 Saxoni, Mr. G. Hutton's, the Craven Stakes
at Skipton, and the Stand Plate at York... 2

3 Sir Launcelot, Sir M. Sykes's, the Craven
Stakes at Malton, and 80gs at Beverley..... 2

4 Vesta, Mr. Garforth's, 110gs, 250gs, and one
of the three Subscription Purses, at York ... 3

BY DON QUIXOTE.

3 Artichoke, Mr. Forth's, 5ol. at Canterbury.. 1

4 La Mancha, Col. Kingscote's, 25gs at Bibury,
70gs and 5ol. at Worcester.............. 3

4 Miss Coiner, Mr. Fenwick's, 5ol. at Epsom,
135gs and 5ol. at Ascot, 5ol. at Stockbridge,
5ol. at Winchester, two fifties at Blandford,
and the Cup at Oxford 8

4 Sancho, Mr. Mellish's, 200gs and 500gs at
Newmarket, 1000gs at Brighton, 3000gs and
200gs at Lewes............................. 5

BY DRIVER.

3 Dora, Mr. Ladbroke's, 100gs at Newmarket 1
Pigmy, Mr. Lushington's, 55gs at Canterbury 1

BY DUBSKELPER.

B. g. Mr. Burton's, 400gs at Catterick...... 1

BY FORTUNIO.

3 Parſon Horne, Mr. Hurſt's, 100gs at Newmarket, 50gs at Aſcot, and 50l. at Haverford-
weſt... 3

BY GAY.

You know me, D. of Richmond's, 50gs at
Goodwood 1

BY GEORGE.

3 Georgina, Ld Stamford's, 50l. at Cheſter, and
50l. at Bridgnorth 2

BY GOHANNA.

3 Cardinal Beaufort, Ld Egremont's, the Derby
Stakes at Epſom, the Pavilion Stakes and
200gs at Brighton............................... 3
2 Jerboa, Ld Egremont's, 250gs at Egham 1
3 Prodigal, Ld Egremont's, 80gs at Brighton .. 1
2 Wretch, Mr. Boyce's, 100gs at Newmarket 1

BY GOUTY.

3 Graffini, Gen. Groſvenor's, 100gs at Newmarket... 1
3 B. c. Mr. Lake's, 60gs at Epſom........... 1

BY GROUSE.

3 B. c. Mr. Watſon's, 100gs at Newmarket .. 1
2 B. c. Mr. Watſon's, 25gs at Newmarket 1
5 Duckling, Mr. Cruckſhank's, 50gs at Taunton;
Mr. Skinner's, 50l. at Reading, 50l. at Warwick, the King's Plate at Lichfield, and 50l.
at Walſal. 5
4 Lumbago, Mr. Waſtell's, 50gs, 100gs, and
50gs, at Newmarket; D. of Grafton's, 50gs
at ditto... 4

BY GUILDFORD.

3 Dudley, Mr. Ladbroke's, 81l. 10s. at Abingdon 1

5 Gipsy, Mr. Emden's, 100gs at Epsom, and
 10gs at Egham..... 2

2 Quarter Master, Mr. Durand's, 25gs at Epsom 1

4 Woodcot, Mr. Branthwayt's, 25gs at Newmarket, 50l. at Ascot, the Cup and 50l. at
 Southampton 4

BY HAMBLETON.

3 Silver-heels, Mr. Wentworth's, 70gs at Catterick 1

BY HAMBLETONIAN.

3 Pufs, Sir J. Shelley's, 80gs and 80gs at Newmarket 2

BY HAMMER.

4 B. c. Mr. Harris's, 50l. at Newton 1

BY HUBY.

Hudibras, Mr. T. Sykes's, the Hunters Stakes
 at Malton.. 1

Rinaldo, Mr. W. Burrell's, 50gs and a Handi.
 cap Plate at Goodwood 2

BY HYPERION.

Angelica, Ld Boringdon's, 100gs at Exeter.. 1

BY JOHN BULL.

4 Agincourt, Ld Grosvenor's, 100gs at Newmarket; Gen. Gower's, 50gs at ditto...... 2

5 Albion, H. R. H. the Prince's, 600gs at Brighton, and 300gs at Lewes.................. 2

O 2   B. m.

5 B. m. Mr. David's, 5ol. (difputed) at Wincheſter 1

6 Captain Abſolute, Ld Foley's, 8ogs, 5gs, 15ogs,
5ol. and 2oogs, at Newmarket.. 5

4 Jack Tar, Mr. Tarleton's, the Earl of Cheſter's Plate and 1oogs at Cheſter 2

6 Margery, Mr. Abbey's, 6ogs .at Wincheſter,
and 5ol. at Oxford 2

4 Mony Muſk, Ld Groſvenor's, 7ol. at Mancheſter............................. 1

2 Norah, Ld Groſvenor's, 5ol. at Newmarket . 1

6 Northampton, D. of St. Albans's, 25gs and 5ogs
at Bibury; Mr. Cholmondeley's, 15gs at ditto 3

3 Plantagenet, Ld Groſvenor's, the July Stakes
at Newmarket...................... 1

4 Vandal, Ld Groſvenor's, 4ogs at Cheſter, 5ol.
at Knutsford, and 5ol. at Worceſter. 3

3 Violantè, Ld Groſvenor's, three fifties, 1oogs,
and the October Oatlands, at Newmarket.. 5

BY JUPITER.

Bay Devil, Ld Middleton's, the Welter Stakes
at Beverley......... 1

5 Norval, Mr. Andrew's, 15ogs, 5ogs, and 8ogs,
at Northampton, 16ogs at Warwick, 1oogs
at Lichfield, 1oogs, 35gs, 35gs, and 25gs, at
Newmarket.............. 9

BY KING FERGUS.

5 Ferguſon, Mr. Peirſe's, one of the three Subſcription Purſes at York; Ld Darlington's,
the Cup at Pontefract.. 2

BY LAUREL.

6 Creeping Gin, Mr. Bayzand's, 5ol. at Worceſter 1

BY MAGIC.

3   Mountaineer, Mr. Browne's, two fifties at Derby   2

BY MAGPIE.

8   Black Dick, Major Pigot's, 50gs at Goodwood   1

BY METEOR.

3   Meteora, Ld Grosvenor's, 100gs, 50gs, 125gs, and 100gs, at Newmarket, the Oaks Stakes at Epsom, 135gs at Ascot, and the Queen's Plate at Chelmsford........ 7

BY MR. TEAZLE.

4   Ch. c. Mr. Hyde's, 50l. at Canterbury; Mr. Doughty's, 50gs at Blickling.............. 2
6   Pic Nic, D. of Grafton's, 50l. at Newmarket   1
5   Slate, Sir H. Lippincott's, 95gs at Bibury, and 50l. at Newbury 2

BY MOORCOCK.

5   Cockspinner, Mr. Billington's, 50l. at Hereford, and a Sweepstakes at Shrewsbury; Mr. Lord's, 50l. and 60gs at Oswestry....... 4
3   Goosecap, Mr. Sitwell's, 60l. 10s. at Nottingham, the Cup and 50l. at Chesterfield 3
3   Gr. c. Mr. Anson's, 50l. at Tenbury....... 1
4   Heathpolt, Sir J. Mawbey's, 40gs at Egham.. 1
4   Principle, Mr. Fermor's, 50l. at Winchester, 50l. at Southampton, 50l. at Newbury, and the King's Plate at Warwick............,..... 4
4   Skylark, Mr. Glossop's, 50l. and 60gs at Chesterfield.................,................. 2

BY MUFTI.

7   Marianne, Mr. Wyndham's, 100gs at Newmarket; Mr. Wilson's, 100gs and 100gs at ditto... ....,................... 3

BY NEWBYTH.

Young Newbyth, Mr. Baird's, 50gs at Kelso, and 50l. at Fife. 2

BY OAK.

Misfortune, Mr. Cripps's, the Welter Stakes at Kingscote 1

BY OBERON.

4 Buckram, Mr. Baker's, 100gs at Newcastle... 1
4 Damper, Mr. Peverall's, 50l. at Newcastle .. 1

BY OLD TAT.

5 Dutchess, Mr. Day's, 50l. at Hereford...... 1
4 Forester, Sir H. Mainwaring's, a Match at Tarporley.. 1

BY ORMOND.

5 Br. h. Ld Darlington's, the Craven Stakes at Catterick, and 50l. at Boroughbridge...... 2
3 Diogenes, Mr. Hutty's, 50l. at Durham... 1

BY OVERTON.

3 B. c. (out of Fanny) Mr. Robinson's, 200gs at York.............................. 1
3 Barouche, Sir W. Gerard's, 90gs at Manchester, 50gs at Newton, 100gs at Preston, and 90gs at Pontefract................ 4
B. g. Sir F. Boynton's, the Welter Stakes at Doncaster.......................... 1
3 Br. c. (Henry) Mr. Riddell's, 60gs at Middleham 1
3 Capias, Mr. Wardell's, 50l. at Guildford, and 50l. at Ipswich; Ld Sackville's, two fifties at Bedford. 4
3 Cleveland, Mr. Hutton's, 80gs at Skipton, 60gs and 50l. at Malton................... 3
3 Didapper, Mr. W. Hutchinson's, 50l. at Skip-
ton,

ton, the King's Plate and 50l. at Carlifle, and
50l. at Penrith.............. 4

3 Gallina, Sir W. Hunloke's, 100gs at Doncafter 1

4 Hebe, Mr. Ackers's, 80gs at Newcaftle, and
100gs at Knutsford; Mr. Smith's, the King's
Plate at Lincoln, and two fifties at Shrewfbury 5

3 Honefty, Mr. Mellifh's, 100gs at Newmarket,
and 5gs at Brighton 2

4 Orphan, Mr. Baillie's, 70l. at Manchefter, 50gs
and 50gs at Edinburgh, and 50l. at Kelfo.. 4

3 Othello, Mr. Egerton's, 50l. at Nottingham,
and 50gs at Tarporley.................... 2

5 Sufan, Mr. Bowman's, 50l. at Newcaftle..... 1

BY PATRIOT.

2 B. f. Sir H. Vane's, 100gs at York, and 100gs
at Pontefract.... 2

BY PEGASUS.

5 B. m. Sir M. Sykes's, the Welter Stakes at Lincoln, and 40gs at Doncafter 2

4 Didler, Mr. Mellifh's, 100gs, 200gs, and 50gs,
at Newmarket, and 50gs at York.......... 4

4 Eunuch, Mr. Fenwick's, 50l. at Egham, and
50l. at Litchfield... 2

Glider, Gen. Grofvenor's, 25gs at Lincoln.... 1

6 Louifa, Col. Thornton's, 500gs at York...... 1

3 Southton, Mr. Branthwayt's, 50gs at Southampton................................... 1

BY PETWORTH.

4 Alaric, Mr. Kellermann's, the firft Clafs of
the Oatlands Stakes at Newmarket 1

BY PICKLE.

Piccalilly, Captain Sutton's, 50l. at Haverfordweft............... 1

BY PIPATOR.

4 Antipator, Mr. Hutchinfon's, 5ol. at Carlifle   1

3 Ch. c. Mr. Lonfdale's, 5ol. at Durham, and
5ol. at Newcaſtle 2

7 Chilton, Mr. Harrifon's, 5ol. at Bibury 1

3 Lavinia, Mr. Birch's, 5ol. at Ludlow, and 5ol.
at Hereford 2

   Quill-driver, Mr Burrell's, 5ol and 25gs at
Totnes, and 5ol. at Exeter; alfo 5ol. at Jump,
Devon. (July 24) beating Ironfides........ 4

3 Welfh Harp, Mr. Hodgfon's, 75gs at Cheſter;
Mr. Clifton's, 5ol. at Preſton 2

BY POTOOOOOOOO.

6 Enchanter, Ld Sackville's, 5ogs, 1oogs, and
5ogs, at Newmarket 3

14 Oliver, Mr. Parker's, 25gs at Newmarket... 1

5 Parafol, D. of Grafton's, two of the King's
Plates, 5ol. the Jockey-club Plate, 1 rogs, 5ogs,
5ogs, and 125gs, at Newmarket.......... 8

4 Timidity, Mr. Golding's, 5ol. at Chelmsford 1

BY PRECIPITATE.

   Bayard, Mr. Lennox's, 9ogs at Lewes....,.. -

4 B. c. Sir A. Don's, 5ol. at Stirling 1

10 Bobtail, Mr. R. Boyce's, 5oogs, 5oogs, 25gs,
and 5ogs, at Newmarket, and 2oogs at Lewes 5

3 Ch. f. Sir T. Gafcoigne's, 13ol. at Newcaſtle,
and 1oogs at Pontefract..... 2

3 Langton, Col. Childers's, 14ogs at Malton,
1ool. and 15ogs at Doncaſter 3

3 Mariner, Sir R. Winn's, 5ol. at Pontefract .. 1

4 Mirror, Sir H. Lippincott's, 165gs at Maddington, 5ogs at Stockbridge, 5ol. at Taunton, 6ogs and 5ol. at Salifbury, 1oogs and the
Kingfcote Stakes at Kingfcote 7

Rolla,

8 Rolla, D. of Richmond's, the Skirters Plate
at Goodwood 1

3 Sir Reginald, Sir M. Sykes's, 120gs at Beverley........ 1

4 Slipper, Ld Egremont's, the Petworth Stakes
at Brighton 1

BY QUETLAVACA.

Dare Devil, Capt. French's, 80gs at Totnes.. 1

BY RAMAH DROOG.

5 Creeping Jane, Capt. Mathias's, 50l. at Haverfordweft........................... 1

BY RESTLESS.

B. g. Capt. Cathcart's, 50l. at Fife........ 1
3 Fanny Fancy, Mr. Bayly's, the Cup at Lincoln 1
6 Brotherton, Mr. Goulburn's, 250gs at Leicefter 1

BY ST. GEORGE.

3 Bumper, Ld Darlington's, 50gs and 100gs at
Newmarket.. 2

4 Zodiac, Ld Darlington's, 300gs at Brighton 1

BY SAXE COBOURG.

2 Czarina, Col. Harbord's, 48gs and 60gs at
Blickling 2

BY SCREVETON.

3 Mifs Welham, Mr. Acred's, 100gs at York;
Mr. Bower's, 50l. at Beverley 2

BY SELIM (AN ARABIAN)

4 Sir Charles, Mr. Dent's, 50l. at Catterick, and
two fifties at Prefton.................. . 3

BY SHUTTLE.

4 Gratitude, Mr. Wardell's, 170gs and 50l. at Lewes, 120gs at Egham; Ld Barrymore's, 25gs at Newmarket..... 4

3 Staveley, Mr. W. Fletcher's, the Produce Stakes at Catterick, and 100gs at York; Mr. Mellish's, the St. Leger Stakes at Doncaster......... 3

BY SIR PETER TEAZLE.

4 Bagatelle, Ld Grosvenor's, the Claret Stakes at Newmarket; Ld C. Somerset's, 110gs at Kingscote........................... 2

3 Barbaroffa, H.R.H. the Prince's, the Egremont Stakes at Brighton....... 1

3 B.c. (out of Æthe) Ld Darlington's, 120gs at Lewes............ . ....,......... 1

2 B.f. Ld Fitzwilliam's, 80gs at Doncaster 1

3 Caleb Quotem, Ld Fitzwilliam's, 200gs and 225gs at York, and the Cup at Doncaster... 3

Cockaboop, Mr. Hawke's, a Sweepstakes at Lewes..... 1

4 Coriolanus, Mr. Clifton's, 50l. at Newcastle.. 1

4 Czar Peter, Ld Foley's, 200gs, 60gs, 25gs, and 25gs, at Newmarket.................... 4

5 Ditto, Sir H. Williamson's, the Craven Stakes at Newmarket, and the King's Plate at Guildford 2

6 Duxbury, Mr. Watson's, 15gs, 50gs, and 5gs, at Newmarket....................... 3

3 Goth, Ld Grosvenor's, the First Class of the Prince's Stakes at Newmarket............ 1

3 Hadley, Col. Kingscote's, 50l. at Ludlow 1

4 Houghton Lass, Mr. Wardell's, 70gs at Newmarket; Sir J. Shelley's, the King's Plate at Ipswich................. 2

3 Jasper, Ld Grosvenor's, 60gs and 30gs at Newmarket 1½

4 Josephina,

4 Jofephina, Mr. Clifton's, 5ol. at Bridgnorth, 5ol. at Nottingham, and 5ol. at Walfal.... 3

3 Iris, Ld Grofvenor's, 75gs at Newmarket ... 1

3 Knight Errant, Ld Grofvenor's, 45gs and 30gs at Newmarket... ,................ .... 1½

3 Little Peter, Ld Foley's, 5ogs, 300gs, 200gs, and 100gs, at Newmarket, and 200gs at Epfom 5

4 Maiden, Mr. Wilfon's, 100gs and 25gs at Newmarket; Mr. Elwes's, 5ol. at Huntingdon, and 5ol. at Northampton 4

4 Mafter Betty, Sir H. Vane's, the Great Produce Stakes and 300gs at York 2

3 Mifs Hornpipe Teazle, Mr. Hewett's, the Produce Stakes and 30gs at York, 120gs and 5ogs at Doncafter.................. 4

6 Pipylin, Major Pigot's, 5oogs at Bibury; Mr. Mellifh's, 55gs at ditto..... 2

5 Sally, Ld Fitzwilliam's, 6ogs at York, and 5ol. at Doncafter.................. 2

5 Sir Harry Dimfdale, Ld Foley's, 2cogs, 75gs, and 5ogs, at Newmarket, 100gs and 25ogs at Bibury.................. 5

3 Sir Paul, Ld Fitzwilliam's, 150gs at York.... 1

5 Starling, Sir H. Williamfon's, the Cup at Middleham, the King's Plate at Newcaftle, 5ol. at York, 7ol. at Richmond, 40gs, the King's Plate, 5ogs, and 5ogs, at Kelfo............ 8

4 Virgin, Mr. Abbey's, 5ol. at Oxford. 1

6 Walton, Sir H. Williamfon's, 200gs, 100gs, 5ol. and the King's Plate, at Newmarket, 5ol. and 6ogs at Lewes..................... 6

4 Wafhington, Mr. Biggs's, 5cl. at Bibury, the Cup at Kingfcote, and 5ogs at Dorchefter... 3

4 Welfh Rabbit, Mr. C. Cholmondeley's, 5ol. at Newcaftle, and 5ol. at Nantwich.... ... 2

4 Witchcraft, Ld Sackville's, the Maddington Stakes at Maddington, 5ogs at Bibury, 5ol. at Stockbridge, the King's Plates at Winchefter

and

and Salisbury, 100gs, 50gs, and 100gs, at Newmarket 8

3 Young Roscius, Ld Stamford's, 60gs at Bridgnorth........ ..../........ 1

3 Yorkshire, Ld Strathmore's, the Cup at Boroughbridge ,........................ 1

BY SKYSCRAPER.

3 C. Mr. Howorth's, 30gs at Newmarket...... 1
5 Paul, Mr. Fellowes's, 50gs at Exeter........ 1

BY SLOPE.

Why-not, Capt. Chamberlain's, 50gs at Skipton 1

BY SPECULATOR.

B. m. Sir W. Wynn's, 50gs at Holywell....... 1

BY STANDARD.

5 Striver, Mr. Rushton's, 80gs at Manchester . 1

BY STAR.

3. B. c. Ld Belhaven's, 80gs at Lamberton, and
75gs at Ayr.................... 2
Ch. g. Mr. Baillie's, 40gs at Lamberton, and
50gs at Edinburgh........................ 2
Ch. h. Ld Belhaven's, 50l. at Ayr.......... 1

4 Quid, Mr. Norton's, 50gs and 100gs at Newmarket; Mr. Mellish's the King's Plate at
Doncaster... 3

BY STICKLER.

4 Mary, Mr. Philipps's, 50gs at Swansea. 1

BY STRIDE.

2 Baronet, Mr. Walker's, 120gs at York...... 1
4 Lady Brough, Mr. Mellish's, 25gs, 125gs, and
200gs, at Newmarket, and 100gs at Lewes 4

4 Petruchio,

4 Petruchio, H. R. H. the Prince's, 50l. at Bibury,
and 50l. at Brighton 2

5 Stretch, Mr. Wardell's, the Ladies Plate at
York, and 50l. at Pontefract ; Mr. Browne's,
the Cup, 50gs, and 150gs, at Newmarket.. 5

BY TELESCOPE.

4 Optician, Mr. Brooke's, 50l. at Chester ; Mr.
Denham's, 50l. at Nantwich, 130gs at Warwick, and 150gs at Lichfield 4

3 Royal Oak, Mr. Bowker's, 70gs at Lichfield,
50l. at Shrewsbury, and 50l. at Oswestry ... 3

BY TOTTERIDGE.

2 Merrythought, D. of Grafton's, 25gs at Newmarket........ 1

3 Tallboy, Mr. Wyndham's, 100gs and 50l. at
Newmarket..... 2

3 Truth, Mr. Nalton's, 50l. at Malton, and 50l.
at Lincoln................................ 2

BY TRAVELLER.

3 Laura, Mr. Garforth's, 60gs at Malton...... 1

BY TRIMMER.

5 Young Trimmer, Mr. Baird's, 50l. at Edinburgh 1

6 Chancellor, Ld Cassillis's, the Cup at Ayr. ... 1

BY TRUMPATOR.

3 Fathom, Mr. Andrew's, 50l. at Stamford, 50l.
at Northampton, and 70gs at Lincoln.,.... 3

7 Giles, Mr. Lake's, the second Class of Oatlands
at Newmarket...................... 1

9 Rebel, H. R. H. the Prince's, the Craven Stakes
and part of the Barrington Stakes at Bibury,
the Smoaker Stakes at Brighton, and 50l. at
Lewes.................................... 4

4 Sir David, Mr. R. Boyce's, 20gs, 50gs, 110gs,
100gs, 200gs, and 100gs, at Newmarket.... 6

7 Trombone, Mr. Watson's, 100gs at Newmarket 1

BY VOLUNTEER.

Annette, Mr. Child's, 50l. at Chelmsford.... 1

8 Black Strap, Mr. Flint's, 100gs at York...... 1

9 Eagle, Mr. Mellish's, 200gs, 100gs, and 200gs, at Newmarket................................. 3

5 Enchantefs, Mr. Martin's, 60gs at Goodwood 1

4 Sorrel, Mr. Watfon's, 200gs and 25gs at Newmarket.. 2

6 Sylvanus, Ld E. Somerfet's, 90gs at Maddington, 25gs at Bibury, and 100gs at Oxford.. 3

BY WALNUT.

4 Hafty, D. of Hamilton's, 50l. at Penrith.... 1

8 Lignum Vitæ, Mr. Watfon's, 10gs at Newmarket.................................... 1

BY WAXY.

5 Delegate, Sir H. Lippincott's, 45gs at Stockbridge, 50l. (difputed) at Taunton........ 2

3 Dodona, D. of Grafton's, 400gs, 65gs, and 50gs, at Newmarket.. 3

5 Elizabeth, Ld F. Ofborne's, 50l. and 50gs at Newmarket 2

4 Heeltap, Mr. Howorth's, 100gs and 20gs at Newmarket; Mr. Kellermann's, 50l. at Warwick...... 3

4 Latitat, Mr. Emden's, 50gs at Afcot...,..... 1

5 Marplot, Ld Brooke's, 50l. at Kingfcote. . . 1

4 Newcaftle, Mr. Thompfon's, 50l. at Durham, 80l. at Manchefter, and 50l. at Newton ; Mr. Ackers's, the King's Plate at Nottingham, and 50l. at Derby...................... 5

3 Newmarket, Mr. Wilfon's, 100gs at Newmarket...... 1

4 Pavilion, Ld D ington's, the New Claret Stakes and 400gs at Newmarket 2

4 Watery, Ld Foley's, 200gs, 50gs, 100gs, and 50gs, at Newmarket........................ 4

BY WHIRLWIND.

6 Tornado, Mr. Morris's, 55gs at Leicefter.... 1

BY WHISKEY.

2 Ch. f. Mr. Barnes's, 20gs at Newmarket 1

7 Eleanor, Sir C. Bunbury's, the Cup, 50l. and
100gs, at Egham, and 100gs at Newmarket 4

6 Julia, Sir J. Shelley's, 100gs at Newmarket.. 1

3 Lydia, Sir C. Bunbury's, 400gs, the Newmarket Stakes, 500gs, 80gs, and 50gs, at
Newmarket.......... 5

6 Midas, Mr. Collins's, 50gs at Swanfea, and 50l.
at Haverfordweft ..... ,...... 2

3 Mouftache, Mr. Moorhpule's, 50l. at Newmarket 1

4 Peliffe, D. of Grafton's, 100gs at Newmarket 1

3 Rofabella, Mr. Lake's, 180gs at Epfom...... 1

5 Sir Ulic M'Killigut, Mr. Clifton's, two fifties
at Chefter, and 60l. at Knutsford......... 3

3 Tramper, Mr. Howorth's, 90gs at Newmarket 1

7 Whirligig, Ld Sackville's, 110gs and 50l. at
Maddington, 50gs and 55gs at Bibury, and
50l. at Winchefter 5

BY WOODPECKER.

6 B. h. H. R. H. the Prince's, 70gs at Bibury.. 1

BY WORTHY.

2 Jumper, Mr. Watfon's, 150gs at Newmarket 1

BY YOUNG ECLIPSE.

6 Young Eclipfe, Mr. Goddard's, 50l. at Maddington, and 50l. at Kingfcote.. 2

BY YOUNG PUMPKIN.

Ironfides (late Gourd) Capt. Wall's, a Sweepftakes at Totnes, and 50l. at Exeter........ 2

BY YOUNG WOODPECKER.

3 Punch, Mr. R. Boyce's, 50gs at Newmarket,
and 42gs at Epfom....................... 2

5　Wheatear, Mr. Howorth's, the Sherborne Stakes, 175gs, and 50gs, at Bibury, and the Woburn Stakes at Bedford 4

3　Wormwood, Mr. Ladbroke's, 50l. at Afcot, the Magna Charta Stakes at Egham, 50gs, 25gs, and 50gs, at Newmarket 5

WINNING HORSES,

OMITTED IN THE PRECEDING LIST.

　B. m. Mr. Kincaid's, a Purfe at Edinburgh ... 1

6　Blickling, Col. Wyndham's, the Welter Stakes at Blickling 1

　Br. g. (Blue Peter, by Magnum Bonum) Mr. Acklom's, 100gs at Beverley. ... ,....... 1

　Br. m. Sir J. Maxwell's, a Match at Kelfo .. 1

　Ch. p. Mr. Bailey's, 100gs at Doncafter 1

　Ch. p. Mr. Hanfon's, 120gs at Manchefter .. 1

　Creeping Jenny, Capt. Fellowes's, 50gs at Totnes 1

　Cyclops, Mr. Burrell's, 40gs at Totnes 1

　Grafshopper, Mr. Bunce's, 50gs at Abingdon 1

　Hackney, Mr. Wilfon's, the Hunters Cup at Northampton 1

　Lady Rufhmere, Mr. Neale's, 50l. at Ipfwich 1

　Louifa, Mr. Seddon's, 50l. at Manchefter ... 1

　Maid of all Work, Mr. Fofter's, 50gs at Totnes 1

　Millintr, Mr. Heron's, 60gs at Tarporley 1

5　Mifs Beverley, Mr. Thompfon's, a Sweepftakes at Beverley 1

5　Nimrod, Mr. Youd's, a Cup at Ofweftry 1

　Peggy O'Rafferty, Mr. Hill's, 100gs at Malton 1

　Pouy, Mr. Sitwell's, three Matches at Chefterfield 3

5　Reclufe (by a brother to Druid) Sir H. Lippincott's, 30gs at Kingfcote. 1

　IRELAND,

IRELAND,

1805.

[*Extracted from the Irish Sheet Calenders.*]

CURRAGH April Meeting.

SATURDAY, April 20, Sweepstakes of 50gs each, h. ft. over the Courfe. (3 Subfcribers.)

Mr. Hamilton's ch. c. Fitz-Emily, by Chanticleer, 4 yrs old, 8ft........ 1

Mr. Batterfby's b. h. Jerry Sneak, aged, 8ft. 7lb. 2

Monday 22d, the Kildare Stakes of 10gs each, for two yr olds, 6ft. three yr olds, 8ft. 3lb. four yr olds, 8ft. 12lb. five yr olds, 9ft. 4lb. fix yr olds and aged, 9ft. 7lb. Three yr old Courfe.   (9 Subfcribers.)

Mr. Edwards's ch. c. Efcape, by Commodore, 2 yrs 1

Capt. Caldwell's b. c. Pipes, 3 yrs old... 2

Mr. Hamilton's b. c. Babe, 4 yrs old........... 3

Mr. Whaley's b. f. Stella, 4 yrs old..... 4

Mr. Ormfby's b. m. Proferpine, 5 yrs old. 5

Col. Lumm's ch. c. Cockahoop, 2 yrs old...... 6

Sweep-

Sweepftakes of 30gs each, h. ft. for three yr old colts, 8ft. 7lb. fillies, 8ft. 4lb. two miles. (3 Subfcribers.) Capt. Caldwell's f. by Cornet, on Loyal's dam, walk-ed over.

Mr. Hawkes's gr. h. Blacklegs, by Deceiver, 8ft. 7lb. recd. a compromife from Mr. Kelly's Proferpine, 8ft. over the Courfe, 100gs.

Mr. Hamilton's Fitz-Emily, by Chanticleer, 4 yrs old, 7ft. 11lb. recd. from Mr. Gore's Loyal, by Bagot, aged, 9ft. over the Courfe, the Cup and 200gs.

Tuefday the 23d, His Majefty's Plate of 100gs, for four yr old mares, 8ft. 7lb. each, four miles.

Mr. Whaley's ch. f. Louifa, by Commodore, 3 yrs	1
Mr. Hunter's b. f. Pandora, 3 yrs old.....	2
Mr. Edwards's gr. f. Hannah.	3
Col. A. Daly's gr. f. by Hero, 3 yrs old........	4
Mr. Batterfby's ch. f. Patty, 3 yrs old...........	5

The firft year of the Lumm Stakes of 25gs each, for two yr old colts, 8ft. and fillies, 7ft. 11lb. Sir Ralph's Poft. (8 Subfcribers.)

Mr. Edwards's ch. c. Efcape, by Commodore....	1
Mr. Kelly's b. c. Pilot....	2

Wednefday 24th, His Majefty's Plate of 100gs, for Irifh-bred horfes; three yr olds, a feather; four yr olds, 7ft. 2lb. five yr olds, 8ft. fix yr olds and aged, 8ft. 7lb. mares allowed 3lb. four miles.

Mr. Hamilton's Fitz-Emily, by Chanticleer, 4 yrs	1
Capt. Caldwell's b. c. Pipes, 3 yrs old..........	2
Mr. Kelly's b. c. Midfhipman, 3 yrs old.	3
Col. A. Daly's gr. f. by Hero, 3 yrs old........	4

Thurfday, His Majefty's Plate of 100gs, for Irifh-bred horfes, 5 yrs old, 10ft. each;—4-mile heats.

Mr. Hawkes's Blacklegs, by Deceiver, 5 yrs .	1	1
Mr. Ormfby's b. m. Proferpine, 5 yrs old . .	2	2
Capt. Caldwell's b. g. Paddy-oats, 4 yrs old	3	3

Friday

Friday 26th, a Handicap Plate of 50gs, heats.
Col. Lumm's b. c. Sir Walter Raleigh, by
    Waxy, 3 yrs old, 6ft. 7lb. . . . . ; 1   1
Mr. Hamilton's b. c. Babe, 4 yrs, 8ft. 2lb. . 5   2
Ld Belmore's b. h. Lambinos, aged, 8ft. 4   3
Mr. Whaley's b. f. Stella, 4 yrs old, 7ft. 2lb. . 3   4
Mr. Hunter's b. h. First Fruits, aged, 8ft. 2lb. 2   5

Saturday the 27th, His Majesty's Plate of 100gs,
for 3 yr old colts, 8ft. and fillies, 7ft. 11lb. three miles.
Capt. Caldwell's b. c. Tom Pipes, by Commodore 1
Col. Lumm's b. c. Sir Walter Raleigh. 2
Mr. Whaley's ch. f. Louisa 3
Mr. Hunter's b. f. Pandora 4
Col. A. Daly's b. c. Partner 5
Mr. Kelly's b. c. Midshipman 6
    Pandora's rider broke his stirrup in running, and
    Sir Walter lost ground at starting.

Col. Lumm's ch. c. Cockahoop, by Honest Tom,
2 yrs old, 7ft. 4lb. beat Mr. Kirwan's b. c. Merryman, 2 yrs old, 6ft. 11lb. Yearling Course, 20gs.

Monday 29th, Mr. Hawkes's gr. h. Blacklegs, by
Deceiver, 5 yrs old, beat Mr. Battersby's Jerry Sneak,
aged, 10ft. 7lb. each, over the Course, 100gs, 25 ft.

    Mr. Hawkes's gr. h. Blacklegs, by Deceiver, 5 yrs
old, beat Mr. Battersby's b. h. Jerry Sneak, aged, 12ft.
each, over the Course, 100gs.

Forced Handicap, 10gs each, Three yr old Course.
Mr. Hawkes's Captain, by Commodore, 2 yrs, 6ft, 1
Mr. Hunter's b. h. First Fruits, aged, 7ft. 7lb. . . 2
Capt. Caldwell's br. c. Menody, 5ft. 11lb. 3
Capt. Caldwell's b. c. Tom Pipes, 3 yrs, 8ft. 10lb. 4
Mr. Whaley's ch. f. Louisa, 3 yrs old, 8ft. 2lb. Mr.
    Gore's b. m. Proserpine, 5 yrs old, 8ft. Mr. Bat-
    tersby's ch. f. Patty, 3 yrs old, 6ft. 13lb. and Mr.
    Blake's b. g. Paddy-oats, 4 yrs old, 6ft. 11lb. also
    started, but the Judge could place only the first four.
                                        CHARLEVILLE.

CHARLEVILLE.

[King's Plate Articles, 3lb. to mares and geldings.]

MONDAY, May 13th, 5ol. for three yr olds, 6ft. four yr olds, 7ft. 2lb. five yr olds, 7ft. 13lb. fix yr olds, 8ft. 7lb. and aged, 9ft.—3-mile heats.

Mr. Hunter's b. h. Firft Fruits, byGroufe, aged	1	1
Col. A. Daly's b. h. Chanter, 5 yrs old....	2	2
Mr. Dogherty's b. m. by Falcon, 5 yrs old ..	3	dis

Tuefday, 5ol. for any horfe, 9ft. each; 3-mile heats.

Col. A. Daly's ch. h. Sweet Robin, aged..	0	1	1
Mr. Hunter's b. h. Firft Fruits, aged....	0	2	2

Wednefday, 5ol. for three yr olds, 7ft. 2lb. four yr olds, 8ft. 3lb. five yr olds, 8ft. 12lb. fix yr olds, 9ft. 7lb. and aged, 10ft —four-mile heats.

Mr. Croker's ch. c. Superior, 4 yrs old...	3	1	1
Col. A. Daly's gr. f. by Hero, 4 yrs old..	1	2	2
Mr. Fitzgibbon's gr. g. Rebel, aged.....	2	3	3

MALLOW.

Monday, May 20th, 5ol. for three yr olds, 7ft. 10lb. and four yr olds, 8ft. 12lb.—two-mile heats.

Mr. Croker's ch. c. Superior, by Turnip, 4 yrs	1	1
Col. A. Daly's gr. f. by Hero, 4 yrs old....	2	2
Major Atkins's b. c. Hypocrite, 4 yrs old...	3	dr

Wednefday 22d, 5ol. for five yr qlds, 8ft. 5lb. fix and aged, 9ft.—four-mile heats.

Mr. Hunter's b. h. Firft Fruits, aged.......	1	1
Col. A. Daly's ch. h. Sweet Robin, aged....	2	2

Friday 24th, 5ol. for three yr olds, 7ft. four yr olds, 8ft. 4lb. five yr olds, 8ft. 12lb. fix and aged, 9ft. 4lb.—three-mile heats.

Mr.

Mr. Hunter's b. h. First Fruits, aged... ...   1   1
Col. A. Daly's ch. h. Sweet Robin, aged....   2   2

Saturday 25th, 50l. Handicap, given by William Wrixon Beecher, Esq.

Mr. Hunter's b. h. First Fruits, aged, 9ft. 2lb.   1   1
Mr. Croker's ch. c. Superior, 4 yrs, 8ft. 4lb.   2   2

DROGHEDA.

(BELLEWSTOWN COURSE.)

Monday, May 27th, Sweepstakes of 5gs each, and 50gs added, for three yr olds, 8ft. 4lb. those that never won, allowed 3lb. a winner of 50l. in Plate, &c. carrying 3lb. extra.—heats, one mile and half.

Mr. Kelly's b. c. Pilot, by Commodore ..   1   1
Mr. Whaley's gr. f. Nanny (bolted)...... ..   2   2

Tuesday, Sweepstakes of 5gs each, 50gs added, four yr olds, 8ft. five yr olds, 8ft. 12lb.—two-mile heats. Winner of a King's Plate in 1805, 5lb. extra. or 50l. in Plate, &c. 2lb. extra.

Mr. Kelly's b. c Midshipman, 4 yrs old   2   1   1
Mr. Whaley's ch. f. Louisa, 4 yrs old ...   3   2   2
Mr. Hamilton's b. h. Babe, 5 yrs (fell)   1   dis

Thursday 30th, Sweepstakes of 5gs each, and 50gs added; five yr olds, 7ft. 11lb. six yr olds, 8ft. 7lb. aged, 8ft. 11lb.—three-mile heats. Winner of a race in 1805, above 20l. value, 3lb. extra. maiden horses, &c. allowed 3lb.—four-mile heats.

Mr. Hamilton's b. h. The Babe, 5 yrs old...   1   1
Mr. Coot's ch. m. Royal Fanny, aged...... ,   2   2

Saturday, June 1st, Sweepstakes of 5gs each, 50gs added; weight for age, &c.—3-mile heats.

Mr. Hamilton's b. c. Babe, 5 yrs old.... ..   1   1
Mr. Whaley's ch. f. Louisa, 4 yrs old   2   2

CURRAGH

CURRAGH June Meeting.

ON Saturday, June 8, a Sweepstakes of 25gs each, 15 ft. Two yr old Course. (3 Subscribers.)

Mr. Hawkes's ch. c. Captain, by Commodore, 8ft. 3lb. walked over.

Sweepstakes 25gs each, 15 ft. three miles.

Mr. Battersby's Jerry Sneak, 9ft. 7lb.   1
Mr. Caldwell's Menody, 7ft. 8lb.   2
Mr. Whaley's Stella, 8ft. 10lb.   3

Monday 10th, Sweepstakes for three yr olds, 8ft. each, the Three yr old Course, 50gs each, 30 ft. (5 Subscribers.)

Mr. Daly's c. Erin, by Commodore, out of Ierne   1
Mr. Hamilton's c. by Sir Peter, out of Georgiana   2

Kirwan Stakes, 50gs each, 10 ft. (9 Subscribers.)

Mr. Hamilton's ch. h. Fitz-Emily, by Chanticleer,
    5 yrs old, 8ft. 9lb.   1
Col. Lumm's b. c. Sir Walter, 4 yrs old, 6ft. 2lb.   2
Mr. Edwards's ch. c. Escape, 3 yrs old, 6ft. 4lb. .   3
Mr. Daly's ch. c. Cockatoo, 5 yrs old, 7ft. 5lb. . .   4
Mr. Hawkes's gr. h. Blacklegs, 6 yrs old, 8ft. 3lb.   5

Tuesday, King's Plate of 100gs, for four yr olds; colts, 8ft. 7lb. fillies, 8ft. 4lb. two-mile heats.

Capt. Caldwell's Tom Pipes, by Commodore   1   1
Col. A. Daly's b. c. Partner.   4   2
Col. Lumm's b. c. Sir Walter Raleigh.   2   3
Mr. Daly's ch. c. Little Tom (rider fell) . . .   3 dis

Wednesday, Sweepstakes for three yr old colts, 8ft. fillies, 7ft. 9lb. Post on the Flat, 50gs, h. ft. 3lb. to untried mares, and 3lb. to untried stallions. (3 Subscribers)

Mr.

Mr. Daly's ch. c. Erin, by Commodore......... 1
Mr. Kelly's b. c. Pilot........ 2

Sweepftakes for Irifh-bred fillies, 3 yrs old, 7ft. 1 1lb.
each, Three yr old Courfe, 50gs, h. ft. (3 Subfcribers.)
Mr. Kelly's, by Commodore, on Louifa, walked over.

Fifty Guineas Handicap Plate, Red Poft heats.

Ld Belmore's b. h. Lambinos, aged, 8ft. 5lb.   3   1   1
Mr. Kirwan's b. c. Merryman, 3 yrs, 6ft 2lb.   2   2   2
Mr. Daly's ch. h. Cockatoo, 5 yrs old, 8ft.   1   dis
Col. Lumm's b. c. by Moorcock, 3 yrs, 6ft.   dis
Mr. Kelly's f. by Commodore, 3 yrs, 5ft. 1 1lb dis

The three that were diftanced ran on the wrong
   fide of one of the Pofts.

Thurfday, King's Plate of 100gs, for fix yr olds,
12ft. 4lb. each; 4-mile heats.
Mr. Hawkes's gr. h. Blacklegs, by Deceiver, 6 yrs old,
walked over.

Poft Sweepftakes, for three yr old colts, 8ft. and
fillies, 7ft. 10lb. the Three yr old Courfe, 50gs each.

Mr. Daly's ch. c. Erin, by Commodore. 1
Col. Lumm's ch. c. Cockahoop... 2
Mr. Kirwan's b. c. by Drone............... 3

Friday, King's Plate of 100gs, for five yr olds, 9ft.
each; three-mile heats.

Mr. Hamilton's Fitz Emily, by Chanticleer..   1   1
Mr. Whaley's b. m. Stella, by Star.........   3   2
Mr. Bateman's br. b. h. Inftructor   2   dr

Mr. Batterfby's Patty, beat Mr. Caldwell's Menody,
8ft. each, 25gs, 10 ft. Yearling Courfe.

Saturday, King's Plate of 100gs, for Irifh-bred
horfes, &c. 9ft.—4-mile heats.
Mr. Hawkes's gr. h. Blacklegs, by Deceiver,
   6 yrs old...............................   1   1
                                              Mr.

Mr. Battersby's b. h. Jerry Sneak, aged. 3 2

Ld Belmore's ch. h. Traveller, aged 2 3

Mr. Battersby's b. h. Jerry Sneak, by Chocolate, beat Mr. Graydon's gr. h. 18ft. each, over the Courfe, 100gs.

Sweepftakes of 25gs each, 15 ft. Two yr old Courfe.

Mr. Hunter's br. f. Pandora, by Sir Peter, 4 yrs old, 8ft. 4lb. 1

Mr. Gore's b. f. by Mafter Bagot, 3 yrs, 5ft. 12lb. 2

Mr. Faunt's b. c. by Ringleader, 3 yrs, 5ft. 10lb. 3

Mr. Blennerhaffet's b. g. Jug, aged, 12ft. beat Mr. Englifh's ch. m. by Tug, 11ft. over the Courfe, 100gs.

Monday 17th, Mr. Kirwan's b. c. by Drone, 7ft. 8lb. beat Col. Lumm's ch. c. Cockahoop, 7ft. 13lb. Sir Ralph's Poft, 50gs, h. ft.

Sweepftakes, from Hamilton's Poft to Sir Ralph's Poft, 25gs each, 15 ft.

Mr. Hawkes's gr. h. Blacklegs, 6 yrs old, 8ft. 4lb. 1

Col. A. Daly's b. c. Partner, 4 yrs old, 7ft. 7lb. 2

Mr. Hamilton's b. h. Babe, 8ft. 7lb.... .....bolted

Sweepftakes 10gs each, 7 ft. Two yr old Courfe.

Mr. Daly's gr. c. Cockfure, 3 yrs old, 8ft....... 1

Col. Lumm's b. c. by Moorcock, 3 yrs old, 8ft... 2

Mr. Kirwan's b. c. by Drone, 3 yrs old, 8ft. 2lb. 3

Mr. Hughes's ch. g. Bonaparte, aged, 8ft. 7lb... 4

Capt. Caldwell's Pipes, 8ft. 8lb. recd. ft. from Col. A. Daly's Partner, 7ft. 10lb. 50gs, h. ft. two miles.

Mr. Daly's gr. c. Cockfure, 3 yrs old, 7ft. 7lb. beat Mr. Hamilton's b. f. Jefly, by Lambinos, 2 yrs old, 5ft. 7lb. Yearling Courfe, 25gs.

Capt. Caldwell's Menody, 8ft. beat Mr. Gore's b. f. by Mafter Bagot, 7ft. 8lb. Three yr old Courfe, 10gs.

ENNIS.

ENNIS.

Tuesday, July the 16th, 50gs for three yr olds, 6ft. 4lb. four yr olds, 7ft. 4lb. and five yr olds, 8ft. 2lb. —3-mile heats.

Col. A. Daly's gr. f. Juliet, by Hero, 4 yrs old   1   1
Mr. Hunter's b. c. Stranger, by Sir Peter, 3 yrs   2   2

Thursday the 18th, 50gs, weight for age; three yr olds, 6ft. 4lb. four yr olds, 7ft. 2lb. five yr olds, 7ft. 12lb. six yr olds, 8ft. 4lb. and aged, 8ft. 7lb.—3-mile heats.

Mr. Hunter's b. h. First Fruits, by Grouse,
   aged . . . . ; 1   1
Col. A. Daly's gr. f. Juliet, 4 yrs old 2   dr

Friday the 19th, 50gs for six yr olds, 8ft. 10lb. and aged, 9ft.—4-mile heats.

Mr. Hunter's b. h. First Fruits, walked over.

RATHKEAL.

Monday, July the 22d, 50l. for three yr olds, 6ft. 4lb. four yr olds, 7ft. 2lb. five yr olds, 7ft. 12lb. six yr olds, 8ft. 3lb. and aged, 8ft. 7lb.—3-mile heats.

Mr. Hunter's b. h. First Fruits, by Grouse,
   aged 2   1   1
Mr. Battersby's b. h. Jerry Sneak, aged . .   1   2   2

Tuesday the 23d, 50l. for three yr olds, 7ft. 10lb. and four yr olds, 8ft. 12lb. two-mile heats.

Mr. Croker's ch. c. Superior, by Turnip, 4 yrs   1   1
Mr. Watts's b. c. Partridge, 4 yrs old 2   dr

Thursday the 25th, 50l. for five yr olds, 8ft. 5lb. six yr olds, 8ft. 11lb. and aged, 9ft.—4-mile heats.

Mr. Hunter's b. h. Firſt Fruits, by Grouſe, aged   1   1
Mr. Batterſby's b. m. Miſs Newcome, 6 yrs..   2   dr

Friday the 26th, 50l. Handicap, given by the Stewards; heats, two miles and a half.

Mr. Croker's ch. c. Superior, 4 yrs old, 8ſt. 2lb.   1   1
Mr. Hunter's b. h. Firſt Fruits, aged, 9ſt. 4lb.
(fell)..   2   2

ROYAL CORPORATION,

HILLSBOROUGH MAZE COURSE.

Monday, July the 22d, His Majeſty's Plate of 100gs, for Iriſh-bred horſes, &c. not exceeding ſix yrs old, 9ſt. 7lb.—4-mile heats.

Mr. Hamilton's ch. h. Fitz-Emily, by Chanticleer, 5 yrs old, walked over.

Tueſday the 23d, 50gs for County of Down bred horſes, &c. 2-mile heats.

Ld Donegall's br. c. Abbot, 3 yrs old, 6ſt. 7lb.   1   1
Mr. Douglas's b. c. by Marquis, 3 yrs old,
.6ſt. 7lb. (bolted) ....   2 dis
Mr. May's ch. m. Averina, 5 yrs old, 8ſt. 11lb.   3   dr
Mr. Pottinger's gr. m. by Harlequin, 5 yrs
old, 8ſt. 11lb.   4   dr
Mr. Martin's br. c. by Marquis, 3 yrs old,
.6ſt. 7lb. (bolted) ....   dis

Wedneſday the 24th, 60gs for five, ſix, and aged; 4-mile heats.

Mr. Hamilton's Fitz-Emily walked over.

Thurſday the 25th, 60gs for three yr olds, 6ſt. 7lb. and four yrs old, 8ſt.—2-mile heats.

Ld Donegall's br. c. Abbot, 3 yrs old   1   1
  Col.

Col. Lumm's ch. c. Cockahoop, 3 yrs old....   2   2
Mr. Martin's br. c. by Marquis (reftive).. .   dis .

Friday the 26th, His Majefty's Plate of 100gs, for four yr olds, 7ft. 11lb. five yr olds, 9ft.—2-mile heats:
Mr. Hamilton's Fitz-Emily, 5 yrs old, walked over.

Saturday the 27th, a Sweepftakes of 5gs each, with 25gs added by the Governor; 2-mile heats.

Mr. Pottinger's b. g. by Vefper, 6 yrs old,   8ft. 11lb.   2   1   1
Ld Donegall's ch m. Averina, 5 yrs, 8ft. 1lb.   3   2   2
Mr. Scott's br. g. aged, 9ft. 1lb. (fell)   1   dis

LIMERICK.

(NEWCASTLE COURSE.)

Tuefday, July the 30th, 50l. for three yr olds, 7ft. 10lb. and four yr olds, 8ft. 12lb.—two-mile heats.
Mr. Croker's ch. c. Superior, by Turnip, 4 yrs   1   1
Mr. Hunter's b. c. Stranger, 3 yrs old.......   2   2
Capt. Kelly's ch. f. by Commodore, 3 yrs old   3   3

Thurfday, Auguft the 1ft, 50l. for five yr olds, 8ft. 7lb. fix yr olds and aged, 9ft.—4-mile heats.
Mr. Batterfby's b. h. Jerry, by Chocolate, aged · 1   1
Mr. Hunter's b. h. Firft Fruits, aged..   2   2

Saturday, Auguft the 3d, 50l. for three yr olds, 6ft. four yr olds, 7ft. 7lb. five yr olds, 8ft. 4lb. fix, and aged, 8ft. 10lb.—4-mile heats.

Mr. Croker's ch c. Superior, by Turnip, 4 yrs   1   1
Mr. Hunter's b. c. Stranger, 3 yrs old.......   2   2
Mr. Batterfby's b. h. Jerry, aged (rider fell)   dis

Monday the 5th, 50l. Handicap Plate; 2-mile heats.

Q 2   Mr. Croker's

Mr. Croker's ch. c. Superior, 9ft. 7lb. 1 1
Major Macnamara's ch. f. Fanny, 3 yrs old, a
    feather 2 2

An objection was made against Superior, for not
    carrying the proper weight.

ROSCOMMON.

TUESDAY, August the 13th, Dillon Stakes, 25g.
   each, to which the Stewards added 50gs; two
miles. (18 Subscribers.)

Mr. Hamilton's b. h. Babe, by Swindler, 5 yrs old,
    8ft. 10lb. 1
Mr. Hawkes's gr. h. Blacklegs, by Deceiver, 6 yrs
    old, 8ft. 10lb. 2
Mr. Carrol's b. f. Pandora, by Sir Peter, 4 yrs old,
    7ft. 7lb. 3
Ld Belmore's b. h. Traveller, by Chanticleer,
    aged, 9ft. 4
Mr. Fallon's ch. c. Captain, by Commodore 3 yrs old,
    6ft. 12lb. Mr. Daly's gr. c. Cocksure, by Chan-
ticleer, 3 yrs old, 6ft. 2lb. Mr. St. George Caul-
field's b. c. Partner, by Drone, 4 yrs old, 7ft. 12lb.
Mr. Caldwell's b. c. Pipes, by Commodore, 4 yrs
old, 8ft. 9lb. and Mr. Fleeming's b. h. Curbs, by
Dungannon, aged, 8ft. also started, but the Judge
could place only the first four.

Fifty Pounds for three yr olds, 6ft. 10lb. and four
yr olds, 8ft.—2-mile heats.

Mr. Caldwell's b. c. Pipes, by Commodore,
    4 yrs old 1 1
Mr. Hawkes's ch. c. Captain, 3 yrs old 3 2
Ld Donegall's b. c. Abbot, 3 yrs old 2 3

Wednesday,

Wednesday the 14th, 5ol. for five yr olds, 8ft. 7lb. six and aged, 9ft.—3-mile heats.

Ld Belmore's ch. h. Traveller, by Chanticleer, aged	2	1	1
Mr. Hawkes's gr. h. Blacklegs, 6 yrs old	1	2	2

Friday the 16th, 5ol. for three yr olds, 6ft. 2lb. four yr olds, 7ft. 8lb. five yr olds, 8ft. 3lb. six and aged, 8ft. 9lb. four miles.

Mr. Caldwell's b. c. Pipes, 4 yrs old	1
Mr. Hawkes's ch. c. Captain, 3 yrs old	2
Ld Donegall's b. h. Curbs, aged	3
Mr. Kelly's b. c. Midshipman, 4 yrs old	4

Fifty Pounds for the beaten horses of the week that saved their distance; 3-mile heats.

Mr. Hawkes's gr. h. Blacklegs, 6 yrs old, 8ft. 1olb.	1	1
Ld Donegall's b. h. Curbs, aged, 8ft. 7lb.	3	2
Mr. Kelly's b. c. Midshipman, 4 yrs, 7ft. 7lb.	2	3

TRALEE.

Monday, August 26th, 5ol. for three yr olds, 8ft. 1olb. and four yr olds, 8ft. horses, &c. that never won a Plate or Match, allowed 3lb. The winner of 5ol. carrying 3lb. extra.

Mr. Croker's ch. c. Superior, by Turnip, 4 yrs	1	1
Mr. Hunter's b. c. Stranger, 3 yrs old	2	2

Tuesday 27th, 5ol. for five yr olds, 8ft. six yr olds, 8ft. 5lb. and aged, 8ft. 7lb. horses to be allowed and winners to carry extra as on Monday; 3 mile heats.

Mr. Hunter's b. h. First Fruits, by Grouse, aged	1	2	1

Q 3   Mr. Bate-

Mr. Bateman's b. h. Inftructor, 5 yrs old   2   1   2
Mr. Dennis's b. h. Anchor, aged...........   3   3   dr
Mr. Croker's ch. c. Superior, 4 yrs old   4   dr

Thurfday the 29th, 60l. given by the Gentlemen of the profeffion of the Law, of the county of Kerry, for all horfes, &c. carrying 9ft.—4-mile heats. Horfes, &c. ftarting for this Plate, muft be bona fide the property of a gentleman who has, prior to the firft day of the Meeting, actually expended in fair adverfe litigation, the fum of 200l. Horfes, &c. of perfons who have fo expended 1000l. allowed 3lb. all horfes, &c. to be qualified upon the honor of an Attorney, if required by the Steward. As the Plate is intended folely for amateurs, no practifing profeffional gentleman will be allowed to ftart a horfe. Horfes to be allowed, and winners to carry extra. as on Monday.

Mr. Dennis's b. h. Anchor, by Tug, aged,
   8ft. 6lb...........................   3   1   1
Mr. Hunter's b. h. Firft Fruits, aged,
   9ft. 3lb...........................   2   3   2
Mr. Bateman's br. h. Inftructor, 5 yrs old,
   8ft. 6lb.........   1   2   dr

Fruits's jockey pulled up by miftake the fecond heat, after running three miles, and was joftled the third heat by Anchor's jockey. The facts and ftatement to be determined by the Stewards of the Turf-club.

Saturday 31ft, 50l. Ladies Plate, for three yr olds, 6ft. four yr olds, 7ft. 5lb. five yr olds, 8ft. 3lb. fix yr olds, 8ft. 12lb. and aged, 9ft. Horfes to be allowed, and winners to carry extra, as on Monday.—3-mile heats.

Mr. Croker's ch. h. Superior, 4 yrs old....... 1   1
Mr. Dennis's b. h. Anchor, aged 3   2
Mr. Hunter's b. c. Stranger, 3 yrs old........ 2   3

TUAM.

TUAM.

Monday, August 26th, Sweepstakes of 25gs each, to which the Stewards added 50gs; two miles. (6 Subscribers.)

Mr. Hunter's br. b. f. Pandora, by Sir Peter, 4 yrs old, 7ft. 1lb..................... 1
Mr. Caldwell's b. c. Tom-pipes, 4 yrs, 8ft. 8lb. . 2
Mr. Hawkes's ch. c. Captain, 3 yrs old, 6ft. 9lb. 3
Mr. Hamilton's b. c. Babe, 4 yrs old, 8ft. 4lb... 4

Fifty Pounds for horses, &c. that have not won 50l. this season in Plate, Match, or Sweepstakes; three yr olds, 7ft. four yr olds, 8ft. 4lb. five yr olds, 8ft. 12lb. six, and aged, 9ft. 2lb. Any horse that never won 50l. allowed 4lb. two-mile heats.

Col. Daly's Chanter, by Drone, 5 yrs old.... 1 1
Ld Donegall's Curbs, aged.............. 2 2
Mr. Kirwan's Merryman, 3 yrs old 3 3
Mr. Batterfby's Patty, 4 yrs old........... 4 dr

Tuesday the 27th, 50l. for three yr olds, 7ft. and four yr olds, 8ft. 5lb.—two-mile heats.

Mr. Hawkes's Captain, by Commodore,
  3 yrs old 3 1 1
Mr. Caldwell's Tom Pipes, 4 yrs old ... 2 3 2
Mr. Hunter's Pandora, 4 yrs old (broke
  her leg) .... 1 2 dis
Col. A. Daly's gr. f. Juliet, 4 yrs old.... 4 dr

Wednesday the 28th, 50l. for five yr olds, 8ft. 7lb. six yr olds, 8ft. 13lb. and aged, 9ft. three-mile heats.

Ld Belmore's ch. h. Traveller, by Chanticleer,
  aged............................ 1 1
Mr. Hamilton's b. c. Babe, 5 yrs old ...... 2 dr

Friday,

Friday the 30th, 60l. given by the Town of Tuam, for three yr olds, 6ft. 5lb. four yr olds, 8ft. five yr olds, 8ft. 8lb. fix and aged, 9ft. three-mile heats.

Ld Belmore's Traveller, aged.	1	1
Mr. Hawkes's Captain, 3 yrs old............	3	2
Col. A. Daly's Partner, 4 yrs old..........	2	3

A Handicap of 5gs each, for the beaten horfes of the week, to which the Stewards added 30gs.

Mr. Caldwell's Tom Pipes, 4 yrs old, 8ft. 7lb.	1	1
Ld Donegall's Curbs, aged, 8ft. 4lb...	3	2
Col. A. Daly's f. 4 yrs old, 6ft.............	4	4
Mr. Batterfby's Patty, 4 yrs old, 6ft. 10lb	2	dr

CURRAGH September Meeting.

ON Monday, September 9th, Mr. Whaley's ch. c. Little Harry, by Mafter Bagot, recd. a compromife from Mr. Daly's ch. c. Tom, 8ft. 7lb. each, Hamilton Courfe, 100gs.

Tuefday 10th, 50gs Handicap Plate, Poft on the Flat, heats.

Mr. Whaley's gr. f. Nanny, by Commodore, 3 yrs old, 6ft.	3	1	1
Mr. Gore's ch. f. Mrs. Leigh, 4 yrs old, 7ft.	1	2	3
Ld Belmore's b. h. Lambinos, aged, 8ft. 11lb.	4	3	2
Mr. Hamilton's b. h. William, aged, 9ft. 7lb.	2	dr	
Mr. Kelly's b. c. Midfhipman, 4 yrs, 8ft.	5	dr	
Mr. Fennelly's b. c. by Auguftus, 3 yrs old, 6ft. 7lb.....	dis		

Wednefday 11th, His Majefty's Plate of 100gs, for any horfe, &c. 12ft.—4-mile heats.

Mr. Hamilton's b. h. Sweetwilliam, by Tug, aged.............	1	1
Mr. Batterfby's b. h. Jerry Sneak, aged......	2	2

Thurf.

Thursday 12th, His Majesty's Plate of 100gs, for three yr old colts, 8ft. and fillies, 7ft. 11lb. two miles.

Mr. Edwards's ch. c. Escape, by Commodore 1
Mr. Daly's gr. c. Cockfure. 2
Mr. Whaley's Nanny........................ 3

Friday 13th, His Majesty's Plate of 100gs, for mares, 10ft. each; 4-mile heats.

Mr. Gore's b. m. Proserpine, by Tug, 6 yrs old   1   1
Mr. Whaley's b. m. Stella, 5 yrs old......... 2   2
Mr. Batterfby's ch. f. Patty, 4 yrs old......... dis

Saturday 14th, Lord Lieutenant's Plate of 100gs, four yr olds, 7ft. 11lb. five yr olds, 8ft. 8lb. six yr olds, 8ft. 13lb. and aged, 9ft. four miles.

Mr. Hamilton's ch. h. Fitz-Emily, by Chanticleer, 5 yrs old 1
Mr. Whaley's ch. c. Little Harry, 4 yrs old...... 2
Mr. Batterfby's b. h. Jerry Sneak, aged......... 3

Tit Stakes (third and laft year) for two yr old colts, 7ft. and fillies, 6ft. 10lb. Two yr old Courfe, 25gs each, 15 ft. (5 Subfcribers.)

Mr. Hamilton's b. f. by Swindler, dam by Tug, on Harmony.. 1
Mr. Caldwell's b. c. by Cornet, on La-la....... 2
Mr. Kelly's b. c. by Mock, on Mifs Bagot (bolted) 3

ENNISKILLEN.

Monday, September 23d, 50l. for three yr olds, 7ft. four yr olds, 8ft. 4lb. and five yr olds, 9ft.—2-mile heats.

Mr. Batterfby's ch. f. Patty, by Tug, 4 yrs old   1   1
Mr. Caldwell's b. g. Paddy-oats, 5 yrs old   2   2

Wed.

Wedne[ſ]day 25th, 5ol. for five yr olds, 8[ſt]. 7lb. [ſix]
yr olds, 9[ſt]. and aged, 9[ſt]. 4lb.—4-mile heats.

Mr. Batter[ſby]'s b. h. Jerry Sneak, by Chocolate 1 1
Mr. Lough's b. m. 2 2

Friday 27th, 5ol. Handicap Plate; 2-mile heats.

Mr. Batter[ſby]'s Jerry Sneak, 10[ſt]. 4lb. recd. half the
Plate to withdraw.

For the other half.

Mr. Caldwell's Paddy-oats, 8[ſt]. 1 1
Mr. Lough's b. m. aged, 8[ſt]. 3 2
Major Bredju's bl. m. 7[ſt]. 7lb. 2 3

LOUGHREA.

Thur[ſday], September 26th, 5ol. for three yr olds,
7[ſt]. 11lb.—one-mile heats.

Mr. Daly's gr. c. Cock[ſure], by Chanticleer,
   3 yrs old. 1 1
Mr. Bodkin's b. c. Bagatelle. 3 2
Col. Daly's b. f. by High[flyer], 3 yrs old. . . . 2 3
Mr. Hunter's b. c. Stranger, 3 yrs old. 4 4

Sweep[ſtakes] of 25gs each, to which the Stewards
added 50gs; two miles. (7 Sub[ſcribers].)

Mr. Caldwell's b. c. Pipes, by Commodore, 4 yrs
   old, 8[ſt]. 9lb. 1
Mr Whaley's ch. c. Little Harry, 4 yrs old, 8[ſt]. 2
Mr. M. Blake's b. c. Partner, 4 yrs old, 7[ſt]. 12lb. 3
Mr. Hamilton's b. h Babe, 5 yrs old, 8[ſt]. 10lb. 4
Mr. Daly's ch. h. Cockatoo, 5 yrs old, 8[ſt]. 2lb. . . 5
Mr. Hawkes's gr. h. Blacklegs, 6 yrs old, 8[ſt]. 10lb. 6

Friday 27th, 5ol. for four yr olds, 8[ſt]. each; 2-mile
heats.

Capt.

Capt. Caldwell's b. c. Pipes, by Commodore   1   1
Col. Daly's b. c. Partner   2   2

Fifty Pounds, for five yr olds, 8ft. and fix yr olds, 8ft. 7lb. three-mile heats.

Col. Daly's b. h. Chanter, by Drone........   1   1
Mr. Hamilton's b. h. Babe, 5 yrs old...   3   2
Mr. Whaley's ch. c. Little Harry, 4 yrs old..   2   dr

Saturday the 28th, 50l. given by the Marquis of Clanricarde, for any horse, &c. carrying 9ft.—4-mile heats. Horses, &c. having won 100l. this year, 7lb. extra.

Col. Daly's b. h. Chanter, by Drone........   1   1
Mr. Hunter's b. h. First Fruits.......   2   2

Fifty Pounds for all ages; four miles.

Mr. Caldwell's b. c. Tom Pipes, 4 yrs, walked over.

ROYAL CORPORATION.

TUESDAY, October the 8th, Sweepstakes of 5gs each, with 30gs added, for maiden horses, &c. fix and aged, 8ft. 7lb. all others, 8ft.—2-mile heats.

Mr. Joyce's ch. g. Duke, by Premier, 6 yrs   1   1
Mr. Pottinger's b. g. by Vesper, 6 yrs old ..   2   2

Thursday the 10th, 30gs for three and four yr olds; mile-and-half heats.

Ld Donegall's br. c. Abbot, by Marquis, 3 yrs old, 7ft. 11lb......   1   1
Mr. Pottinger's b. f. by Bob Booty, 3 yrs old, 7ft. 11lb............   2   dr

Friday 11th, 30gs, for five, fix, and aged;—3-mile heats.

Ld

Ld Donegall's b. h. Curbs, by Dungannon,
    aged, 9ft. 1 1
Mr. Pottinger's b. g. Smoke, aged, 8ft. 11lb. 2 2

    Saturday 12th, 30gs, weight for age.
Ld Donegall's Abbot, walked over.

    Thirty Guineas, Handicap, 5gs each; heats, two
miles and a half.
Ld Donegall's Curbs, 9ft. 1
Mr. Scott's Smoke, 8ft. 7lb. 2
Mr. Pottinger's b. g. by Vesper, 7ft. 7lb.... ... 3
            3 to 1 on Curbs.
    Night coming on, this race was adjourned.

    Monday 14th, the weights to be handicapped over
again.
Ld Donegall's Curbs, 9ft. 1
Mr. Scott's Smoke, 7ft. 10lb. 2
Mr. Pottinger's b. g. by Vesper, 6ft. 8lb......... 3

CURRAGH October Meeting.

    Monday, October 14th, Sweepstakes of 50gs each,
30 ft. for two yr old colts, 8ft. and fillies, 7ft. 10lb.
Two yr old Course. 3lb. each allowed to untried
stallions and mares. (4 Subscribers.)

Mr. Daly's c. by Cornet, on Young Louisa 1
Mr. Hamilton's f. by Swindler, on a Tug mare.. 2

    Long Stakes of 25gs each, 15 ft. for two yr olds.
Two yr old Course. (11 Subscribers.)

Mr. Hamilton's b. f. Noony, by Swindler, out of
    St. Bridget, 7ft. 13lb.......................... 1
Mr. Daly's b. c. by Cornet, out of Young Louisa,
    7ft. 11lb...... 2
Mr. Edwards's ch. c. Hollowback, by Commo-
    dore, on Buffer's dam, 8ft. 3lb................. 3
                            Mr.

Mr. Caldwell's b. c. by Cornet, out of La-la, 7ft. 11lb.
Col. Lumm's b. c. by Swindler, out of Hydropho-
bia, 7ft. 11lb. Mr. Batterfby's gr. c. by Soldier,
out of Crazy Jane, 7ft. 11lb. and Ld Belmore's
ch. f. by Commodore, out of a gr. m. bought from
Mr. Bateman, 7ft. 10lb. also started, but the Judge
could place only the first three.

Kirwan Stakes, 50gs each, h. ft. Red Poft: thofe
who declared ft. on Monday, laft September Meeting, pay but 10gs; the winner to run on Wednefday,
with as many of the beaten horfes, &c. as may challenge him, for 100gs each, he carrying 3lb. more,
and they 3lb. lefs than the weight they originally ran
at; the 10gs fts. to go to the winner of the challenge;
if no challenge, to go to the original winner. (13
Subfcribers.)

Mr. Edwards's ch. c. Efcape, by Commodore,
   3 yrs old, 7ft. 11lb...................... 1
Col. Lumm's b. c. Sir Walter, 4 yrs old, 7ft. 2lb. 2
Mr. Daly's ch. c. Erin, 3 yrs old, 6ft. 11lb.. 3
Ld Belmore's ch. h. Traveller, aged, 8ft. 8lb.... 4
Mr. Hamilton's ch. h. Fitz-Emily, 5 yrs old, 9ft. 4lb.
  Mr. Caldwell's b. c. Tom Pipes, 4 yrs old, 8ft. 4lb.
  Mr. Hamilton's b. h. Babe, 5 yrs old, 8ft. 4lb.
  Mr. Kelly's b. c. Pilot, 3 yrs old, 6ft. 4lb. alfo
ftarted, but the Judge could place only the firft
four.—The reft pd 10gs each.

Mr. Hamilton's William, 8ft. recd. ft. from Mr.
Hawkes's Blacklegs, 8ft. 7lb. over the Courfe, 100gs,
h. ft.

Tuefday 15th, 50gs, for three yr olds, 7ft. 5lb.
and four yr olds, 8ft. 7lb. Firft poft on the Flat, home,
heats. The winner with his engagements to be fold
for 150gs, if demanded, &c.

Mr. Kelly's b. c. Pilot, by Commodore, 3 yrs
old, 7ft. 6lb. .... I I
Mr. Whaley's ch. c. Little Harry, 4 yrs, 8ft. 9lb. 3 2
Mr. Edwards's b. c. by Auguftus, 3 yrs old,
7ft. 2lb............................ ... 2 3
Col. Lumm's b. c. by Moorcock, 3 yrs, 7ft. 2lb. 5 dr
Mr. Daly's ch. c. Tom, 4 yrs old, 8ft. 3lb. (re-
fufed to ftart the fecond heat)........... 4 dis
Mr. Batterfby's ch. f. Patty 4 yrs old, 8ft. 6lb. dis

The winner was claimed.

Wednefday 16th, 50gs, for five yr olds, 8ft. fix yr
olds and aged, 8ft. 7lb. Red Poft, heats. The winner with his engagements to be fold as on Tuefday,
&c. &c.

Mr. Whaley's b. m. Stella, by Star, 5 yrs old,
7ft. 8lb. .... I I
Ld Belmore's b. h. Lambinos, aged, 8ft. 9lb . 3 2
Mr. Bateman's b. h. Inftructor, 5 yrs, 7ft. 11lb. 4 3
Mr. Daly's ch. h. Cockatoo, 5 yrs, 7ft. 10lb. 2 4
Mr. Gore's b. m. Proferpine, aged, 8ft. 7lb. and Mr.
Hamilton's b. h. Babe, 5 yrs old, 8ft. 6lb. alfo
ftarted, but the Judge could place only the firft four.

Mr. Edwards's ch. c. Efcape, by Commodore,
3 yrs old, 8ft. beat Col. Lumm's b. c. Sir Walter,
4 yrs old, 6ft. 13lb. Red Poft, the challenge in the
Kirwan Stakes, roogs each, and the 10gs forfeits.

Thurfday 17th, 50gs, for three yr olds, 6ft. 4lb.
four yr olds, 7ft. 6lb five yr olds, 8ft. 2lb. fix yr olds
and aged, 8ft. 7lb. Hamilton Courfe.

Ld Belmore's ch. h. Traveller, by Chanticleer,
aged, 8ft. 13lb............................ 1
Mr. Hamilton's b. h. William, aged, 8ft. 11lb.
(broke down) 2
Mr. Daly's ch. c Erin, 3 yrs old, 6ft. 10lb...... 3
Mr. Whaley's ch. c. Little Harry, 4 yrs, 7ft. 8lb. 4

Fifty

Fifty Guineas, for two yr olds, 8ft. each, Two yr old Courfe.

Mr. Hamilton's b. f. Noony, by Swindler...... 1
Mr. Daly's b. c. by Cornet.................... 2
Mr. Caldwell's b. c. by Cornet........... 3
Mr. Gore's br. c. by Mock 4

Friday 18th, 50gs Handicap Plate, Firft poft on the Flat, home, heats.

Mr. Whaley's gr. f. Nanny, 3 yrs, 6ft.2lb.   4 1 1
Ld Belmore's ch. h.Traveller, aged, 9ft.7lb. 1 2 2
Mr. Daly's gr. c. Cockfure, 3 yrs, 6ft. 10lb. 3 3 3
Mr. Batterfby's b. h. Jerry, aged, 8ft. 7lb. 5 5 4
Col. Lumm's b.c. Sir Walter, 4 yrs, 7ft.5lb. 2 4 dis

Sweepftakes of 25gs each, Conolly's Mile.

Ld Belmore's f. Pigmy, by Commodore, 8ft...... 1
Mr. Batterfby's c. Recruit, by Soldier, out of Crazy Jane, 8ft. 3lb....................... 2
Mr. Whaley's f. by Bacchus, out of Abbot's dam, 8ft.............. 3

Ld Belmore's b. h. Lambinos, aged, 8ft. 5lb. beat Mr. Whaley's b. m. Stella, 5 yrs old, 7ft. 13lb. Red Poft, 25gs.

Saturday 19th, the Grinder Stakes (renewed for three years) 20gs, h. ft. Red Poft, heats; four yr olds, 12ft. five yr olds, 13ft. fix yr olds and aged, 13ft. 7lb.—5lb. to mares. No horfe to run who has won 50l. in Plate, Prize, or Sweepftakes, except the winner of this Stakes, who muft carry 7lb. extra. for every time he wins it; to be rode by Members of Daly's, Sackville-ftreet, Kildare-ftreet, or Turf-club.

Mr. Gore's ch. f. Mrs. Leigh, 4 yrs old. .. 1 1
Mr. Graydon's gr. g. aged..... .... 2 2
Mr. Daly's ch. h. 5 yrs old .... dis

Mr. Hamilton's Fitz-Emily, 9ft. beat Mr. Caldwell's Tom Pipes, 7ft. 12lb. Red Poft, 200gs, h. ft.

A LIST

OF

WINNING HORSES,

IN

Ireland,

IN THE YEAR 1805.

Years Old.	GOT BY BOXER.	No. of Prizes.

5 PADDY-OATS, Mr. Caldwell's, 25l. at Ennifkillen........................... 1

BY CHANTICLEER.

5 Fitz-Emily, Mr. Hamilton's, two of the King's Plates, the Lord Lieutenant's Plate, 75gs, the Cup with 200gs, the Kirwan Stakes, and 200gs, at the Curragh, two of the King's Plates and 60gs, Royal Corporation .,...... 10

3 Cockfure, Mr. Daly's, 30gs and 25gs at the Curragh, and 50l. at Loughrea 3

8 Tra-

8 Traveller, Ld Belmore's, 50l. at Roſcommon, 50l. and 60l. at Tuam, and 50gs at the Curragh 4

BY CHOCOLATE.

9 Jerry Sneak, Mr. Batterſby's, 50gs and 100gs at the Curragh, 50l. at Limerick, 50l. and 25l. at Enniſkillen 5

BY COMMODORE.

3 Eſcape, Mr. Edwards's, the Kildare Stakes, the Lumm Stakes, one of the King's Plates, the Kirwan Stakes, and the Challenge of ditto, at the Curragh.... 5

4 Louiſa, Mr. Whaley's, one of the King's Plates at the Curragh................... 1

4 Tom Pipes, Capt. Caldwell's, two of the King's Plates and 25gs at the Curragh, two fifties at Roſcommon, 45gs at Tuam, two fifties and 200gs at Loughrea 9

3 Captain, Mr. Hawkes's, 70gs and 30gs at the Curragh, and 50l. at Tuam.............. 3

3 Pilot, Mr. Kelly's, 55gs at Drogheda, and 50gs at the Curragh 2

4 Midſhipman, Mr. Kelly's, 60gs at Drogheda 1

3 Erin, Mr. Daly's, 140gs, 75gs, and 100gs, at the Curragh 3

3 Ch. f. Mr. Kelly's, 50gs at the Curragh.. . 1

3 Nanny, Mr. Whaley's, 50gs and 50gs at the Curragh 2

2 Pigmy, Ld Belmore's, 50gs at the Curragh,. 1

BY CORNET.

4 F. Capt. Caldwell's, 30gs at the Curragh,.... 1
2 B. c. Mr. Daly's, 110gs at the Curragh...... 1
3 Menody, Capt. Caldwell's, 10gs at the Curragh 1

BY DECEIVER.

6 Blacklegs, Mr. Hawkes's, a compromife, three of the King's Plates, 100gs, 100gs, 50gs, and 100gs, at the Curragh, and 50l. at Rofcommon 9

BY DRONE.

3 B. e. Mr. Kirwan's, 50gs at the Curragh..., 1
5 Chanter, Col. Daly's, 50l. at Tuam, and two fifties at Loughrea 3

BY DUNGANNON.

7 Curbs, Ld Donegall's, 30gs and 40gs Royal Corporation.... :................. 2

BY GROUSE.

8 Firft Fruits, Mr. Hunter's, 50l. at Charleville, three fifties at Mallow, two fifties at Ennis, two fifties at Rathkeal, and 50l. at Tralee.. 9

BY HERO.

4 Juliet, Col. A. Daly's, 50gs at Ennis 1

BY HONEST TOM.

3 Cockahoop, Col. Lumm's, 20gs at the Curragh 1

BY LAMBINOS.

8 Lambinos, Ld Belmore's, 50gs and 25gs at the Curragh............... 2

BY MARQUIS.

3 Abbot, Ld Donegall's, 60gs, 50gs, 30gs, and 30gs, Royal Corporation 4

BY MASTER BAGOT.

7 Sweet Robin, Col. A. Daly's, 50l. at Charleville 1

4 Little Harry, Mr. Whaley's, a compromise at the Curragh 1

BY PREMIER.

6 Duke, Mr. Joyce's, 35gs Royal Corporation 1

BY SIR PETER TEAZLE.

4 Pandora, Mr. Hunter's, 50gs at the Curragh, and 175gs at Tuam...... 2

BY STAR.

5 Stella, Mr. Whaley's, 50gs at the Curragh . 1

BY SWINDLER.

5 Babe, Mr. Hamilton's, 55gs and 55gs at Drogheda, and the Dillon Stakes at Roscommon 3

2 B. f. Mr. Hamilton's, the Tit Stakes at the Curragh 1

2 Noony, Mr. Hamilton's, the Long Stakes and 50gs at the Curragh 2

BY TUG.

7 Anchor, Mr. Dennis's, 60l. at Tralee........ 1

7 Sweetwilliam, Mr. Hamilton's, one of the King's Plates and 50gs at the Curragh...... 2

6 Proserpine, Mr. Gore's, one of the King's Plates at the Curragh.... 1

4 Patty, Mr. Battersby's, 25gs at the Curragh, and 50l. at Enniskillen 2

BY

BY TURNIP.

4 Superior, Mr. Croker's, 50l. at Charleville, 50l. at Mallow, two fifties at Rathkeal, two fifties at Tralee, and three fifties at Limerick   9

BY VESPER.

6 B. g. Mr. Pottinger's, 35gs Royal Corporation 1

BY WAXY.

4 Sir Walter Raleigh, Col. Lumm's, 50gs at the Curragh 1

Jug, Mr. Blennerhassett's, 100gs at the Curragh 1

4 Mrs. Leigh, Mr. Gore's, the Grinder Stakes at the Curragh........................... 1

COCKING,

1805.

CHESTER.

DURING the Race-week a Main was fought between Sir Peter Warburton, Bart. and Sir Windfor Hunloke, Bart. which was won by the former, as follows :

Cheshire.			*Derbyshire.*		
	M.	B.		M.	B.
Monday........	3	2	....	2	0
Tuesday	4	1	....	1	1
Wednesday....	1	0	....	5	1
Thursday......	3	1	....	2	1
Friday........	3	1	....	3	1
	14	5		13	4

N. B. There was a drawn battle in the Main on Thursday.

YORK

During the Spring Meeting, a Long Main was fought between Sir F. Boynton, Bart. (Thompson, feeder)

feeder) and H. F. Mellifh, Efq. (Sunley, feeder) which was won by the former, as follows:

	Sir F. Boynton.				Mr. Mellifh.	
	M.	B.			M.	B.
Monday	3	2	....		3	1
Tuefday	5	2	....		1	1
Wednefday ...	2	2	....		4	1
Thurfday	3	2	....		3	1
Friday	3	1	....		3	2
Saturday	3	2	....		3	2
	19	11			17	8

NEWTON.

During the Races, a Main was fought between the Earl of Derby (Goodill, feeder) and Richard Crofs, Efq. (Gilliver, feeder) for 10gs a battle, and 200gs the Main, which was won by the latter, as follows:

	Ld Derby.				Mr. Croffe.	
	M.	B.			M.	B.
Tuefday	3	0	....		5	1
Wednefday ...	5	1	....		3	0
Thurfday	6	1	....		8	1
Friday	2	0	....		6	1
	16	2			22	3

MANCHESTER.

During the Race week, a Main was fought between Sir W. Hunloke, Bart. (Harrifon, feeder) and R. G. Hopwood, Efq. (Potter, feeder) for 10gs a battle, and 100gs the Main, which was won by the latter, two a-head.

NEW-

NEWCASTLE-UPON-TYNE.

The Main fought during the Races, between Charles Brandling, Efq. (Sunley, feeder) and H. F Mellifh, Efq (Small, feeder) for 20gs a battle, and 1000gs the Main, was won by the latter, one a-head. Byes, eight each.

MORPETH.

On the 2d, 3d, and 4th of July, was fought a Main between C. Brandling, Efq. (Sunley, feeder) and Rob. Storey, Efq. (Small, feeder) which was won by the latter, 14 to 9.

PRESTON.

During the week of the Races, a Main was fought between the Earl of Derby (Goodill, feeder) and Richard Croffe, Efq. (Gilliver, feeder) for 10gs a battle, and 200gs the Main, which was won by the latter, as follows :

	Ld Derby.			Mr. Croffe.		
	M	B.			M.	B.
Monday	6	4	....		7	1
Tuefday	4	0	....		3	1
Wednefday ...	3	1	....		4	0
Thurfday	3	0	....		4	1
	16	5			18	3

RACES.

RACES TO COME.

NEWMARKET

Craven Meeting, 1806.

MONDAY, April 7th.

THE Craven Stakes, a Subfcription of 10gs each, for all ages; two yr olds carrying 6ft. three yr olds, 8ft. four olds, 8ft. 9lb. five yr olds, 9ft. 1lb. fix yr olds, 9ft. 5lb. and aged, 9ft. 7lb. Acrofs the Flat.

This Subfcription to clofe on the Thurfday before running, and the horfes to be entered on the Saturday before running, between eleven and one o'clock, at the King's ftables, Newmarket.

Subfcriptions received at the Coffee-houfe, Newmarket; at No. 7, Oxenden-ftreet; and at Mr. Tatterfall's. Horfes, &c. which have never run at Newmarket, muft be fhewn at the time of entrance.

Sweepftakes of 100gs each, h. ft. for colts, 8ft. 4lb. fillies, 8ft. 1lb. rifing three yrs old, Acrofs the Flat.

Mr. Wilfon's b. c. by Hambletonian, out of Surprize's dam

Mr. Wilfon's brother to Merryman

Ld Sackville's b. c. by Buzzard, out of Offian's dam

Mr. Panton's brother to Dilettante

Gen.

Gen. Grofvenor's b. c. by Hambletonian, bought of Sir J. Eden

Gen. Grofvenor's ch. c. by Gouty, out of a fifter to Mother Bunch

Ld G. H. Cavendifh's b. c. by Worthy, out of Mrs. Candour

Mr. Waftell's brother to Lumbago

Sir C. Bunbury's b. c. by Whifkey, dam by Diomed, out of Trombone's dam

Sir C. Bunbury's ch. c. brother to Eleanor

Mr. D. Radcliffe's ch. c. by Beningbrough, out of Dick Andrews's dam

D. of Grafton's c. by Worthy, out of Prunella

Sir F. Standifh's brother to Stamford

Mr. Lake's c. by Gouty, out of a fifter to Oatlands

Mr. H. F. Mellifh's b. c. Luck's-all, by Stamford, out of Marchionefs

Mr. H. F. Mellifh's b. f. Off-fhe-goes, by Shuttle, dam by Highflyer, out of Dido

Ld Grofvenor's b. c. by John Bull, out of Tulip

Ld Grofvenor's b. c. by John Bull, out of Cælia

Sweepftakes of 100gs each, for colts and fillies warranted untried, 17th of April, 1805; colts carrying 8ft. 5lb. fillies, 8ft. 1lb. Ab. Mile, rifing three yrs old.

Ld Foley's c. by Zachariah, dam by Fortitude, bought of Mr. Buckle

Ld Darlington's b. c. by Sir Peter, dam by Paymafter

Ld G. H. Cavendifh's f. by Coriander, out of Fairy

Mr. Sitwell's c. Clafher, by Sir Peter, out of Hyale

Ld F. G. Ofborne's ch. c. Superftition, by Buzzard, out of Vixen

Mr. Howorth's f. by Coriander, out of Mifs Green

D. of Grafton's Parafol, 8ft. 5lb. agft Ld Foley's Hippocampus, 8ft. B. C. 200gs, h. ft.

Sir H. T. Vane's Mafter Betty agft Ld Foley's Hippoeampus, 8ft. 7lb. each, B. C. 1000gs, h. ft.

D. of Grafton's Peliſſe, 8ft. 10lb. agſt Ld Foley's Little Peter, 8ft. D. I. 200gs.

Ld Darlington's c. by Sir Peter, dam by Paymaſter, agſt Mr. Sitwell's Claſher, by Sir Peter, Ab. Mile, 100gs, 25gs ft.—(No weights mentioned.)

Ld Grosvenor's Meteora agſt Ld Barrymore's Gratitude, 8ft. each, Ab. Mile, 200gs, h. ft.

Mr. Melliſh's Staveley, 8ft. 7lb. agſt Mr. R. Boyce's Brainworm, 7ft. 12lb. Ab. Mile, 100gs.

Mr. F. Neale's br. h. Meagrums, by Boxer, out of a Snap mare, bought of Mr. Harris, agſt Mr. Abbey's b. h. Brown Stout, bought of Mr. Tuting, got by Calomel, out of a Metaphyſician mare, called Chambermaid, for 25gs, h. ft. owners are to ride; Mr. Neale is to ride 7lb. under Mr. Abbey's weight. To ſtart at Two yr old Courſe, and run half a mile, croſſing and joſtling.

The firſt Claſs of the Oatlands Stakes of 50gs each, h. ft. D. I.

	AGES.	ft. lb.
Ld Foley's Sir Harry Dimſdale....	5 yrs	9 6
Sir J. Shelley's Houghton Laſs.. ..	4 yrs	8 8
Mr. Ladbroke's Proſpero.........	4 yrs	8 6
Mr. Melliſh's Quid....	4 yrs	8 5
Ld Grosvenor's Goth	3 yrs	8 3
Mr. Jones's Junius	3 yrs	7 8
Mr. Andrew's Fathom	3 yrs	6 11
Mr. Frogley's ch. f. by a ſon of Cignet....................	3 yrs	6 6

TUESDAY.

Sweepſtakes of 100gs each, h. ft. for the produce of untried mares covered in 1802 by untried ſtallions; colts, 8ft. 3lb. and fillies, 8ft. Acroſs the Flat.

Mr. Hallett's f. by Stickler, out of Quiz

Mr.

- Mr. Wilfon's f. by Worthy, out of Comedy
Mr. Lake's f. by Gouty, out of Mademoifelle

Ld Grofvenor's br. c. by Sir Peter, out of Cælia, agft Mr. Elwes's b. c. by Buzzard, dam by Highflyer, out of a Goldfinder mare, 8ft. 7lb. each, D. I. 200gs, h. ft.

Ld F. G. Ofborne's ch. c. Superftition, by Buzzard, out of Vixen, agft Gen. Grofvenor's Richard, by His Lordfhip, out of Nelly, 8ft. 2lb. each, R. M. 200gs, h. ft.

D. of Grafton's b. f. Merrythought, by Totteridge, out of Woodbine, agft Mr. Craven's br f. Bronze, fifter to Caftrel, 8ft. 3lb. each, R. M. 200gs, h. ft.

Ld Sackville's Witchcraft, 8ft. 4lb. agft Mr. Mellifh's Quid, 8ft. B. C. 200gs.

Mr. Watfon's f. (dead) by Sir Peter Teazle, out of Gaoler's dam, 8ft. 4lb. agft Mr. Whaley's b. c. by His Lordfhip, out of Nelly, 8ft. 3lb. D. M. 200gs, h. ft.

The fecond Clafs of the Oatlands Stakes of 50gs each, h. ft. D. I.

	AGES.	ft. lb.
Mr. Watfon's Duxbury	6 yrs	8 10
Mr. Mellifh's Staveley	3 yrs	8 8
Mr. Lake's Watery..............	4 yrs	8 2
Sir J. Shelley's Sir Launcelot... ..	3 yrs	8 2
Gen. Gower's Swinley	3 yrs	7 12
Mr. B. Craven's br. c. Henry, by Overton, bought of Mr. Riddell..	3 yrs	7 5
Mr. Howorth's Scrip.............	3 yrs	6 9
Mr. Biggs's Margaretta	3 yrs	6 7

WEDNESDAY.

The third Clafs of the Oatlands Stakes of 50gs each, h. ft. D. I.

S 2

Mr.

	AGES.	ft.	lb.
Mr. F. Neale's Quiz.	aged	9	4
Sir H. Vane's Master Betty	4 yrs	8	11
Mr. Lake's Giles	aged	8	10
Mr. W. Fenwick's Mifs Coiner ...	4 yrs	8	4
Mr. Watfon's Yorkshire, brother to Witchcraft	3 yrs	7	10
Sir J. Shelley's Mouftache	3 yrs	7	9
Mr Frogley's b. c Triptolemus ...	4 yrs	7	5
Mr. Smith's b. c. Prodigal, bought of Mr. Howorth	3 yrs	6	11

The following having declared forfeit within the time prefcribed, are to pay only 10gs each, to be divided between the owners of the fecond horfes.

	AGES.	ft.	lb.
Mr. F. Neale's Trombone........	aged	8	12
Ld Grofvenor's Meteora	3 yrs	8	7
Mr. Ladbroke's c. by Pipator, bought of Mr. Hutchinfon	4 yrs	8	3
Mr. W. Fenwick's b. g. Eunuch..	4 yrs	8	6
Ld Grofvenor's Iris..............	3 yrs	7	9
Mr. Kellermann's Heeltap........	4 yrs	7	5
Mr. Elwes's Chriftopher..........	3 yrs	7	4
Ld F. G. Ofborne's br. c. by Overton	3 yrs	6	12
Ld Stawell's Gloriana............	3 yrs	6	9

Poft Sweepftakes of 200gs each, h. ft. colts, 8ft. 3lb. fillies, 8ft. D. M. rifing three yrs old.

Ld Grofvenor's three colts, by John Bull, out of Tulip, Cælia, and Ifabella

Mr. Sitwell's c. Clafher, by Sir Peter, out of Hyale; Pipylina, fifter to Pipylin; or his c. Cocolobo, by Moorcock, out of St. George's dam

Mr. Watfon's f. by Sir Peter, out of Dreadnought's dam; c. by Sir Peter, out of Doubtful; or his f. by Sir Peter, out of Faunus's dam

Gen.

Gen. Grofvenor's br. c. by Hambletonian, dam by Sir Peter, bought of Sir J. Eden, agft Ld Sackville's b. c. by Buzzard, out of Offian's dam, 8ft. 7lb. each, Ab. Mile, 100gs, h. ft.

Mr. Tolley's Foreft Lady, 7ft. 11lb. agft Mr. Emden's Poll Thompfon, 6ft. 7lb. B. C. 70gs, h. ft.

THURSDAY.

Mr. Cave Browne's c. Mountaineer, by Magic, out of Amelia, agft Mr. Andrew's Fathom, 8ft. 2lb. each, D. I. 200gs, h. ft.

Mr. R. Boyce's Sir David, 8ft. 7lb. agft Sir J. Shelley's Sir Launcelot, 7ft. 11lb. D. I. 200gs.

First Spring Meeting, 1806.

MONDAY, April 21ft.

SWEEPSTAKES of 100gs each, h. ft. for the produce of mares covered in 1802; colts carrying 8ft. 4lb. and fillies, 8ft. Acrofs the Flat.

Sir F. Standifh's b. f. by Sir Peter, or Mr. Teazle, out of Eagle's dam
Sir F. Standifh's br. c. by Sir Peter, out of Horatia
Mr. Watfon's b. c. by Sir Peter, out of Doubtful
Mr. Whaley's b. c. by His Lordfhip, out of Nelly
Sir C. Bunbury's ch. c. by Whifkey, out of Giantefs
Ld Grofvenor's ch. c. by John Bull, out of Ifabella
Ld Grofvenor's ch. f. by John Bull, out of Mifseltoe
Mr. Coventry's b. f. by Buzzard, out of Neriffa
Mr. Lake's b. c. by Gouty, out of a fifter to Oatlands

The firft Clafs of the Prince's Stakes of 100gs each, h. ft. colts carrying 8ft. 7lb. and fillies, 8ft. 4lb. Acrofs the Flat, rifing three yrs old.

S 3

Mr.

Mr. Panton names Gen. Grofvenor's br. c. Have-at-
'em, by Hambletonian, dam by Sir Peter, out of
Windleftone's dam

Mr. Wilfon's b. c. by Coriander, dam by Highflyer,
out of Sincerity

Mr. Watfon names the D. of Grafton's c. by Whifkey,
out of Sea-fowl

Ld Grofvenor's b. c. by John Bull, out of Popinjay's
dam

Mr. Glover did not name

Sweepftakes of 100gs each, h. ft. Ab. M. 8ft. 2lb.
each.

Mr. Lake's b. f. Romance, by Gouty, out of Mademoifelle

Mr. Sitwell's b. f. by Moorcock, out of Palmflower

Mr. H. F. Mellifh's b. f. Flighty, by Traveller, out of
a fifter to Fidget

Sweepftakes of 100gs each, Two middle miles B. C.

	ft.	lb.
Mr. Mellifh's Quid	8	8
Ld Darlington's Zodiac	8	7
Ld Barrymore's Gratitude	7	7

Sweepftakes of 100gs each, h. ft. for colts and fillies unbacked at the time of naming (May 4th, 1805)
colts, 8ft. 3lb. fillies, 8ft. R. M.

Ld Grofvenor's b. c. by John Bull, out of Tulip
Gen. Gower's b. c. by Buzzard, out of Marcella
Mr. Watfon's b. c. by Worthy, out of Mrs. Candour
Ld Foley's b. c. by Zachariah, bought of Mr. Buckle

Sweepftakes of 200gs each, h. ft. B. C.

Sir H. Williamfon's Walton ⎫
D. of Grafton's Parafol...... ⎬ 8ft. 7lb. each.
Ld Foley's Hippocampus... ⎭

Mr.

Mr. Biggs's ch. c. brother to Phœnix, agft Mr. D. Radcliffe's c. by Gohanna, out of Trumpetta, 8ft. each, Acrofs the Flat, 100gs, h. ft.

Mr. Sitwell's c. by Moorcock, out of St. George's dam, agft Mr. Mellifh's b. c. Companion, by Beningbrough, dam by Lurcher, 8ft. 1lb. each, Acrofs the Flat, 200gs, h. ft.

Mr. Cave Browne's b. c. by Magic, bought of Sir C. Bunbury, agft Mr. Sitwell's Goofecap, 8ft. each, D. I. 100gs, h. ft.

Mr. Mellifh's Staveley, 8ft. agft Sir J. Shelley's Mouftache, 7ft. D. I. 200gs.

TUESDAY.

The Claret Stakes of 200gs each, h. ft. for colts carrying 8ft. 7lb. and fillies, 8ft. 2lb. D. I. rifing three yrs old. The owner of the fecond horfe to receive back his ftake.

Ld F. G. Ofborne's Don Felix, brother to Hippocampus

Mr. Smith's Hippomenes

Col. Childers's Langton

Mr. Wardell's b. c. by Pipator, dam by Drone, bought of Sir J. Lawfon

Ld Grofvenor's b. c. Plantagenet, by John Bull, out of Tulip

Ld Foley's Little Peter

Gen. Grofvenor's Richard, agft Mr. Howorth's Courtier, by John Bull, out of a fifter to Skyfcraper, 8ft. each, Ab. M. 200gs, h. ft.

WEDNESDAY.

The third and laft year of the Newmarket Stakes of 50gs each, h. ft. for colts, 8ft. 7lb. fillies, 8ft. 2lb. D. M. rifing three yrs old.

D. of

D. of Grafton's c. by Worthy, out of Prunella

D. of Grafton's c. Trafalgar, by Whiſkey, out of Seafowl

Sir C. Bunbury's b. f. ſiſter to Orlando

Sir C. Bunbury's b. f. by Whiſkey, out of Orange-bud

Mr. Wilſon's br. c. by Sir Peter, out of a ſiſter to Peter Pindar

Mr. Wilſon's brother to Merryman

Mr. Waſtell's own brother to Lumbago

Mr. Lockley's b. f. Princeſs Royal, by Teleſcope, out of Queen Charlotte

Ld Darlington's b. c. by Sir Peter, dam by Paymaſter, out of Pomona

Mr. F. Neale names Mr. Ladbroke's ch. c. by Young Woodpecker, out of Platina

Mr. Norton names Mr. Dawſon's b. f. by Coriander, out of Fairy

Mr. Watſon names Mr. Elton's c. by Worthy, out of a ſiſter to Barnaby

Ld Groſvenor's b. c. by John Bull, out of Cælia

Ld Groſvenor's b. c. by John Bull, out of Popinjay's dam

Sir F. Standiſh's f. by Sir Peter, or Mr. Teazle, out of Eagle's dam

Mr. Panton's ch. c. Amateur, brother Dilettante

Mr. Glover names Mr. Perren's ch. f. by Buzzard, out of Gipſy, by Trumpator

Ld Milſintown, and Mr. Whaley (who has two Subſcriptions) did not name.

The Port Stakes of 100gs each, h. ft. for colts and fillies, then riſing four yrs old, to run the Two middle miles; colts, 8ſt. 7lb. fillies, 8ſt. 4lb. The owner of the ſecond horſe to withdraw his Stake.

Gen. Gower's b. c. Swinley, by Coriander, out of Lady Mary

Mr. R. Jones's ch. c. Junius

Ld Groſvenor's b. f. Violantè

Ld

Ld Grofvenor's b. c. Goth
Mr. Biggs's ch. c. Baffanio
D. of Grafton's b. f. Dodona
Mr. Glover's ch. f. by Buzzard, out of Camilla.

Sweepftakes of 50gs each, h. ft. D. I.

	ft.	lb.
Mr. Mellifh's Lady Brough...	8	5
Mr. Ladbroke's Profpero......	8	1
Ld Foley's Czar Peter	8	0
Mr. W. Fenwick's Mifs Coiner	7	11

THURSDAY.

The fecond Clafs of the Prince's Stakes of 100gs each, h. ft. for colts carrying 8ft. 7lb. fillies, 8ft. 4lb. Acrofs the Flat; rifing three yrs old.

Mr. Panton's c. by Whifkey, dam by Pot8o's, out of Dutchefs
Sir C. Bunbury's ch. c. by Whifkey, dam by Diomed, out of Trombone's dam
D. of Grafton's brother to Hornby Lafs
Ld Grofvenor's b. c. by John Bull, out of Cælia
Mr. Whaley did not name.

Gen. Gower's b. f. Sprite, by Buzzard, out of Sylph, by Saltram, agft Mr. Sitwell's f. Ofier, by Moorcock, out of Palmflower, 8ft. each, Acrofs the Flat, 100gs, h. ft.

Sweepftakes of 50gs each, h. ft. Two yr old Courfe.

	ft.	lb.
Mr. Mellifh's Staveley	8	12
Sir C. Bunbury's Lydia...................	8	8
Mr. Ladbroke's Wormwood...	8	1
Mr. Delmè Radcliffe's Pedeftrian...........	7	10
Gen. L. Gower's Swinley...	7	7
Ld F. G. Ofborne's Don Felix........, ...	7	5
Mr. Bartley's Hippomenes .. ..:	7	3

Ld

ft. lb.

Ld Grofvenor's Iris 7   3
Mr. Elwes's Chriftopher 7   0
Mr. Wilfon's Newmarket........ 7   0

FRIDAY.

Mr. R. Boyce's Sir David, 8ft. 9lb. agft Ld Grofvenor's Plantagenet, 8ft. Acrofs the Flat, 200gs, h. ft.

Second Spring Meeting, 1806.

MONDAY, May 5th.

MR. Cave Browne's c. Mountaineer, by Magic, agft
Ld F. G. Ofborne's Don Felix, brother to Hippocampus, 8ft. 2lb. each, D. I. 200gs, h. ft.

Ld Grofvenor's Plantagenet, 8ft. 7lb. agft Ld Foley's
Little Peter, 7ft. 13½lb. from the Starting Poft of the
T. M. M. to the End of the Flat, 200gs.

Mr. Mellifh's Staveley, 4 yrs old, agft Mr. R.
Boyce's Sir David, 5 yrs old, 8ft. each, Ab. M. 200gs.

TUESDAY.

Ld F. G. Ofborne's Superftition, by Buzzard, out
of Vixen, agft Mr. Panton's Tamburro, by Whifkey,
out of Tamborine, R. M. 100gs, h. ft. (no weights
mentioned.)

THURSDAY.

Sweepftakes of 50gs each, h. ft. B. C.   ft. lb.

Ld Foley's Sir Harry Dimfdale 9   3
Mr. F. Neale's Quiz 8   13
Mr. Delmè Radcliffe's Orville 8   7
Mr. Howorth's Norval 7   3

NO

NO DAY MENTIONED.

Mr. Craven's Frolick, aged, 9ft. 4lb. agft Mr. R. Jones's b. c. Freedom, by Buzzard, 6ft. Laft two miles of the B. C. 300gs, h. ft.

July Meeting, 1806.

MONDAY, JULY 7th.

FIRST year of a renewal of the July Stakes, a Subfcription of 50gs each, 30gs ft. for two yr old colts carrying 8ft. 6lb. fillies, 8ft. 4lb. Two yr old Courfe.

D. of Grafton's c. by Worthy, out of Hornby Lafs
Sir C. Bunbury's b. c. brother to Orlando
Mr. Wilfon's ch. f. by Buzzard, out of Totterella
Ld Stawell's f fifter to Ringtail
Mr. Panton's b. f fifter to Dilettante
Mr. Watfon's b. f. fifter to Merryman
Ld Clermont's c. by Trumpator, out of Beda, by Delpini
Mr. Mellifh's gr. c. Bedale
Sir F. Standifh's c. by Mr. Teazle, out of a fifter to Gouty, fold to Mr. Cholmondeley
Mr. Abbey's b. c. by Ambrofio, dam by Highflyer, grandam by Matchem, great grandam by Blank
Mr. Golding's b. f. by Buzzard, out of Vixen
Mr. R. Prince's b. c. by Stamford, out of Companion's dam

Ld Foley's Blowing agft Mr. R. Boyce's Wretch, 8ft. each, Ab. M. 200gs.

TUES-

TUESDAY.

July Three yr old Stakes of 100gs each, h. ft. for colts carrying 8ft. 7lb. and fillies, 8ft. 3lb. Across the Flat.

D. of Grafton's br. c. by Grouse, out of Rattle
Mr. Watson's c. by Sir Peter, out of Doubtful
Ld Grosvenor's b. c. by John Bull, out of Popinjay's dam
Ld Grosvenor's ch. c. by John Bull, out of Isabella
Sir C. Bunbury's b. f. sister to Orlando

Sweepstakes of 10gs each, for three yr olds carrying 6ft. 9lb. four yr olds, 8ft. 1lb. five yr olds, 8ft 10lb. six yr olds, 9ft. and aged, 9ft. 2lb. the Two middle miles. The winner to be sold for 300gs, if demanded, &c.

The horses to be named at the Coffee-house, before dinner, on the day before running. To continue in the year, 1807.

SUBSCRIBERS.

Mr. Wilson	Mr. Watson
D. of Grafton	Ld G. H. Cavendish
Mr. Howorth	Ld F G. Osborne
Sir C Bunbury	Mr. Lake
Gen. Grosvenor	Ld Grosvenor
Mr. Elwes	

First October Meeting, 1806.

MONDAY, 29th SEPTEMBER.

THE second year of a renewal of the Subscription of 5gs each, for four yr olds carrying 7ft. 7lb. five yr olds, 8ft. 6lb. six yr olds, 8ft. 13lb. and aged, 9ft 2lb. B. C. To be the property of a Subscriber, or pay 50gs entrance.

To

The horſes, &c. to be entered at the King's ſtables, Newmarket, on the Saturday before running, between eleven and one o'clock, with proper certificates.— To continue in 1807.

SUBSCRIBERS.

Sir C. Bunbury	Mr. Melliſh
Mr. Wilſon	Mr. Ladbroke
Sir F. Standiſh	Mr. Watſon
Ld Sackville	Mr. Norton
Ld G. H. Cavendiſh	Mr. R. Boyce
D. of Grafton	Mr. J. Browne
Ld Groſvenor	Mr. Elwes
Ld Stawell	Ld F. G. Oſborne
Mr. Delmè Radcliffe	Gen. L. Gower,
Sir H. Williamſon	Sir J. Shelley
Ld Foley	

Sweepſtakes of 100gs each, h. ft. for colts and fillies then three yrs old, Acroſs the Flat; colts carrying 8ſt. 7lb. fillies, 8ſt. 3lb.

Ld Groſvenor's ch. c. by John Bull, out of Iſabella
Ld Groſvenor's b. c. by John Bull, out of Tulip
Sir C. Bunbury's b. c. by Whiſkey, dam by Diomed, out of Trombone's dam
Sir C. Bunbury's b. f. ſiſter to Orlando
Mr. Wilſon's b. c. by Hambletonian, out of Surprize's dam
Mr. Watſon's b. c. by Worthy, out of Mrs. Candour
Sir F. Standiſh's brother to Stamford
D. of Grafton's b. c. by Worthy, out of Prunella
Mr. Elwes's br. c. by Sir Peter, out of a ſiſter to Peter Pindar

Ld Foley's Blowing agſt Mr. R. Boyce's Wretch, 8ſt. each, Ab. M. 200gs.

TUESDAY.

(Second year). One-third of a Subscription of
25gs each, for four yr old colts carrying 8ft. 7lb. and
fillies, 8ft. 4lb. D. I. The horses, &c. to be bona
fide the property of Subscribers.

To be entered at the King's stables, Newmarket,
on the day before running, between eleven and one
o'clock.

SUBSCRIBERS.

Sir C. Bunbury	Mr. Mellish
Mr. Wilson	Gen. L. Gower
Ld Sackville	Sir J. Shelley
D. of Grafton	Mr. Norton
Ld Grosvenor	Mr. Watson
Mr. Ladbroke	Ld F. G. Osborne
Ld Foley	Sir H. Williamson
Mr. Delmè Radcliffe	

WEDNESDAY.

One-third of a Subscription of 25gs each, for three
yr old colts carrying 8ft. 6lb. and fillies, 8ft. 3lb.
D. I. The horses, &c. to be bona fide the property
of Subscribers, and to be entered at the King's stables,
Newmarket, between eleven and one o'clock, on the
day before running.

Subscribers, the same as on Tuesday.

Mr. Panton's Tamburro, then 3 yrs old, 8ft. 7lb.
agst Ld F. G. Osborne's f. Sour Crout, then 2 yrs old,
7ft. Two yr old Course, 100gs, h. ft.

NO DAY MENTIONED.

Ld Sackville's b. c. by Buzzard, out of Offian's dam,
agst Mr. Elwes's ch. c. by Buzzard, out of Totterella,
8ft. 1lb. each, Across the Flat, 100gs, h. ft.

Second

Second October Meeting, 1806.

MONDAY, 13th October.

SECOND YEAR. One-third of a Subfcription of 25gs each, for five yr olds carrying 8ft. 5lb. fix yr olds, 8ft. 11lb. and aged, 9ft. B. C. The horfes, &c. to be bona fide the property of Subfcribers.

To be entered at the King's ftables, Newmarket, between eleven and one o'clock, on the Saturday before running.

Subfcribers, the fame as on Tuefday in the Firft October Meeting.

Mr. Mellifh's Sancho, 8ft. agft Mr. Delmè Radcliffe's Orville, 7ft. 7lb. Ab. M. 200gs.

Mr. R. Boyce's b. c. by Precipitate, out of Albatrofs's dam, agft Ld Stawell's brother to Ringtail, 8ft. 3lb. each, Ab. M. 100gs.

WEDNESDAY.

The firft year of a renewal of the October Oatlands Stakes, B. M. a Subfcription of 30gs each, 10gs ft. if declared by one o'clock on Tuefday, for three years, commencing in 1806. To be run for by horfes of all ages, two yr olds excepted. To be named at the Coffee-houfe, by and the weights to be fixed by the Stewards or whom they fhall appoint, by half an hour after twelve o'clock on Tuefday. If there fhould be 10 Subfcribers or more after the 10gs forfeits are declared, the Stakes are to be divided, and two Claffes to be formed, and drawn after the manner of the Prince's Stakes; the fecond Clafs to be run for on the Thurfday in the fame Meeting, R. M. If 25 Subfcribers or more,

T 2   after

after the 10gs forfeits are declared, a third Clafs is to be formed, and the horfes in it are to run on the Friday, Ditch Mile.

To clofe at the end of the Second Spring Meeting, 1806.

PRESENT SUBSCRIBERS.

Sir C. Bunbury Mr. Wyndham
Ld G. H. Cavendifh Mr. Watfon
Mr. Wilfon Mr. Delmè Radcliffe
Mr. Ladbroke Ld F. G. Ofborne
Mr. Mellifh Ld Grofvenor
Gen. L. Gower Mr. Howorth
Ld Barrymore Mr. Lake
Ld Foley D. of Grafton

Houghton Meeting, 1806.

MONDAY, 27th October.

MR. R. Boyce's Wretch, 8ft. 3lb. agft Mr. Mellifh's Off-fhe-goes, 8ft. Ab. M. 200gs.

Ld Darlington's Pavilion, 5 yrs old, agft Mr. Mellifh's Staveley, 4 yrs old, 8ft. each, Ab. M. 500gs.

Craven Meeting, 1807.

MONDAY;

SWEEPSTAKES of 100gs each, h. ft. 8ft. 2lb. each, R. M.

D. of St. Albans's f. by Coriander, out of Fairy
D. of Grafton's f. by Groufe, out of Rattle
Sir J. Shelley's f. Wood Nymph, by Trumpator, bought of Ld Clermont

Sweep.

Sweepstakes of 150gs each, h. ft. colts, 8ft. 3lb. and fillies, 8ft. Across the Flat.

Ld Grosvenor's b. c. by Sir Peter, out of Lady Bull
Mr. Sitwell's ch. f. by Beningbrough, out of Hyale
Mr. Watson's b f. by Sir Peter, dam by Dungannon, out of Rutland's dam

Ld Grosvenor's br. f. by Sir Peter, out of Olivia, agst Mr. Watson's b. f. by Sir Peter, out of Doubtful, 8ft. each, Across the Flat, 150gs, h. ft.

Ld Grosvenor's b. f. by Sir Peter, out of Misseltoe, agst Mr. Sitwell's br. b. f. by Sir Peter, out of Palm-flower, 8ft. each, Across the Flat, 150gs, h. ft.

TUESDAY.

Sweepstakes of 100gs each, h. ft. colts carrying 8ft. 4lb. and fillies, 8ft. Across the Flat.

Mr. Watson's b. f. by Sir Peter, out of Doubtful
Ld Grosvenor's br. f. by Sir Peter, out of Olivia
Ld Grosvenor's b. f. by Sir Peter, out of Misseltoe
D. of Grafton's c. by Whiskey, out of Prunella

Sweepstakes of 100gs each, h. ft. for colts carrying 8ft. 5lb. and fillies, 8ft. 2lb. R. M. then rising three yrs old.

Ld Grosvenor's br. c. by Sir Peter, out of Cælia
Ld Grosvenor's b. c. by Sir Peter, out of Ibis
Mr. Wilson's b. c. by Sir Solomon, out of Lignum's dam
Mr. Biggs's br. c. Rosario, by Ambrosio, out of Portia
Mr. Elwes's b. c. by Whiskey, out of a sister to Flintilla
D. of Grafton's own brother to Pelisse
Sir C. Bunbury's b. c. by Whiskey, out of Amelia
Sir F. Standish's brother to Duxbury

T 3   Gen.

Gen. Gower's ch. c. Gladiator, by Buzzard, out of a
fifter to Champion

Mr. Forth's b. f. by Whifkey, dam by Pot8o's, out of
Maid of all Work

Ld Grofvenor's fifter to Meteora, agft Ld F. G.
Ofborne's Sour Crout, by Beningbrough, out of Quid's
dam, 8ft. 2lb. each, Two yr old Courfe, 100gs, h. ft.

THURSDAY.

Ld Foley's br.c. Chaife and-one, by Whifkey, out of
Xenia, agft Mr. Biggs's br. c. Rofaiio, by Ambrofio,
out of Portia, 8ft. 5lb. each, Acrofs the Flat, 200gs,
h. ft.

Gen. Grofvenor's b. f. by Beningbrough, out of
Lady Jane, 8ft. 4lb. agft Ld F. G. Ofborne's Sour
Crout, 8ft. 1lb. R. M. 100gs, h. ft.

Mr. Mellifh's b. f. Darling, by Patriot, dam by
Highflyer, out of Tiffany, 8ft. 7lb. agft Sir J. Shel-
ley's br. f. Wood Nymph, by Trumpator, dam by
Highflyer, 8ft. Ab. M. 200gs, h. ft.

First Spring Meeting, 1807.

MONDAY.

RENEWAL of the Prince's Stakes, a Subfcription
of 100gs each, h. ft. for colts and fillies, then rifing
three yrs old; colts carrying 8ft. 7lb. fillies, 8ft. 4lb.
Acrofs the Flat. This Subfcription to continue on the
fame conditions in the years 1808-9, and to name in
the July Meeting, when yearlings.

Ld Grofvenor's b. c. by Sir Peter, out of Ibis
D. of Grafton's c. by Worthy, out of Woodbine
Gen. Gower's br. f. Marcellina, by Worthy, out of
Marcella

Mr.

Mr. Mellish's ch. c. Harry-long-legs, by Bening-
brough, out of the dam of Off-she-goes
Mr. Mellish's b. f. Darling, by Patriot, dam by High-
flyer, out of Tiffany
Mr. Mellish's b. f. Miss Buckle, by Precipitate, out of
Plaistow's dam

TUESDAY.

Mr. Northey's c. by Lop, out of Jockey's dam,
8ft. 4lb. agst Sir J. Shelley's f. by Trumpator, dam by
Highflyer, out of Othëa, 8ft. D. I. 200gs, h. ft.

WEDNESDAY.

Renewal of the Newmarket Stakes of 50gs each,
h. ft. for colts and fillies then rising three yrs old; colts
carrying 8ft. 7lb. and fillies, 8ft 2lb. D. M. To continue on the same conditions in the years 1808-9, and
to name in the July Meeting, when yearlings.

Ld Grosvenor's b. c. by John Bull, out of Isabella
Ld Grosvenor's b. f. sister to Meteora
Ld Grosvenor's f. by Sir Peter, out of Popinjay's dam
D. of Grafton's c. by Worthy, out of Woodbine
D. of Grafton's brother to Duckling
Sir C. Bunbury's b c. brother to Orlando
Mr. Wilson's ch. f. by Buzzard, out of Totterella
Mr. Mellish's gr c. Bedale, by Star, dam by Stride,
grandam by Drone, out of Dimsdale's dam
Sir J Shelley's f. Wood Nymph, by Trumpator, dam
by Highflyer, out of Othëa
Mr. Watson's ch. c. by Hambletonian, dam by Buz-
zard, out of Calash, by Herod
Ld Darlington's brother to Expectation, bought of Ld
Derby
Gen. Gower's ch c. Gladiator, by Buzzard, out of a
sister to Champion
Ld

Ld Foley's a Chaise-and-one, by Whiſkey
Mr Delmè Radcliffe's c. by Beningbrough, out of
Mulespinner
Mr. Delmè Radcliffe's ſiſter to Caſtrel
Ld F. G. Oſborne's b c. by Trumpator, out of Beda,
bought of Ld Clermont

LAST DAY.

Mr. Sitwell's f. by Beningbrough, out of Hyale,
agſt Mr. Melliſh's b. f. Darling, by Patriot, 8ſt. 2lb.
each, D. M. 100gs, b. ft.

NO DAY MENTIONED.

Sweepſtakes of 50gs each, Acroſs the Flat. No
weights mentioned.

D. of St. Albans's b. f. by Coriander, out of Fairy
Sir G. Heathcote's b. f. by Warter, dam by Highflyer
Gen. Groſvenor's Briſeïs, by Beningbrough, out of
Lady Jane

July Meeting, 1807.

TUESDAY.

THE firſt year of a renewal of the July Three yr old
Stakes, a Sweepſtakes of 100gs each, b. ft. for
colts carrying 8ſt. 7lb. and fillies, 8ſt. 3lb. Acroſs the
Flat. The winner of the Derby or Oaks, to carry 5lb.
extra. To continue in the year 1808, and to name
in the July Meeting, when yearlings.

Ld Groſvenor's b. c. by John Bull, out of Iſabella
Ld Groſvenor's br. c. by Sir Peter, out of Lady Bull
D. of Grafton's c. by Worthy, out of Woodbine

Sir.

Sir C. Bunbury's b. c. brother to Orlando

Mr. Howorth's b. f. by Sir Peter, out of Violante's dam

Gen. Gower's ch. c. Gladiator, by Buzzard, out of a sister to Champion

Mr. Mellish's b. f. Miss Buckle, by Precipitate, out of Plaistow's dam

First October Meeting, 1807.

MONDAY.

MR. Delme Radcliffe's sister to Castrel, agst Ld Grosvenor's sister to Meteora, both then three yrs old, 8ft. 2lb. each, Across the Flat, 200gs, h. ft.

Second October Meeting, 1807.

TUESDAY.

SWEEPSTAKES of 50gs each, h. ft. for fillies then three yrs old, D. I. 8ft. 3lb. each. A winner of the Derby, Oaks, Ascot, or Pavilion Stakes, to carry 7lb. extra.

D. of Grafton's f. by Grouse, out of Rattle

Ld Grosvenor's b. f. by Sir Peter, out of Popinjay's dam

Ld Grosvenor's b. f. by Meteor, out of Maid-of-all-work

Gen. Grosvenor's f. Brisess, by Beningbrough, out of Lady Jane

Gen. Gower's br. f. by Worthy, out of Marcella

Mr. Wilson's b. f. by Hambletonian, out of Surprize's dam

Mr.

Mr. Watson's f. by Sir Peter, out of Doubtful

Mr. Lake's b. f. by Gouty, out of Mademoiselle

Mr. Lake's b. f. by Gouty, out of Mameluke's dam

Mr. F. Bott's ch. f. by Ambrosio, dam by Highflyer

Mr. F. Bott's gr. f. by Ambrosio, dam by the Arcot Arabian, out of Black Deuce

Mr. J. Forth's b. f. by Whiskey, dam by Potßo's, out of Maid-of-all-work

Houghton Meeting, 1807.

MONDAY.

THE Gogmagog Stakes of 100gs each, h. ft. Across the Flat, 8ft. 2lb. each, then three yrs old.

Ld Grofvenor's fifter to Meteora

Mr. Delmè Radcliffe's fifter to Caftrel

Gen. Grofvenor's b. f. by Beningbrough, out of Lady Jane

Ld F. G. Ofborne's Sour Crout, by Overton, out of Quid's dam

Craven Meeting, 1808.

MONDAY.

PRODUCE Sweepftakes of 100gs each, h. ft. for the produce of mares covered in 1804; colts carrying 8ft. 4lb. fillies, 8ft. Across the Flat.

Ld Grofvenor's f. (dead) by Sir Peter, out of Miftletoe

Sir F. Standifh's f. by Sir Peter, out of Eagle's dam

Sir F. Standifh's f. by Sir Peter, out of Storace

Mr. Wilfon's b. c. by Hambletonian, out of Pavilion's dam

Mr.

Mr. Wilson's b. c. by Hambletonian, out of Surprize's dam.

Mr. Watson's ch. f. by Coriander, out of Lilly

Mr. Browne's f. by Teddy the Grinder, out of Countess

Mr. Biggs's c. by Kill Devil, out of Portia

Sweepstakes of 100gs each, h. ft. for colts and fillies, then rising three yrs old; colts carrying 8ft. 7lb. and fillies, 8ft. 4lb. D. M. Those out of untried mares allowed 3lb. those got by untried horses, allowed 2lb. and those got by untried horses out of untried mares, allowed 5lb.

Sir C. Bunbury's bl. c. by Sorcerer, out of Wowskey, both untried

Mr. Wilson's b. c. by Hambletonian, out of Surprize's dam

Mr. Lake's bl. c. Noyeau, brother to Rumbo

Gen. Gower's b. f. by Worthy, dam, Thistle, by Woodpecker, out of a sister to Mother Bunch, both untried

D. of Grafton's f. by Sorcerer, out of Hornby Lass, both untried

Sir F. Standish's c. by Mr. Teazle, dam by Volunteer, out of Storace, an untried mare

Ld Grosvenor's b. c. by Sir Peter, out of a Woodpecker mare, dam by Sweetbriar, the mare untried

Mr. Mellish's b. c. by Shuttle, out of Strap's dam.

THURSDAY.

Sweepstakes of 100gs each, h. ft. Across the Flat, 8ft. each.

Gen. Gower's ch. c. by Buzzard, out of a sister to Champion

Mr. Biggs's c. by Kill Devil, out of Portia

Mr. Sitwell's c. by Sir Peter, out of Hyde.

First Spring Meeting, 1808.

MONDAY.

SWEEPSTAKES of 100gs each, h. ft. for the produce of untried mares, or of tried mares covered by untried ftallions; colts carrying 8ft. 4lb. and fillies, 8ft. Acrofs the Flat.

Ld Grofvenor's f. by Sir Peter, out of Ibis
D. of Grafton's f. (dead) by Coriander, out of Drab
D. of Grafton's c. by Sir Peter, out of Dabchick
Mr. Browne's f. by Teddy the Grinder, out of Phantafmagoria
Sir F. Standifh's c. by Mr. Teazle, out of Parifot
Mr. Lake's b. f. by Sorcerer, out of Deceit
Sir C. Bunbury's f. by Sorcerer, out of Amelia

First October Meeting, 1808.

TUESDAY.

SWEEPSTAKES of 100gs each, h. ft. for fillies then three yrs old, carrying 8ft. 3lb. each, D. I. The winner of the Oaks Stakes to carry 4lb. extra.

Mr. Mellifh's b. f. by Worthy, out of a fifter to Chippenham
Ld Grofvenor's b. f. by Sir Peter, out of Popinjay's dam
Ld Grofvenor's b. f. by Alexander, out of Nimble
Gen. Gower's b. f. by Worthy, dam by Woodpecker, out of a fifter to Mother Bunch
Mr. Wilfon's b. f. by Stamford, out of Lignum's dam
Sir F. Standifh's f. by Sir Peter, out of Eagle's dam

Craven

Craven Meeting, 1809.

MONDAY.

SWEEPSTAKES of 100gs each, h. ft. for the produce of mares covered in 1805. To run Rowley's mile—colts, 8ft. 4lb. and fillies, 8ft. No produce, no forfeit. The produce, or failure of produce, to be declared to Mr. Weatherby, in the July Meeting, 1806, or before; if not declared by that time, to be considered as a forfeit.

Mr. Watson's Lily, covered by Trumpator
Mr. Wilson's dam of Stately, covered by Hambletonian
Sir C. Bunbury's Giantess, covered by Whiskey
Mr. Mellish's sister to Chippenham, covered by Eagle
Ld Grosvenor's Maid of all Work, covered by Sir Peter
Ld Grosvenor's Olivia, covered by Sir Peter
D. of Grafton's Prunella, covered by Waxy
Sir F. Standish's Storace, covered by Sir Peter

TUESDAY.

Produce Sweepstakes of 200gs each, h. ft. Across the Flat. No produce, no forfeit. No weights mentioned.

Gen. Grosvenor's Lady Jane, covered by Asparagus
Ms. Northey's Macaria, covered by Lop
Mr. Howorth's Louisa, covered by Waxy

Firſt Spring Meeting, 1809.

MONDAY.

THE Produce of Sir J. Shelley's Julia, covered by Waxy, 8ft. 2lb. agſt the produce of Mr. Lake's ſiſter to Oatlands, covered by Guildford, 7ft. 13lb. Two yr old Courſe, 200gs, h. ft. No produce, no forfeit.

Second Spring Meeting, 1809.

MONDAY.

THE produce of Mr. Watſon's Scotia, covered by Trumpator, agſt Mr. Howorth's Canary, covered by Sorcerer; colts, 8ft. 7lb. fillies, 8ft. 4lb. R. M. 200gs, 50gs ft.

EPSOM, 1806.

THURSDAY.

THE ſecond and laſt year of a renewal of the Derby Stakes of 50gs each, h. ft. for colts, 8ft. 5lb. and fillies, 8ft. then three yrs old; the laſt mile and half. The owner of the ſecond horſe to receive 100gs out of the Stakes.

N. B. The Stakes to be made before ſtarting, to Mr. Weatherby, No. 7, Oxenden-ſtreet, or at the Oaks, under the ſame penalty for non-performance, as is eſtabliſhed at Newmarket, by the rules of the Jockey Club.

Ld Derby names Sir F. Standiſh's ch. f. by Mr. Teazle, out of the Yellow mare

Ld

Ld Egremont's b. c. by Gohanna, out of Catherine

Ld Egremont's ch. c. brother to Trinidada

Ld Egremont's b. c. Trafalgar, by Gohanna, out of
Humbug's dam

Ld Egremont's ch. c. by Waxy, out of Gohanna's
dam

Mr. Norton names Mr. Batson's b. c. Rapture, by Sir
Harry, out of Juliana

Sir C. Bunbury's ch. c. by Whiskey, dam by Diomed,
out of Trombone's dam

Ld G. H. Cavendish's c. by Waxy, dam by Sir Peter,
bought of Ld Fitzwilliam

Sir F. Standish's brother to Stamford

Mr. Watson's c. by Sir Peter, out of Doubtful

Sir J. Shelley's c. by Sir Peter, out of Emigrant's dam

Mr. Lake's b. c. by Gouty, out of a fister to Oatlands

Mr. D. Radcliffe's ch. c. by Beningbrough, out of Dick
Andrews's dam

D. of Grafton's c. by Worthy, out of Prunella

Mr. Panton names Mr. Wastell's brother to Lumbago

Mr. Howorth names Ld Stawell's brother to Ringtail

Ld Darlington's b. c. by Sir Peter, dam by Paymaster,
out of Pomona

Mr. Glover names Gen. Grosvenor's br. c. Have-at-
'em, by Hambletonian, dam by Sir Peter, out of
Windlestone's dam

Mr. Robert Jones names Mr. Elton's b. c. by Worthy,
out of a fister to Barnaby

Mr. Robert Jones names Mr. Sitwell's br. c. Clasher,
by Sir Peter, out of Hyale

Ld Foley names Sir C. Bunbury's b. f. fister to Orlando

Ld Grosvenor's b. c. by John Bull, out of Cælia

Ld Grosvenor's b. c. by John Bull, out of Popinjay's
dam

Ld Grosvenor's ch. c. by John Bull, out of Isabella

Ld Grosvenor names Gen. Grosvenor's b. c. Richard,
by His Lordship, out of Nelly, the dam of Kill Devil

Ld

Ld Sp. Chichester names the Margrave of Anspach's gr. c. by Highover, out of Augusta

Gen. L. Gower's b. c. by Buzzard, out of Marcella

Mr. Wilson's b. c. by Hambletonian, out of Surprize's dam

Mr. Wilson's b. c. by Gohanna, dam by Highflyer, out of Merliton

Mr. C. Fisher's b. c. by Precipitate, out of Albatross's dam

Mr. C. Fisher's ch. c. by Precipitate, dam by Trumpator, out of a sister to Colibri

Mr. H. F. Mellish's b. c. Luck's-all, by Stamford, out of Marchioness

Mr. H. F. Mellish's b. f. Off-she-goes, by Shuttle, dam by Highflyer, out of Dido

Mr. Biggs's Cerberus, own brother to Phœnix

Mr. Burton names Mr. Elwes's b. c. by Sir Peter, out of a sister to Peter Pindar

Mr. Harris's c. Ploughboy, by Volunteer, out of Allegranti's dam

Col. O'Kelly's b. c. by Sir Harry, out of Flirtilla

Mr. Whaley }
Mr. Whaley } did not name,

FRIDAY.

The second and last year of a renewal of the Oaks Stakes of 50gs each, h. ft. for fillies carrying 8st. then three yrs old; the last mile and half. The owner of the second filly to receive 100gs out of the Stakes.

N. B. The Stakes to be made before starting, &c. the same as for the Derby.

Ld Derby names Sir C. Bunbury's b. f. by Whiskey, out of Orange-bud

Ld Egremont's b f. Jerboa, by Gohanna, out of Camilla

Ld Egremont's b. f. by Gohanna, out of Fraxinella

Ld Egremont's gr. f. by Gohanna, out of the dam of Nitre

Mr.

Mr. Norton names Mr. Perren's ch. f. by Buzzard, out of Gipfy, by Trumpator

Ld G. H. Cavendiſh names Mr. Melliſh's b. f. Off-ſhe-goes, by Shuttle, dam by Highflyer, out of Dido

Sir F. Standiſh's f. by Mr. Teazle, out of the Yellow mare

Mr. Watſon names Mr. T. Bird's ch. f. Wretch, by Gohanna, out of Brainworm's dam

Sir J. Shelley names a f. Princeſs Royal, by Teleſcope, out of Queen Charlotte

Mr. Lake's b. f. Romance, by Gouty, out of Mademoiſelle

Mr. Lake's b. f. Roſabella, by Whiſkey, dam by Diomed, out of Harriet

Mr. Delmè Radcliffe names the D. of Queenſberry's br. f. Bronze, by Buzzard, dam by Alexander

D. of Grafton's br. f. by Buzzard, out of Dab Chick

Mr. Panton's ch. f. by Beningbrough, out of Didapper

Mr. Howorth names Mr. Dawſon's ſiſter to Hippocampus

Sir C. Bunbury's b. f. ſiſter to Orlando

Mr. Glover's b. f. by Teleſcope, out of Queen Charlotte

Ld Foley's f. by Sir Peter, dam by Highflyer, bought of Mr. Vernon

Ld Groſvenor names Sir F. Standiſh's f. by Sir Peter, or Mr. Teazle, out of the dam of Eagle

Ld Groſvenor's ſiſter to Georgiana

Ld Groſvenor's ch. f. Norah, by John Bull, out of Nimble

Mr. Sitwell's b. f. Oſier, by Moorcock, out of Palm-flower

Gen. L. Gower's f. by Buzzard, out of Sylph, by Saltram

Sir T. Gaſcoigne's b. f. by Hambletonian, out of Goldenlocks

Sir H. Williamſon's b. f. by Gohanna, out of Kezia

Mr. Hallett's br. f. by Stickler, out of Quiz

Col. O'Kelly's b. f. by Sir Harry, dam by Volunteer

U 3   SATURDAY.

SATURDAY.

Sweepstakes of 50gs each, 30gs ft. for the produce of mares covered in 1802 ; to run the Derby Stakes Course. Those out of untried mares or got by untried stallions at the time of naming the mares (January 1st, 1803) allowed 3lb. and those got by untried stallions, and out of untried mares, allowed 5lb. colts carrying 8ft. 5lb. fillies, 8ft. 2lb.

Ld Egremont's b. c. by Gohanna, out of Colibri
Ld Egremont's b. c. by Gohanna, out of Catherine, sister to Colibri
Mr. Durand's ch. c. by Guildford, out of Bellissima
Mr. Durand's b. c. by Guildford, out of Miss Slammerkin
Mr. Whaley's gr. c. by His Lordship, or Guildford, out of Grey Gawkey
Mr. Whaley's b. c. by His Lordship, out of Nelly
Mr. Elton's b. c. by Worthy, out of a sister to Barnaby
Sir F. Standish's b. f. by Sir Peter, or Mr. Teazle, out of the dam of Eagle
Sir F. Standish's br. c. by Sir Peter, out of Horatia

Mr. Ladbroke's f. by Sir Peter, out of Æthe, agst
Mr. Howorth's f. by Whiskey, out of Orange-bud, 8ft. each, Woodcot Course, 100gs, h. ft.

A Sweepstakes of 20gs each, for two yr old colts, 8ft. 2lb. and fillies, 8ft. the last half mile.
The Subscription to close the first of March, and the horses to be named to Mr. Weatherby, Oxenden-street, on or before that day.

PRESENT SUBSCRIBERS.
Mr. Ladbroke
Mr. Lake
Mr. Durand

A Sweep-

A Sweepſtakes of 10gs each, for three yr old colts, 8ft. 2lb. and fillies, 8ft. the laſt mile. The winner to be ſold for 200gs, if claimed within a quarter of an hour, the owner of the ſecond horſe, being firſt entitled, &c: &c.

The Subſcription to cloſe on the firſt of March. The colts, &c. to be named by eight o'clock on the evening before running, to the Clerk of the Courſe at Epſom.

PRESENT SUBSCRIBERS.
Mr. Ladbroke
Mr. Lake
Sir J. Mawbey.

A Sweepſtakes of 10gs each, for hunters of all ages, that never won 100gs at any one time, and that have been regularly hunted ten times the preceding ſeaſon, and a certificate to be produced from the owner of the hounds, that they have been hunted with: four yr olds, 10ft. 4lb. five yr olds, 11ft. 6lb. ſix yr olds, 12ft. and aged, 12ft. 2lb.—2-mile heats.

To cloſe on the 1ſt day of March, and the horſes to be named to Mr. Weatherby, No: 7, Oxendon ſtreet, or to Mr. Sanders, Clerk of the Courſe, Epſom, on or before that day. Five Subſcribers, or no race.

PRESENT SUBSCRIBER.
Mr. Ladbroke

1807.

THURSDAY.

THE firſt year of a renewal of the Derby Stakes of 50gs each, h. ft. for three yr old colts, 8ft. 7lb. and fillies, 8ft. 2lb.—the other conditions as before.
Ld

Ld Derby's b. c. by Sir Peter, out of Zilia

Ld Darlington's b. c. by St. George, dam by Mercury

Ld G. H. Cavendish's c. by Sir Peter, out of Alexina

Mr. Panton names Mr. Abbey's b. c. by Ambrosio, dam by Highflyer, grandam by Matchem

Ld Egremont's br. c. by Gohanna, out of the dam of Cyprefs

Ld Egremont's b. c. by Gohanna, out of Catherine

Ld Egremont's b. c. by Gohanna, out of a fifter to Humbug's dam

Ld Egremont's ch. c. by Gohanna, out of a fifter to Nitre's dam

Mr. Watfon names the D. of Grafton's c. by Worthy, out of Woodbine

Mr. Howorth's br. c. by Whifkey, out of Thalia

Mr. Howorth's br. b. c. Tony Lumpkin, by Ambrofio, dam by Highflyer, out of Shark's dam

Mr. Wilfon's b. c. by Sir Solomon, out of Lignum's dam

Mr. Wilfon's b. f. by Hambletonian, out of Surprize's dam

Mr. Norton names b. c. Wrynofe, by Worthy, dam by Coriander

Mr. Lake names Sir F. Standifh's c. by Sir Peter, dam by Volunteer, out of Storace

Sir F. Standifh's c. by Sir Peter, out of Storace

Mr. Northey names Dr. J. Willis's c. by Warter, out of a Dungannon mare, fifter to Minimus

Sir C. Bunbury's b. c. by Whifkey, out of Amelia

Ld Foley's c. Chaife-and-one, by Whifkey, out of Xenia

Mr. Mellifh's gr. c. Bedale, by Star, dam by Stride, grandam by Drone, out of Sir Harry Dimfdale's dam

Mr. Mellifh's ch. c. Harry-long-legs, by Beningbrough, out of the dam of Off-fhe-goes

Gen. L. Gower's ch. c. Gladiator, by Buzzard, out of a fifter to Champion

Mr. Biggs's br. c. Rofario, by Ambrofio, out of Portia

Mr.

Mr. Biggs's b. c. by Y. Woodpecker, out of Equity

Ld F. G. Osborne's c. by Beningbrough, out of Mule spinner

Mr. D'Arley's br. c. by Oscar, out of Nelly, the dam of Kill Devil

D. of Grafton's brother to Pelisse

D. of Grafton's c. by Worthy, out of Minion

Mr. Delmè Radcliffe's c. by Gohanna, out of Trumpetta

Ld Grosvenor's b. c. by John Bull, out of Esther

Ld Grosvenor's b. c. by Sir Peter, out of Ibis

Ld Grosvenor's b. c. by Sir Peter, out of Lady Bull

Mr. Hall's ch. c. by Hyperion, out of Vivaldi's dam

Mr. Durand's b. c. by Guildford, out of Ramschoondra, by Sir Peter, grandam by Dungannon

Ld Clermont's c. by Trumpator, dam by Mark Anthony, out of Young Doxy

Mr. Lord's b. c. by Totteridge, out of Sweet Reseda

Mr. Wardell's b. c. by Expectation, dam by Marske, bought of Mr. Mackall

Mr. Wardell's br. c. by Oberon, dam by Spanker, bought of Mr. Mackall

Mr. Wardell's b. c. by Hambletonian, dam by Gunpowder, out of Suwarrow's dam

FRIDAY.

The first year of a renewal of the Oaks Stakes of 50gs each, h. ft. for three yr old fillies carrying 8ft. 4lb.—the other conditions as usual.

Ld Derby's br. f. by Sir Peter, out of Brown Bess

Mr. Panton's b. f. by Buzzard, dam by Trumpator, out of Crane

Ld Egremont's ch. f. by Y. Woodpecker, out of Hannibal's dam

Ld Egremont's ch. f. by Y. Woodpecker, out of a sister to Petworth

Ld

Ld Egremont's b. f. by Waxy, out of Gohanna's dam

Mr. Watson names Capt. Vyse's f. Fillikins, by Gouty, dam by King Fergus

Mr. Howorth's b. f. by Sir Peter, out of a fister to Skyscraper

Mr. Howorth's br. f. by Trumpator, out of Othëa

Mr. Lake's b. f. by Gouty, out of a fister to Oatlands

Mr. Lake's b. f. by Mr. Teazle, out of Y. Maiden (Walnut's fister)

Sir F. Standish names Mr. Lake's b. f. by Whiskey, out of Admiral's dam

Mr. Northey names Ld Rous's ch. f. fister to Trinidada

Sir C. Bunbury names Mr. Wilson's b. f. by Hambletonian, out of Surprize's dam

Ld Foley names Mr. Sitwell's ch. f. by Beningbrough, out of Hyale

Mr. Mellish's b. f. Darling, by Patriot, dam by Highflyer, out of Tiffany

Mr. Mellish's b. f. Miss Buckle, by Precipitate, out of Plaistow's dam

Gen. L. Gower's br. f. Marcellina, by Worthy, out of Marcella

Ld Stawell's b. f. fister to Ringtail

Ld F. G. Osborne's f. Sour Crout, by Overton, out of Quid's dam

Mr. Kellermann's gr. f. Thalestris, fister to Iphigenia

D. of Grafton's f. by Grouse, out of Rattle

Mr. Wilson's ch. f. by Buzzard, out of Totterella

Mr. Delmè Radcliffe's fister to Castrel

Mr. Forth's b. f. by Whiskey, dam by Pot8o's, bred by Mr. R. Prince

Ld Grosvenor's b. f. fister to Meteora

Ld Grosvenor's b. f. by Sir Peter, out of Mistletoe

Ld Grosvenor's b. f. by Sir Peter, out of Popinjay's dam

Sir J. Shelley names a ch. f. Emily, by Ambrosio, dam by Highflyer, out of Lily of the Valley

Sir J. Shelley names a gr. f. Euphrasia, by Ambrosio, dam by the Arcot Arabian, out of Black Deuce

Gen.

Gen. Grofvenor's f. by Beningbrough, out of Lady
  Jane
Mr. Golding's b. f. by Buzzard, out of Vixen

1808.

FRIDAY.

THE produce of Ld Egremont's dam of Hannibal,
covered by   8ft. 7lb. agft the
produce of Sir J. Shelley's Julia, covered by Waxy,
8ft. from Tattenham Corner to the end of the Courfe,
200gs, h. ft. No produce, no forfeit.

ASCOT-HEATH, 1806.

SECOND DAY.

SWINLEY STAKES of 25gs each, 15gs ft. for
three and four yr olds; three yr olds to carry
7ft. 4lb. four yr olds, 8ft. 11lb. Three yr old filies
to be allowed 3lb. To run the laft mile and half of
the Courfe. Four Subfcribers, or no race.

To clofe, and the horfes to be named to Mr. Weatherby, in Oxenden-ftreet, on or before the 1ft of
March, 1806.

PRESENT SUBSCRIBERS.
Mr. Kellermann
Sir J. Mawbey

Same day, Sweepftakes of 10gs each, for a Gold
Cup, 80gs value, the remainder, if any, in fpecie.
Three yr olds, 6ft. four yr olds, 7ft. 11lb. five yr
olds, 8ft. 7lb. fix yr olds and aged, 9ft. To ftart at
the

the King's Stand, and go once round. Eight Subscribers, or no race.

To close, and the horses to be named to Mr. Weatherby, Oxenden-street, on or before the 1st of March, 1806.

PRESENT SUBSCRIBER.
Sir J. Mawbey.

1807.

FIRST DAY.

SIR J. Shelley's Trumpator f. bought of Ld Clermont, agst Mr. Lake's f. by Gouty, out of sister to Oatlands, 8st. each; the New Mile, 100gs.

FRIDAY.

Sir J. Shelley's Trumpator f. agst Mr. Lake's f. by Gouty, of Mademoiselle, 8st. each, the New Mile, 100gs.

1808.

FIRST DAY.

PRODUCE Sweepstakes of 100gs each, h. ft. the New Mile; colts, 8st. 7lb. fillies, 8st. 4lb. The Arabian mare's produce to be allowed 7lb.

	Covered by
Mr. Northey's Highflyer mare	Lop
Mr. Page's Woodpecker mare, out of Precipitate's dam.................	Gouty
Mr. Culling Smith names Mr. Wellesley's Arabian mare........................	Gouty

BRIGHTON,

BRIGHTON, 1806.

FIRST DAY.

THE Silver Cup of 50gs value, the furplus in fpecie, a Subfcription of 5gs each, for three yr olds, 7ft. four yr olds, 8ft. 3lb. five yr olds, 8ft. 10lb. fix yr olds, 9ft. 1lb. and aged, 9ft. 3lb. the New Courfe. The winner to be fold for 200gs, if demanded within a quarter of an hour after the race, the owner of the fecond horfe being firft entitled, &c.

To name on the day preceding, by eight o'clock. This Subfcription is clofed.

H. R. H. the P. of Wales	Mr. Mellifh
Ld Darlington	Sir F. Evelyn
Ld Barrymore	Mr. Lloyd
Ld G. H. Cavendifh	Mr. Egerton
Sir J. Shelley	Mr. Goddard
Gen. Grofvenor	Mr. Blachford
Ld Fitzwilliam	Mr. Batfon
Mr. Watfon	Mr. Germain
Mr. Norton	Sir J. Honywood
Mr. Shakefpear	Ld Egremont
Mr. Ladbroke	Mr. Howorth
Ld Foley	

The firft year of a renewal of the Sweepftakes of 10gs each, for three yr olds. To be named by eight o'clock in the evening before running: colts, 8ft. 7lb. fillies, 8ft. 4lb. the laft mile of the Courfe. The winner to be fold for 150gs, if demanded within a quarter of an hour after the race, the owner of the fecond horfe being firft entitled, &c. To continue in the year 1807.—Clofed.

SUBSCRIBERS.

H. R. H. the P. of Wales	Sir C. Bunbury
H. R. H. the P. of Wales	Mr. Shakespear
Ld Darlington	Ld Barrymore
Mr. Mellish	Ld Egremont
Mr. Ladbroke	Mr. Howorth
Mr. Watson	

Sweepstakes of 100gs each, New Course.

	ft.	lb.
Mr. Mellish's Didler	8	8
H. R. H. the P. of Wales's Petruchio.........	8	0
Mr. Watson's Dreadnought.....	7	11
Mr. Howorth's Honesty	6	8

Ld Foley's Watery, 8ft. 9lb. agst Sir J. Shelley's Currycomb, 7ft. 4lb. the last mile, 200, h. ft.

Sir J. Shelley's Houghton Lass, 8ft. 3lb. agst Ld Foley's Little Peter, 7ft. last three miles, 200, h. ft.

Mr. R. Boyce's Sir David, agst Mr. Mellish's Staveley, 8ft. each, to start at the turn, and run a mile homewards, 200gs.

The first year of the Pavilion Stakes of 100gs each, h. ft. (to continue in 1807 and 1808, and to name when yearlings, in the First October Meeting) for three yr old colts, 9ft. fillies, 8ft. 9lb. The winner of the Derby, Oaks, or Ascot Stakes, to carry 7lb. extra. the last mile.

H. R. H. the P. of Wales's ch. c. by Beningbrough, out of Dick Andrews's dam

H. R. H. the P. of Wales's b. c. by Gohanna, out of Trumpetta

Sir C. Bunbury's ch. c. by Whiskey, out of Giantess

Mr. Howorth names Mr. H. F. Mellish's b. c. Luck's-all, by Stamford, out of Marchioness

Mr. Ladbroke names Sir C. Bunbury's b. f. sister to Orlando

Mr. Watson's c. by Sir Peter, out of Doubtful

Mr.

Mr. H. F. Mellifh's b. f. Off-fhe-goes, by Shuttle, dam by Highflyer, out of Dido

Mr. Wilfon's b. c. by Hambletonian, out of Surprize's dam

Ld F. G. Ofborne's ch. c. by Buzzard, out of Vixen, bought of Gelding

D. of Grafton's b. c. by Whiſkey, out of Tyrant's dam

Ld Grofvenor's b. c. by John Bull, out of Cælia

Ld Grofvenor's b. c. by John Bull, out of Popinjay's dam

Ld Egremont's b. c. by Gohanna, out of Catherine

Ld Egremont's b. c. Trafalgar, by Gohanna, out of Humbug's dam

Ld Egremont's ch. c. by Waxy, out of Gohanna's dam

Ld Darlington's b. c. by Sir Peter, out of Mendoza's dam

Ld Darlington's ch. c. by Star, dam by Highflyer, bought of Robfon

SECOND DAY.

The firſt year of a renewal of the Petworth Stakes of 10gs each, for horfes to be named by eight o'clock the evening before running. Four yr olds to carry 7ft. 7lb. five yr olds, 8ft. 7lb. fix yr olds, 9ft. and aged, 9ft. 3lb.—four miles. Mares allowed 3lb. The winner to be fold for 250gs, if demanded within a quarter of an hour after the race, the owner of the fecond horfe being firſt entitled, &c. To continue in 1807.—Clofed.

SUBSCRIBERS.

H. R. H. the P. of Wales	Mr. Watfon
H. R. H. the P. of Wales	Sir J. Shelley
Ld Darlington	Mr. Shakefpear
Ld Foley	Sir J. Honywood
Mr. Mellifh	Ld Egremont
Mr. Ladbroke	Mr. Howorth

X 2   The

The Somerset Stakes of 50gs each, h. ft. for four yr olds, 7ft. 7lb. five yr olds, 8ft. 5lb. fix yr olds, 8ft. 11lb. and aged, 8ft. 13lb.—four miles. Mares allowed 3lb. and horſes bred in Ireland, allowed 5lb.

To cloſe the laſt day of the Second Spring Meeting, and the horſes to be named on or before that day, to Mr. Weatherby, at Newmarket, or in Oxenden-ſtreet, London.

PRESENT SUBSCRIBERS.

H. R. H. the P. of Wales	Mr. Mellifh
H. R. H. the P. of Wales	Ld Foley
Ld Fitzwilliam	Ld Darlington
Sir J. Shelley	Mr. D. B. Daly
Mr. Ladbroke	Mr. Latouche
Mr. R. Boyce	

Mr. R. Boyce's Sir David, 8ft. 7lb. agſt Mr. Mellifh's Lady Brough, 7ft. 13lb. New Courſe, 200gs, h. ft.

The Hippocampus Stakes of 50gs each, h. ft. for three yr old colts, 8ft. 5lb. and fillies, 8ft. The winner of the Derby, Oaks, Aſcot, or Pavilion Stakes, to carry 7lb. extra.—the New Courſe.

H. R. H. the P. of Wales's ch. c. by Beninghrough, out of Dick Andrews's dam

Ld F. G. Oſborne's ch. c. by Buzzard, out of Vixen, bought of Golding

Mr. Wilſon's b. c. by Hambletonian, out of Surprize's dam

Sir J. Shelley's c. by Sir Peter, out of Emigrant's dam

Mr. H. F. Mellifh's b. c. Luck's-all, by Stamford, out of Marchioneſs

Mr. Ladbroke's ch. c. by Waxy, bought at Sir F. Poole's ſale

Mr. Watſon names Ld Sondes's c. by Schedoni, out of Gift's dam

Ld Egremont's b. c. by Gohanna, out of Catherine

Ld Egremont's ch. c. by Waxy, out of Gohanna's dam

Ld

Ld Stawell's brother to Ringtail

Sir W. W. Wynn's b. c. by Waxy, bought at Sir F.
Poole's fale

THIRD DAY.

The Egremont Stakes of 200gs each, h. ft. colts,
8ft. 7lb. fillies, 8ft. 3lb. warranted never to have
been fweated or tried before the 1ft of Auguft, 1805;
the laft mile and half.

H. R. H. the P. of Wales's b. c. by Gohanna, out of
Colibri

H. R. H. the P. of Wales's fifter to Caftrel

Mr. Mellifh's Luck's-all, by Stamford, out of Marchionefs

Ld Foley's Zachariah colt, bought of Mr. Buckle

Ld G. H. Cavendifh's c. by Waxy, dam by Sir Peter,
bought of Ld Fitzwilliam

Gen. Grofvenor's Richard, by His Lordfhip, out of
Nelly

Ld Egremont's b. c. Trafalgar, by Gohanna, out of
Humbug's dam

Mr. Howorth's c. by Sir Peter, out of Gnat

LAST DAY.

Mr. Mellifh's Sancho, 9ft. agft Mr. Ladbroke's
Wagtail, 7ft. 2lb. the laft mile, 200gs.

Mr. Mellifh's Sancho, 8ft. 7lb. agft Ld Darlington's
Pavilion, 8ft. laft mile, 2000gs.

Sweepftakes of 100gs each, h. ft. 8ft. the laft mile.

H. R. H. the P. of Wales's ch. c. by Beningbrough,
out of Dick Andrews's dam

Ld Stawell's b. c. brother to Ringtail

Ld Sackville's br. c. by Trumpator, out of Young
Noifette

A Gold

A Gold Cup, given by H. R. H. the P. of Wales, and a Subfcription of 10gs each, for three yr olds, 6ft. four yr olds, 7ft. 8lb. five yr olds, 8ft. 6lb. fix yr olds and aged, 8ft. 12lb. mares allowed 3lb. four miles. The Subfcription clofed on the 1ft of January, 1806; the horfes to be named on the day of entrance for the Plates at Brighton, to the Clerk of the Courfe, and to be, bona fide, the property of the Subfcribers.

SUBSCRIBERS.

H. R. H. the P. of Wales	Mr. Cav. Bradfhaw
H. R. H. the P. of Wales	Mr. Payne
Ld Fitzwilliam	Mr. Latouche
Ld G. H. Cavendifh	Mr. Delmè Radcliffe
Sir J. Shelley	Mr. Craven
Gen. Grofvenor	Ld Barrymore
Sir C. Bunbury	Ld Darlington
Mr. D. B. Daly	Mr. Howorth
Mr. Shakefpear	Mr. Douglas
Mr. Ladbroke	Ld Egremont
Mr. Mellifh	Mr. Wilfon
Ld Foley	Ld Grofvenor
Mr. Cholmondeley	Mr. Fermor

· 1807

FIRST DAY.

THE fecond year of the Pavilion Stakes of 100gs each, h. ft. the laft mile.

H. R. H. the P. of Wales's b. c. by Gohanna, out of Trumpetta

H. R. H. the P. of Wales's b. c. by Beningbrough, out of Mulefpinner

Sir C. Bunbury's b. c. brother to Orlando

Mr. Howorth's br. c. by Whifkey, out of Thalia -

Mr.

Mr. Watfon names Mr. Heworth's b. f. by Sir Peter, out of a fifter to Skyfcraper

Mr. H. F. Mellifh's gr. c. Bedale, by Star

Mr. Wilfon's b. c. by Sir Solomon, out of Mifs Judy

Ld F. G. Ofborne's b c. by Trumpator, dam by Mark Anthony, bought of Ld Clermont

D. of Grafton's b. c. by Worthy, out of Woodbine

Ld Grofvenor's b. c. by John Bull, out of Ifabella

Ld Grofvenor's b. c. by Sir Peter, out of Lady Bull

Ld Egremont's b. c. by Gohanna, out of Skyfweeper

Ld Egremont's ch. c. by Gohanna, out of Prodigal's dam

Ld Egremont's ch. f. by Young Woodpecker, out of Fractious

Ld Darlington's brother to Expectation

Ld Darlington's c. by St. George, out of a Mercury mare

Mr. Ladbroke did not name

THIRD DAY.

H. R. H. the P. of Wales's fifter to Caftrel, agft Mr. Mellifh's f. Darling, by Patriot, dam by High-flyer, out of Tiffany, 8ft. 3lb. each, laft mile, 200gs, h. ft.

1808.

FIRST DAY.

PRODUCE Match. Mr. Blachford's Javelin mare, covered by Worthy, agft Mr. Page's mare, out of the dam of Precipitate, covered by Teddy the Grinder, 8ft. each; fillies allowed 3lb. laft three quarters of a mile, 100gs, h. ft. No produce, no forfeit.

Produce Match.—Sir J. Shelley's Julia, covered by Waxy, agft Mr. Mellifh's Lady Cow, covered by

Don

Don Quixote ; colts, 8ft. 4lb. fillies, 8ft. laft half
mile, 200gs. No produce, no forfeit. The produce,
or failure of produce, to be declared to Mr. Weatherby, on or before the 1ft day of the July Meeting,
1806.

THIRD DAY.

H. R. H. the P. of Wales's brother to Caftrel, agft
Mr. Mellifh's c. Bradbury, by Delpini, dam by Young
Marfk, 8ft. 3lb. each, laft mile, 200gs, h. ft.

LAST DAY.

Produce Match.—Mr. Mellifh's Lady Cow, covered by Don Quixote, 8ft. 4lb. agft Sir J. Shelley's b. m.
by Pipator, dam by Slope, covered by Don Quixote,
7ft. 4lb. the laft mile, 200gs.

NO DAY MENTIONED.

The Darlington Stakes of 200g's each, h. ft. for
three yr old colts, 8ft. 7lb. and fillies, 8ft. 3lb. the
laft mile.

H. R. H. the P. of Wales's f. by Whifkey, out of
    Trumpetta
Mr. Mellifh's b. f. by Shuttle, out of Plaiftow's dam
Mr. Mellifh's b. f. by Coriander, dam by Highflyer,
    out of Tiffany
Mr. Wilfon's b. c. by Hambletonian, out of Sur-
    prize's dam
Mr. Wilfon's b. c. by Hambletonian, out of Totterella
Mr. Norton's c. by   out of Quid's dam
Sir C. Bunbury's f. by Sorcerer, out of Amelia
Mr. Panton's c. by Worthy, out of Crane
Ld Grofvenor's f. (fince dead) by Sir Peter, out of
    Mifletoe

Ld Grofvenor's f. by Sir Peter, out of Popinjay's dam
Mr. Peirfe's b. c. by Hambletonian, out of Conftantia
Ld Egremont's b. c. by Gohanna, out of Catherine
Ld Egremont's b. f. by Driver, out of Fractious
Ld Darlington's c. by St. George, out of his Mercury
    mare
Ld Stawell's c. by Buzzard, out of Ringtail's dam
Ld Stawell's c. by Buzzard, out of Gipfy, by Trumpator

1809.

FIRST DAY.

THE Darlington Stakes of 200gs each, h. ft. for
the produce of mares covered in 1805; colts,
8ft. 7lb. fillies, 8ft. 3lb. the laft mile. No produce,
no forfeit. The produce, or failure of produce, to
be declared to Mr. Weatherby, at Newmarket, or in
Oxenden-ftreet, on or before the laft day of the July
Meeting, 1806.

H. R. H. the P. of Wales's Trumpetta, covered by
    Waxy
H. R. H. the P. of Wales's dam of Dick Andrews,
    covered by Waxy
Ld Darlington's Æthe, covered by Sir Peter
Ld Egremont's Amazon, covered by Gohanna
Ld Egremont's b. m. by Sir Peter, out of Nimble,
    covered by Gohanna
Ld Foley's Mifs Fuery, covered by Eagle
Ld Foley's Xenia, covered by
Sir C. Bunbury's Giantefs, covered by Whifkey
Mr. Mellifh's fifter to Chippenham, covered by Eagle
Mr. Mellifh's Sancho's dam, covered by Don Quixote
Mr. Mellifh's Plaiftow's dam, covered by Don Quixote
Mr. Watfon's Lily, covered by Trumpator
D. of Grafton's Woodbine, covered by Waxy
                                    Ld

1807.

FIRST DAY.

SIR J. Shelley's f. by Trumpator, bought of Ld Clermont, agst Mr. Lake's br. f. by Mr. Teazle, out of fister to Walnut, 8ft. each, the laft mile, 100gs, h. ft.

1810.

LAST DAY.

POST Produce Match.—Ld Egremont's Amazon, Fractious, Sir Peter mare out of Nimble, and Trinidada; agst Ld Stawell's Gipfy, Ringtail, Ringtail's dam, and Sir David's dam; all to be covered in 1806; colts, 8ft. 5lb. fillies, 8ft. Ld Egremont's to carry 4lb. extra, one mile, 200gs, h. ft.—Foals to live a fortnight, or no match; produce, or failure, to be declared to Mr. Weatherby, in the July Meeting, 1807.

GOODWOOD, 1806,

ARE TO BE THE WEEK AFTER THE FIRST NEWMARKET SPRING MEETING.

THE Goodwood Club Subfcription Plate of 50gs, 12ft.—two-mile heats; Firft Day, for horfes, bona fide the property of Subfcribers, and to be rode for by Members of the Club. The nominations to be made to Mr. Weatherby, or the Clerk of the
Courfe,

Courfe, on or before the 1ſt of March, 1806; and
the Subſcriptions to be paid into the Chicheſter Old
Bank, previous to ſtarting.

SUBSCRIBERS.

Lt. Gen. Lennox	Lieut. Col. Newbery
Sir C. Merrik Burrell	Mr. Percy Burrell
Mr. J. L. Newnham	Mr. Reed Kemp
Mr. Michael Barnes	Mr. Charles Harriſon
Mr. Walter Burrell	Mr. J. M. Cripps

Hunters Plate, 50gs;—2-mile heats, 12ſt.   No
day fixed.

The horſes to have been hunted ten different days
with the Goodwood hounds previous to the 15th of
March, 1806, and to have been rode on thoſe days
either by the owner or his groom, or by a Subſcriber
of 2gs, or his groom.   To have been at the death of
four foxes, two of which muſt be after Chriſtmas.
But ſuch horſes as are at the death of more foxes,
after having completed the number required above,
to be allowed 1lb. for every ſuch fox, not exceeding
ſeven.   The horſes for the above Plate, are to have
been bona fide the property of ſome Subſcriber of 5gs,
from the 1ſt of November, 1805, but transferring
between Subſcribers of the above ſum, before the
day of naming, to be allowed.   Not to have a ſweat
between Chriſtmas and the 15th of March, 1806.
To be named to the Clerk of the Courſe; and the
Subſcription to be paid into one of the Chicheſter
Banks, on or before Eaſter Monday.   But any perſon
who ſhall complete the qualification of his horſe after
the 15th of March, or wiſh to name after Eaſter
Monday, may enter on the Saturday before running,
by ſhewing the horſe on that day at Waterbeach, and
paying an additional Subſcription of 5gs.

A Subſcriber of 5gs may name for any Free Plate
without paying entrance.

1. A Match of 100gs, the laſt mile, play or pay, between Mr. Sadlier Bruere and Mr. J. M. Cripps.—The horſes not yet named.

The Second Goodwood Club Subſcription Plate of 50gs, Laſt Day, under the ſame weights and qualifications as the former, except that the winner of the firſt Plate is to carry 7lb. extra.

Skirters Plate. No day fixed. A Subſcription of 10gs each, h. ft. with ſo much to be added from the fund as ſhall make it 70gs, for horſes, bona fide the property of any Subſcriber, from the 1ſt of December, 1805, and who ſhall never have ſtarted before that day, to carry 13ft.—two-mile heats. The horſes to be named to Mr. Weatherby, or the Clerk of the Courſe, on or before the 1ſt of March, 1806; and not-to have a ſweat before that day. The Subſcription to be paid on naming. Not naming to be conſidered as declaring forfeit. To cloſe the 1ſt of March, 1806. Ten Subſcribers, or no race.

A Match of 100gs, the laſt mile, between Mr. J. M. Cripps and Mr. T. Reed Kemp.—Horſes not yet named.

No Day fixed—Ladies Plate, 60gs, free for all horſes;—2-mile heats; King's Plate weights. Three guineas entrance, but to Subſcribers of 5gs to the fund, entrance free.

No jockies to be allowed to ride at theſe races, but with the ſpecial permiſſion of the Duke of Richmond, which, if given, may be obtained by application to the Clerk of the Courſe, any time before ſtarting; but had better be applied for a week before; if refuſed, no reaſon will be given.

All diſputes to be decided by the Steward of the Races.

MAD-

MADDINGTON, 1806.

STOCKBRIDGE COURSE.

FIRST DAY (*Wednesday in Whitsun Week.*)

THE Maddington Stakes of 25gs each, 15 ft. and only 5gs if declared at the Thatched house, by eight o'clock in the evening of Saturday, in the New-market Second Spring Meeting.

The Subscription to close, and the horses to be named to Mr. Weatherby, on the Saturday in the Newmarket First Spring Meeting. The weights to be declared at Mr. Weatherby's Office, Oxenden-street, by twelve o'clook on the Saturday following.—Four miles.—50gs added by the Club.

PRESENT SUBSCRIBERS.

Col. Kingscote	Mr. Elton
Mr. Howorth	Mr. Germain
Ld Brooke	Mr. Goddard
Mr. Biggs	Sir H. Lippincott
Mr. Byndloss	Mr. Douglas

Sweepstakes of 10gs each, with 50gs added by the Club, for four yr olds, 10st. 7lb. five yr olds, 11ft. 6lb. six yr olds, 12ft. and aged, 12ft. 2lb. mares and geldings allowed 3lb. two miles.

To close on Saturday in the Newmarket Second Spring Meeting, and the horses to be named at the Thatched-house, by eight o'clock in the evening of that day.

PRESENT SUBSCRIBERS.

Col. Kingscote	Mr. Byndloss
Mr. Howorth	Mr. Elton
Mr. Biggs	Mr. Germain

Y 2 Sweep-

Sweepſtakes of 10gs each, with 50gs added by the Club, for horſes that never ſtarted or received forfeit before the day of naming; four yr olds, 11ſt. five yr olds and upwards, 11ſt. 8lb. mares and geldings allowed 3lb.—2-mile heats.

To cloſe on Saturday in the Newmarket Second Spring Meeting, and the horſes to be named at the Thatched-houſe, by eight o'clock that evening. Five Subſcribers, or no race.

PRESENT SUBSCRIBERS.

Col. Kingſcote	Sir H. Lippincott
Ld Brooke	Mr. Douglas
Major Pigot	

SECOND DAY.

Sweepſtakes of 5gs each, with 100gs added by the Club, for horſes that never won 100gs at any one time, except at Maddington, Bibury, or Kingſcote; four yr olds, 10ſt. 7lb. five yr olds, 11ſt. 6lb. ſix yr olds and aged, 12ſt. three miles. Horſes that never won, to be allowed 4lb. mares and geldings allowed 3lb. To be named at the Thatched houſe, by eight o'clock, on Saturday in the Newmarket Second Spring Meeting.

PRESENT SUBSCRIBERS.

Col. Kingſcote	Sir H. Lippincott
Ld Brooke	Mr. Douglas
Mr. Biggs	Mr. Villebois
Mr. Byndloſs	Mr. Miles
Mr. Scrope	Mr. Elton
Mr. Goddard	Mr. Germain
Mr. Græme	Ld Sackville
Mr. Howorth	Mr. Delmè Radcliffe

A Plate, value 50l. for horſes of all ages; heats, about two miles and a quarter: four yr olds, 10ſt.

five

five yr olds, 11ft. six yr olds and aged, 11ft. 6lb. Horses that never won any thing, allowed 4lb. mares and geldings allowed 3lb, The winner of the open 10gs Stakes, the first day, to carry 7lb. extra.

To be named to the Steward, or whom he shall depute, by eight o'clock the evening before running, paying 2gs entrance.

THIRD DAY.

A Handicap Plate of 50l. free for all horses; heats, the last mile.

To be named by eight o'clock the evening before running, and the weights fixed as foon after as possible. Entrance 2gs.

WILLIAM SCROPE, Esq. Steward.

BIBURY, 1806.

(WEEK AND DAYS ALTERED.)

MONDAY, JUNE 23d.

THE Craven Stakes, a Subscription of 10gs each, with 25gs added by the Club, for three yr olds carrying 10ft. four yr olds, 11ft. five yr olds, 11ft. 6lb. six yr olds and aged, 11ft. 12lb. the New Mile. The winner to be sold for 250gs, if demanded within a quarter of an hour, the owner of the second horse being first entitled, &c. &c.

To be named at Mr. Weatherby's, on the Monday before Epsom.

The Sherborne Stakes, a Subscription of 50gs each, 30 ft. and only 10gs ft. if declared by eight o'clock, at the dinner at the Thatched-house, on the Saturday

Y 3 before

before Afcot; the weights to be publifhed at Mr. Weatherby's, the preceding Tuefday; to run four miles. Three yr olds are excluded.

To clofe on the laft day of the Maddington Meeting, and the horfes to be named to Mr. Weatherby, on or before that day.

PRESENT SUBSCRIBERS.

H. R. H. the P. of Wales	Sir S. R. Glynn
Ld Foley	Mr. Lindow
D. of St. Albans	Mr. Mellifh
Gen. Grofvenor	Mr. Howorth
Ld F. Bentinck	Mr. Kellermann

The Welter Stakes, a Subfcription of 20gs each, for horfes that never won before the day of naming; five yr olds, 11ft. 6lb. fix yr olds, 12ft. and aged, 12ft. 2lb.—3-mile heats. Horfes that never ftarted before the day of naming, allowed 5lb. mares and geldings allowed 3lb.

To clofe on the laft day of the Craven Meeting, and the horfes to be named at the Thatched-houfe, on the Monday before Epfom.

PRESENT SUBSCRIBERS.

H. R. H. the P. of Wales	Ld Brooke
Ld Foley	Ld F. Bentinck
D. of St. Albans	Mr. Mellifh
Gen. Grofvenor	Mr. Howorth
Major Draper	Mr. Stratton
Col. Kingfcote	

TUESDAY.

Handicap Plate of 50l. by horfes of all denominations; 2-mile heats.

To be named to the Steward, or whom he fhall depute, by eight o'clock the evening before running. Entrance 2gs.

A Sweep-

A Sweepſtakes of 5gs each, with 50gs added by the Club, for horſes, &c. that never won more than 100gs at any one time, except at Bibury, Maddington, or Kingſcote; four yr olds to carry 10ft. 7lb. five yr olds, 11ft. 5lb. ſix yr olds, 11ft. 12lb. and aged, 12ft. three miles. Thoſe that never won any thing before the day of naming, to be allowed 3lb. and thoſe that never ſtarted, paid or received forfeit, before the day of naming, allowed 5lb.

To cloſe, and the horſes to be named to Mr. Weatherby, on the Monday before Epſom.

PRESENT SUBSCRIBERS.

H. R. H. the P. of Wales	Mr. Biggs
Gen. Groſvenor	Capt. F. B. Hervey
Ld Sackville	Sir J. Hawkins
Mr. Germain	Ld Ch. Manners
D. of St Albans	Sir R Leighton
Mr. Elton	Mr Cholmondeley
Gen. Lumley	Mr. Melliſh
Col. Kingſcote	Mr. Newton
Sir H. Lippincott	Mr. Egerton
Mr. Douglas	Ld F. Bentinck
Mr. Græme	Ld Brooke
Major Barnard	Mr. Howorth
Mr. Scrope	Mr. Kellermann

A Sweepſtakes of 25gs each, 15 ft. with 100gs added by the Club, for horſes, &c. of different ages and qualifications. Thoſe that never won a Plate or Sweepſtakes; four yr olds, 9ft. 10lb. five yr olds, 10ft. 10lb. ſix yr olds, 11ft. 1lb. and aged, 11ft. 3lb. Thoſe that have won one Plate or Sweepſtakes; four yr olds, 10ft. 2lb. five yr olds, 11ft. 2lb. ſix yr olds, 11ft. 8lb. and aged, 11ft. 9lb. Thoſe that have won two Plates or Sweepſtakes; four yr olds, 10ft. 4lb. five yr olds, 11ft. 4lb. ſix yr olds, 11ft. 9lb. and aged, 11ft. 11lb. Thoſe that have won three or more;

four

four yr olds, 10ft. 5lb. five yr olds, 11ft. 5lb. fix yr olds, 11ft. 10lb. - and aged, 11ft. 12lb. mares and geldings allowed 2lb. four miles.

Clofed on the 1ft of January, and the horfes to be named at Mr. Weatherby's on the Monday before Epfom.

SUBSCRIBERS.

H.R.H. the P. of Wales	Mr. Elton
Ld Foley	Mr. Mellifh
D. of St. Albans	Mr. Howorth
Gen. Grofvenor	Mr. Andrew
Ld Sackville	

WEDNESDAY.

A Handicap Sweepftakes of 10gs each; two miles. To name to Mr. Weatherby, on or before the Saturday preceding Afcot Races, till which time the Subfcription will remain open; the weights to be fixed at Bibury on the Monday evening of the Meeting. Five Subfcribers, or no race.

It is intended there fhall be a Free Handicap of 10gs each, for horfes that have run at Maddington and Bibury, in 1806, to be divided into two Claffes, with 25gs added by the Club to each, both to be run on the Wednefday. The number of acceptances neceffary to make a race, &c. &c. to be previoufly fettled by the Handicappers and the Steward, of which timely notice will be given.

THURSDAY.

Fifty Pounds, by horfes of all denominations; heats, the New Mile.

To be named to the Steward, or whom fhall depute, by eight o'clock the evening before running; and the weights to be fixed the fame evening.—Entrance 3gs.

The

The Barrington Stakes of 25gs each, 10gs ft. for all ages; two miles. Three yr olds to carry 9ft. 7lb. four yr olds, 10ft. 10lb. five yr olds, 11ft. 4lb. six yr olds and aged, 11ft. 9lb. The winner to be fold for 150gs, if demanded within a quarter of an hour, &c. To clofe and name on the Monday before Epfom.

CHARLES GRÆME, Efq. Steward.

1807.

FIRST DAY.

A SWEEPSTAKES of 100gs each, h. ft. colts, 10ft. 5lb. and fillies, 10ft. four yrs old, two miles and a half. Thofe that have won once, to carry 3lb. extra, twice, or more, 5lb. receiving forfeit not deemed winning.

H. R. H. the P. of Wales's ch. c. by Beningbrough, out of Dick Andrews's dam
Ld Sackville's br. c. brother to Fathom
Mr. Howorth's fifter to Hippocampus
Ld Foley's c. by Zachariah, bought of Mr. Buckle
Mr. Mellifh's Luck's-all, by Stamford
Gen. Grofvenor's b. c. Richard, by His Lordfhip

1808.

FIRST DAY.

MR. Elton's c. by Ambrofio, out of a fifter to Barnaby, 10ft. agft Mr. Scrope's f. by Dotterell, dam by Highflyer, out of Nutcracker, 9ft. 9lb. both then 3 yrs old, Red Poft, in, 100gs, h. ft.

KINGS-

KINGSCOTE, 1806,

THIRD TUESDAY IN SEPTEMBER,

FIRST DAY.

MR. Goddard's b. c. Guido, by Tranfit, out of Betty Brampton, agſt Col. Kingſcote's ch. c. Reſerve, by Volunteer, both then 4 yrs old, 10ſt. each, one mile, 50gs, h. ft.

The Kingſcote Stakes of 25gs each, 15 ft. and only 5gs, if declared by eight o'clock in the evening of Whit-Monday, at the Thatched-houſe. The weights will be declared at Mr. Weatherby's Office, one week before. To run three miles.

The horſes to be named, and the ſtake to cloſe, on the Friday before Epſom Races.—To this Sweep-ſtakes, 50gs will be added by the Club.

PRESENT SUBSCRIBERS.

Ld C. H. Somerſet   Mr. Miller
Mr. Germain   Ld de Clifford
Mr. Lindow   Capt. Hervey
Ld Arthur Somerſet   Mr. Goddard
Col. Kingſcote   Mr. Biggs
Sir H. Lippincott   Mr. Herbert
Mr. Douglas   Mr. E. Cripps

The Welter Stakes of 5gs each, for horſes that never ſtarted or received forfeit before the firſt day of the Maddington Meeting, 1805, carrying 12ſt.— 2-mile heats; mares and geldings allowed 5lbs.

The horſes to be named to Mr. Weatherby, by eight o'clock in the evening of Whit-Monday, till which time the Subſcription will remain open. The

winner

winner of the Welter at Bibury, to carry 7lb. extra. and the winner of any Stakes at Maddington, 7lb. extra.

PRESENT SUBSCRIBERS.

Mr. E. Cripps	Mr. I. Cripps
Col. Kingfcote	Mr. Moreton
Mr. Sheppard	Mr. Crefswell
Mr. Miller	Mr. Wallinton
Ld de Clifford	Mr. Whorwood
Mr. Bacon	Mr. Windfor

A Plate of 100gs; 2-mile heats; 5gs entrance, to go to the fecond horfe; three yr olds, 9ft 3lb. four yr olds, 10ft. 7lb. five yr olds, 11ft. 3lb. fix yr olds and aged, 11ft. 9lb. Thofe that have won once in 1806, to carry 3lb. twice, 5lb. and three times, 7lb. extra. mares and geldings allowed 3lb.

The horfes to be entered before eight o'clock the evening before running.

SECOND DAY.

Fifty Pounds for horfes of all denominations; heats, the laft mile

The horfes to be named by feven o'clock the evening before running, and the weights to be fixed and declared the fame evening, by eight o'clock. To pay 2gs entrance.

A Sweepftakes of 10gs each, with 50gs added by the Club; four yr olds, 10ft. 7lb. five yr olds, 11ft. 7lb. fix yr olds, 12ft. and aged, 12ft. 2lb three miles. Horfes that have won once in 1806, to carry 3lb. extra. twice, 5lb. thrice, or more, 7lb. mares and geldings allowed 3lb. Five Subfcribers, or no race.

To be named to Mr. Weatherby, on or before the laft day of the Bibury Meeting, 1806.

, PRESENT

PRESENT SUBSCRIBERS.
Ld Frederick-Bentinck
Col. Kingfcote
Mr. Goddard

The Cup, a Subfcription of 10gs each, to be paid
in fpecie, for horfes that never ftarted or received
forfeit before the firft day of Maddington Meeting,
1806 ; four yr olds, 11ft. five yr olds, 12ft. 2lb. fix
yr olds, 12ft. 11lb. and aged, 13ft. three miles; mares
and geldings allowed 3lb. If above 15 Subfcribers,
the owner of the fecond horfe to receive 20gs out of
the Stakes.

To name to Mr. Weatherby, by eight o'clock in
the evening of Whit-Monday, till which time the
Subfcription will remain open.

PRESENT SUBSCRIBERS.
Mr. Biggs
Col. Kingfcote

A Sweepftakes of 10gs each, with 100gs added by
the Club, for horfes that never won 100gs at any one
time, except at Bibury or Maddington ; four miles ;
four yr olds, 10ft. 2lb. five yr olds, 11ft. fix yr olds,
and aged, 11ft. 7lb. horfes that never won a Plate
(Handicap Plates excepted) to be allowed 4lb. mares
and geldings allowed 3lb. The winner of the 5gs
Stakes at Maddington or Bibury in 1806, to carry
5lb. extra. the winner of both, 8lb. extra.

To clofe on Monday in the Whitfun week, and the
horfes to be named to Mr. Weatherby, on or before
that day.

PRESENT SUBSCRIBERS.
Mr. Herbert
Col. Kingfcote
Mr. Douglas

THIRD

THIRD DAY.

Fifty Pounds for horfes on the fame terms as the Handicap Plate the fecond day;—heats, two miles each.

Ld C. H. SOMERSET,
THOMAS GODDARD, Efq. } Stewards.

Mr. KIRKBY, at Hunters Hall, Clerk of the Courfe,

ABINGDON, 1806.

FIRST DAY.

A Sweepftakes of 10gs each, for three yr old colts to carry 8ft. and fillies, 7ft. 11lb. once round the Courfe.

The colts, &c. to be named on or before the 1ft day of March, 1806, to Mr. Weatherby, Oxenden-ftreet, and the Stakes clofed. Five Subfcribers, or no race.

PRESENT SUBSCRIBERS.

The Earl of Abingdon
Sir George Bowyer
C. Dundas

The two Sweepftakes which clofed January 1ft, did not fill.

BLANDFORD, 1806.

SWEEPSTAKES of 10gs each; four yr olds to carry 10ft. 12lb. five yr olds, 11ft. 8lb. fix yr olds and aged, 12ft. heats, four miles. Horfes having

won once, 3lb. extra. twice, 5lb. and three times, 7lb.
To be rode by Gentlemen. Six Subfcribers, or no
race.

PRESENT SUBSCRIBERS.
——— Farquharfon
——— Mills
Drax Grofvenor

A Sweepftakes of 5gs each, for Hunters, the property of Freeholders of the county of Dorfet; five yr
olds to carry 11ft. 10lb. fix yr olds, 12ft. 2lb. and
aged, 12ft. 4lb. heats, four miles. To be rode by
Gentlemen.

Horfes to be named at Mr. Weatherby's, on or before the 1ft of June, 1806. Owners to bring certificates of their horfes having been regularly hunted,
and been at the death of three foxes during the feafon,
and not to be put in training before the 1ft of April,
1806.

PRESENT SUBSCRIBERS.
Drax Grofvenor
H. Sturt
——— Farquharfon

BRIDGNORTH, 1806.

ARE FIXED FOR THE THURSDAY AND FRIDAY AFTER
BIBURY.

FIRST DAY.

A Sweepftakes of 10gs each, for three and four yr
olds; three yr olds, 7ft. 7lb. four yr olds, 8ft. 9lb.
fillies and geldings to be allowed 3lb. one 2-mile heat.

PRESENT SUBSCRIBERS.
Francis Edward Holyoake, Efq.
Ld Stamford

A Sweep-

A.Sweepstakes of 10gs each, for horses that have never started, paid or received forfeit before the 1ft day of March, 1806; four yr olds, 10ft. 4lb. five yr olds, 11ft. 5lb. fix yr olds, 11ft. 12lb. and aged, 12ft. 2lb. mares and geldings to be allowed 3lb. one 4-mile heat. To be rode by Gentlemen.

PRESENT SUBSCRIBERS.

Thomas Whitmore, Efq.
S. Emden, Efq.

FRIDAY.

A Sweepftakes of 10gs each, for all ages; three yr olds, 6ft. 10lb. four yr olds, 8ft. five yr olds, 8ft. 8lb. fix yr olds, 9ft. and aged, 9ft. 2lb. mares and geldings to be allowed 3lb. one 4-mile heat.

PRESENT SUBSCRIBERS.

Ld Stamford	C. Whitmore, Efq.
Thomas Whitmore, Efq.	W. L. Child, Efq.

Thefe Subfcriptions to clofe on the 1ft day of May, 1806. The horfes to be named to Mr. Weatherby, London, or to Mr. Richard Dukes, Bridgnorth, on, or before the day above mentioned. Five Subfcribers, or no race. Five fhillings to be paid to the Clerk of the Courfe, on nomination of each horfe; and the winner is expected to pay him one guinea. Stakes to be made the evening before running.

CHARLES WHITMORE, Efq. } Stewards.
W. L. CHILD, Efq.
RICHARD DUKES, Clerk of the Courfe.

CANTERBURY.

THE fecond and laft year of a Sweepftakes of 10gs each, free for all ages; three yr olds, 7ft. four yr olds, 8ft. 4lb. five yr olds, 8ft. 12lb. fix yr olds,

9ft.

9ft. 1lb. and aged, 9ft. 2lb. mares and geldings allowed
3lb. two miles.

The horses, &c. to be named on Thursday before
the races, to Mr. Weatherby, in London, or to Mr.
H. Crosoer, at Bridge.

SUBSCRIBERS.

Geo. Harris	Robert Jones
Sondes	H. Crosoer
G. Watson	— Duppa
J. W. Brydges	— Icosle

CHESTER, 1806,

EARLY IN MAY.

MONDAY.

SWEEPSTAKES of 25gs each, for fillies then three
yrs old, 8ft. each, once round the Course and a
distance. To start at the Distance Chair. Five Subscribers, or no race. To close on the 1st of March,
1806.

PRESENT SUBSCRIBER.
Mr. Tarleton

TUESDAY.

A Sweepstakes of 15gs each, for maiden horses
that never won either Match, Plate, or Sweepstakes;
two miles: three yr olds to carry 6ft. 12lb. four yr
olds, 8ft. five yr olds, 8ft. 10lb. six yr olds, 9ft. and
aged, 9ft. 2lb. mares allowed 3lb.

To close on the 1st of March, 1806. Horses to be
named on the day of entry for the Plates. Four Subscribers, or no race. Five Shillings to be paid to Mr.
Jackson

Jackſon on nomination of each horſe, and the winner to pay him one guinea. Stakes to be paid to Mr. Jackſon before ſtarting, or forfeit 3gs to the winning horſe.

PRESENT SUBSCRIBERS.

Sir Thos. Stanley   Earl Groſvenor
Mr. F. R. Price   Mr. Wilb. Egerton

WEDNESDAY.

A Sweepſtakes of 20gs each, for three yr olds, once round the Courſe, and a diſtance. To ſtart at the Diſtance Chair. The horſes to be bona fide the property of Subſcribers ; colts to carry 8ſt. 7lb. fillies, 8ſt. 3lb. Four Subſcribers, or no race.

To name on the day of entry for the Plates ; to pay Mr. Jackſon five ſhillings on the nomination of each horſe, and the winner to pay him one guinea. Stakes to be paid to Mr. Jackſon before ſtarting, or forfeit 3gs to the winning horſe. To cloſe on the 1ſt of March, 1806.

PRESENT SUBSCRIBERS.

Mr. Tarleton
Earl Groſvenor

THURSDAY.

A Sweepſtakes of 20gs each, two miles, bona fide the property of the Subſcribers ; four yr olds to carry 7ſt. 12lb. five yr olds, 8ſt. 10lb. ſix yr olds, 9ſt. 2lb. and aged, 9ſt. 5lb. mares and geldings allowed 3lb. Three Subſcribers, or no race.

To name on the day of entry for the Plates. To pay to Mr. Jackſon five ſhillings on nomination of each horſe, and the winner to pay him one guinea. Stakes to be paid to Mr. Jackſon before ſtarting, or forfeit 3gs to the winning horſe. To cloſe on the 1ſt of March, 1806.

PRESENT SUBSCRIBER.

Earl Grofvenor

FRIDAY.

A Handicap Stake of 10gs each, with 20gs added by the Stewards; two miles. The horfes to be bona fide the property of the Subfcribers.

To name before ten o'clock on Thurfday morning, and to be handicapped before ten o'clock that evening by the Stewards, or whom they fhall appoint. Three Subfcribers, or no race. Subfcriptions paid to Mr. Jackfon before ftarting, and the winner to pay him one guinea. To clofe on the 1ft of March, 1806.

PRESENT SUBSCRIBER.

Earl Grofvenor

*** Subfcribers names for any of the above Sweep-ftakes taken at Mr. Jackfon's, Royal Hotel, Chefter, or at Mr. Weatherby's, Oxenden-ftreet, London.

Ld Grey's ch. c. by Beningbrough, dam by Coriander, agft Mr. Brooke's ch. c. by Telefcope, out of a fifter to Emigrant, 7ft. 7lb. each, two miles, 100gs, h. ft.

The produce of Mr. Brooke's m. Mrs. Jordan, covered by Beningbrough, agft that of Sir W. W. Wynn's Nina, covered by Sir Peter; colt, 7ft. 10lb. filly, 7ft. 7lb. one mile, 100gs, h. ft.—Produce to live 10 days, or no forfeit.

Sir THOMAS STANLEY, Bart. ⎱ Stewards.
F. R. PRICE, Efq.   ⎰

1807.

FIRST DAY.

MR. J. Egerton's b. c. Oulton, by Beningbrough, out of Cordelia, 8ft. 3lb. agft Mr. Langford Brooke's f. by Beningbrough, out of Mrs. Jordan, 8ft. two miles, 100gs, h. ft.

CHELMSFORD, 1806.

MR. Child's b. c. Ofmyn, by Ofcar, dam, Dairy-maid, by Diomed, out of Nelly, by Conductor, 8ft. 3lb. agft Mr. Morland's bl. f. Honeyfuckle, by Ofcar, out of Meliffa, own fifter to Tuneful, 8ft. then 3 yrs old, once round the Courfe, 50gs. h. ft.

DERBY, 1806.

FIRST DAY.

A Sweepftakes of 5gs each, for Hunters that have been regularly hunted the preceding feafon, bona fide the property of the Subfcribers: the beft of three 2-mile heats. Four yr olds to carry 10ft. 10lb. five yr olds, 11ft. 6lb. fix yr olds, 11ft. 12lb. and aged, 12ft. Certificates of each horfe never having won Match, Plate, or Sweepftakes, or had any fweat previous to the 1ft day of March, 1806, to be produced before ftarting.

This Subfcription to clofe on the 10th day of May, 1806, and the horfes to be named to the Clerk of the Courfe at Derby, the Keeper of the Match-book as

New.

Newmarket, or Mr. Rhodes, at York, on or before the 10th day of May, 1806. A winner of one Sweep-stakes to carry 3lb. extra. a winner of two, 5lb. extra. a winner of three, 7lb. extra. The winner to pay 2gs to the Clerk of the Course, for extra. expences. Ten Subscribers, or no race.

PRESENT SUBSCRIBERS.

Devonshire.	D. Curzon
G. H. Cavendish	J. B. Story
Scarsdale	J. C. Girandot
Oswald Mosley	Charles Broadhurst

LAST DAY.

A Sweepstakes of 10gs each, for horses of all ages; three yr olds to carry 6ft. 4lb. four yr olds, 7ft. 4lb. five yr olds, 8ft. 2lb. six yr olds, 8ft. 10lb. and aged, 9ft. the best of three 2-mile heats. The Subscriptions to be paid to the Clerk of the Course before running, or to pay double.

This Subscription to close the 10th day of May, 1806, and the horses to be named on or before that day to the Clerk of the Course at Derby, the Keeper of the Match-book at Newmarket, or Mr. Rhodes at York. Five Subscribers, or no race.

PRESENT SUBSCRIBERS.

Scarsdale
J. B. Story
T. Cave Browne

EGHAM, 1806.

FIRST DAY.

THE Gold Cup of 100gs value, and the surplus to be paid to the winner in specie, a Subscription of 10gs each; being above 12 Subscribers, the owner

of

of the second horfe to receive back his Stake; for horfes of all ages, viz. three yr olds to carry 6ft. 3lb. four yr olds, 7ft. 10lb. five yr olds, 8ft. 6lb. fix yr olds, 8ft. 12lb. and aged, 9ft. mares and geldings to be allowed 2lb.—one 4-mile heat.

PRESENT SUBSCRIBERS.

Mr. T. Wood, jun.	Sir C. Bunbury
Mr. F. Bathurft Hervey	Sir J. Shelley
Mr. B. Torin	Mr. Howorth
Mr. R. Tayler	Mr. Branthwayt
Mr. J. Coggan	Mr. Ladbroke
Sir W. Abdy	Ld Egremont
Sir J. Mawbey	Mr. H. Villebois
Mr. Chas. Culling Smith	Ld Afhbrook
Mr. J. Blake	

SECOND DAY.

The Magna Charta Stakes of 50gs each, h. ft. for three yr old colts to carry 8ft. 5lb. fillies, 8ft. 2lb. the New Mile. The winner of the Derby, Oaks, Afcot, or Pavilion Stakes at Brighton, to carry 6lb. extra.

PRESENT SUBSCRIBERS.

Ld Egremont
Mr. Ladbroke
Sir John Shelley

A Sweepftakes of 20gs each, for horfes of all ages; two yr olds to carry a feather; three yr olds, 7ft. 7lb. four yr olds, 8ft. 9lb. five yr olds, 9ft. 3lb. fix yr olds, 9ft. 7lb. and aged, 9ft. 10lb.—one 2-mile heat.

PRESENT SUBSCRIBERS.

Mr. F.-Bathurft Hervey
Sir Jofeph Mawbey

THIRD

THIRD DAY.

A Sweepstakes of 30gs each, 20gs ft. for two yr old colts to carry 8ft. 5lb. and fillies, 8ft. 2lb. the laſt half of the New Mile. The winner of any Two yr old Stakes to carry 4lb. extra.

PRESENT SUBSCRIBERS.
Ld Egremont
Mr. Chas. Culling Smith
Sir C. Bunbury

All the above Stakes to cloſe the 1ſt day of March, 1806. The horſes for the Magna Charta Stakes, the All-age Stakes the ſecond day, and the Two yr old Stakes, are to be named on or before the 1ſt day of March, to Mr. Weatherby, No. 7, Oxenden-ſtreet, London, or to Stephen Sims, Clerk of the Courſe at Egham. The Subſcription for the Cup cloſes at the ſame time; but the horſes for the Cup are allowed to be named on or before the firſt Monday after Aſcot-Heath Races.

FOURTH DAY.

A Subſcription of 25gs each; four yr olds to carry 7ft. 11lb. five yr olds, 8ft. 7lb. ſix yr olds, 8ft. 12lb. and aged, 9ft. four yr old fillies to be allowed 3lb.— one 3-mile heat. The horſes to be bona fide the property of Subſcribers. If there ſhould be 12 Subſcribers, to be equally divided into two claſſes, and the ſecond claſs to be run for by four yr old colts, 8ft. 7lb. fillies, 8ft. 4lb. the ſame day; one 3-mile heat. To continue in the year 1807.

The Subſcription to cloſe the 1ſt day of May, 1806. The horſes to be named to the Clerk of the Courſe, on the day of entrance for the Plates, each year.

PRESENT SUBSCRIBER.
Sir Joſeph Mawbey

A Sub-

A Subfcription of 10gs each, for two and three yr olds; two yr olds to carry 7ft. 2lb. and three yr olds, 9ft. 2lb. fillies to be allowed 2lb. the New Straight Mile.

To clofe the 1ft day of May next. The colts to be named to the Clerk of the Courfe, by fix o'clock the evening before running. Five Subfcribers, or no race.

A Handicap Subfcription of 20gs each, with 20gs added by the town of Egham. Four Subfcribers, or no race; if five Subfcribers, the owner of the fecond horfe is to receive back his ftake, for horfes of all ages; to run the beft of three heats, two miles and a diftance to each heat: to ftart at the Diftance Poft.

To clofe the Monday after Afcot-Heath Races, and the horfes to be named to the Clerk of the Courfe, the day of entrance for the Plates; and the weights to be fixed by the Steward, or whom he fhall appoint, by four o'clock the day before running.

The Stakes to be paid to the Clerk of the Courfe, by ten o'clock the day of running.

BENJAMIN TORIN, Efq. Steward.

S. SIMS, Clerk.

EXETER, 1806.

ON THE MONDAY AND TUESDAY NEXT AFTER THE SUMMER ASSIZE WEEK (UNLESS HEREAFTER ALTERED) AND IN THAT CASE NOTICE WILL BE GIVEN.

FIRST DAY.

A Sweepftakes of 5gs each, to name by the day next before the races, for horfes carrying the New-

Newmarket October King's Plate weights, one 4-mile heat.

PRESENT SUBSCRIBERS.

Clifford	Boringdon
Graves	Ebrington
Lawrence Palk	Wm. Veale
Charles Hayne	Samuel Kekewick
Percy Burrell	H. A. Morshead
Wm. Hamilton	Edward Lee
Courtenay	W. T. Pole
Mont. Parker, jun.	Peter Ilbert
George Herbert	John Osborne
Henry Weir	Geo. War. Bampfylde
Newton Fellowes	Arth. Champernowne
Alex. Cockburn	Man. Lopes
Charles H. Somerset	Alexander Hamilton
Edm. Bastard, jun.	Charles Lennox

Also on the same day, a Sweepstakes of 25gs each, to name to Mr. Weatherby, Oxenden--street, London, on or before the 1st of March next, and then to close, for horses which have never started, paid or received forfeit, before the day of naming; three yr olds to carry 7st. 7lb. four yr olds, 8st. five yr olds, 9st. 3lb. six yr olds and aged, 10st. 3lb. mares and geldings to be allowed 4lb.—one 2-mile heat. Stakes to be made to the Clerk of the Course before running, or double afterwards.

C. H. Somerset	Graves
Newton Fellowes	G. Herbert
Boringdon	

SECOND DAY.

A Sweepstakes of 10gs each, with 20gs added from the Race-fund. To name to Mr. Weatherby, Oxenden-street, London, on or before the 1st of March next, and then to close, for horses which have never ftarted, paid or received forfeit, before the day of naming; three yr olds to carry 10ft. 4lb. four yr olds, 11ft. 4lb. five yr olds, 12ft. fix yr olds and aged, 12ft. 4lb. mares and geldings to be allowed 4lb.— 2-mile heats. To be ridden by Gentlemen. Stakes to be made to the Clerk of the Courfe before running, or double afterwards.

C. H. Somerfet   Graves
Newton Fellowes   G. Herbert
Boringdon

Ld Boringdon's Raphael, by Hyperion, dam by Pegafus, agft Mr. Fellowes's c. by Dragon, out of Cælia's dam, 8ft. each, two miles, 100gs.

Ld EBRINGTON, } Stewards.
Sir L. PALK, Bart. }

1807.

LORD Boringdon's c. by Hyperion, dam by Pegafus, agft Mr. Fellowes's c. by Dragon, dam by the Woburn Arabian, out of Cælia, the beft of three 2-mile heats, 100gs.

GLAMORGANSHIRE, 1806.

A Sweepftakes of 10gs each, for horfes, &c. bred in Glamorganfhire and Monmouthfhire; three yr olds to carry 6ft. 10lb. four yr olds, 8ft. 3lb. five yr olds, 9ft. fix yr olds, 9ft. 7lb. and aged, 9ft. 9lb. the beft of three 2-mile heats. To be named to Mr. Weatherby, or the Clerk of the Courfe, on or before the 1ft day of May, 1806.

H. Hurſt	J. Wood, jun.
Rt. Jones	R. Jones
Rt. Jones	W. B. Grey
J. B. Knight	Robert Lynch Bloſſe.

On the Firſt Day, Mr. Jones's ch. c. Junius, four yrs old, 9ſt. agſt Mr. Hurſt's b. c. Parſon Horne, by Fortunio, 8ſt.—2-mile heats, 200gs.

A Sweepſtakes of 5gs each, for horſes, &c. that ſhall not have been in training before the 1ſt day of May, 1806 ; three yr olds to carry 7ſt. four yr olds, 8ſt. 6lb. five yr olds, 9ſt. ſix yr olds, 9ſt. 4lb. and aged, 9ſt. 7lb. the beſt of three 2-mile heats. To be named to the Clerk of the Courſe on or before the 1ſt day of May, at which time the Subſcription muſt be paid.

I. Homfray	Robert Jones
Robert Jones	R. H. Jenkins
H. Hurſt	R. Lynch Bloſſe
R. M. Philipps	J. B. Knight
W. B. Grey	

KNUTSFORD, 1806.

WEDNESDAY.

THE ſecond day of the Races, to be run for by all ages, a Sweepſtakes of 10gs each ; three yr olds to carry 6ſt. 10lb. four yr olds, 8ſt. five yr olds, 8ſt. 10lb. ſix yr olds, and aged horſes, 8ſt. 12lb. mares and geldings allowed 2lb. one heat, three times round the Courſe. The horſes to be bona fide the property of the Subſcribers at the time of naming; and the Stakes to be paid to the Clerk of the Races, before ſtarting.

The

The horses to be named to the Clerk of the Races, on or before the Thursday after the next Chester Races.

PRESENT SUBSCRIBERS.

Ld Stamford and Warrington   Mr. Blackburne
Sir Peter Warburton   Sir Richard Brooke
Sir M. M. Sykes   Mr. Clifton
Mr. Brooke   Mr. Egerton
Mr. Wilb. Egerton

LEICESTER, 1806.

FIRST DAY.

THE Belvoir Stakes, a Subscription of 5gs each, with 20gs added by His Grace the Duke of Rutland, Lord Lieutenant of the County, by horses, &c. that have regularly hunted the preceding season, and which have never started, paid or received ft. or been put in training before the 2d of May, 1806; on or before which day the horses to be named and Subscriptions paid to Mr. Weatherby, or the Clerk of the Course at Leicester; to be bona fide the property of a Subscriber at the time of naming.

This Subscription to be classed in two Stakes, by lottery, to be drawn by the Steward of the Race, to be run after the heats for the Plate;—one 2-mile heat each Stake. The winners of these Stakes to run a heat for 25gs each, on the second day of the Races. To carry, four yr olds, 10st. 12lb. five yr olds, 11st. 7lb. six and aged, 12st.

C. Morris   C. W. Pochin
G. Payne   T. Palmer
F. W. Woollaston   R. Andrew, jun.
E. C. Hartopp   J. L. Simpson

LICHFIELD, 1806.

SWEEPSTAKES of 10gs each, for feven years, for horfes bred in the county of Stafford, to carry 12ft. each;—one 4-mile heat. The horfes to have been in the poffeffion of the Subfcribers on or before the 1ft day of March, in each year, and to be bona fide their property, on the day of naming, which will be on the 1ft day of June, in each year, and never to have been in training before that time; a lofing horfe that has run for this Stake only, fhall be allowed to ftart in any fubfequent year; mares and geldings allowed 3lb. Nominations to be made to Mr. Weatherby, in London, or to Mr. Allport, in Lichfield, on or before the 1ft day of June, 1806. This Subfcription is clofed.

R. Dyott	Paget
R. H. Harper	Thos. Anfon
Henry Cafe	Geo. Pigot
Edw. Grove	J. Glover
Uxbridge	Wm. Keene

FIRST DAY.

A Sweepftakes of 10gs each, for three and four yr old horfes, &c. three yr olds to carry 6ft. 11lb. and four yr olds, 8ft. 2lb. the laft mile on Lichfield Race Courfe; mares and geldings allowed 3lb. To name on or before the 1ft of July, 1806, at Mr. Weatherby's, in London, or at Mr. Allport's, in Lichfield. Five Subfcribers, or no race.

T. Cave Browne

SECOND DAY.

A Sweepftakes of 10gs each, to be run for at Lichfield, by horfes, &c. of all ages;—one 2-mile heat.

heat. Two yr olds to carry a feather; three yr olds, 6ft. 11lb. four yr olds, 8ft. 2lb. five yr olds, 9ft. six yr olds and aged horfes, 9ft. 5lb. Mares and geldings allowed 3lb. All horfes running for the above Sweepftakes muft be bona fide the property of a Subfcriber, on or before the day of naming; and the nominations to be made at Mr. Allport's, in Lichfield, or at Mr. Weatherby's, in London, on or before the 25th day of March, 1806.

To the above Sweepftakes, the Stewards and Truftees for the regulation of all matters concerning Lichfield Races will add the fum of 50gs. The Subfcriptions to be paid into the hands of Mr. Allport, before ftarting, under a penalty of 5gs to the fecond horfe.

Grey   R. Peele
T. Cave Browne   T. Gillibrand
T. L. Brooke

LAST DAY.

A Sweepftakes of 10gs each, for horfes, &c. that have never ftarted or recd. ft. before the 1ft of March, 1806; and to be rode by Gentlemen;—one 2-mile heat. Four yr olds to carry 10ft. five yr olds, 10ft. 9lb. six yr olds, 11ft. 1lb. and aged horfes, 11ft. 3lb. Five Subfcribers, or no race.

To name on or before the faid 1ft day of March, at Mr. Weatherby's, in London, or at Mr. Allport's, in Lichfield. Mares and geldings allowed 3lb.

Gower   R. Andrew
Lewifham   R. Dyott

A Sweepftakes of 10gs each, for three yr olds; colts to carry 8ft. fillies, 7ft. 11lb. one 2-mile heat. To name on or before the 1ft day of July, 1806, to Mr. Weatherby, in London, or to Mr. Allport, in Lichfield, when this Subfcription will clofe.

Gower	John Swinfen
E. Monckton, jun.	T. Cave Browne
Geo. Pigot	Grey
Henry Cafe	

LUDLOW, 1806.

THE WEEK AFTER BRIDGNORTH.

FIRST DAY.

BETWEEN the heats of the Maiden Plate, a Sweep-ftakes of 10gs each, to which will be added 10gs by the town of Ludlow, for all ages; three yr olds, 6ft. four yr olds, 7ft. 6lb. five yr olds, 8ft. 4lb. fix yr olds, 8ft. 12lb. and aged, 9ft. 2lb. one 4-mile heat. mares and geldings allowed 3lb. The winner of one Plate or Sweepftakes, this year, to carry 3lb. of two, 5lb. of three or more, 7lb. extra. Four Subfcribers, or no race.

To be named on or before the 1ft of May next, to Mr. Weatherby, or the Clerk of the Courfe.

PRESENT SUBSCRIBERS.
Robert Clive
Clive

A Sweepftakes of 5gs each, by horfes bred within twenty miles of the town of Ludlow, and that have never ftarted for Plate, Match, or Sweepftakes, but have hunted the preceding feafon with hounds kept within the above fpecified diftance of the town of Ludlow; four yr olds, 10ft. 4lb. five yr olds, 11ft. 6lb. fix yr olds, 12ft. and aged, 12ft. 2lb. mares allowed 4lb. one 4-mile heat.

To

To be named on or before the 1st of May next, to Mr. Weatherby, or the Clerk of the Course, and the horses at the time of naming to be bona fide the property of the Subscribers. Certificates of their age and qualifications to be produced on the day of entrance for Ludlow Races. Ten Subscribers, or no race.

PRESENT SUBSCRIBER.
Bernard Coleman

SECOND DAY.

To be run between the heats of the Plate, a Sweepstakes of 10gs each, to which will be added 10gs by the town of Ludlow, for three yr old colts to carry 8ft. 3lb. fillies, 8ft. one 3-mile heat, the same as the Maiden Plate. The winner of one Plate or Sweepstakes, this year, to carry 3lb. of two, 5lb. of three, or more, 7lb. extra. Four Subscribers, or no race.

To be named on or before the 1st of May next, to Mr. Weatherby, or the Clerk of the Course

PRESENT SUBSCRIBERS.
Edward Rogers
John Sayer

A Sweepstakes of 5gs each, by horses that have been regularly hunted with any hounds, whose usual place of throwing off is not more than fifty miles from the town of Ludlow; certificates of their having hunted at least ten times, to be produced to the Clerk of the Course, on the day of entrance for Ludlow Races; to be bona fide the property of the Subscriber at the time of naming, and to be named on or before the 1st of May next, to Mr. Weatherby, or the Clerk of the Course; weights the same as above, only

mares

mares and geldings allowed 3lb. one 4-mile heat. Ten Subfcribers, or no race.

Robert Clive Wm. Adams
Clive S. Emden
Edward Rogers

Lord CLIVE, Steward.

MANCHESTER, 1806.

A Sweepftakes of 10gs each, for horfes, mares, &c. then three yrs old, to carry 8ft. 3lb. mares allowed 3lb. The winner of any Match, Plate or Sweepftakes, in that year, to carry 3lb. extra. one mile.

To name to the Clerk of the Courfe at Manchefter, or Meffrs. Weatherby, London, on or before the firft of March, 1806. Five Subfcribers, or no race.

PRESENT SUBSCRIBERS.

Edward Hanfon William Crefwell
Francis Dukin. Aftley Jofeph Hanfon
Samuel Taylor

A Sweepftakes of 20gs each; one 4-mile heat, for all ages; three yr olds to carry a feather; four yr olds, 7ft. 12lb. five yr olds, 8ft. fix yr olds and aged, 8ft. 12lb.

To name, as above, on or before the 1ft of March, 1806, and the Subfcription to clofe on that day; mares and fillies to be allowed lb. Three Subfcribers, or no race.

SUBSCRIBERS.
Francis Dukinfield Aftley
Samuel Taylor
Charles Smith

A Hun-

A Hunters Sweepstakes of 10gs each, for horses, &c. that never started for Plate, Match, or Sweepstakes, or have been put in training before the time of naming, to carry 12ft. each; four miles. A certificate to be produced (if required) from the owners of the hounds before the time of running, that the horse, &c. has been regularly hunted in Lancashire or Cheshire the preceding season. To name on or before the 1st of March, 1806, to the above-mentioned persons, and the Subscription to close on the 1st day of March. Five Subscribers, or no race.

PRESENT SUBSCRIBERS.

Edward Hanson	Edward Rushton
Francis Dukin. Astley	Peter Marsland
Samuel Taylor	George Hornsby

A Sweepstakes of 10gs each, for horses, &c. not exceeding 13½ hands; under 13 hands to carry a feather; 13 hands, 6ft. those above 13 hands to carry 7lb. for an inch, and so in proportion for each inch or half inch above; the best of three 2-mile heats.

To name on or before the 1st of March, 1806, to the Clerk of the Course, or Messrs. Weatherby.— Closed. Five Subscribers, or no race.

Edward Hanson	William Seddon
Francis Dukin. Astley	William Nabb
Samuel Taylor	Joseph Kershaw
Edward Rushton	William Creswell

A Hunters Sweepstakes of 10gs each, for horses, &c. that had never started for Plate, Match, or Sweepstakes, paid or received forfeit, or been put in training, before the time of naming; to carry 13ft. each; four miles, and rode by Gentlemen. A certificate to be produced from the owners of the hounds, before the time of running, that the horses, &c. have been regularly hunted in Lancashire the preceding season.

To

To name as within, and the Subscription to close on the first day of March next. Five Subscribers, or no race.

PRESENT SUBSCRIBERS.

Edward Rushton   Samuel Taylor
Francis Dukin. Astley   Joseph Hanson
Charles Smith

NANTWICH, 1806.

THE TIME ALTERED TO THE WEEK BEFORE KNUTSFORD.

FIRST DAY.

AFTER the second heat for a Maiden Plate of 50l. a Sweepstakes of 15gs each, for three yr olds; one 2-mile heat; colts to carry 8st. 3lb. fillies, 8st.

To close to Mr. Gardner or Mr. Weatherby, on or before the 1st day of April, 1806, and to be named to Mr. Gardner on the day of entrance for the Plates.

One Subscriber

A Hunters Sweepstakes of 10gs each. Five Subscribers, or no race; one 4-mile heat; four yr olds to carry 10st. 4lb. five yr olds, 11st. 2lb. six yr olds, 11st. 10lb. and aged horses, 12st. mares and geldings allowed 3lb. to be bona fide the property of the Subscriber six months before running, and to be regularly hunted the preceding season. To be free to any horse that has never started, paid or received forfeit, before the 1st day of May, 1806, and to remain open until that time.

To be named to Mr. Gardner, on the Monday before running, or the day of entrance for the Plates.

One Subscriber

SECOND

SECOND DAY.

A Sweepſtakes of 10gs each, with 20l. added by the Town, for all ages; 3-mile heats; three yr olds to carry 6ft. 5lb. four yr olds, 7ft. 8lb. five yr olds, 8ft. 4lb. ſix yr olds, 8ft. 10lb. and aged, 9ft. a winner of one Plate or Stake in the preſent year (ſince January 1ſt, 1806) to carry 3lb. extra. of two or more, 5lb. mares and geldings allowed 2lb.

To cloſe to Mr. Gardner or Mr. Weatherby, on or before the 1ſt day of April, 1806. To be named to Mr. Gardner, on the day of entrance, and the Stakes to be paid into his hands before ſtarting, under a penalty of 5l. to the ſecond horſe.

Two Subſcribers

A Sweepſtakes of 5gs each, with 10l. added by the Town, for ponies that never ſtarted, paid or received forfeit; 2-mile heats; thirteen hands to carry 6ft. and 7lb. extra for every inch up to fourteen hands, or more or leſs in proportion to an inch; under thirteen hands, to carry a feather.

One Subſcriber.

In the above Sweepſtakes, the weighing fees to be paid by the winner.

Ten pounds will be paid to the ſecond horſe, if three or more ſtart, for each of the Plates. The ſecond day will be an All-age Plate as uſual.

NEWBURY, 1806.

FIRST DAY.

MR. Dundas's b. c. by Pencil, out of Drug, agſt Mr. Cally's b. f. by Cardock, dam by Magnet, both 3 yrs old, 8ft. each, 50gs, h. ft, over the Newbury Courſe.

A Sweep-

A Sweepſtakes of 5gs each, with 20gs added by the fund, for horſes, mares, or geldings, bona fide the property of Subſcribers at the time of naming, and bred in the counties of Berks, Hants or Wilts; three yr olds to carry 6ſt. 7lb. four yr olds, 8ſt. five yr olds, 8ſt. 13lb. ſix yr olds and aged, 9ſt. 5lb. the winner of Plate, Match or Sweepſtakes, to carry 3lb. extra, or 5lb. having won more than once; 2-mile heats.

To be named on or before the 25th day of March, 1806, to Mr. Baily, or Mr. Weatherby. Ten Sub-ſcribers, or no race.

C. Dundas	P. H. Wroughton
A. Bacon	M. Montague

SECOND DAY.

The firſt year of a Sweepſtakes of 10gs each, for three yr old colts, 8ſt. 5lb. and fillies, 8ſt. 2lb. two miles. To continue in 1807.

To be named to Mr. Baily, or Mr. Weatherby, on the 1ſt of January of each year.

Mr. Dundas's Rubens, by Pencil
Mr. Bacon's br. c. Fingal, by Oſcar
Mr. Biggs's brother to Phœnix
Mr. Silvertop names Sir H. Lippincott's gr. c. by His
    Lordſhip, or Guildford, out of Grey Gawkey
Mr. Croft's ſiſter to Houghton Laſs
Mr. Backhurſt's gr. c. by Highover, out of Auguſta
Mr. Ladbroke's ch. c. by Waxy, dam by Mentor
Mr. Frogley's ch. c. by a ſon of Cygnet, dam by
    Protector

A Hunters Sweepſtakes of 10gs each, carrying 12ſt. each; 2-mile heats.

To be named to Mr. Baily, or Mr. Weatherby, on or before the 25th day of March, 1806. This Stake to extend to horſes that have been regularly hunted

in Berks, Hants, Wilts, or Bucks, and to thefe counties only; and that have never ftarted before the
day of naming, for Sweepftakes, Plate, or Match.
No horfe to be deemed qualified to ftart for this Stake,
unlefs a certificate is produced of his having been
hunted twelve times with fox hounds, which certificate is to be figned by the manager of the hounds
the horfe has been hunted with.

C. Dundas   H. M. Craven

T. S. Stead   M. Peirce

A. Bacon   C. B. Long

M. Montague

This Stake is clofed.

The Hon. K. CRAVEN, ⎫ Stewards.
A. BACON, Efq.   ⎭

C. Baily, Clerk.

NEWCASTLE-UNDER-LYME, 1806.

FIRST DAY.

SWEEPSTAKES of 10gs each; one 4-mile heat,
for all ages; three yr olds, 6ft. 3lb. four yr olds,
7ft. 9lb. five yr olds, 8ft. 8lb. fix yr olds and aged,
9ft. mares and geldings to be allowed 2lb. The
winner of one Plate, Match, or Sweepftakes, in the
fame year, to carry 3lb. extra. and of two, 5lb. extra.

This Subfcription to clofe 25th March next, at
which time the horfes to be nominated to the Clerk
of the Courfe, or Mr. Weatherby, and the Subfcriptions then paid.

PRESENT SUBSCRIBERS.

J. F. Boughey Fletcher   Edward Downes

E. Wilb. Bootle   John Clifton

H. M. Mainwaring

THIRD DAY.

A Sweepſtakes of 5gs each; one 2-mile heat, for all ages; the winning horſe to be ſold for 100gs, if demanded within one hour after the race, the owner of the ſecond horſe being firſt entitled, and ſo on in rotation. Ten Subſcribers, or no race. This Sub-ſcription to cloſe on the evening before running, at which time the nominations are to be made, and the money paid, to the Clerk of the Courſe.—Weights as follows; three yr olds, 6ft. 9lb. four yr olds, 8ft. five yr olds, 8ft. 11lb. ſix yr olds and aged, 9ft. 2lb.

PRESENT SUBSCRIBERS.

H. M. Mainwaring   Edward Downes
E. Wilb. Bootle   J. B. Baſnett
J. F. Boughey Fletcher

Right Hon. Earl GOWER,   }
Sir H. M. MAINWARING, Bt. } Stewards.

NEWTON, 1806.

A Sweepſtakes of 10gs each, for colts and fillies three yrs old, with 20gs added by the Clerk of the Courſe, to be run for the Firſt Day of the Races; one 2-mile heat.

This Subſcription to remain open till the 1ſt day of March, 1806, and the horſes to be named to Mr. Weatherby, in London, or to the Clerk of the Courſe, on or before that day; and the money to be paid to the Clerk of the Courſe before ſtarting, or double afterwards. Four Subſcribers, or no race. Colts to carry 8ft. 3lb. fillies, 8ft.

E. N. Kerſhaw

A Sweepſtakes of 10gs each, for horſes, &c. that never won, carrying 12ft. one 4-mile heat; mares and geldings allowed 3lb.

To

To be named to Mr. Weatherby, in London, or to the Clerk of the Course, on or before the 1st day of March, 1806. Five Subscribers, or no race. To be run for on the Third Day of the Races, 1806. The money to be paid before starting, or double afterwards.

Thos. Gillibrand

T. Claughton

A Subscription of 10gs each, for four, five, six yr old, and aged horses, with 20gs added by the Clerk of the Course, to be run for the Last Day of the Races; four yr olds to carry 7st. 7lb. five yr olds, 8st. 4lb. six yr olds, 8st. 12lb. and aged horses, 9st. mares and geldings allowed 2lb.

This Subscription to remain open till the 1st day of March, 1806, and the horses to be named to Mr. Weatherby, in London, or to the Clerk of the Course, on or before that day; and the money to be paid to the Clerk of the Course before starting, or double afterwards. Four Subscribers, or no race; one 4-mile heat.

Thos. Gillibrand

NOTTINGHAM, 1806.

WE, whose names are hereunto subscribed, do agree to run for a Hunters Stakes, over Nottingham Course, the second race day, one 4-mile heat; to carry 12st. each. The winner of the Welter Stakes at Bibury, to carry 7lb. extra; for 10gs each. To be bona fide the property of the Subscriber at the time of naming—any horse, &c. ever having won one Plate, to carry 3lb. extra. if two, 5lb. extra. mares and geldings to be allowed 3lb. and to have been regularly hunted with some pack of hounds this last season, of which a certificate from the huntsman is to be produced before starting.

B b 2

To

To be named to Mr. Dear, Nottingham, or Mr. Weatherby, Oxenden-ftreet, London, on or before the 1ft day of June, 1806. Unlefs there are 5 Subfcribers, it is no race.

Scott Titchfield
S. Duncombe

OSWESTRY, 1806.

MONDAY.

A Sweepftakes of 15gs each; one mile. To clofe the 14th of Auguft, 1806. Three yr olds to carry 7ft. four yr olds, 8ft. 2lb. five yr olds, 8ft. 9lb. fix yr olds and aged, 9ft. Horfes, &c. that win once after naming, to carry 3lb. twice, 5lb. thrice or more, 7lb. extra; and horfes that have ftarted twice fince naming, without winning, to be allowed 3lb. thrice or more, 5lb. Four Subfcribers, or no race.

Sir W. W. Wynn, Bart.
W. W. Wynn, Efq.

WEDNESDAY.

A Sweepftakes of 10gs each, for half-bred horfes, that never ftarted, paid or received forfeit, before the 1ft of May; to be bona fide the property of the Subfcribers the 1ft of January; the winner of either Ofweftry Cup, to carry 5lb. extra. To clofe and name the 1ft of May. Five yr olds, 10ft. 7lb. fix yr olds, 11ft. 2lb. and aged, 11ft. 7lb. mares and geldings allowed 2lb.—2-mile heats.

Sir W. W. Wynn, Bart.   F. P. Price, Efq.
Hon. Thomas Kenyon   W. Lloyd, Efq.
E. Lloyd Lloyd, Efq.

A Sweep-

A Sweepstakes of 5gs each, with 20gs added by the fund; four yr olds to carry 10ft. 7lb. five yr olds, 11ft. 5lb fix yr olds, 11ft. 12lb. and aged, 12ft.— one-mile heats. The winner to be fold for 50gs; the owner of the fecond horfe firft entitled, and the other Subfcribers in rotation as their horfes come in. To clofe on the Saturday evening preceding the races.

Sir W. W. Wynn, Bt.	F. P. Price, Efq.
Hon. Thomas Kenyon	W. Wynne, Efq.
C. W. W. Wynn, Efq.	Richard Lovett, Efq.
W. Lloyd, Efq.	Charles Saxton, Efq.
E. Lloyd Lloyd, Efq.	

OXFORD, 1806.

FIRST DAY.

A Cup of 100gs value, by Subfcribers of 10gs each; if more than ten Subfcribers, the furplus to be paid the winner in fpecie. Four yr olds to carry 7ft. 7lb. five yr olds, 8ft. 7lb. fix yr olds, 9ft. and aged, 9ft. 4lb. one 4-mile heat. If only one horfe fhall appear to ftart, he will be allowed 25gs only; two horfes belonging to the fame perfon, if no others ftart, will not be allowed to run, but will be entitled to the 25gs; and, in either cafe, all the remaining Stakes will be added to the next year's Cup.

Mr. Fane names Enchantrefs, by Volunteer, 6 yrs old

Mr. Wright's Rumbo, by Whifkey, 6 yrs old

Mr. Stratton's ch. f. by Buzzard, out of Totterella, 4 yrs

Major Stratton's b. h. by Conftitution, dam by Amaranthos, 5 yrs old

Mr. Langfton names Marplot, 6 yrs old

Ld F. Spencer names Bagatelle, by Sir Peter, 5 yrs

Ld C. Spencer's b. m. Duckling, 6 yrs old

Ld Jerfey names Langton, by Precipitate, 4 yrs old

Mr.

Mr. W. Fenwick's Mifs Coiner, 5 yrs old

Mr. Bacon's b. m. Little Peggy, 5 yrs old

Mr. F. Neale's ch. h. Quiz, aged

Mr. R. Boyce's King Charles, by Pipator, **dam by** Drone, 4 yrs old

Mr. Abbey's Scampfton (late Mr. Flint's) **4 yrs old**

Mr. Fermor's b. h. Principle, by Moorcock, **5 yrs**

Mr. Ladbroke's Profpero, 5 yrs old

D. of Marlborough
Col. Parker } are Subfcribers, but **did not** name.
Mr. Burton

OXFORD, 7th Auguft, 1805.

SECOND DAY.

We whofe names are hereunto fubfcribed, do agree to run for a Sweepftakes of 10gs each, by horfes that fhall produce a certificate of having been regularly hunted the preceding feafon, from the owner of the hounds with which they have hunted, and have never been entered, trained, or paid or received forfeit for any Stake before the laft day of naming. All horfes above 5 yrs old to carry 11ft. 7lb. mares allowed 3lb. five yr old horfes, 2lb. and five yr old mares, 5lb. one 4-mile heat. To be rode by Gentlemen. The Subfcription to clofe, and the horfes, &c. to be named to the Clerk of the Courfe, or Mr. Weatherby, on or before the 1ft day of March next. The Subfcription to be paid to the Clerk of the Courfe, before ftarting, otherwife not to be entitled to the Stakes, though a winner.

PRESENT SUBSCRIBERS.

D. of Marlborough	Hon. Col. Parker
Mr. Atkins Wright	Mr. Harrifon
Mr. Stratton	Ld C. Spencer
Mr. J. Stratton	Ld Jerfey

PRESTON,

PRESTON, 1806.

FIRST DAY.

LORD Derby's b. c. Grazier, by Sir Peter, out of a fister to Aimator, agft Sir W. Gerard's b. c. by Beningbrough, out of Mary Ann, both 3 yrs old, 8ft. 4lb. each, two miles, 200gs, h. ft.

The Sweepftakes for three yr olds did not fill.

SECOND DAY.

Sir T. D. Hefketh's c. by Sir Peter, agft Sir W. Gerard's ch. f. by Mr. Teazle, both 3 yrs old, 8ft. each, two miles, 50gs, h. ft.

The Union Cup, value 100gs, to be added to a Sweepftakes of 10gs each; three yr olds, 6ft. 6lb. four yr olds, 8ft. five yr olds, 8ft. 10lb. fix and aged, 8ft. 12lb. mares allowed 2lb. four miles.

D. of Hamilton's ch. h. Why-not, by Walnut, dam by Bourdeaux, 6 yrs old

D. of Hamilton's br. c. Governor, by Trumpator (bought of Ld Clermont) 4 yrs old

Ld Derby's br. c. brother to Agoniftes, 4 yrs old

Ld Stanley's br. c. by Sir Peter, out of Mifs Piper, 3 yrs old

Mr. Horrocks's gr. c. Trafalgar, by Delpini, 4 yrs

Mr. R. Croffe's b. h. Jack Tar, by John Bull, 5 yrs

Col. Watfon's gr. h. Starling, by Sir Peter, 6 yrs old

Sir P. Warburton's b. f. by Meteor, dam by Sir Peter, 3 yrs old

Mr. Cafe's ch. c. Sapling, brother to Royal Oak, by Telefcope, 3 yrs old

Mr. James Forfhaw's br. c. by Overton, dam by Phœnomenon, 4 yrs old

Mr.

Mr. Clifton's b. m. by Sir Peter, dam by Diomed,.
   5 yrs old

Sir T. D. Hesketh's ch. c. Welsh Harp, by Pipator,
   4 yrs old

Mr. Gillibrand's gr. c. Atlas, by Sir Peter, 3 yrs old

Mr. Smith's br. m. Hebe, by Overton, 5 yrs old

Sir W. Gerard's br. c. by Alexander, dam by Sir
   Peter, 3 yrs old

Mr. Dalton's br. c. Warrior, by Sir Peter, 3 yrs old

Mr. Jones's br. c. by a brother to Eagle, out of Sir
   Charles's dam, 3 yrs old

Mr. Hopwood's br. h. Newcastle, by Waxy, 5 yrs

Ld Grosvenor's b. f. Meteora, by Meteor, 4 yrs old

Ld Grosvenor's br. c. Knight Errant, by Sir Peter,.
   4 yrs old

Ld Stamford's br. c. Young Roscius, by Sir Peter,
   . 4 yrs old

THIRD DAY.

Sweepstakes of 20gs each, for all ages; three yr
olds, 6ft. 7lb. four yr olds, 8ft. five yr olds, 8ft. 10lb.
six and aged, 8ft. 12lb. mares allowed 2lb. four miles.

D. of Hamilton's b. c. Grazier, by Sir Peter, 3 yrs

Ld Derby's brother to Agonistes, 4 yrs old

Mr. Clifton's b. m. Josephina, 5 yrs old

Mr. Hutton's br c. Cleveland, 4 yrs old

Mr. Gillibrand's b. f. by Meteor, 3 yrs old

Mr. Lonsdale's b. c. by a brother to Eagle, 3 yrs old

Mr. Tarleton's b. h. Jack Tar, 5 yrs old

Ld Grosvenor's b. f. Meteora, by Meteor, 4 yrs old

Ld Grosvenor's br. c. Knight Errant, 4 yrs old

Sweepstakes of 10gs each, for horses that never won
the value of 50l. before the day of nomination, carrying 12ft.—one 4-mile heat.

To name to Mr. Brade at Preston, Mr. Weatherby
in London, or Mr. Rhodes at York, on or before the
1st of May. Five Subscribers, or no race.

PRESENT

PRESENT SUBSCRIBERS.
Mr. Gillibrand
Mr. Horrocks
Mr. Yates

1807.

FIRST DAY.

PRODUCE Sweepftakes of 50gs each, two miles;
colts, 8ft. 4lb. fillies, 8ft.

Mr. Clifton's b. c. Bryan, brother to Monica, by Sir
Peter

Mr. E. L. Hodgfon's b. f. by Patriot, out of Mifs Mufton

Sir W. Gerard did not name

1808.

FIRST DAY.

PRODUCE Stakes of 50gs each, for colts, 8ft. 4lb.
fillies, 8ft. two miles.

Sir W. Gerard's ch. c. by Hambletonian, out of Mary
Ann

Mr. Tarleton's br. f. by Mr. Teazle, out of Jack Tar's
dam

Mr. E. L. Hodgfon's gr. f. by Shuttle, dam by Sir
Peter, out of Bab

Mr. Clifton's b. c. own brother to Sir Oliver, by Sir
Peter

1809.

FIRST DAY.

SWEEPSTAKES of 50gs each, for the produce of
mares covered in 1805, no produce, no forfeit;
colts, 8ft. 4lb. fillies, 8ft. two miles. The defcription

tion of produce, or failure of produce, to be mentioned to Mr. Brade at Prefton, Mr. Weatherby in London, or Mr. Rhodes at York, on or before the laft
day of the York Auguft Meeting, 1806.

	Covered by
Ld Derby's fifter to Petworth...	Sir Peter
Mr. Ogle's Mary Gray.........	Chefhire Cheefe
Mr. Clifton's Fanny...........	Sir Peter
Mr. Clifton's Lurcher mare.....	Sir Peter
Mr. Clifton's dam of Capias....	Sir Peter
Mr. Horrocks's Dungannon mare	Delpini
D. of Hamilton's br. Javelin mare	Sir Peter
D. of Hamilton's Mifs Pratt.....	Sir Peter
Mr. Tarleton's Jack Tar's dam..	Shuttle
Sir W. Gerard's Conftantia	Beningbrough

READING, 1806.

FIRST DAY.

THE fecond year of the Gold Cup of 8ogs value,
being a Subfcription of 10gs each, the remainder, if any, in fpecie. Eight Subfcribers, or no
race; if above 16 Subfcribers, the owner of the
fecond horfe to receive back his ftake. Three yr olds
to carry 6ft. 3lb. four yr olds, 7ft. 10lb. five yr olds,
8ft. 6lb. fix yr olds, 8ft. 12lb. and aged, 9ft. Three
and four yr old fillies to be allowed 2lb.—one 4-mile
heat. The Subfcription to clofe the 25th of March,
1806, and the horfes to be named to Mr. Weatherby,
Oxenden-ftreet, on or before the 1ft of July next.
The Stakes to be made before ftarting, under the fame
penalty for non-performance as eftablifhed by the
Jockey-club.

R. Neville   H. Howorth
Braybrooke   W. Lake

          H. Van-

H. Vanfittart	Foley
Barrymore	Rd. Simeon
C. S. Lefevre	H. F. Mellifh
W. Abdy	H. F. Mellifh
R. Ladbroke	

SECOND DAY.

A Hunters Sweepftakes of 5gs each, for horfes that never ftarted, or recd. ft. before the 1ft of January, 1806;—two-mile heats; mares and geldings allowed. 3lb. five yr olds, 11ft. 9lb. fix yr olds, 11ft. 12lb. and aged, 12ft. Ten Subfcribers, or no race.

The horfes to be named, and the Subfcription paid, to Mr. Weatherby, on or before the 25th of March, 1806.

R. Neville	Barrymore.
H. Vanfittart.	Mountmorris.
H. Piggot	C. Dundas
Braybrooke	C. Bentinck
Ch. Hervey	W. Abdy

THIRD DAY.

A Sweepftakes of 20gs each, for three, four, and five yr olds; three yr olds to carry 6ft. 4lb. four yr olds, 7ft. 9lb. five yr olds, 8ft. 6lb.—one 3-mile heat; mares and geldings allowed 3lb. the winner of the Cup on the firft day, to carry 5lb. extra.

The horfes to be named to Mr. Weatherby, and the ftakes to clofe on or before the laft day of the July Meeting at Newmarket, 1806. Five Subfcribers, or no race.

Barrymore

Ld BARRYMORE, } Stewards.
Ld ABINGDON,

J. Becher, Clerk.

SALISBURY,

SALISBURY, 1806.

SWEEPSTAKES of 10gs each, for four yr olds, 10ft. 7lb. five yr olds, 11ft. 6lb. fix yr olds, 12ft. and aged, 12ft. 2lb. horfes that have won once during the year (Handicaps excepted) to carry 3lb. extra. twice, 5lb. three times, or more, 7lb. extra.—2-mile heats. To be rode by Gentlemen.

The Subfcription to be clofed on the 1ft of April, 1806, and the horfes to be named to Mr. Weatherby, on or before the 1ft of May, 1806. The Stakes to be made before ftarting, to the Clerk of the Courfe, and no horfe entitled to win who negle¢ts making them. Five Subfcribers, or no race.

William Scrope M. G. Eyre
Thomas Cally H. C. Lippincott
T. Goddard

SHREWSBURY, 1806.

A Hunters Sweepftakes of 10gs each; to carry 12ft. the beft of three 2-mile heats. To be rode by Gentlemen; free for any horfe that never won before the time of naming, and has been regularly hunted the laft feafon, a certificate of which muft be produced on the day of entrance for the Plates; and to be named on or before the firft day of May, to Mr. James Ralphs, Clerk of the Courfe. Five Subfcribers, or no race.

STAM-

STAMFORD, 1806.

FIRST DAY.

SWEEPSTAKES of 20gs each, for three old colts, 8ft. 2lb. and fillies, 8ft. To ftart at the Diftance Poft, and to run once round and the diftance, ending at the Ending Poft. Colts and fillies having won once, to carry 3lb. twice, 5lb. thrice or more, 7lb. extra.

Mr. Sitwell's br. f. Pipylina, by Sir Peter, out of Rally

Ld Fitzwilliam's b. f. Mary, by Sir Peter, out of a Diomed mare

Mr. Hartopp's b. f. Merrymaid, by Buzzard

Ld Henniker's b. f. by Worthy, out of Comedy

Mr. Wentworth Bayly's b. f. Eliza, by Moorcock, out of Mulefpinner

Gen. Grofvenor's ch. f. Norah, by John Bull

Ld Sondes's b. c. Empingham, by Schédoni, out of Gift's dam

SECOND DAY.

A Gold Cup of 100gs value, by Subfcribers of 10gs each, the furplus in fpecie; three yr olds, 6ft. four yr olds, 7ft. 7lb. five yr olds, 8ft. 7lb. fix yr olds, 9ft. and aged, 9ft 2lb. mares and geldings allowed 4lb. four miles.

Mr. Sitwell's br. f Pipylina, 3 yrs old

Mr. Sitwell's Goofecap, by Moorcock, 4 yrs old

Mr. Cave Browne's b. c. by Magic, out of Amelia, 4 yrs old

Dr. J. Willis's ch. g. by Vertumnus, 5 yrs old

Mr. Wentworth Bayly's ch. g. Monarch, by Ormond, out of Recovery, aged

Mr. Andrew's br. c. Trafalgar, by Moorcock, dam
  by Alexander, out of Kifs-my-lady, 4 yrs old
Ld Grofvenor's Goth, by Sir Peter, 4 yrs old
Mr. Hartopp's b. c. brother to Tuneful, by Trum-
  pator, 4 yrs old
Ld Henniker's b. f. by Worthy, out of Comedy, 3 yrs
Sir G. Heathcote's b. g. Chicken, by Moorcock, dam
  by Coriander, 3 yrs old
Mr. Morris's b. m. Two-fhoes, 5 yrs old
Mr. Wilfon's b. f. Merrymaid, by Buzzard, 3 yrs old
Mr. Watfon's b. c. Empingham, 3 yrs old
Mr. Thorold's gr. c. Aylefby, by Aimator, dam by
  Delpini, 4 yrs old

The Sweepftakes of 10gs each, for all ages, did
not fill.

LAST DAY.

Sweepftakes of 10gs each, for horfes that have
regularly hunted the preceding feafon, and which
have never ftarted, paid or received forfeit, before
the day of naming. To be bona fide the property of
the Subfcriber at the time of naming; to carry 12ft.
each; mares and geldings allowed 3lb. twice round
the Courfe; the beft of three heats.

Horfes to be named to Mr. Weatherby, or Mr.
Saile, Clerk of the Courfe at Stamford, on or before
the 1ft of March, 1806.

PRESENT SUBSCRIBERS.

Ld Henniker	Ld Harborough
Mr. Hartopp	Mr. Went. Bayly
Mr. Andrew	Ld Lowther
Mr. Allix	

Lord HENNIKER, } Stewards.
E. HARTOPP, Efq. }

R. SAILE, Clerk.

STOCK.

STOCKBRIDGE, 1806.

FIRST DAY.

SWEEPSTAKES of 10gs each, for three yr olds, 6ft. four yr olds, 7ft. 6lb. five yr olds, 8ft. 4lb. six yr olds, 8ft. 12lb. and aged, 9ft. mares and geldings allowed 3lb. one 3-mile heat; the winner of one Plate this year, to carry 3lb. of two, 5lb, of three or more, 7lb. extra. horses that have run in 1806, and not won, to be allowed 3lb. five Subscribers, or no race. To be named to Mr. Weatherby, or Mr. Cole, Clerk of the Course, Stockbridge, on or before the last day of the Maddington Meeting, 1806.

SECOND DAY.

Sweepstakes of 5gs each, for horses that never won 100gs at any one time, before the day of nomination; four yr olds, 10ft. 4lb. five yr olds, 11ft. 2lb. six yr olds, 11ft. 10lb. and aged, 11ft. 12lb. the best of heats, two miles and a quarter. Those that never won any thing before the day of running, allowed 3lb. and those that never started, or recd. ft. allowed, 5lb. Ten Subscribers, or no race.

To close, and the horses to be named to Mr. Weatherby, or the Clerk of the Course, Stockbridge, on or before the last day of the Maddington Meeting, 1806. Mares and geldings allowed 3lb.

Gen. Porter	Mr. Douglas
Mr. Powlett	Mr. Branthwayt
Mr. Græme	Mr. Powell
Mr. Byndlofs	Mr. James
Sir H. Lippincott	Mr. Hart

WALSALL, 1806.

FIRST DAY.

A Sweepstakes of 10gs each, by horses of all ages; three yr olds, 6ft. four yr olds, 7ft. 4lb. five yr olds, 8ft. 4lb. fix yr olds, 9ft. and aged, 9ft. 4lb. (bridle and saddle included) a winner of one Plate, Match, or Sweepstakes, in 1806, to carry 3lb. of two or more, 5lb. extra. one 3-mile heat; mares and geldings allowed 3lb. five shillings to be paid upon the nomination of each horse, and the winner to pay the Clerk one guinea. Five Subscribers, or no race.

· This Subscription to remain open, and the horses to be named to Mr. Weatherby in London, or Mr. Hawkes in Walsall, on or before the 1ft day of May next; and the Stakes to be made to Mr. Hawkes before starting, or not entitled, though a winner

SECOND DAY.

A Sweepstakes of 10gs each, for three yr olds only, carrying 7ft. distance and other conditions and particulars, the same as the first day's Sweepstakes.

JAMES ADAMS, Esq. } Stewards.
RICHARD ADAMS, Esq. }
   JOHN HAWKES, Clerk of the Races.

WARWICK, 1806. ·

SWEEPSTAKES of 10gs each, for any horse, mare, or gelding, that never won before the day of naming, and that has been regularly hunted the
pre-

preceding feafon, carrying 12ft. each; the beft of three 2-mile heats; to ftart at the ufual place, once round the Courfe, and end at the Stand; mares and geldings allowed 2lb. To be rode by Gentlemen.

To be named to Mr. Weatherby, or Mr. Bevan, Clerk of the Courfe, Warwick, on or before the 1ft day of May, 1806.

PRESENT SUBSCRIBERS.

Ld Warwick	Hon. Col. Greville
Ld Clonmell	Mr. J. Suckburgh
Ld Brooke	Mr. D. S. Dugdale
Sir J. Throckmorton	Mr. R. Canning
Sir S. Suckburgh	Mr. H. Ryder
Mr. J. Fullerton	

A Sweepftakes of 10gs each; the beft of three 2-mile heats, for all ages; free for any horfe, mare, or gelding; four yr olds carrying 7ft. 7lb. five yr olds, 8ft. 4lb. fix yr olds, 8ft. 10lb. and aged horfes, 9ft. To ftart at the ufual place, once round the Courfe, and end at the Stand.

To be named to Mr. Weatherby, or Mr. Bevan, Clerk of the Courfe, Warwick, on or before the 1ft of May, 1806.

PRESENT SUBSCRIBERS.

Ld Warwick	Sir S. Suckburgh
Ld Clonmell	Mr. J. Fullerton

WINCHESTER, 1806.

FIRST DAY.

A Cup of 100gs value, a Subfcription of 10gs each, and the furplus to be paid the winner in fpecie; to carry Richmond Cup weights, except mares

C c 3

`and

and geldings to be allowed 2lb. for all ages, viz.
three yr olds to carry 6ft. 3lb. four yr olds, 7ft. 10lb.
five yr olds, 8ft 6lb. fix yr olds, 8ft. 12lb. and aged,
9ft. one 4-mile heat.

To clofe the 1ft day of March, 1806; the horfes,
&c. to be named to Mr. Weatherby, on the Monday
preceding Afcot Races. The Subfcriptions to be paid
to Mr. Weatherby, or Mr. Weftlake, Clerk of the
Courfe, on the Monday before ftarting. Ten Subfcribers, or no race.

N. B. The above Stake has been re-opened, having had but eight Subfcribers on the 1ft of January,
the day originally fixed for clofing.

WORCESTER, 1806.

FIRST DAY.

A Sweepftakes of 10gs each; three yr olds, 6ft.
four yr olds, 7ft. 4lb. five yr olds, 8ft. 2lb. fix
yr olds, 8ft. 10lb. and aged, 9ft. mares and geldings
allowed 3lb. the beft of three 2-mile heats.

To be named on or before the 1ft of May, to Mr.
Weatherby, or Mr. Cobley, Newport-ftreet, Wor-
cefter. Five Subfcribers, or no race.

PRESENT SUBSCRIBERS.
Hon. G. W. Coventry
Jos. Scott, Efq. M. P.
Hon. J. W. Ward, M. P.

Hon. Col. COVENTRY, Steward.

YORK

YORK

Spring Meeting, 1806.

ENTERING DAY, June 2.

MR. Clifton's Fyldene, brother to Sir Oliver, age Mr. Walker's Baronet, brother to Brough, 8ft. each, the laſt mile and half, 100gs, h. ft.

FIRST DAY.

Sweepſtakes of 20gs each, for all ages; two miles.

	ft.	lb.
Ld Fitzwilliam's b. m. Sally	9	1
Mr. Melliſh's Sir Launcelot, by Delpini	8	5
Mr. G. Hutton's c. Cleveland, by Overton	8	5
Mr. Burton's ch. c. Percy, by Stamford, out of Belle Fille	6	11

SECOND DAY.

Sweepſtakes of 20gs each, for colts and fillies then three yrs old; colts, 8ft. fillies, 7ft. 12lb. laſt mile and half.

Mr. Melliſh's b. f. Flighty, by Traveller
Mr. Grimſton's b. c. Woldſman, by Sir Peter
Mr. Clifton's b. c. Fyldene, by Sir Peter
Ld Fitzwilliam's b. f. fiſter to Sir Solomon
Sir W. Gerard's c. by Alexander, dam by Sir Peter
Mr. Walker's c. Baronet, brother to Brough
Mr. Burton's b. c. Holderneſs, by Beningbrough

The Stand Plate of 50l. for all ages.

JOHN GRIMSTON, Eſq. {
R. C. BURTON, Eſq. } Stewards.

Auguſt

Auguſt Meeting, 1806.

THE firſt year of a renewal of the Subſcription of 25gs each divided into three purſes, with 50l. added to each by the City of York; to be run for on the Wedneſday, Thurſday, and Friday in the Auguſt Meetings, 1806, 1807, 1808, and 1809.

SUBSCRIBERS.

H. R. H. the P. of Wales	Mr. Lumley Savile
Ld Fitzwilliam	Mr. Wentworth
Ld Darlington	Mr. Garforth
D. of Hamilton	Mr. Clifton
Ld Strathmore	Mr. Wilſon
Ld Groſvenor	Mr. Peirſe
Ld Milton	Mr. E. L. Hodgſon
Sir G. Armytage	Mr. Melliſh
Sir M. M. Sykes	Mr. Watt
Sir F. Standiſh	Mr. Hewett
Sir T. Gaſcoigne	Mr. Brandling
Sir W. Gerard	Mr. Burton
Sir H. T. Vane	Mr. N. B. Hodgſon

SATURDAY BEFORE THE MEETING.

Sir T. Gaſcoigne's ch. c. by Timothy, out of Violet, agſt Mr. Melliſh's b. c. by Stamford, out of Marchioneſs, by Lurcher, out of Miſs Cogden, 8ſt. 3lb. each, two miles, 200gs, h. ft.

Mr. Grimſton's br. c. Woldſman, by Sir Peter, dam by Volunteer, 8ſt. 3lb. agſt Mr. Croft's b. c. by Cardinal, out of Luna, 8ſt. two miles, 100gs, h. ft.

Sir M. M. Sykes's b. c. Sir Scudamore, by Stamford, out of Stella, 8ſt. 3lb. agſt. Mr. Melliſh's Off-ſhe-goes, by Shuttle, 8ſt. two miles, 200gs, h. ft.

Sir

Sir M. M. Sykes's Sir Reginald, agft Ld Darlington's c. Trafalgar, by Sir Peter, out of Æthe, 8ft. 7lb. each, four miles, 200gs.

Mr. Hill's c. Talifman, agft Mr. Burton's ch. c. by Stamford, out of Belle Fille, 8ft. 4lb. each, two miles, 200gs, h. ft.

Sir M. M. Sykes's Sir Sacripant, agft Mr. Watt's c. by Beningbrough, dam by Young Marfk, 8ft. 4lb. each, three miles, 100gs.

MONDAY.

The fecond year of the renewed Subfcription of £5gs each, for any horfe, &c. the property of the Subfcriber three months before the time of running ; four yr olds, 7ft. 9lb. five yr olds, 8ft. 5lb fix yr olds and aged, 8ft. 10lb. four yr old fillies allowed 4lb. four miles.

The horfes, &c. to be named between the hours of two and fix o'clock on the Saturday afternoon before the time of running. To be continued in 1807.

SUBSCRIBERS.

Ld Fitzwilliam	Ld Darlington
D. of Hamilton	Ld Grey
Sir M. M. Sykes	Sir T. Gafcoigne
Mr. Mellifh	Sir H. T. Vane
Mr. Garforth	Mr. N. B. Hodgfon

Produce Stakes of 100gs each, h. ft. colts, 8ft. 7lb. fillies, 8ft. 4lb. Thofe marked * allowed 3lb. four miles.

*Ld Fitzwilliam's br. c. Norval, by Hambletonian, out of Evelina

*Ld Fitzwilliam's b. c. by Moorcock, out of Matron,

Ld Fitzwilliam's b. c. Caleb Quotem, by Sir Peter, dam by Diomed

*Mr. Wilfon's b. c. Newmarket, by Waxy, dam by Highflyer, grandam by Marfk

*Mr.

*Mr. Sitwell's b. f. Goofecap, fifter to Regina, by
  Moorcock
*Mr. Hewett's b. f. Mifs Hornpipe Teazle, by Sir
  Peter, out of Hornpipe
D. of Hamilton's b. f. by Walnut, dam by Javelin
D. of Hamilton's b. c. by Walnut, out of Mifs Pratt
Ld Strathmore's b. c. by Sir Peter, out of Queen Mab
Sir T. Gafcoigne's b. f. by Sir Peter, out of Violet
*Mr. Hill's b. f. by Ormond, out of St. Anne
*Mr. Acred's b. f. Mifs Welham, by Screveton, out
  of Mifs Cogden

Mr. N. B. Hodgfon's Brafferton, by Beningbrough,
agft Mr. Watt's Shuttlecock, by Schedoni, 8ft. each,
the laft mile, 100gs, h. ft.

TUESDAY.

Sweepftakes of 20gs each, for two yr old colts,
8ft. fillies, 7ft. 12lb. Two yr old Courfe.

Ld Darlington's b. c. brother to Bumper
Ld Fitzwilliam's dark b. f fifter to Sir Paul
Sir T. Gafcoigne's ch. f. by Timothy, out of Violet
Sir W. Gerard's b. f. by Expeƈation, out of Lady
  Brough's dam
Mr. Mellifh's f. Mifs Buckle, by Precipitate, out of
  Plaiftow's dam
Ld Strathmore's b. f. by Enchanter, out of Viciffitude,
  by Pipator
Sir H. T. Vane's c. by Patriot, out of Hyperion's dam

WEDNESDAY.

Ld Fitzwilliam's b. c. Caleb Quotem, agft Sir H. T.
Vane's b. c. (fince dead) by Hambletonian, 8ft. 7lb.
each, four miles, 200gs, h. ft.

Sweepftakes of 50gs each, h. ft. for three yr old
colts, 8ft. 2lb. fillies, 7ft. 13lb. two miles.

Mr.

Mr. Mellish's b. f. Off-she-goes, by Shuttle, dam by Highflyer, out of Dido, by Eclipse

Sir H. T. Vane's br. c. by Hambletonian, out of Lady Sarah

Sir H. T. Vane's b. f. by Hambletonian, out of Lopcatcher

Mr. Brandling's b. c. by Shuttle, dam by Walnut, out of Little Scot's dam

Mr. T. Hutchinson's ch. c. by Beningbrough, out of Lardella

Ld Grosvenor's b. c. by John Bull, out of Cælia

Mr. W. Hutchinson's ch. c. by St. George, dam by Young Mark, grandam by Silvio

Mr. Clifton's b. c. Fyldene, by Sir Peter, out of Fanny

Mr. Clifton's br. c. Warrior, by Sir Peter, out of Monica's dam

Mr. T. Robinson's b. c. by Beningbrough, out of Belle Vue's dam

Mr. J. Grimston's Woldsman, by Sir Peter, dam by Volunteer

Sweepstakes of 100gs each, h. ft. 8ft. 4lb. three miles.

Mr. Mellish's b. c. True Briton, by St. George

Mr. Mellish's ch c. Honesty, by Overton

Ld Grosvenor's b. c. by Sir Peter, out of Cælia

Ld Grosvenor's br. c. by Sir Peter, out of Leveret

Ld Strathmore's b. c. by Pipator, out of Heroine

Sir M. M. Sykes's b. c. Sir Reginald, by Precipitate

THURSDAY.

Produce Stakes of 100gs each, h. ft. colts, 8ft. 2lb. fillies, 8ft. those marked * allowed 3lb. two miles.

*D. of Hamilton's b. c. by Beningbrough, dam by Walnut, out of Rosaletta

D. of Hamilton's b. f. by Spadille, dam by Javelin, out of Walnut's sister

Ld Fitzwilliam's b. c. Delville, by Beningbrough, out of Evelina

Ld

Ld Fitzwilliam's b. f. by Sir Peter out of Matron

*Mr. Hewett's b. f. by Sir Peter, out of Eliza

*Mr Hewett's br. f. by Sir Peter, out of Hornpipe

*Sir M. M. Syke's b. c. Sir Scudamore, by Stamford, out of Stella

Mr. T. Hutchinson's f. by Sir Peter, out of Constitution's sister

Ld Strathmore's b. c. by Sir Peter, out of Queen Mab

*Ld Strathmore's b. f. by Sir Peter, out of Heroine

Sir H. T. Vane's br. c. by Hambletonian, out of Lady Sarah

Mr. W. Lee's b. c. by Beningbrough, out of Strap's dam

Mr. Peirse's b. c. by Beningbrough, out of Constantia

FRIDAY.

Sweepstakes of 50gs each, 10gs ft. for fillies three yrs old, 8ft. each, the last mile and three quarters.

Ld Fitzwilliam's bay, Mary, sister to Sally

Mr. Hewett's bay, Miss Eliza Teazle

Mr. Jaques's chesnut, by Star, dam by Marsk, bought of Mr. R. Linton

Mr. Peirse's brown, by Beningbrough, out of Rosamond

Mr. Mellish's Streatlam Lass, by Sir Peter

Mr. Richardson's bay, by Sir Peter, dam by Pegasus

Mr. G. Hutton's bay, by a brother to Eagle, dam by Star

SATURDAY.

Sweepstakes of 30gs each, 10gs ft. for three yr old colts, 8ft. 2lb. fillies, 7ft. 12lb. the last mile and three quarters.

Ld Darlington's ch. c. Well-enough, by Star, dam by Highflyer, bought of Mr. Robson

Ld Fitzwilliam's b. c. Delville, by Beningbrough, out of Evelina

D. of

D. of Hamilton's b. c. Crafty, by Walnut, dam by
  Javelin, out of Spadille's fifter
Sir T. Gafcoigne's ch. c. by Timothy, out of Violet
Ld Belhaven's b. c. by Beningbrough, out of Lady
  Mary's dam
Ld Hawke's ch. c. by Stamford, dam by Morwick
  Ball
Mr. N. B. Hodgfon's ch. c. Brafferton

      Sir T. GASCOIGNE, Bart. }
      P. WENTWORTH, Efq. } Stewards.
      JOHN CLIFTON, Efq.   }

Auguft Meeting, 1807.

SATURDAY BEFORE THE MEETING.

SIR T. Gafcoigne's b. f. by Hambletonian, out of
Goldenlocks, agft Mr. Mellifh's b. f. by Shuttle,
dam by Highflyer, out of Dido, 8ft. 4lb. each, four
miles, 200gs, h. ft.

  Mr. Clifton's c. Warrior, by Sir Peter, out of
Mary Ann, 8ft. 3lb. agft Mr. Mellifh's c. by Stamford,
out of Marchionefs, by Lurcher, 8ft. four miles.

  Mr. Watt's b. c. Shuttlecock, by Schedoni, agft
Mr. Grimfton's b. c. Woldfman, by Sir Peter, 8ft. 7lb.
each, the laft mile, 500gs.

MONDAY.

Produce Stakes of 100gs each, h. ft. colts, 8ft. 7lb.
fillies, 8ft. 4lb. thofe marked * allowed 3lb. four
miles.

*D. of Hamilton's b. c. by Beningbrough, dam by
  Walnut, out of Rofaletta
*D. of Hamilton's b. f. by Walnut, out of Mifs Pratt
Ld Fitzwilliam's b. c. by Beningbrough, out of Evelina

Ld Fitzwilliam's b. f. by Sir Peter, out of Matron

Ld Fitzwilliam's b. f. by Sir Peter, out of a Diomed mare

Sir J. Lawfon's ch. c. by Stride, out of a Drone mare

Sir F. Standifh's c. by Sir Peter, out of Horatia

Sir F. Standifh's b f. by Sir Peter, or Mr. Teazle, out of Eagle's dam

*Mr. Hewett's b. f. by Sir Peter, out of Eliza

*Mr. Hewett's br. f. by Sir Peter, out of Hornpipe

*Sir M. M. Sykes's ch. c. by Stamford, dam by King Fergus, bought of Mr. Nalton

*Sir H. T. Vane's b. f. by Hambletonian, out of Lopcatcher

*Sir H. T. Vane's b. f. by Hambletonian, out of Hyperion's dam

*Sir H. T. Vane's br. c. by Hambletonian, out of Lady Sarah

Mr. W. Lee's b. c. by Beningbrough, out of Strap's dam

*Mr. Peirfe's b. c. by Beningbrough, out of Conftantia

Sweepftakes of 100gs each, h. ft. two miles.

Col. Childeis's c. by Stamford, out of a Bourdeaux mare, 8ft. 2lb.

Mr. Denifon's c. by Beningbrough, out of Rofamond, 8ft. 2lb.

Sir M. M. Sykes's f. by Precipitate, out of a Volunteer mare, 8ft.

WEDNESDAY.

Sweepftakes of 50gs each, h. ft. 8ft. 2lb. two miles.

Mr. Brandling's c. by Beningbrough, out of Strap's dam

Mr. W. Hutchinfon's b. c. Silvio, by St. George, dam by Young Marfk

Mr. Kirby's gr. c. by Beningbrough, dam by Delpini, out of Nanny

Mr.

Mr. N. B. Hodgſon's b. c. by Beningbrough, out of Eliza, by Alfred

Sweepſtakes of 100gs each, h. ft. 8ſt. 4lb. three miles.

Ld Fitzwilliam's b. c. Delville, by Beningbrough, out of Evelina

Sir M. M. Sykes's b, c. Sir Scudamore, by Stamford, out of Stella

Mr. Brandling's c. by Star, dam by Mercury

Ld Darlington's ch. c. by Star, dam by Highflyer, .. bought of Mr. Robſon

Ld Darlington's b. c. by Sir Peter, out of Pedlar's dam

Mr. Wilſon's b. c. by Hambletonian, out of Surprize's dam

Mr. Grimſton's b. c. Woldſman, by Sir Peter, out of Young Rachel

Mr. Clifton's b. c. Fyldene, brother to Sir Oliver

Ld Groſvenor's br. c. by John Bull, out of Cætia

Sir F. Standiſh's brother to Stamford

Mr. Peirſe's b. c. by Beningbrough, out of Conſtantia

THURSDAY.

Produce Stakes of 100gs each, h. ft. colts, 8ſt. 2lb. fillies, 8ſt. thoſe marked * allowed 3lb. two miles.

Ld Fitzwilliam's b f. by Beningbrough, out of Evelina

*Ld Fitzwilliam's b. f. by Sir Peter, out of Pewet

Ld Strathmore's b. f. by Pipator, out of Queen Mab

*Ld Strathmore's ch. f. by Pipator, dam by Dragon, out of Queen Mab

Mr. Peirſe's b.c. by Beningbrough, out of Conſtantia

*Mr. Peirſe's b. c. by Waxy, dam by Delpini, out of Tuberoſe

Mr. Melliſh's ch. c. by Beningbrough, dam by Highflyer, out of Dido

*Mr. Hewett's b. c. Scud, by Beningbrough, out of Eliza

*Mr.

*Mr. Walker's ch. c. by Star, dam by Young Mark, out of Gentle Kitty

*Mr Pickering's b. f. by Beningbrough, out of St Anne

*D. of Hamilton's b. c. by Hambletonian, out of Louisa, by Javelin

D of Hamilton's br. b. c. by Walnut, dam by Javelin, out of Young Maiden

*Sir H. T. Vane's b. c. by Hambletonian, out of Lopcatcher

*Sir H. T. Vane's br. f. by Hambletonian, out of Lady Sarah

Mr. T. Hutchinson's br. c. by Sir Peter, out of Alexina

Ld Grosvenor's br. f. by Sir Peter, out of Olivia

Ld Grosvenor's b. f. by Sir Peter, out of Mistletoe

*Ld Grosvenor's b. c. by Sir Peter, out of Ibis

Ld Grosvenor's br. c. by Sir Peter, out of Cælia

*Mr. G. Linton's b. c. by Star, dam by Walnut

*Mr. E. L. Hodgson's b. f. by Patriot, out of Miss Muston

Mr. Clifton's br. c. Bryan, by Sir Peter, out of the dam of Monica

Sir M. M. Sykes's b. f. Statira, by Beningbrough, out of Stella

August Meeting, 1808.

SATURDAY BEFORE THE MEETING.

MR. Hewett's b. c. by Sir Peter, out of Hornpipe, 8ſt. 4lb. agſt Mr. Mellish's f. by Shuttle, out of Plaiſtow's dam, 8ſt. two miles, 1000gs, h. ft.

MONDAY.

Produce Stakes of 100gs each, h. ft. colts, 8ft. 7lb. fillies, 8ft. 4lb. thoſe marked * allowed 3lb. four miles.

Ld

Ld Fitzwilliam's b. f. by Beningbrough, out of Evelina

Mr. Wilſon's b. f. by Hambletonian, out of Maria

Mr. Mellifh's b. f by Precipitate, out of Plaiſtow's dam

Mr. Mellifh's b. f. by Patriot, dam by Highflyer

Mr. Pickering's b. f by Beningbrough, out of St. Anne

D. of Hamilton's br. b. c. by Walnut, dam by Javelin, out of Young Maiden

D. of Hamilton's b. f. by Hambletonian, dam by Javelin, out of Spadille's fifter

Sir H. T. Vane's br. f. by Hambletonian, out of Lady Sarah

Sir H. T. Vane's b. c. by Hambletonian, out of Lopcatcher

Sir F. Standifh's b. c. by Sir Peter, out of Storace

Sir F. Standifh's b. c. by Sir Peter, dam by Volunteer

Ld Grofvenor's br. f by Sir Peter, out of Olivia

Ld Grofvenor's b. f. by Sir Peter, out of Miftletoe

Ld Grofvenor's b. c. (dead) by Sir Peter, out of Shipton's fifter

Ld Strathmore's b. f. by Pipator, out of Queen Mab

Ld Strathmore's ch. f. by Pipator, dam by Dragon, out of Queen Mab

Mr. Hewett's b. c. Scud, by Beningbrough, out of Eliza

Mr. Hodgfon's b. f. by Patriot, out of Mifs Mufton

Mr. Wilfon's ch. f. by Buzzard, out of Totterella

Sir M. M. Sykes's b. f. Statira, by Beningbrough, out of Stella

Sir M. M. Sykes's b. f. Harriet, by Precipitate, dam by Volunteer, out of Rachel

WEDNESDAY.

Sweepftakes of 50gs each, h. ft. for three yr old colts, 8ft. 2lb. and fillies, 7ft. 13lb. two miles.

Ld Fitzwilliam's b. c. by Buftard, out of Fanny

Sir T. Gafcoigne's ch. c. by Hambletonian, out of Goldenlocks

Mr.

Mr. Mellifh's b. c. Experiment, by Hambletonian, out of Lady Cow

Sir H. T. Vane's b. f. by Hambletonian, out of Lady Sarah

Sweepftakes of 100gs each, h. ft. for four yr old colts, 8ft. 4lb. and filhes, 8ft. three miles.

Ld Darlington's brother to Expectation

Sir T. Gafcoigne's ch. f. by Hambletonian, out of Goldenlocks

Mr. Wilfon's b. c. by Sir Solomon, out of Lignum Vitæ's dam

Mr. Lonfdale's br. by Ambrofio, dam by Pot8o's, out of Editha

Sir W. Gerard's b. c. by Beningbrough, out of Mary Ann

Mr. Mellifh's b. c. Harry-long-legs, by Beningbrough, out of the dam of Off-fhe-goes

Mr. Watt's b. c. by Beningbrough, dam by Slope, bought of Mr. Nalton

Mr. Watt's b. c. by Beningbrough, dam by Delpini, bought of Mr. Kirby

THURSDAY.

Produce Stakes of 100gs each, h. ft. colts to carry 8ft. 2lb. fillies, 8ft. thofe marked * allowed 3lb. two miles.

Ld Fitzwilliam's br. c. by Sir Peter, out of Evelina

Ld Fitzwilliam's b. f. by Sir Peter, dam by Diomed

*Ld Fitzwilliam's b. f. by Beningbrough, out of Cecilia

*Mr. Mellifh's b. f. by Hambletonian, out of a fifter to Fidget

*Mr. Brandling's b. f. by Expectation, dam by Star

*Ld Strathmore's b. f. by Sir Solomon, out of Queen Mab

*Ld Strathmore's b. f. (fince dead) by Sir Solomon, out of his Dragon mare

*Sir

*Sir M. M. Sykes's b. c. by Stamford, out of Rachel

Sir M. M. Sykes's b. f. by Hambletonian, out of Sancho's dam

D. of Hamilton's br. b. c. by Walnut, out of Brown
Javelin

Mr. Wentworth's b. f. by Shuttle, out of a sister to
Ambrosio

*Mr. Peirse's b. f. by Pipator, dam by Delpini

*Mr. Peirse's b. c. by Expectation, out of Rosamond

*Mr. Kirby's b. f. by Delpini, dam by Trumpator

Sir T. Gascoigne's b. f. by Hambletonian, out of
Violet

Mr. Clifton's c. Alexander the First, by Sir Peter,
dam by Diomed

Spring Meeting, 1809.

PRODUCE Sweepstakes of 100gs each; fillies allowed 3lb. two miles. No produce, no forfeit.

	ft.	lb.
Sir H. T. Vane's Lady Sarah.............. .	8	2
Mr. Beckwith's mare, by Precipitate, out of Everlasting....	8	6
Mr. C. Mason's mare, own sister to Honest John........	8	6

All covered by Shuttle in 1805.

August Meeting, 1809.

SATURDAY PRECEDING.

PRODUCE Match.—Ld Strathmore's Queen Mab,
covered by Coriander, agst Mr. Mellish's dam of
Plaistow, covered by Don Quixote; colts, 8ft. 4lb.
fillies, 8ft. 200gs each, two miles. The produce, or
failure of produce, to be declared to Mr. Weatherby,
on or before the 1st day of the July Meeting, 1806.

MONDAY.

MONDAY.

Produce Stakes of 100gs each, h. ft. colts, 8ft. 7lb.
fillies, 8ft. 4lb. thofe marked * allowed 3lb. four
miles.

Ld Fitzwilliam's b. f. by Sir Peter, dam by Diomed

*Ld Fitzwilliam's b. f. by Beningbrough, out of Cecilia

Ld Milton's br. c. by Sir Peter, out of Evelina

*Mr. Mellifh's b. f. by Hambletonian, out of a fifter
to Fidget

*Mr. Mellifh's b. c. by Stamford, out of Marchionefs

*Sir M. M. Sykes's b. f. by Stamford, out of Young
Rachel

Sir M. M. Sykes's b. f. by Hambletonian, out of Sancho's dam

D. of Hamilton's br. b. c. by Walnut, out of Brown
Javelin

*Mr. Wentworth's b. f. by Shuttle, out of a fifter to
Ambrofio

Mr. Wilfon's b. c. by Hambletonian, out of Surprize's
dam

*Ld Strathmore's b. f. by Sir Solomon, out of Queen
Mab

*Ld Strathmore's b. f. (fince dead) by Sir Solomon,
out of his Dragon mare

*Mr. Peirfe's b. c. by Hambletonian, out of Con-
ftantia

*Mr. Peirfe's b. c. by Expectation, out of Rofamond

*Mr. E. L. Hodgfon's ch. f. by Shuttle, out of Mifs
Mufton

*Sir H. T. Vane's b. f. by Hambletonian, out of
Lady Sarah

*Sir H. T. Vane's br. c. by Hambletonian, out of
Lopcatcher

Ld Grofvenor's f. (fince dead) by Sir Peter, out of
Miftletoe

Sir F. Standifh's b. f. by Sir Peter, out of Storace

Sir

Sir F. Standifh's b. f. by Sir Peter, out of Eagle's dam
Sir T. Gafcoigne's ch. c. by Hambletonian, out of
Goldenlocks

THURSDAY.

Produce Stakes of 100gs each, h. ft, mares covered
in 1805; colts, 8ft. 2lb. fillies, 8ft. two miles.—3lb.
allowed to thofe got by untried ftallions, or out of
mares whofe produce never won before the day of
naming, or to thofe bred in Ireland; but none to be
allowed more than 3lb. No produce, no forfeit.
A defcription of the produce, or failure of produce,
to be delivered to Mr. E. W. Rhodes at York, on or
before the laft day of the York Auguft Meeting, 1806,
otherwife it will be confidered as a forfeit.

	Covered by
Ld Fitzwilliam's Fanny	Beningbrough
Ld Fitzwilliam's Cecilia	Don Quixote
Ld Milton's Evelina	Don Quixote
D. of Hamilton's b. m. by Javelin, out of Spadille's fifter	Hambletonian
D. of Hamilton's br. m. by Javelin, out of Walnut's fifter	Sir Peter
D. of Hamilton's b. m. by Walnut, out of Rofaletta	Beningbrough and Shuttle
Mr. Mellifh's dam of Junius	Stamford
Mr. Mellifh's fifter to Spadille	Don Quixote
Mr. Mellifh's gr. m. by Highflyer, out of Tiffany	Don Quixote
Mr. Hewett's Eliza	Shuttle
Mr. Hewett's Hornpipe	Sir Peter
Mr Hewett's Mifs Zilia Teazle	Shuttle
Sir T. Gafcoigne's Teoe	Sir Solomon
Sir W. Gerard's Conftantia, by Sir Peter	Beningbrough
Mr Brandling's mare, by Star	Alonzo
Mr. Peirfe's Conftantia	Hambletonian
Mr. Peirfe's Rofamond	Shuttle

Ld

Covered by

Ld Strathmore's Queen Mab ..... Coriander
Mr. Clifton's Fanny, by Diomed .. Sir Peter
Mr. E. L. Hodgson's Miss Muston... Shuttle
Mr. E. L. Hodgson's gr. m. by Sir
   Peter .... Shuttle
Mr. Watt's m. by Saltram .. .. Delpini
Sir M. M. Sykes's Volunteer mare.. Sir Peter
Sir H. T. Vane's Shuttle's dam .... Cockfighter
Sir H. T. Vane's Lady Sarah....... Shuttle
Sir H. T. Vane's b. m. by Drone,
   dam by Dux................. Shuttle

August Meeting, 1810.

MONDAY.

PRODUCE Stakes, to run when four yrs old:—
A Sweepstakes of 100gs each, h. ft. mares covered in 1805; colts, 8ft. 7lb. fillies, 8ft. 4lb. four
miles.—3lb. allowed to those got by untried stallions,
or out of mares whose produce never won before the
day of naming, or to those bred in Ireland; but none
to be allowed more than 3lb. No produce, no forfeit. A description of the produce, or failure of
produce, to be delivered to Mr. E. W. Rhodes at York,
on or before the last day of the York August Meeting, 1806, otherwise it will be considered a forfeit.

Covered by

Ld Fitzwilliam's Fanny .... Beningbrough
Ld Fitzwilliam's Cecilia.. .... Don Quixote
Ld Milton's Evelina............. Don Quixote
D. of Hamilton's b. m. by Javelin,
   out of Spadille's fister . ... Hambletonian
D. of Hamilton's br. m. by Javelin,
   out of Walnut's fister .... Sir Peter
D. of Hamilton's b. m. by Walnut,⎫ Beningbrough
   out of Rosaletta............ :..⎭ and Shuttle

Mr.

	Covered by
Mr. Mellish's sister to Chippenham	Eagle
Mr. Mellish's Marchioness........	Stamford
Mr. Mellish's dam of Off-she-goes...	Don Quixote
Sir M. M. Sykes's Rachel.........	Don Quixote
Sir H. T. Vane's Shuttle's dam	Cockfighter
Sir H. T. Vane's Lady Sarah......	Shuttle
Sir H. T. Vane's b. m. by Drone, dam by Dux.......	Shuttle
Sir F. Standish's b m. by Volunteer, out of Storace.................	Sir Peter
Mr Hewett's Eliza	Shuttle
Mr. Hewett's Hornpipe	Sir Peter
Mr. Hewett's Miss Zilia Teazle....	Shuttle
Mr. Wilson's Totterella	Sir Solomon
Sir T. Gascoigne's Violet....	Timothy

MALTON

Craven Meeting, 1806.

TUESDAY, MARCH 25th.

THE Craven Stakes, a Sweepstakes of 10gs each, for all ages, usual weights; last mile and half.

Ld Fitzwilliam's Sir Paul, 3 yrs old

Mr. Watt's ch. c. by Harrison's Trumpator, dam by King Fergus, 2 yrs old

Sir M. M. Sykes's Sir Scudamore, by Stamford, 2 yrs

Mr. N. B. Hodgson's gr. c. Snap, by Delpini, 3 yrs

Mr. Bower's Miss Welham, 3 yrs old

Mr. Barton's b. c. by Stamford, dam by Rockingham, 2 yrs old

Mr. Lumley Savile's br. c. by Ld Egremont's Arabian, 2 yrs old

Sweepstakes of 20gs each, rising 3 yrs old, 8st. 3lb. mile and half.

Mr.

Mr. Brandling's br. c. by Star, dam by Mercury

Mr. Clifton's br c. Warrior, by Sir Peter

Mr. Watt's b. c. Beningbrough, dam by Y. Mark

Mr. Grimston's Woldsman, by Sir Peter

Sir M. M. Sykes's Sir Scudamore

Sir F. Boynton's c. Integrity, by Totteridge, brother
to Truth

₊ The Filly Sweepstakes did not fill.

SECOND DAY.

Sweepstakes of 20gs each; colts, 8ft. 4lb. fillies,
8ft. rising 4 yrs old; three miles.

Ld Fitzwilliam's Sir Paul, by Sir Peter

Mr. Robinson's b. f. Imma, by Beningbrough, out of
Belle Fille's dam

Mr. Burton's b. f. by Beningbrough, sister to Primrose

Sir. M. M. Sykes did not name

Sweepstakes of 10gs each, for fillies rising 3 yrs
old; to carry 8ft. each, last mile. Five Subscribers,
or no race.

PRESENT SUBSCRIBERS.
Mr. E. L. Hodgson
Mr. John Richardson

The above Stakes to close on the 1st day of March
next, and to be named to Mr. Mark Smith at Malton,
or to Mr. E. W. Rhodes, at York.

LAST DAY.

Sir M. M. Sykes's ch. c. Sir Sacripant, by Stamford,
agst Mr. N. B. Hodgson's ch. c. by Beningbrough, out
of Eliza, by Alfred, two miles, 100gs, h. ft.

Mr. T. Robinson's b. c. by Traveller, dam by
True Blue, 8ft. agst Mr. Acred's Miss Welham,
8ft. 7lb. two miles, 50gs each, h. ft.

Sweep-

Sweepstakes of 5gs each, for horses, &c. not thorough-bred, 12ft. each, to be rode by Gentlemen; two miles.

Mr. Bower's b. g. by Cavendish
Mr. Barlow's b. g. Percival, by Overton
Mr. Burton's b. g. by Windlestone
Mr. Bowes Foord's Rudiger
Mr. M. Hawke's br. g. Prince Bangradion
Mr. Thompson's br. g. by Askham
Sir M. M. Sykes's b. h. by John Bull, rising 6 yrs
Mr. Acklom's b. g. by Traveller
Mr. Smith's m. Tittle Tattle
Sir F. Boynton, Mr. Watt, Mr. Darley, Mr. Hartley, Mr. Teasdale, and Mr. Leathem, did not name

1807.

SWEEPSTAKES of 20gs each, for colts, 8ft. 2lb. fillies, 7ft. 13lb.—one mile and a half; if no Spring Meeting at Malton, to be run at York Spring Meeting.

Mr. N. B. Hodgson's b. c. by Beningbrough, out of Eliza, by Alfred
Mr. T. Robinson's b. f. by Stamford, out of Belle Fille
Mr. J. Nalton's b. c. by Beningbrough, dam by Slope
Mr. T. Kirby's gr. c. by Beningbrough, dam by Delpini
Mr. S. Pickering's b. f. by Beningbrough, out of St. Anne

1808.

PRODUCE Stakes of 50gs each, h. ft. for three yr old colts, 8ft. fillies, 7ft. 12lb. two miles.

Major Bower's ch. f. by Stamford, out of Belle Fille
Ld Fitzwilliam's b. f. by Sir Peter, dam by Diomed

Ld Milton's b. c. by Sir Peter, out of Evelina
Sir M. M. Sykes's ch. f. by Stamford, out of Stella
Ld Middleton's b. c. by Stamford, out of Rachel
Mr. T. Kirby's b. c. by Agonistes, out of a fifter to Kilton
Mr. J. Thompfon's ch. c. by Stamford, out of Welto-nian, by King Fergus
Mr. S. Pickering's b. f. by Sir Solomon, out of St. Anne
Mr. Acred's gr. f. by Delpini, out of Mifs Cogden
Mr. T. Sykes's and Mr. Grimfton's mares had no produce

LAST DAY.

Sir M. M. Sykes's ch. f. by Stamford, out of Stella, agft Major Bower's ch. f. by Stamford, out of Belle Fille, laft mile and a half, 100gs, h. ft.

1809.

PRODUCE Stakes of 50gs each, h. ft. mares co-vered in 1805; colts, 8ft. 3lb. fillies, 8ft. two miles. The produce to be declared on or before the laft day of the Auguft Meeting at York, 1806.

	Covered by
Ld Fitzwilliam's Fanny...........	Beningbrough
Ld Milton's Evelina.............	Don Quixote
Mr. Darley's m. by Sir Peter.......	Delpini
Sir T. Gafcoigne's Wryneck......	Delpini
Mr. Livefey's Young Marfk mare..	Delpini
Mr. Watt's b. m. by Saltram......	Delpini
Mr. Grimfton's fifter to Efcape....	Hambletonian
Mr. Lee's b. m. by Pot8o's, out of Winifred................	Shuttle
Sir M. M. Sykes's m. by Volunteer	Sir Peter
Mr. Dinfdale's b. m. by Weafel....	Delpini
Mr. Burton's Sir Launcelot's dam..	Stamford
Mr. Teafdale did not name	

1810.

1810.

SIR M. M. Sykes's dam of Woldsman, agst Mr. Thompson's Miss Eliza Overton, to be covered in 1806; colts, 8st. 3lb. fillies, 8st. once round the Course, 50gs. No produce, no forfeit. To run the last day.

CATTERICK-BRIDGE, 1806.

WEDNESDAY, April 9th.

PRODUCE Stakes of 25gs each, h. ft. colts, 8st. 3lb. fillies, 8st. two miles; those marked * allowed 3lb.

*Ld Strathmore's f. by Sir Peter, out of Heroine
Sir J. Lawson's c. by Stride, dam by Drone
*Ld Strathmore's f. by Pipator, dam by Dragon
Sir W. Gerard's c. by Beningbrough, out of Mary Ann
Mr. T. Robinson's c. by Beningbrough, out of a sister to Fanny
*Ld Belhaven's f. by Beningbrough, out of his black Highflyer mare
Mr D. M'Queen's c. by Beningbrough, out of his bay Highflyer mare.

Sweepstakes of 5gs each, for horses, &c. not thorough-bred; to be rode by Gentlemen, 12st.—2-mile heats.

Mr. Bower's b. g. by Cavendish, aged
Mr. Burton's b. g. by Windlestone, 5 yrs old
Mr. Barlow's b. h. Percival, by Overton
Sir M. M. Sykes's b. h. by John Bull, 6 yrs old, bred by Mr. Watt

Mr. R. W. Peirfe's b. g. Mafter Slender, by Weafel

Mr. Smith's br. m. Mifs Appleby, by Hermes, dam
by Tandem

Mr. Chamberlain's b. g. bought of Mr. Simpfon

Mr. W. Chaytor's b. h. by Conftitution

Mr. Trotter's b. m. by Reftlefs

Mr. Witham's b. g. by Pipator

Mr. J. Morley's ch. h. by Apollo

Mr. G. Hutton did not name

THURSDAY.

The Gold Cup, value 100gs, the remainder in
fpecie, a Subfcription of 10gs each, for all ages, Craven weights; three miles. To be named between
the ufual hours of entrance for the Plate.

SUBSCRIBERS.

D. of Leeds	Mr. R. C. Burton
Sir J. Lawfon	Mr. Bower
Sir W. Gerard	Mr. Watt
Ld Darlington	Mr. Melliff
Mr. Clifton	Mr. W. Hutchinfon
Mr. R. W. Peirfe	

Sweepftakes of 10gs each; colts, 8ft. 3lb. and fillies, 8ft. rifing three yrs old; two miles.

Sir J. Lawfon's b. c. by Stride, dam by Abba Thulle

Mr. Field's ch. c. by Buzzard, dam, Spinetta

Mr. Hirft's b. c. by Buftard, dam by Sir Peter

Mr. G. Linton's b. c. by Star, out of Baron Nile's dam

Mr. Watt's ch. c. by Trumpator, dam by K. Fergus

Mr. Baillie's ch. c. by Star, dam by Walnut, bought
of Mr. G. Linton

Mr. Brandling's b. c. by Shuttle, dam by Walnut

Mr. Lee's b. c. by Beningbrough, dam by Highflyer

Mr. Burton's b. c. by St. George, dam by Woodpecker

Mr. Wentworth's b. c. Centurion, by Beningbrough,
dam by Highflyer

Mr.

Mr. Mellith's b. f. Streatlam Lass, by Pipator
Mr. Lonsdale's b. c. by a brother to Eagle, dam by
  King Fergus

  Sweepstakes of 20gs each, for fillies rising three,
88. one mile and a half.

Mr. Mellith's b. Streatlam Lass, by Pipator
Mr. Field's b. by Beningbrough, dam by Drone
Mr. Jaques's ch. by Star, dam by Mark, bought of
  Mr. R. Linton
Mr. R. W. Peirfe's b. by Sir Peter, dam by Delpini
Mr. S. Duncombe's b. by Sir Peter, dam by Drone,
  out of Lardella
Mr. Peirfe's br. by Beningbrough, out of Rosamond

1807.

PRODUCE Stakes of 25gs each, h. ft. colts, 8ft. 3lb
    fillies, 8ft. those marked * allowed 3lb. two
miles.

*Sir J. Lawfon's f. by Expectation, dam by Drone.
Mr. Grimston's f. by Precipitate, out of Alonzo's dam
Sir A. Don's c. by Spadille, out of Rofalind, by Vo-
  lunteer
Sir W. Gerard's b. c. by Beningbrough, out of Mary
  Ann
*Mr. Baillie's f. by Delpini, dam by Beningbrough,
  out of Euftatia
Mr. G. Linton's c. by Star, out of his chefnut Walnut
  mare
Mr. T. Hutchinfon's c. by Sir Peter, out of Alexina
Mr. W. Fletcher's f. by Shuttle, dam by Drone
*Mr. J. Robfon's c. by Expectation, out of Heirefs,
  by Highflyer
*Mr. J. Robfon's c. by Expectation, out of his bay
  Ruler mare

      Sir

Sir W. Gerard's b. c. by Beningbrough, out of Mary Ann, 8ſt. agſt Sir J. Lawſon's ch. c. by Expectation, out of his Drone mare, bought of Mr. E. Burke, 7ſt. 11lb. both riſing 3 yrs old, two miles, 100gs, h. ft.

1808.

PRODUCE Stakes of 25gs each, h. ft. mares covered in 1804, two miles; colts, 8ſt. 3lb. fillies, 8ſt.

Sir J. Lawſon's b. f. by Expectation, dam by Drone
Sir W. Gerard's c. by Sir Peter, out of Mary Ann
Mr. W. Coulſon's ch. f. by Expectation, out of Tipple Cyder
Mr. S. Coulſon's ch. c. by Expectation, out of Bonny Kate
Mr. Baillie's br. b. c. by Delpini, dam by Beningbrough

1809.

SWEEPSTAKES of 25gs each, h. ft. for the produce of mares covered in 1805; colts, 8ſt. 3lb. fillies, 8ſt. two miles.—3lb. allowed to untried ſtallions, &c. Produce, or failure of produce, to be declared to Mr. Ferguſon, on or before the laſt day of the Richmond Races 1806.

	Covered by
Sir J. Lawſon's Drone mare...... ..	Stride
D. of Leeds's Mother Red Cap....	Shuttle
Mr. Dinſdale's m. by Weaſel.... .	Delpini
Sir W. Gerard's Mary Ann... ...	Hambletonian
Mr. W. Hutchinſon's m. by a brother to Eagle.	Don Quixote
Mr. W. Hutchinſon's Màrſk mare...	Cockfighter
Mr. B. Howes's br. m. by Sir Peter, dam by Engineer......	Shuttle

Mr.

	Covered by
Mr. Danby's Drone mare.........	Stride
Mr. J. Robfon's Heirefs..........	Cockfighter
Mr. L. Seymour's Oberon mare....	Stride
Mr. Wetherell's Paymafter........	Shuttle
Mr. M. Brown's b. m. by Weafel, out of the Old Mare, by Ancafter	Shuttle
Mr. G. Cock's m. by Beningbrough, out of Expectation...	Shuttle

BEVERLEY, 1806.

FIRST DAY.

SWEEPSTAKES of 20gs each, for three yr old colts, 8ft. 3lb. and fillies, 8ft. one mile and half.

Mr. Watt's ch. c. by Harrifon's Trumpator, out of a Fergus mare

Mr. Richardfon's b. f. by Sir Peter, dam by Pegafus, out of Mendoza's dam

Sir M. M. Sykes's ch. c. Sir Sacripant, by Stamford

Mr. Nalton's c. Integrity, brother to Truth

Mr. Burton's ch. c. by Stamford, out of Belle Fille

Sir F. Boynton did not name.

Sweepftakes of 20gs each, for all ages; three yr olds, 5ft. 12lb. four yr olds, 8ft. 4lb. mares allowed 3lb. four miles.

Mr. Watt's Evander, by Delpini, 5 yrs old

Mr. Thompfon's b. c. by Traveller, out of Palmflower's dam, 3 yrs old

Sir M. M. Sykes's Sir Scudamore, by Stamford, 3 yrs

Mr. Burton's b. c. by St. George, dam by Woodpecker, 3 yrs old

Mr. Uppleby's b. f. by Stamford, dam by Toby, 3 yrs old

The

The Subfcription for a Gold Cup, did not fill.

The Welter Stakes clofes the 1ft of March.

NEWCASTLE, 1806.

MONDAY,

A Sweepftakes of 20gs each, for three yr old colts, 8ft. 4lb. and fillies, 8ft. two miles.

Mr. Brandling's br. c. by Star, dam by Mercury

Mr. Storey's b. c. Cramlington, by Pipator, dam by ———

Mr. Burton's b. c. Rofeden, by Archduke, dam by Drone

Ld Belhaven's b. c. by Beningbrough, out of Lady Mary's dam

Mr. Lumley Savile's b. c. by Screveton, out of Thefpis, by Delpini

Mr. Baillie's ch. c. by Star, dam by Walnut

A Sweepftakes of 10gs each, with 25l. added, for three yr old fillies, 8ft. each, two miles.

Mr. G. Hutton's b. by a brother to Eagle, dam by Star

Mr. Fenton's b. by Beningbrough, dam by Sir Peter

Mr. Jaques's ch. by Star, dam by Mafk

Mr. Field's b. by Beningbrough, dam by Drone

Mr. Ellifon's ch. by Beningbrough, out of Cockfeeder's dam

TUESDAY.

A Sweepftakes of 10gs each, for horfes not thorough bred; three yr olds, 6ft. 10lb. four yr olds, 8ft. five yr olds, 8ft. 10lb. fix yr olds, 9ft. 2lb. and aged, 9ft. 5lb. the horfes never to have a fweat before May, 1806, and never to have been in public training ftables; 2-mile heats.—To clofe on the 1ft of March.

WED-

WEDNESDAY.

The Macaroni Stakes of 20gs each, for any horse, &c. five yr olds, 11ft. 10lb. six yr olds and aged, 12ft. mares and geldings allowed 3lb. four miles. To be rode by Gentlemen. Horses having won one Plate or Stakes, to carry 4lb. and two or more, 7lb. extra. and horses that never started, allowed 4lb. Five Subscribers, or no race.—To close on the 1st of March.

R. C. Burton.

THURSDAY.

The Gold Cup, value 100gs, a Subscription of 10gs each, the surplus to be paid the winner in specie, for three yr olds, 6ft. 3lb. four yr olds, 7ft. 12lb. five ys olds, 8ft. 8lb. six yr olds and aged, 9ft. four miles.

Mr. Brandling's b. c. by Shuttle, 3 yrs old
Sir H. Williamson's gr. h. Starling, 6 yrs old
Mr. M. W. Ridley's, gr. c. by Delpini, dam by Weathercock, 4 yrs old
Mr. Bell's br. c. by Star, dam by Mercury, 3 yrs old
Mr. Storey's b. c. Cramlington, by Pipator, 3 yrs old
Mr. Ellison's ch. c. The Dean, by Pipator, 4 yrs old
Mr. Riddell's br. c. by Overton, dam by Spadille, 4 yrs
Mr. Baker's gr. m. Marcia, by Coriander, aged
Mr. Clowes's b. h. Firelock, by Beningbrough, 5 yrs
Mr. Burton's b. c. by Stamford, out of Belle Fille
Mr. Hodgson's gr. m. Priscilla, by Delpini, 5 yrs old
Mr. Ord's b. c. Cleveland, by Overton, 4 yrs old
Sir C. Monck's br. h. Chariot, 5 yrs old
Mr. Ilderton's b. c. Roseden, 3 yrs old
Mr. Lumley Savile's b. c. by Screveton, out of Thespis, 3 yrs old
Mr. Baillie's ch. c. by Star, dam by Walnut, 3 yrs old

The particulars of produce, for the Sweepstakes in 1808, had not been received when it was necessary to go to press with this part of the book.

RICH.

RICHMOND, 1806.

SECOND DAY.

SWEEPSTAKES of 20gs each, for three yr old colts, 8ft. 1lb. and fillies, 7ft. 12lb. once round.

D. of Leeds's ch. c. by Star, dam by Walnut

Ld Fitzwilliam's b. f. Minstrel, by Sir Peter, out of Matron

Mr. Field's b. f. by Beningbrough, dam by Drone

Ld Dundas did not name

The Cup, a Subscription of 10gs each; to name on the entrance day.

D. of Leeds	Hon. G. H. L. Dundas
Ld Strathmore	Mr. E. Hewgill
Ld Dundas	Mr. R. Chaloner
Sir W. Gerard	Mr. H. Witham
Sir J. Lawson	

N. B. There is a collection in hand of 15gs for the Cup for 1806.

The All-age Stake did not fill, and will therefore continue open till the 1st of March next.

PONTEFRACT, 1806.

FIRST DAY.

SWEEPSTAKES of 10gs each, with 20gs added, four miles. The winner to be fold for 300gs, if demanded in half an hour, &c. three yr olds, 6ft.2lb. four yr olds, 7ft. 10lb. five yr olds, 8ft. 5lb. six yr olds and aged, 8ft. 12lb. mares allowed 3lb. the winner of a Plate, Sweepstakes, or Subscription, this year, to carry 3lb. extra.

Ld

Ld Fitzwilliam's Sir Paul, 4 yrs old

Sir T, Gafcoigne's br. g. by Sir Peter, out of Goldenlocks, 5 yrs old

Mr. Bland's c. Talifman, by Totteridge, 3 yrs old

Mr. Wentworth's ch. c. Hyppolitus, 4 yrs old

Mr. Medley's gr. m. Prifcilla, 5 yrs old

Mr. Thornhill's b. c. by Stamford, dam by Adamant

Mr. Dinfdale's br. c. by Stamford, dam by Rockingham, 3 yrs old

Mr. Mellifh's b. f. Streatlam Lafs, 3 yrs old

Sweepftakes of 30gs each, 10gs ft. colts, 8ft. 3lb.
fillies, 8ft. laft mile and three quarters.

Ld Darlington's c. Well-enough, by Star, bought of
Mr. Robfon

Mr. Sitwell's c. Clafher, by Sir Peter, out of Hyale

Ld Hawke's ch. c. by Stamford, dam by Morwick
Ball

Mr. Lee's brother to Strap

Sir W. Gerard's br. c. by Alexander, out of Conftantia, by Sir Peter

Mr. E. L. Hodgfon's b. f. by Moorcock, out of Mifs
Mufton

Sir H. T. Vane's b. c. by Hambletonian, out of Lady
Sarah

Mr. Nalton's b. c. Integrity, own brother to Truth

Mr. Mellifh's b. f. Streatlam Lafs, by Pipator

Mr. Lonfdale's b. c. by brother to Eagle, out of Lavinia

Mr. J. Robinfon's ch. c. Norton, by Beningbrough

SECOND DAY.

Sweepftakes of 20gs each, for fillies, 8ft. laft mile
and three-quarters.

Mr. Sitwell's b. Pipylina, by Sir Peter, out of Rally

Ld Fitzwilliam's b. Minftrel, by Sir Peter

Mr. Wilfon's b. by Hambletonian, out of Goldenlocks

Mr.

Mr. Wetherell's bl. by Sir Peter, sister to Doncaster

Ld Strathmore's br. by Sir Peter, out of Heroine

Mr. Jaques's ch. by Star, dam by Mark, bought of Mr. Linton

Mr. E. L. Hodgson's b. by Moorcock, out of Miss Muston

Mr. Mellish's b. Streatlam Lass

Mr. G. Hutton's b. by brother to Eagle, dam by Star

The Gold Cup, a Sweepstakes of 10gs each, with 20gs added, for three yr olds, 6ft. 2lb. four yr olds, 7ft. 10lb. five yr olds, 8ft. 5lb. six yr olds, 8ft. 12lb. and aged, 9ft. four miles; mares and geldings allowed 3lb. and the winner of any of the Subscriptions or Sweepstakes at York, in 1806, to carry 7lb. extra.

Ld Darlington's b. h. Ferguson, 6 yrs old

Ld Darlington's b. c. Trafalgar, by Sir Peter, out of Æthe, 4 yrs old

Sir T. Gascoigne's gr. c. by Delpini, dam by Weathercock, out of Cora, 4 yrs old

Mr. Bland's br. c. Talisman, 3 yrs old

Mr. Wilson's b. c. Newmarket, 4 yrs old

Mr. Thornhill's brother to Strap

Sir W. Gerard's Barouche, 4 yrs old

Mr. E. L. Hodgson's b. f. by Moorcock, out of Miss Muston

Sir H. T. Vane's Master Betty, 5 yrs old

Mr. Mellish's Quid, 5 yrs old

Mr. Mellish's Lady Brough, 5 yrs old

Mr. W. Bayly's b. f. by Beningbrough, out of Belle Fille

THIRD DAY.

Sweepstakes of 20gs each, for two yr old colts, 8ft. 2lb. and fillies, 8ft. last mile.

Ld Darlington's brother to Bumper

Ld Fitzwilliam's br. f. by Sir Peter, own sister to Sir Paul

Mr.

Mr. Mellifh's b. f. Mifs Buckle, by Precipitate

Sir W. Gerard's b. f. by Expectation, out of Lady Brough's dam

Sir H. T. Vane's ch. c. by Patriot, out of Hyperion's dam

The Macaroni Stakes clofes the 1ft day of April, 1806.

1810.

PRODUCE Sweepftakes of 50gs each, h. ft. mares covered in 1805; colts, 8ft. 7lb; fillies, 8ft. 4lb. thofe by untried ftallions, or out of mares whofe produce never won, to be allowed 3lb. No produce, no forfeit.

A defcription of produce, or failure of produce, to be made to Mr. J. Tute, at Pontefract, on or before the Laft Day of Pontefract Races, 1806.

	Covered by
Ld Fitzwilliam's Fanny..	Beningbrough
Ld Milton's Evelina......	Don Quixote
Mr. Wilfon's Totterella...........	Sir Solomon
Mr. E. L. Hodgfon's Mifs Mufton..	Shuttle
Mr. E. L. Hodgfon's gr. m. by Sir Peter..................... .	Shuttle
Mr. Mellifh's fifter to Chippenham.	Eagle
Mr. Mellifh's dam of Off-fhe-goes..	Don Quixote

DONCASTER, 1806.

MONDAY, September 22.

SWEEPSTAKES of 20gs each, for two yr old colts, 8ft. and fillies, 7ft. 12lb. laft mile.

Ld Darlington's b. c. brother to Bumper

Ld Fitzwilliam's dark b. f. by Sir Peter, out of Pewet

Sir

Sir T. Gafcoigne's ch. f. by Timothy, out of Violet

Ld Strathmore's b. f. by Enchanter, out of Viciffitude, by Pipator

Mr. Mellifh's f. Mifs Buckle, by Precipitate

Sir H. T. Vane's ch. c. by Patriot, out of Hyperion's dam

TUESDAY.

The St. Leger Stakes of 25gs each, for three yr old colts, 8ft. 2lb. and fillies, 8ft. St Leger Courfe.

D. of Hamilton's b. c. Crafty, by Walnut, dam by Javelin, out of Spadille's fifter

D. of Hamilton's b. c. Banker, by Beningbrough, out of Young Rofaletta

Ld Fitzwilliam's b. f. Mary, by Sir Peter, out of a Diomed mare

Ld Milton's b. c. Delville, by Beningbrough

D. of Leeds's b. c. by Sir Peter, out of Mother Red Cap

Sir T. Gafcoigne's ch. c. by Timothy, out of Violet

Mr. Brandling's br. c. by Star, dam by Mercury

Mr. Peirfe's c. by Beningbrough, out of Conftantia

Ld Strathmore's b. c. by Sir Peter, out of Queen Mab

Ld Belhaven's b. c. by Beningbrough, out of Lady Mary's dam

Mr. Thompfon's b. c. by Traveller, out of Palm-flower's dam

Mr. Mellifh's b. c. Luck's-all, by Stamford

Mr. Mellifh's br. f. Off-fhe-goes, by Shuttle

Mr. Mellifh's b. f. Streatlam Lafs, by Pipator

Ld Derby's c. by Sir Peter, out of Mifs Piper

Mr. Clifton's br. c. Warrior, by Sir Peter

Mr. Clifton's b. c. Fyldene, by Sir Peter

Mr. Croft's b. c. by Cardinal, out of Luna

Mr. Lumley's Savile's b. c. by Screveton, out of Thefpis

Mr.

Mr. Watt's b. c. Shuttlecock, by Schedoni

Mr. Harrison's b. c. by Harrison's Trumpator, out of a sister to Queen Mab

Mr. Grimston's Woldsman, by Sir Peter

Sir M. M. Sykes's c. Sir Scudamore

Sir M. M. Sykes's c. Sir Sacripant

Sir H. T. Vane's b. c. by Hambletonian, out of Lady Sarah

Mr. N. B. Hodgson's ch. c. Brafferton, by Beningbrough, out of Eliza

Mr. Burton's ch. c. by Stamford, dam by Jupiter

Mr. Burton's ch. c. Percy, by Stamford, out of Belle Fille

Mr. R. Wardell's b. c. by Delpini, dam by Pot8o's

Ld Foley's c. by Schedoni, dam by Woodpecker, bought of Mr. Herrick

Sir F. Standish's f. by Mr. Teazle, out of the Yellow mare

Mr. R. Boyce's ch. c. brother to Maidstone

Mr. Clowes's b. f. by Stamford, dam by Y. Marsk

Mr. Hewett's br. f. Miss Teazle Hornpipe

Mr. Hewett's b. f. Miss Eliza Teazle

Mr. W. Hutchinson's ch. c. by St. George, dam by Marsk

Mr. Sitwell's c. Clasher, by Sir Peter, out of Hyale

Sir W. Gerard's c. by Alexander, dam by Sir Peter

Mr. Hirst's ch. c. Baronet, by Stride, dam by Drone

WEDNESDAY.

The renewed Doncaster Stakes, a Subscription of 10gs each, with 20gs added by the Corporation, for horses, &c. of all ages, bona fide the property of the Subscriber, or confederate.—To continue in 1807; three yr olds, 6ft. four yr olds, 7ft. 7lb. five yr olds, 8ft. 3lb. six yr olds and aged, 8ft. 10lb. four miles.

To be named between the usual hours for entering for the Plates.

SUB-

SUBSCRIBERS.

Ld Fitzwilliam	Sir H. T. Vane
Ld Darlington	Mr. Garforth
D. of Hamilton	Mr. Mellish
Ld Strathmore	Mr. Brandling
Sir M. M. Sykes	Mr. N. B. Hodgfon
Sir Thomas Gafcoigne	Sir Wm. Gerard
Mr. E. L. Hodgfon	Mr. Wilfon

THURSDAY.

Sweepftakes of 20gs each, with 20gs added by the Corporation, for three yr old fillies, 8ft. each, two miles.

Ld Fitzwilliam's b. Mary, by Sir Peter

Sir T. Gafcoigne's b. by Hambletonian, out of Golden-locks

Mr. Wetherell's bl. fifter to Doncafter

Ld Strathmore's br. by Sir Peter, out of Heroine

Ld Belhaven's b by Beningbrough, dam by Highflyer, grandam by Conductor

Mr. Mellifh's Streatlam Lafs, by Pipator

Mr. Clowes's br. by Stamford, dam by Young Marfk, out of Overton's dam

Mr. Sitwell's br. Pipylina, by Sir Peter

Mr. Hewett's br. Mifs Teazle Hornpipe

Mr. E. L. Hodgfon's b. by Moorcock

Sir F. Standifh's f. by Mr. Teazle, out of the Yellow mare

The Hunter and North Welter Stakes will clofe on the laft day of March.

Mr. E. L. Hodgfon's f. by Moorcock, out of Mifs Mufton, agft Mr. Hewett's Mifs Eliza Teazle, 100gs each, h. ft. give-and-take weights, higheft, 8ft. 2lb. two miles.

Sir M. M. SYKES, Bart.   ⎫
S. CLOWES, Efq.   ⎬ Stewards.
                     ⎭

1827.

1807.

POST Produce Match.—Mr. E. L. Hodgſon's b. f. by Patriot, out of Miſs Muſton; agſt Ld Darlington's b. f. by St. George, out of Abigail, or his c. by St. George, dam by Mercury; colts, 8ſt. 3lb. fillies, 8ſt. two miles, 100gs, h. ft.

1809.

PRODUCE Stakes of 100gs each, h. ft. colts, 8ſt. 7lb. fillies, 8ſt. 4lb.—3lb. allowed to thoſe got by untried ſtallions, or out of mares that never bred a winner; four miles.

Ld Fitzwilliam's b. f. by Sir Peter, out of a Diomed mare

Ld Fitzwilliam's b. f. by Beningbrough, out of Cecilia

Ld Milton's br. c. by Sir Peter, out of Evelina

D. of Hamilton's br. b. c. by Walnut, out of the brown Javelin mare

Col. Childers's b. f. by Stamford, dam by Pot8o's, out of Editha

Mr. Melliſh's b. f. by Coriander, dam by Highflyer, out of Tiffany

Mr. Melliſh's br. f. by Shuttle, out of Plaiſtow's dam

Mr. Wilſon's b. c. by Hambletonian, out of Surprize's dam

Sir H. T. Vane's b. f. by Hambletonian, out of Lady Sarah

Sir H. T. Vane's b. c. by Hambletonian, out of Lopcatcher

Mr. E. L. Hodgſon's ch. f. by Shuttle, out of Miſs Muſton

1810.

1810.

PRODUCE Stakes of 100gs each, h. ft. colts, 8ft. 7lb. 6 fillies, 8ft. 4lb. those got by untried stallions, &c. allowed 3lb.—four miles. A description of the produce, or failure of produce, to be declared to Mr. Lockwood, Clerk of the Course, at Doncaster, on or before the last day of Doncaster Races, 1806. The winner of the four yr old Produce Stakes at York, to carry 5lb. extra. and the winner of the four yr old Great Subscription at York, to carry 4lb. extra. but the winner of the two to carry no more than 5lb. extra.

	Covered by
D. of Hamilton's br. m. by Walnut, out of Rosaletta..................	Beningbrough and Shuttle
D. of Hamilton's b. m. by Javelin, out of Spadille's sister	Hambletonian
D. of Hamilton's br. m. by Javelin, out of Walnut's sister	Sir Peter
Ld Fitzwilliam's Fanny	Beningbrough
Ld Fitzwilliam's Cecilia	Don Quixote
Ld Milton's Evelina..	Don Quixote
D. of Leeds's Mother Red Cap ...,	Shuttle
D. of Leeds's Elvira.............	Sir Peter
Sir T. Gascoigne's Weathercock m.	Sir Solomon
Mr. Wilson's Totterella	Sir Solomon
Mr. Mellish's sister to Chippenham	Eagle
Mr. Mellish's dam of Off-she-goes..	Don Quixote
Mr. Mellish's br. m. by K. Fergus, out of Camilla	Coriander
Mr. E. L. Hodgson's Miss Muston..	Shuttle
Mr. E. L. Hodgson's gr. m. by Sir Peter	Shuttle
Sir M. M. Sykes's m. by Volunteer	Sir Peter

Mr.

Mr. T. Sykes's Highflyer m. out of
  Juno ....   Sir Peter
Sir H. T. Vane's Shuttle's dam....   Cockfighter
Sir H. T. Vane's Lady Sarah......   Shuttle
Sir H. T. Vane's b. m. by Drone,
  dam by Dux....................   Shuttle
Mr. E. Phillips's ch. m. by Dragon,
  out of Queen Mab...... .....   Coriander
Sir F. Standish's m. by Volunteer,
  out of Storace ....   Sir Peter
Mr. Hewett's Hornpipe.............   Sir Peter
Mr. Hewett's Eliza ....   Shuttle

SKIPTON, 1806.

WEDNESDAY, April 2d.

SWEEPSTAKES of 10gs each, with 20gs added,
for colts, 8ft. and fillies, 7ft. 11lb. twice round
the Course, rather more than two miles.

Ld Ribblesdale's ch. c. by Bishoprick, dam by Phœnomenon

Mr. Birtwhistle's b. c. by Star, dam by Paymaster

Mr. Chamberlain's ro. f. by Hambletonian, dam by Phlegon

Mr. A. Chamberlain's b. c. John Pratt, by Stamford, dam by Rockingham

Mr. G. Hutton's b. f. by a brother to Eagle, dam by Star

Mr. L. Seymour's b. c. Sweetwilliam, by St. George, dam by Ruler

Sir T. Stanley's b. c. by Soldier, dam, Smallbones, by Highflyer

Mr. Wentworth's b. c. Centurion

Capt. C. Parker did not name

Sweepstakes of 10gs each, for horses, &c. not thorough-bred, 12ft. each, rode by Gentlemen. A winner
ner

ner of one Sweepſtakes to carry 3lb. of two or more, 5lb. extra. mares allowed 3lb.—heats, twice round the Courſe.

Mr. Morley's ch. h. by Apollo
Mr. Chamberlain's b. g. 5 yrs old
Mr. J. Dyneley's br. g. by Oberon
Sir M. M. Sykes's gr. g. Confeſſor, by Delpini
Mr. Tatton Sykes did not name

Sweepſtakes of 10gs each, with 20gs added, for all ages; two yr olds, 6ſt three yr olds, 8ſt. four yr olds, 8ſt. 9lb. five yr olds, 9ſt. 1lb. ſix yr olds, 9ſt. 5lb. and aged, 9ſt. 7lb. mares allowed 3lb. twice round the Courſe.

Mr. J. Maſon's gr. c. Trafalgar, by Delpini, out of Dapple's dam
Mr. Lonſdale's gr. c. Young Selim
Mr. C. Simpſon's br. c. by Overton, dam by Phœnomenon
Sir W. Gerard's bl. c. Barouche
Mr. Wentworth's ch. c. Hippolytus

Mr. Chamberlain's ro. f. by Hambletonian, dam by Phlegon, 2 yrs old, 6ſt. agſt Mr. J. Maſon's gr. c. Trafalgar, by Delpini, out of Dapple's dam, 3 yrs old, 7ſt. 9lb. twice round the Courſe, 100gs.

THURSDAY.

Hunters Sweepſtakes of 10gs each, 12ſt. rode by Gentlemen; mares allowed 3lb.—heats, twice round the Courſe; a winner of one Sweepſtakes to carry 3lb. of two or more, 5lb. extra.

Ld Ribbleſdale's br. h. Surrender, by Beningbrough, dam by Highflyer
Mr. Garforth's b. g. 6 yrs old

Mr,

Mr. Tatton Sykes's b. h. Sir Pertinax, by Sir Peter Capt. Parker, Mr. R Wainman, and Mr. Tatton Sykes, are also Subscribers.

CHESTERFIELD, 1806.

A Gold Cup, by Subscribers of 5gs each: if above 20 Subscribers, the cup to be 100gs value, and the remainder to be paid to the winner in specie. Twelve Subscribers, or no race. Three yr olds to carry 6ft. 3lb. four yr olds, 7ft. 7lb. five yr olds, 8ft. 3lb. six yr olds, 8ft. 12lb. and aged, 9ft.—one 4-mile heat; mares and geldings allowed 3lb. the winner of any Subscription at York to carry 4lb. extra. To be named to the Clerk of the Course, or Mr. Weatherby, on or before the 1st of July, 1806, till which time the Subscription will be open.

W. A. Lord	Francis Eyre
Sitwell Sitwell	Gotfrey Meynell
Sitwell Sitwell	W. Hunloke
John Read	

Sweepstakes of 10gs each, all ages, Doncaster Cup weights; four miles. Any horse that wins a Plate, Match, or Sweepstakes, in 1806, to carry 3lb. extra. if twice, 5lb. if thrice, 7lb. mares and geldings allowed 3lb. Seven Subscribers, or no race. To close on the 1st of July, and the horses to be named to the Clerk of the Course, on or before that day.

Sitwell Sitwell

The

The following Matches were made too late to
appear in their proper places.

———

NEWMARKET

Firſt Spring Meeting, 1806.

MONDAY.

LORD Foley's Stretch, 8ft. 7lb. agſt Mr. R. Boyce's
Brainworm, 8ft. 1lb. Ab. M. 100gs.

THURSDAY.

Mr. Mellish's Staveley, 8ft. 5lb. agſt Ld Egremont's
Cardinal Beaufort, 8ft. Ab. Mile, 500gs, h. ft.

Second Spring Meeting.

THURSDAY.

MR. Mellish's Staveley, 8ft. agſt Ld Egremont's
Cardinal Beaufort, 7ft. 7lb. Two yr old Courſe,
500gs.

Mr. R. Boyce's Sir David, 8ft. 5lb. agſt Ld Foley's
Hippocampus, 8ft. 3lb. D. I. 100gs.

Mr. R. Boyce's Sir David, 8ft. 7lb. agſt Ld Barrymore's Gratitude, 7ft. 10lb. Acroſs the Flat, 100gs.

INDEX

INDEX

TO THE

HORSES, &c. IN GREAT BRITAIN,

IN 1805,

MENTIONED IN THIS BOOK.

ANDREWS,

BEL-

BELHAVEN, Ld.—Brandon, 29, 65, 77, 142, 143.
Lady Mary, 29, 49, 57, 105, 126, 126, 134, 134,
134, 143, 143.
  B. c. by Star, 65, 126.
  Ch. h. by Star, 126.

BELL, Mr.—Jack Tar, by Pitch, 3.
  B. f. (4 yrs old) by Abba Thulle, dam by Car-
  buncle, 30.

BENTINCK, Ld Fr.—Lothario, by Chance, 51, 53,
  54, 60, 86, 120.
  Sir Harry, 51.

BENTON, Mr.—B. h. 102.

BEST, T. Esq.—Ch. c. by Dungannon, out of Flirtilla, 32, 36.

BETTISON, J. Esq.—B. f. by Sir Peter, 20.

BIGGS, H. Esq.—Bassanio, by Skyscraper, out of
  Portia, 15, 32.
  Washington, by Sir Peter, out of His Lordship's
  dam, 37, 38, 52, 118, 119, 120, 120, 128.
  Margaretta, by Sir Peter, dam by Highflyer, out
  of Nutcracker, 99, 102.

BILLINGTON, Mr. J.—Forester, 43, 57, 64, 117,
  122, 152.
  Bamford (late Mr. Smith's) 58, 65.
  Ratler, 91.
  Cockspinner, see Lord, Mr.

BIRCH, Thomas, Esq.—Lavinia, by Pipator, out of
  Dick Andrews's dam, 41, 66, 90, 100, 100.

BISHOFFHAUSON, Mr.—Serpent, 70.

BLANDY. A. Esq.—Miss Countryman, 110.

BLOSS, Mr. A.—Master Betty, see Harbord, Col.

BURGH,

BURGH, C. Efq.—B. m. 82.

BURRELL, Sir C. M.—Sarpedon, 22, 23.

BURRELL, Capt. Percy.—Quill-driver, 22, 23, 63, 64, 89, 89.
  Cyclops, 63, 64.

BURRELL, Walter, Efq.—Rinaldo, 22, 22.

BURT, Mr.—Harriet (now Honeyfuckle) 33, 109.

BURTON, R. C. Efq.—Hebe, *fee Ackers, Mr.*
  B. g. 2, 42.
  Off-fhe goes, by Trumpator, 3, 48.
  B. f. (Elizabeth) by Beningbrough, 11, 42, 42, 48, 49, 98, 103.
  B. g by Dubíkelper, 11.
  Ufurper, 43.
  Percy, by Stamford, 96, 112.

BYNDLOSS, E. Efq.—Gary Owen, *fee Pigot, Major.*

CALCRAFT, Mr.—B. f. by Reftlefs, 3.

CARNEGIE, Mr.—B. m. 65, 77, 78, 152.

CASSILLIS, Earl of.—Chancellor, 126.

CATHCART, Major.—Ch. g. by Walnut, 126,

CATHCART, Capt.—B. g. by Reftlefs, 151, 152.

CAVENDISH, Lord G. H.—Duxbury, 44, 139.
  For the reft, fee Watfon, Hon. G.

CHAMBERLAIN, Capt.—Gr. c. by Delpini, dam by Phlegon, 3.
  Why-not, 3.
  Tally O, 125.

CHAPLIN, —— Efq.—B. h. by Spartacus, 116.

CHILD,

COOPER,

DENHAM,

C. by

GER.

H.h.2.   HYDE,

KING,

KING, Col.—Hebe, 43, 115, 116.

KINGSCOTE, Col.—La Mancha, 37, 50, 53, 54,
54, 90, 90, 118, 119.
Hedly, by Sir Peter, out of Improver's dam, 59,
60, 66, 66.
Viper, by Vermin, out of Egham's dam, 37.

KIRBY, Mr.—Elizabeth, by Beningbrough, out of
Judy, 98, 103.
Evander, 95, 104, 122.

KIRKWALL, Lord.—Murphy, 141, 142, 141.

KNAPTON, Mr.—B. f. by a brother to Eagle, 301.

LADBROKE, R. Esq.—Dora, 4, 16, 25, 58, 73, 74.
Bustard, 6, 8, 23, 26, 71, 74, 98, 98, 130, 131,
137, 148, 149.
Sir David, }
Brainworm, } see Boyce, Mr. R.
Prospero (late Sir C. Bunbury's) 27, 67, 108.
Br. c. by Sir Peter, dam by Dungannon, out of
Brown Charlotte, 33, 109.
Dudley, by Guildford, out of Volontiers's dam, 84,
68, 72, 92, 110.
Wormwood (late Wagtail) 44, 45, 80, 109, 110,
139, 141, 146, 150, 150.
Rumbo, 81.
Impostor, 75, 83.—sold to Mr. Bowes Daly.
Rubbish, by Volunteer, 132.

LAKE, W. Esq.—Giles, 7, 28.
Mameluke, 9.
B. c. by Gouty, 34.
Rosabella, by Whiskey, dam by Diomed, out of
Harriet, 34, 109.
Virtuola, 46, 108, 110, 137, 146.
Lynceus, by Buzzard, out of Rose, 66, 131, 199, 147.

MAIN-

True

SADLER,

SITWELL, S. Efq.—Goofecap, by Moorcock, out
of Rally, 4, 7, 16, 25, 39, 85, 91, 103, 103, 116.
Gallina, fifter to Cockfighter, 5, 24, 27, 125.
Pony, 104, 104, 104.

SITWELL, F. H. Efq.—Roan g. 143.

SKINNER, Mr.—Duckling, 67, 84, 85, 102, 107,
113, 117, 127.

SMITH, Sir E.—Betfy, 112, 136.

SMITH, C. C. Efq.—Argus, brother to Peggy, by
Buzzard, 109.

SMITH, Charles, Efq.—Hebe, 57, 78, 115, 117, 117.

SMITH, Thomas, Efq.—Venture, by Volunteer,
45, 103.

SMITH, Mr.—Hippomenes, *fee Todd, Col.*

SMITH, Mr.—Gr. m. 127.

SODEN, Mr.—B. f. by Abba Thulle, 91.

SOMERSET, Lord C. H.—Daify, by Buzzard, out
of Tulip, 37, 39, 53, 70, 71, 115.
Gamboy, by Fidget, dam by Volunteer, 118.
Bagatelle, 50, 118, 119.

SOMERSET, Lord Edw.—Sylvanus, by Volunteer,
out of Dryad, 37, 38, 38, 51, 60, 86, 120.

SPARROW, Gen. (deceafed)—Caftrel, 4, 7, 26.

STACPOOLE, W. Efq.—Ch f. by John Bull, 115, 119

STAGG, Mr.—B. f. 85.

STAMFORD, Earl of.—Georgina, by George, dam,
Petrina, by Sir Peter, 19, 21, 60, 78, 90, 114, 127.
Gayman, 21, 59, 65, 90, 90, 114, 114, 120, 121.

SYKES, Sir M. M.—Sir Reginald, by Precipitate, out of Rachel, by Highflyer, 1, 41, 99, 133.
Sir Launcelot, by Delpini, dam by K. Fergus, 2, 42, 96, 123.
B. m. by Pegasus, out of Y. Magnolia, 43, 116, 125.
Sir Bertrand, by Beningbrough, 95.

SYKES, Tatton, Efq.—Hudibras, 2.

TARLETON, T. Efq.—Jack Tar, 20, 21.

TAYLER, R. Efq.—B. h. 8.

TAYLOR, Mr.—B. c. by Richardfon's fon of Young Marfk, 39, 41.
B. c. by Hammer, 69, 69.

TEASDALE, Mr.—Experiment, by Experiment, 2.

THEAKSTON, Mr.—Ch. c. by Walnut, out of Mifs Pratt, 78, 145.

THOMAS, Sir G.—Leader, 22.

THOMLINSON, J. W. Efq.—B. f. by Wonder, 144.

THOMPSON, Mr. J.—Newcaftle, 12, 31, 40, 41, 85.
Welton, by Antæus, 2.
Mifs Beverley (5 yrs old) 43.
Eliza, by Overton, 99, 123, 134.

THOMPSON, Mr.—Ch. f. by Buzzard, out of Bennington's dam, 132, 140.

THORNTON, Col.—Louifa, 99.

TODD, Col.—Hippomenes, 123, 147, 149, 150.

TOWER, Capt.—Wafhington, *fee Biggs, Mr.*

TRAFFORD, Capt.—Ch. g. 84, 89.

I i 2   TROT-

Capias,

WHITE,

INDEX

TO THE

HORSES, &c. IN IRELAND.

IN 1805,

MENTIONED IN THIS BOOK.

CALD

ED-

A LIST

A LIST OF ROYAL PLATES OF 100gs,

Run for in GREAT BRITAIN, in 1805,

WITH THE NAMES OF THE WINNING HORSES, &c.

	Page
NEWMARKET, April 30.	
PARASOL, by Potso's, 4 yrs old, 10ft. R. C.	15
NEWMARKET, May 2. (Ages as in April)	
Walton, by Sir Peter, 5 yrs, 11ft. 9lb. R. C. —	17
CHESTER, May 7.	
Jack Tar, by John Bull, 4 yrs, 8ft. 12lb. thrice round.	20
GUILDFORD, June 4.	
Ditto, by Sir Peter, 5 yrs, 11ft. 6lb. 4-mile heats. —	36
ASCOT HEATH (Hunters) June 8.	
Lemon-fqueezer, by Coriander, aged, 12ft. 4-m. heats.	44
NEWCASTLE, June 25.	
Starling, by Sir Peter, 5 yrs, 10ft. 3-mile heats. —	47
IPSWICH, July 2.	
Houghton Lafs, by Sir Peter, 4 yrs, 9ft. 2lb. 2-m. hts.	55
WINCHESTER, July 16.	
Witchcraft, by Sir Peter, 4 yrs, 10ft. 4lb. 4-mile heats.	67
EDINBURGH, July 30.	
Brandon, by Beningbrough, 6 yrs, 8ft. 10lb. 4-m. hts.	77
LEWES, August 1.	
Orville, by Beningbrough, 6 yrs, 12ft. 4-mile heats.	81
NOTTINGHAM, August 6.	
Newcaftle, by Waxy, 4 yrs, 10ft. 4lb. 4-mile heats.	85
CHELMSFORD, August 6.	
Meteora, by Meteor, 3 yrs, 7ft. 7lb. 2-mile heats.	88
CANTERBURY, August 14.	
Buftard, by Buzzard, 4 yrs, 10ft. 4lb. 4-mile heats.	92
SALISBURY, August 14.	
Witchcraft, by Sir Peter, 4 yrs, 10ft. 4lb. 4-m. heats.	93
YORK, August 19.	
Evander, by Delpini, 4 yrs, 10ft. 4lb. 4 miles.	95
RICHMOND, Sept. 4.	
Lady Mary, by Beningbrough, 5 yrs, 10ft. 4-m. hts.	105
WARWICK, September 4.	
Principle, by Moorcock, 4 yrs, 10ft. 4lb. 4-m. heats.	106

LICH-

DITTO, IN IRELAND.

Advertisements

OF

STALLIONS

TO COVER IN

1806.

IN ALPHABETICAL ORDER.

At Barham Wood, near Edgware, Middlesex, **AARON** (late Sacripant) at 3gs, and 10s. 6d. the groom.

AMBROSIO, at 10gs, & 10s. 6d. the groom.

KILL DEVIL, at 10gs, and 10s. 6d. the groom.
Good accommodations for mares and foals. All expences to be paid before the mares are taken away. Address (post paid) to Francis Bott, stud-groom.

AGONISTES, at Mr. Morland's, Sutton, Surrey, eleven miles from Westminster Bridge, at 6gs and a half each mare.

He was got by Sir Peter Teazle, his dam, Wren (Belliffima's dam) by Woodpecker, grandam, Papillon (Sir Peter's dam) by Snap; Miss Cleveland,

land, by Regulus; Midge, by a son of Bay Bolton
—Bartlett's Childers—Honywood's Arabian—Dam
of the two True Blues.

Agonistes is 15 hands 3 inches high, one of the
most powerful and best bred sons of Sir Peter, and
was a capital racer.

At Figdale, near Chester, at 5gs each, and half-a-
guinea the groom,

ALEXANDER,

METEOR, and

CESARIO.

ALEXANDER THE GREAT, at Mr. Richard
Goodisson's, Newmarket, at 5gs.

He was got by Lord Grosvenor's Alexander, out
of Fairy, by Highflyer, dam, Fairy Queen.—Being
the finest horse in England, his proprietor, who
would not voluntarily debase the Turf, hopes he
will receive the attention of the public.

AMBROSIO, see page 386.

At Chilton, near Hungerford, Berks, blood mares
at 3gs and 5s. half-bred or country mares at 2gs
and 5s.

APPLEGARTH. For his pedigree, see the General
Stud-Book, and for his performances on the Turf,
see the Racing Calendars of 1798, 1799, 1800,
1801, 1802, and 1803.

Good

Good grafs at 7s. per week.

.All expences for covering, keep, &c. to be paid before the mares are taken away.

Applegarth's ftock, now rifing one year old, are large, bony, and handfome.

———

At Chefhunt, Herts,

A GREY ARABIAN & a CHESNUT ARABIAN, the Grey at 8gs, and the Chefnut at 5gs, and 10s. 6d. the groom.

Thefe horfes are of the firft blood, chofen by Englifh judges, in that part of Arabia where the beft horfes are bred. They are diftinguifhed by fize and power feldom found in any of their fuperior blood.

Good grafs, at 7s. a week, and proper care taken of the mares. All expences for covering, keep, &c. to be paid before the mares are taken away.

Any Gentleman enquiring at the Green Dragon, Chefhunt, will be directed to the horfes.

Chefhunt is nine miles from Hertford, Ware, and Epping, and four from Enfield.

———

ARABIANS, fee pages 391, 395.

———

At Wentworth Caftle, near Barnfley, Yorkfhire, at 2gs, and 5s. the groom.

A GREY COLT, rifing four yrs old, got by Sir George Pigot's Arabian, out of Darling, an Hungarian mare, late the property of Lord Caftlereagh, prefented by the Archduke Charles to Col. Craufoid.

He

He is a remarkably fine ftrong horfe, and ftands full 15 hands and a half high. This is his firft feafon.

Plenty of Grafs at 7s. a week.

***

BEELZEBUB, near 15 hands 1 inch high, at Tollerton, four miles from Nottingham, at 6gs and a half each mare.

He is the beft bred fon of Rockingham, out of an own fifter to Tickle Toby.

He had only one blood mare in 1804, and two the laft feafon (owing to his not being publicly known in the Sporting Calendar as a Stallion) the produce is allowed by judges to be equal to any in the kingdom for fize, ftrength, beauty, and extraordinary good action.

Beelzebub beat Kill Devil at Northampton on the 23d September, 1800, both three yrs old; Kill Devil, on the 1ft of October, 1800, beat Firft Fruits and three others at Newmarket, having before beat all the beft horfes in the fouth.

Grafs and hay at 7s. per week. The money to be paid before the mares are taken away.

***

BENINGBROUGH, at Shipton, fix miles from York, at 10gs a mare, and 10s. 6d. the groom.

ZECHARIAH, own brother to Beningbrough, at the fame place, at 3gs each mare, and 5s. the groom. His ftock are large, handfome, and bony.

***

BOBTAIL, fee page 392.

CESA.

CESARIO, fee page 387.

CHESHIRE CHEESE, at Knutsford, at 5gs and 10s. 6d.

Good grafs and hay, at 7s. 6d. Corn, if required.

COCKFIGHTER, fee page 396.

CORIANDER. This horfe being advertifed for public fale on the 3d of February, the place of his covering cannot be mentioned here, but the earlieft notice will be given of the fame.

DIAMOND, at the Royals, near Nantwich, Chefhire, at 7gs each mare.

Diamond, own brother to Screveton and Stickler, and once the property of Jofeph Cookfon, Efq. was got by Highflyer, dam by Matchem, grandam, Barbara, by Snap—Mifs Vernon, by Cade—Sifter to the Widdrington mare, by Partner, &c. &c.

In 1798, Diamond, 8ft. 6lb. beat Shuttle (now covering at 20gs each mare,) 8ft. four miles, over Doncafter, for 1000gs.

Good grafs for mares, at 7s. per week, and corn, if ordered.

The money for covering and keep, to be paid before the mares are taken away.

The Royals is a farm-houfe, four miles to the left of Nantwich, on the direct road from London to Chefter, five from Whitchurch, 20 from Chefter, 38 from Manchefter, 26 from Stafford, and 25 from Shrewfbury.

DON

DON QUIXOTE, twenty-five mares besides those of his owner, at 20gs each, at Blyth, Nottinghamshire.

DIDLER, at 3gs and 5s.

MAMELUKE, a Grey Arabian, at 3gs and 5s.

The money for covering and mares keep, to be paid before the mares are taken away.

Good accommodation for mares and foals, at 7s. per week.

Blyth is 7 miles from Workfop, 7 from Retford, and 12 from Doncaster.

DUNGANNON and VOLUNTEER will cover at the same place and on the same terms as last year.

EAGLE, thirty mares, besides those of his owner, at 20gs each, at Mr. Richard Prince's, Newmarket. The money to be paid at the time of covering.

YOUNG EAGLE, see page 395.

YOUNG EAGLE, see page 395.

FLAGEOLET, at Swarkstone, near Derby, at 3gs and a crown. Thorough-bred mares which have won a 50l. Prize agst one or more reputed horses, *gratis*, till the end of May, paying groom's fee only.

Good grass to be had at the usual prices.

Enquire for Thomas Munton, at the New Inn, Swarkstone.

At Epfom, or Sutton, Surrey, at 3gs a mare, and 5s. the groom,

GAMENUT, got by Walnut, his dam, Contessina, by Young Mark, grandam, Tuberose, by Herod—
Starling—

Starling---Bartlett's Childers---Counsellor---Snake, &c.

Walnut was got by Highflyer, out of Mr. Pratt's mare, Maiden, own fister to Pumpkin, Purity, Riddle, &c. &c.

There is every accommodation for mares.

Good hay and grafs at 7s. per week. Corn, if ordered.

The money for keep, cover, &c. to be paid before the mares are taken away.

———

At Petworth, from the 1ft of February to the 14th of July,

GOHANNA, at 25gs a mare, and 1g the groom.

BOBTAIL, at 5gs, and 1g the groom.

HANNIBAL, at 5gs, and 1g the groom.

BROTHER TO DRIVER, at 2gs, and 10s. 6d. the groom.

The money to be paid at the time of covering.

———

GOUTY, at Newmarket, at 5gs a mare, and 10s. 6d. the groom.

He was got by Sir Peter Teazle, out of the Yellow mare.

The money to be paid before the mares are taken away.

———

GUILDFORD, fee page 397.

———

HAMBLETONIAN, fee page 396.

HAN-

HANNIBAL, fee page 392.

HIGHLAND FLING, at 5gs and 5s. at C. Day's, Barrow's Brook, near Cirencefter.

He was got by Spadille, his dam, Cælia, by Herod, out of Proferpine, fifter to Eclipfe; is 15 hands 3 inches high, with capital bone and fine action.

Spadille was got by Highflyer, out of Flora, by Squirrel, her dam, Angelica, by Snap—Regulus — Bartlett's Childers——Honywood's Arabian— Dam of the two True Blues.

After the 10th of May he will cover half-bred mares at 3gs and 5s.

PETWORTH, at the fame place, at 3gs and 5s.

Hay and grafs at 8s. per week, and every proper attention paid to mares and foals.

JOHNNY, fee page 399.

At Langham, near Bury St. Edmund's,

YOUNG JUSTICE, a dark Brown Bay Horfe, 15 hands and an inch high, and upwards, by Juftice, out of Dido, 8 years old, and unblemifhed.

Young Juftice is a horfe of remarkable powers and good temper; and of the moft favourite blood, being the immediate defcendant of Herod and Eclipfe, and is well known.

He was bred by Ld Grofvenor; his fire, Juftice, was one of the beft fons of Herod, his dam, Dido, by Eclipfe.

All thorough-bred mares, who have been winners of a 50l. Plate and upwards, will be covered gratis, only paying the groom's fee.

Price

Price 3gs a mare and 5s. the groom.

Money to be paid before the mares are taken away.

Grass will be found mares upon the usual terms, and every attention paid to them.

———

KILL DEVIL, see page 386.

———

'KING BLADUD, at 5gs, and 10s. 6d. the groom, at Mr. Howlum's Training Stables, Littlewick, Maidenhead Thicket, Berks.

He was got by Fortunio, dam, Magnolia, by Marske.

For his performances, see Calendars 1795, 1796, 1797, 1798, 1799, 1800.; in all his running, he has been remarked for his honesty; no horse now living has won more King's Plates, carrying 12ft. than King Bladud.

For action in all his paces, substance, bone, constitution, shape, gentleness, and colour, no horse can excel him.—*A perfect snaffle bridle horse and capital hunter.*

N. B. Repeated letters have been written for the purchase of King Bladud, offering considerable sums, to send abroad.

———

METEOR, see page 387.

———

At Duxbury, near Chorley, Lancashire, MR. TEAZLE, own brother to Stamford, &c. at 5gs a mare and 5s. the groom.

YOUNG

YOUNG EAGLE, own brother to Spread Eagle, and Eagle, at 3gs, and 5s. the groom.

Hay and grafs at 7s. a week.

At Jofeph Rutter's, Whitley, 6 miles from War-rington, 10 from Knutsford, and 16 from Chefter,

OLD TAT, at 5gs a mare, and 5s. to the groom.

He was got by Highflyer, his dam, Plaything, by Matchem—Regulus—Hutton's Spot—Fox Cub—Bay Bolton, &c. &c. is 15 hands 3 inches high, and free from all natural blemiſhes.

Good grafs for mares, at 7s. per week, and corn, if ordered. Every attention will be paid to mares.

The money for covering, &c. to be paid before the mares are taken away.

At Shockerwick, four miles from Bath, and two from Box, at 5gs, and 5s. the groom,

That beautiful Grey Arabian,

OSMYN BEY. The fymmetry of this horfe is fo perfect, and his bone and mufcles fo fuperior to any Arabian ever brought into this country, that breeders will not find their moft fanguine expec-tations difappointed.

N. B. The money to be paid at the time of covering.

Good grafs for mares.

PETWORTH, fee page 393.

REMEMBRANCER, at Streatlam Caftle (near Catterick and Richmond) at 5gs a mare, and 5s. the groom. His performances as a racer (previous to his lamenefs) are well known.

Proper

Proper convenience for mares at the usual prices, and all demands to be paid before the mares are taken away.

————

At Mr. Hornsey's, Middlethorpe, near York,

SHUTTLE, at 20gs each mare, and 1 guinea the groom.

HAMBLETONIAN, at 10gs, and 10s. 6d. ditto.

COCKFIGHTER, at 3gs and 5s.

————

SIR OLIVER, at the Bay Malton, in Altrincham, Cheshire, at 5gs, and 10s. 6d. the groom.

Sir Oliver was got by Sir Peter, out of Fanny, by Diomed.

For his performances on the Turf, vide Racing Calendars, 1803 and 1804.

Good grafs and hay at 7s. 6d. a week, and the utmost attention paid to the mares. Corn, if ordered,

All demands to be paid before the mares are taken away.

————

SIR PETER TEAZLE. The Subscription to the above horse, for 1806, is full.

————

At Oatlands, Surrey, at 10gs a mare, and half-a-guinea the groom,

The Black Horse,

SORCERER, 16 hands and an inch high.

He was got by Trumpator, out of Giantess; she is the dam of Eleanor, Julia, Lydia, &c.

At

At Carr Houfe, near Doncafter, at 5gs, and 5s. the
groom,

STAMFORD, a dark brown horfe, of great fize and
bone; for his performances, fee the Calendars.

Stamford was got by Sir Peter, his dam, Horatia,
by Eclipfe, and is the dam of Archduke and Mr.
Teazle, out of Delpini's dam, which was the dam
of Cobfcar, Vizard, and Greybeard.

All demands for covering, &c. to be paid before
the mares are taken away.

Good grafs and hay—corn, if ordered.

––––––––

At Mr. Durand's Warren, Epfom Downs,

TEDDY THE GRINDER, at 5gs, and 10s. 6d.
the groom.—After the 20th of April he will cover
hunting mares at 3gs, and 5s.

The money for covering and keep, to be paid
before the mares are taken away.

GUILDFORD, at the fame place, at 3gs, and 5s.
each mare.——Guildford will cover hunting mares
at 2gs, and 5s.

––––––––

TOTTERIDGE, at 5gs and a half each mare.

He was got by Dungannon, and is full brother to
Totterella, the dam of Pavilion and Mifs Totteridge; his dam, Marcella, alfo the dam of Magic,
&c. For his performances, vide Racing Calendar,
1795-6-7.

He is a fine dark brown, full 15 hands 3 inches,
compact, with great powers and good action.
His ftock are of great ftrength, and particularly
good goers.

Any Nobleman or Gentleman favouring Mr. Bott with their mares, may depend upon the greatest attention to their being stinted, under his own immediate inspection.

Mr. Bott wishes to impress the attention of those Noblemen and Gentlemen of the Turf, that four only of Totteridge's stock have been trained, three of which have been winners, and the other matched for 200, h. ft. to run next Spring, at York; with confidence he presumes, that from the few thorough-bred mares Totteridge has had, he is equal to any stallion in the kingdom.

A number of good sheds for mares in bad weather, with several roomy boxes, with separate paddocks for mares and foals.

Hay and grass at 8s. per week—corn, if ordered.

N. B. All expences for cover and keep, must be paid at the time of covering, or before the mares are delivered.

TRUMPATOR will cover ten mares beside those of his owner, at Rockingham Castle, Northampton-shire, at 10gs a mare, and 10s. 6d. the groom.

He is sire of Sir David, Penelope, Sorcerer, Spoliator, and many other good runners.

Gentlemen intending to send mares to him, are requested to give notice to James Stevenson, as above.

At Newmarket,
WAXY, at 10gs, and 10s. 6d. the groom.

At Great Barton, near Bury St. Edmund's, at 10gs a mare, and half-a-guinea the groom,
WHISKEY, the sire of Eleanor, Julia, Whirligig, Orlando, Rumbo, Pelisse, Lydia, &c.

Whiskey was a capital racer, got by Saltram, one of the speediest sons of Eclipse, out of Calash.

His

His stock is remarkable for size, bone, beauty and action.

At the same place, at 5gs, and 5s. the groom, YOUNG WHISKEY, got by Whiskey, out of Giantess. He is own brother to Eleanor, Lydia, &c.

Young Whiskey is a horse of great strength and beauty, upwards of 16 hands high, and had uncommon speed before he met with the accident which occasioned his lameness.

The money to be paid before the mares are taken away.

At Padnall's Farm, near Romford, Essex, eight miles from London, on the Whitechapel road, WORTHY, own brother to Waxy, at 10gs a mare, and 10s. 6d. to the groom.—Mares not thoroughbred, at 5gs, and 5s.

The best accommodation will be afforded for mares, with or without foals, and every attention in respect to their being thoroughly stinted, &c.

The money for the cover, and for the keep, to be paid before the mares are taken away.

ZECHARIAH, see page 389.

JOHNNY (late Mr. Durand's) at Broomsthorpe, near Rainham, Norfolk, at 5gs a mare, and a crown the groom.

Mares that have won a fifty, or bred a winner, gratis, those not thorough-bred, at 2gs and a half.

His stock are rising 3 yrs old, and are equal in size and beauty to the get of any horse.

Grass and hay at the usual prices; and the money to be paid before the mares are taken away.

For his pedigree and performance, see the vol. Racing Calendar, 1803.

FOR SALE,

NEAR DORCHESTER, DORSET,

THE Brown Mare, HOPEFUL, 9 years old, near 16 hands high, got by Creeper, dam by Highflyer, out of a Matchem mare; in foal by Skyscraper —price 120gs.

A fine BROWN FILLY, 2 years old, now breaking, not engaged, out of the above mare, and got by Prodligate, who was got by Assassin, dam by Eclipse— price 8ogs.

A GREY FILLY, rising 3 years old, dam by Pickle, and got by Gauger, who was got by Banker by Matchem.—Snip.—Mogul.—Sweepstakes —.Bay Barb—price 60gs.

A BAY YEARLING COLT, out of the above mare by Pickle, and got by Dotterel—price 100gs.

A GREY YEARLING COLT, got by the Ofmyn Bey Arabian, dam by H. R. H. the P. of Wales's Arcot Arabian—price 120gs.

A CHESNUT FILLY YEARLING, got by Applegarth, dam by Pegasus—price 50gs.

For further particulars, enquire by letter (post paid) to Mr. GEORGE CLARK, Dorchester, Dorset.

TO BE SOLD,

A BAY FILLY, rising 3, very strong, well made, and handsome, sound and quiet; unbacked and unengaged; got by Don Quixote, dam by Dungannon, out of Lady Teazle—price 100gs.

Also, a fine FILLY, rising 1, of good shape, size, and substance, got by Pegasus, dam by Dungannon, &c. &c. &c.—price 40gs.

For reference to the proprietor, address, post paid, Mr. WEATHERBY, Oxenden street.

TO

TO BE SOLD,

A BROWN COLT, rifing 4 years old, by Telefcope, his dam (fifter to Louifa) by Cicero, out
of Lapwing. He is very promifing, never ftarted,
paid or received, or was ever in training.

N. B. Louifa was the property of Ld C. Somerfet,
and ran at Bibury, Litchfield, Stafford, &c. &c. he is
worth attention.

For further particulars, apply, poft paid, to Mr.
WEATHERBY, Oxenden-ftreet.

TO BE SOLD,

A Remarkably handfome YEARLING COLT, by
Sir Peter, out of Brown Charlotte, by Highflyer, own fifter to St. George, &c. &c. his fize not
very large, good legs and feet, and good bone, colour
brown, own brother to Lucan.

A large bony COLT FOAL, by Hambletonian,
dam by Dungannon, out of Brown Charlotte, colour
bay, no white, very likely to make a large fine horfe.

Enquire of WILLIAM HERRICK, Efq. Beau Manor,
Loughborough, Leicefterfhire.

WILLIAM RIDETT, No. 36, GEORGE STREET,
PORTMAN SQUARE, being particularly recommended by his friends, begs to inform gentlemen that
he buys Horfes by Commiffion for the Turf, and
other horfes for Hunters, &c. &c. &c.—He bought
Mr. Wardell's famous fillies that were fuch capital
runners at 3 years old.—He bought Mr. Fermor's
Principle, that won feveral fol. Plates, and the King's
Plate at Warwick, 1805.—He alfo bought Mariner
for Capt. Hervey; and being ready to oblige any
nobleman or gentleman by giving his opinion without

L l 3   any

any charge, and can be recommended on the higheſt terms, if required, by applying to William Fermor, Eſq. No. 58, George-ſtreet, Portman-ſquare. It is totally left to generoſity, by thoſe who chuſe to employ him; and was, in the early part of his life, bred up to the Turf, with Mr. Parker, afterwards Lord Boringdon.

———————

TO BE LET, completely furniſhed, for two years, from April 5th, 1806, but immediate poſſeſſion may be had if required,

BULFORD HOUSE,

with twelve acres of excellent meadow land; an extenſive manor, and alſo fiſhery; very large and well planted garden, and walled in part; a large dove-houſe, dog-kennel with a running ſtream through it; farm-yard, barn, and out-buildings of all ſorts, ſtabling for eight horſes, with lofts; ſtanding for three carriages, the ſtables are divided, one in five ſtalls, and one in three; a good granary, larder, dairy, brew-houſe, green-houſe with a ſtove, cold bath nearly finiſhed in garden, &c. &c. two fiſh ponds. The rent one hundred a year, excluſive of taxes, which amount, in toto, to 21l. 19s. annually; no poor rates or tythes payable by tenant. The above is admirably calculated for any gentleman wiſhing to keep harriers, or to train race horſes, there being beautiful downs immediately adjoining, calculated for that purpoſe.

BULFORD HOUSE is ſituate 9 miles from Saliſbury, 3 from Stonehenge, and about 30 from Bath, a good neighbourhood, and good roads. The whole was repaired laſt March.

For particulars, enquire of the occupier, Bulford Houſe, near Ameſbury, Wilts. No letters will be anſwered unleſs poſt paid.

N. B. A rick of excellent Hay may be had if required.

JAMES

JAMES FOZARD,

STABLE KEEPER, OF PARK-LANE,

RESPECTFULLY begs to acquaint all gentlemen, and others, owners of horfes, that he continues to fell thofe invaluable Medicines, as originally invented and prepared by the late Mr. WATSON, Farrier, Norwich, and now by his fon and fucceffor, Mr. RICHARD WATSON.—It would be needlefs to fpeak of the efficacy of medicines which have ftood the teft of thirty years, and were never known to fail in thofe cafes for which they are adapted, when it was in the power of medicine to relieve.

The *Purging Pafte,* fo univerfally known and approved of, may be given with fafety at any feafon of the year, and to horfes and colts at grafs.

The *Anodyne Pafte,* for the Gripes, and all complaints of the Bowels.

The *Diuretic Balls,* for the Greafe and Swelled Legs.

The *Fever Powders,* for all Inflammatory Difeafes.

The above to be had in any quantity, and fent to any part of the united kingdom; if three guineas worth is ordered, a book of directions, as publifhed by the late Mr. WATSON, will be given.

FOR

FOR HORSES.

DR. STEERS'S OPODELDOC.

The following Letter from Mr. COWLING, Master of the Riding-house, Moorfields, will be a further Proof of the superior Efficacy of this Medicine.

To Mr. H. STEERS.

SIR,

HAVING often known the good effects of your Opodeldoc in the human species, I was induced to try it on horses; and I have found it so superior to every other application in bruises, sprains, rheumatisms, and other external complaints, that I think it but justice to give you this testimony. In treads through the coronet, if the wound is immediately filled up with it, and covered with a little bandage, so as to keep the cold out for a day or two, the cure will be perfected without festering, or any other inconvenience. In strains from leaping, or any other violence, where the seat of them could be ascertained, I have, by rubbing in very hard half a bottle at a time, morning and evening, removed the complaint, though ever so bad, in a few days. I have likewise reduced a large callus, or tumour, upon the cap of a horse's hock, which always has been deemed incurable, by rubbing in half a bottle at a time, as above; but this was not effected in less than three weeks. I have also found it equally serviceable when horses have been wrung in the shoulders, or bruised by the saddle, if immediately applied. Any gentleman may be further satisfied, by writing to, or calling upon me, at the Riding-house, Moorfields.

I am, Sir, &c.

WILLIAM COWLING.

This Opodeldoc, in the human species, is universally esteemed, for curing bruises, sprains, and rheumatisms; as also for fresh cuts, burns, and scalds, as well as the sting of wasps, gnats, &c.—It is very pleasant to the smell, and simple in the application, requiring only to be rubbed in with the hand.

CAUTION.

CAUTION.

The innumerable counterfeits and imitations of this medicine, render it absolutely necessary to guard the public against the impositions that are daily practised.

Various druggists, and other designing persons (some taking the advantage of being of the name of Steers, and others venturing to forge both Mr. Newbery's and Mr. Steers's names to their bills) have disseminated throughout the town and country, many spurious sorts of Opodeldoc, totally different, and infinitely inferior in quality to the real preparation.

All purchasers, therefore, who would wish to avail themselves of the virtues of Dr. Steers's genuine Opodeldoc, are requested to observe very particularly, and as the only certain means to prevent the being deceived, that the name of F. Newbery is engraved on the stamps, which are pasted round the directions on the outside of each bottle; and as this distinction has been made by order of the Commissioners of the Stamp-office, no person can imitate it without being guilty of felony.

Sold only by F. Newbery, at the warehouse for Dr. James's Powders, No. 45, in St. Paul's Church-yard, a few doors from Cheapside, London; and by his appointment by Messrs. Jeboult and Co. No. 150, and Dr. Allen, No. 76, Oxford-street; J. Wade, Old Bond-street; Bayley and Co. Cockspur street; Godfrey and Cooke, Southampton-street; J. Ward, Middle-row, Holborn; T. Tutt, Royal Exchange; and W. Clarke, Borough High-street Price 2s. 6d. per bottle, including the stamp, or six for 13s. 6d.

FOXALL,

FOXALL,

OPERATIVE FARRIER,

Preparer and Vender of Genuine Horse Medicines,

LITTLE MOORFIELDS, LONDON,

CONTINUES to give advice, and adminifter relief, in all diforders and cafes of Lamenefs incident to Horfes, founded on the experience of 29 years, in a very extenfive practice.

As a proof of the efficacy and fafenefs of his medicines, prepared from genuine drugs, under his own infpection, the following perfons, his cuftomers, thus publicly fignify their approbation of them, and earneftly recommend them to training grooms, ftable keepers, and all other perfons, entrufted to the care and management of horfes.

> Mr. T. Hull, Repofitory, Chifwell-ftreet
> Mr. T. Marfden, Tottenham-court-road
> Mr. T. James, Worfhip-ftreet
> Mr. J. White, Little Moorfields
> Mr. H. Thrupp, White Lion-ftreet
> Mr. F. Choppin, Park-lane
> Mr. J. Hopkins, Holborn
> Mr. J. Mellows, Curtain-road
> Mr. G. Hart, Holborn
> Mr J. Robfon, Little Britain
> Mr J. I'ons, Riding-houfe, Iflington
> Mr. H. Bradley, King-ftreet, Portman-fquare
> Mr. R. Daniel, Rolls-buildings, Fetter-lane

HORSE

HORSE MEDICINES,

Prepared and fold by

FORSTER AND CRESSEY,

(Late Cecil and Haynes)

Chemists and Druggists

TO HIS ROYAL HIGHNESS THE PRINCE OF WALES,

No. 2, OLD BOND STREET, LONDON.

PHYSIC Balls, from 1s. to 1s. 6d. each.

RHUBARB BALLS, 2s. 6d. each.

DIURETIC BALLS, 6s. to 8s. per dozen.

CORDIAL SAFFRON BALLS, 6s. to 8s. per doz.

PECTORAL BALLS, for Coughs and Epidemic Colds in Horfes, 6s. to 8s. per dozen.

WORM BALLS, 1s. to 1s. 6d. each.

FEVER POWDERS, 6s. per dozen.

OINTMENT FOR BLISTERS, 3s. 6d. per pot.

BLACK OIL, for Strains and Bruifes, 3s. 6d. per pot.

LINIMENT for Cracked Heels, 3s. per pot.

PURGING BALLS for Dogs, 2s. 6d. per box.

Horfe Medicine Chefts fitted up at all prices.

TAPLIN'S, SNAPE'S, BRACKEN'S, and other Horfe Medicines, accurately prepared from the genuine receipts, as publifhed by the refpective proprietors.

By

[By fome accident, the following account never appeared in the Sheet Calendar, and was omitted in its proper place in this book—confequently no reference to it will be found in the index, or in the lift of winning horfes.]

TEWKESBURY RACES, 1805.

ON Tuefday the 24th of September, a Sweepftakes of 10gs each, with 25gs added from the Race-fund, for three yr olds 6ft. 5lb. four yr olds, 7ft. 9lb. five yr olds, 8ft. 4lb. fix yr olds, 8ft. 10lb. and aged, 9ft. 2lb.—2-mile heats.

Ld Brooke's ch. h. Marplot, by Waxy, 5 yrs old	4	1	1
Mr. Herbert's Little Peggy, 4 yrs old	1	3	3
Mr. Kellermann's Mary, 5 yrs old	3	4	2
Mr. Daly's ch. h. Frederick, 5 yrs old	5	2	dr
Mr. Creffwell's b. m. Dutchefs, 5 yrs.	2	dr	

On Wednefday the 25th, a Sweepftakes of 5gs each, with 40gs added, for three yr olds, 7ft. four yr olds, 8ft. 2lb. five yr olds, 8ft. 9lb. fix yr olds, 9ft. 2lb. and aged, 9ft. 3lb.—4-mile heats.

Ld Brooke's Marplot	5	1	1
Mr. Creffwell's Dutchefs	1	2	3
Mr. Kellermann's Heeltap, 4 yrs old	2	3	2
Mr. Daly's Frederick	4	4	dr
Mr. Herbert's Little Peggy	3	dr	

The following Match, with feveral for 1807, &c. came to hand as the laft page was going to prefs.

NEWMARKET JULY MEETING, 1806.

MONDAY.—Ld Grofvenor's Plantagenet, 8ft. 7lb. agft Ld F. G. Ofborne's Don Felix, 7ft. 12lb. Ab. M. 200gs, h. ft.

FINIS.

Printed by H. Reynell, No. 21, Piccadilly.

Lightning Source UK Ltd.
Milton Keynes UK
UKHW010302220119
335963UK00013B/1040/P